SUSAN BOE

purposeful design®
p u b l i c a t i o n s
A Division of ACSI

Colorado Springs, Colorado

Originally published 2000
© 2005 by ACSI/Purposeful Design Publications

Purposeful Design Publications is the publishing division of the Association
of Christian Schools International (ACSI) and is committed to the ministry of
Christian school education, to enable Christian educators and schools world-
wide to effectively prepare students for life. As the publisher of textbooks, trade
books, and other educational resources within ACSI, Purposeful Design Publications strives to produce biblically sound materials that reflect Christian scholar-
ship and stewardship and that address the identified needs of Christian schools
around the world.

References to books, computer software, and other ancillary resources in this
series are not endorsements by ACSI. These materials were selected to provide
teachers with additional resources appropriate to the concepts being taught and
to promote student understanding and enjoyment.

Printed in the United States of America
16 15 14 13   8 9 10 11

Boe, Susan
    Choices for a winning lifestyle: A health textbook for high school
    Second edition
    Total Health series
    ISBN 978-1-58331-225-4   Hardcover edition   Catalog #7606
    ISBN 978-1-58331-226-1   Softcover edition   Catalog #7607

Cover design: Sarah Schultz

Purposeful Design Publications
A Division of ACSI
PO Box 65130 • Colorado Springs, CO 80962-5130
Customer Service: 800-367-0798 • Website: www.acsi.org

To my sons Steven and Christopher

Acknowledgements

This book could not have been written without the contribution and expertise of many people. I wish to give a special thanks to the following people for their involvement in this project.

Consultants:

Colleen Hacker, Ph.D. Professor, Physical Education, Pacific Lutheran University. Tacoma, Washington. Thank you for bringing to the book the challenge, "How can your faith make a difference in your life?" As the result of your challenging, questioning approach, I hope students ask themselves the same question.

George Hamilton, MD. Cardiologist, Instructor for *Healing Touch Ministries*. Your hours of professional input and expertise give the manuscript its depth. I respect your knowledge and appreciate your servant's heart.

Paul Hoseth, Ed.D. Professor, Health Education, Pacific Lutheran University. Tacoma, Washington. Your sincerity of heart and concern for your students is obvious. I appreciate your willingness to be involved in this project and the time you gave me discussing important issues.

Mark Jones, DMD. Author and Seminar Speaker, *Right/Wrong Thinking*. You and your wife, Susan, are quite the team. Thank you for your encouragement in every area of the book. Thank you for your pastor's heart and prayers for both Scott and me.

David Sargent, MD. Portland Adventist Medical Center. Portland, Oregon. Your love and commitment to the Lord is an example to me. You successfully blend your life's work with your love for God and I know your patients feel the same way.

Wendell Smith, Senior Pastor, The City Church. Bellevue, Washington. I have received such a rich deposit in my life because of your example and life message. Thank you for your years of service to Bible Temple and now to The City Church in Bellevue, Washington. Your encouragement and inspiration gave me a vision for this project.

Editor:

Barbara Wright. Thank you for burning the candle at both ends to finish this project. Your professionalism and expertise are evident. Thank you for not letting me quit!

Illustrator:

Lisa Million. Your professional and creative abilities made this book what it is. Thank you for your long hours and endless encouragement.

Health Teachers:

The Teachers at Temple Christian High School: Carol Townsend, Dorcas Mason, Nancy Meechum, Larry Lawson and Phil Zedwick. Thank you for all your input. I appreciate your words of encouragement and for teaching the material in its unfinished form.

Jim Cochran, Barbara Owens and Mitzi Tillstrom. Thank you for viewing the manuscript in the early stages and giving me your personal and professional advice.

Heartfelt thanks goes to the following individuals for their insight and contribution to the manuscript and to me personally:

Dr. Brand. Thank you for your insight and burden for students. You are a deep well from which others can draw.

John Bryan. I am grateful for your vision for quality education. More than thanks to you and Martha.

Heather Cole. You are the nanny above all nannies! My children and I are blessed to have you in our home these past few months. Jackie, do you know what a prize you have?

Missy Conser, Amy Gall, Kim Knoefel. What great neighbors and friends you are! You entertained my boys so I could work on this project.

Tim Hodgson. Thank you for the production of the cover. Unlimited possibilities within limited resources! Thanks for working within our means.

Liz Kitchen. Thank you for working on the design of the layout. Your creativity added to the book.

Lazerquick, Milwaukie Oregon. Dennis Buie and staff. Thank you for your fine quality and service.

Glenda Malmin. My friend and confidant, my thanks to you for all your input into my life. Thank you for looking beyond my weaknesses and helping me grow in the Lord.

Sally Stuart. Thank you for serving the Christian community with your knowledge and insight into the special needs of publishing.

Frosty Westering. Thank you for teaching me to make the big time where I am. Your book continues to motivate me as do my memories from Pacific Lutheran University.

Credits

Art Credits

Cover Design by Tim Hodgson.

Page numbers in *italics* indicate that the illustration has been modified from the original supplied by the art companies.

Illustrations on the following pages are original and copyright ©1995 by Lisa Million:
pages 2 (3 girls), 3, 4, 5 (scales), 6 (girl on stairs), 9 (foundation is the Word, crown), 15 (hand), 16 (thermometer and thinker), 17 (ladder), 18 (cell), 19, 22, 27, 28, 31, 32, 33, 40, 43, 44, 46, 47, 53, 55, 63 (protein), 66, 67, 68 (except as credited to 3G Graphics), 88, 89, 91, 97, 98 (biceps), 99 (scale), 103 (chalkboard), 109, 111, 119, 133, 135 (book and soldier), 154, 166 (cells), 174, 187, 220, 241, 242, 262 (tongue and girl), 287, 310 (water fountain), 317, 325, 326, 328 (books), 331, 333, 340, 343 (books), 345, 350, 363, 375 (girl), 391, 392 (list), 403.

Illustrations on the following pages are copyright Dynamic Graphics, Inc. and are used with their permission:
pages *1*, 2 (bike), 5 (books), 6 (cigarettes), 7 (cheering people), 8, 14, *15* (eye), 16 (outdoor scene), 17 (family), 18 (runner), 20, 21, 23, *29*, 30, 35, 36 (faces), 38, 39, 45, *48*, 50, 54, 62, 63 (pasta), 64, 69, 71, 87, 90, 98 (stethoscope), *99* (flexibility), 102, *103* (walker), 104 (swimmer), *105*, *106*, 113, 115 (soccer and runner), 117 (physical fatigue and emotional fatigue), 118, *126*, 127, 128 (elements of), *132*, 134, 137, *139*, 141, *143*, 147, *153*, 155, 156, 157, 160, 161, 162, 165, 166 (virus and genetic), 167, *169*, 170 (biker), 171, 173, *182*, 183, *184*, 185, 189 (shoes and time management), 190 (tennis), 191, 192 (kids), 193, 195, 197, *201*, *202*, *203*, 204, *207*, *208* (standing figure), 209, 210, *211*, 213 (girls), 216, 218, 219, 221, *227*, 228, *229*, 230 (weightlifters and girl), *232*, 243 (blackboard and garden), *244*, 245, 248, 249 (sparrows), 250 (gloves), 251 (blackboard), *252*, 253, *255* (music and blackboard), 256 (ear exam), 257, *258* (toothbrush and smile), 259 (teeth and dentist), 260, *265*, 272 (crutches), 274, *275*, 276 (fire), 277, 280 (tree), 282, 283 (earthquake), *284*, *288*, *290*, *291*, 300, *301*, 303, 304, 306 (graduates and man), 307 (island and men), 308, 309, 310 (air pollution), 311 (water pollution and recycle), 312, 313 (trash), 314 (popcorn), 318, 319, 332, 334, 336, 337, 343 (smoking), 347, 348, 349, 351, 352, 362 (golf, tennis, skiing, bikes), *364*, 365 (bottom couple), 366, 373, 374, 375 (family), 376, 378, *393*, *394*, 396, 397, 398, *399*, 400, 401 (choir), 404, 405, 406 (hourglass), 411, 414, 415, 416, 418, 419, 420, 423, *429*.

Illustrations on the following pages are copyright Metro ImageBase, Inc. and are used with their permission:
pages 78 (except bread), 188 (wave), *208* (prayer), 214, 215, 217, 222, 233, 247 (man), 254, 263, 280 (school), 283 (jet ski), *313* (consumer), 316,

Foreword

This is a very important book. It is also timely. I am in a good position to know just how timely it is, because I have been in practice as a doctor for more than 50 years and in more than three countries. I have seen and experienced the changing importance of health education and of moral education over the past half century. I can recognize four major changes.

When I was in medical school there was little that doctors could do to cure diseases. The age of antibiotics and of chemotherapy had not started yet. We gave advice, and in most cases we told patients that they would recover, because we knew that the human body had wonderful power to heal itself. Doctors often gave moral advice; not because they were Christians, but because they knew how serious and mostly incurable were diseases like syphilis and gonorrhea that resulted from immoral behavior.

Soon after we became doctors, during World War II, came the explosion of new medications and vaccines that were called miracle drugs because nobody had ever imagined that so much power over germs would come into our hands. Health education in those days was devoted to teaching people to come to the doctor soon so that some new miracle drug could be chosen to fit their need.

It was during this exciting stage that my wife and I went to India as missionaries. I was asked to become a member of the Indian Council of Medical Research. The members met as a group once each year and discussed new advances and new medicines that could be applied to diseases like malaria, dysentery, typhoid, leprosy and tuberculosis. All of these diseases were due to germs and it was good to be able to announce that each, in its turn, was being brought under control.

Finally, as our children grew up, we left India and joined the

United States Public Health Service. Here too all the epidemiologists and Public Health experts met together for a week every year for a conference. We spent our time reviewing new patterns of disease and new advances in treatment that had been developed during the previous year. We were specially alert to new problems and the possible emergence of germs and viruses that had not been recognized before. These were good meetings and I was proud to be able to attend and to feel part of such a body of experts.

Just a few years ago, at one such conference, I remember a sudden sense of *deja vu* as I saw myself in one of our similar conferences in India, and even more as I recollected England before antibiotics. Here in America we scarcely mentioned the diseases that had taken most of our time and discussion in India. They were no longer a problem in America, having fallen before the miracle drugs. But we spent hours and days talking about the new plagues that were spreading in our land. Some were really new, like AIDS. Others were old, like alcoholism, drug addiction, and the crimes of violence that came along with them. Though old they were on the increase because of the way people were choosing to behave. Sexually Transmitted Diseases were increasing to epidemic proportions. We had cures for most of them, but the net result of the availability of cures had been a sense that it was acceptable to be promiscuous because resulting disease could be cured. Unwanted pregnancy didn't matter because abortion was easily available. Broken marriages didn't matter because divorce was available. The children of broken homes formed gangs to give themselves a sense of belonging. Their new loyalty to the gang led them to murder members of rival gangs and to rape and rob at the ages too young for the judicial system to deal with. Suicide between ages 18 and 22 had reached new record highs.

All sorts of programs were discussed that might slow down or reverse these epidemics that were so clearly based on behavior. But it saddened me to sense the concern in the Public Health Service that they should use only "politically correct speech" which meant that they should not speak of <u>moral </u>decline in case it should be interpreted as a call for religion and moral teaching in schools.

Yet nothing could be more obvious. Seen from my bird's-eye view of fifty years in medicine, we do not need more medicines or more vaccines or more condoms, but a new concern for behavior and respect for the moral law that God gave us as a guidebook for health and happiness.

I observe a new serpent calling to our new generation of children and teenagers who live in our scientific Garden of Eden and saying, as the old serpent did, "You shall NOT surely die. Science has made moral restraint unnecessary. If it feels good — do it."

It is in the context of today's new epidemics of behavior-related diseases and misery that Susan Boe has had the insight to undertake the writing of a guidebook about what she calls *TOTAL HEALTH*. To her and to me also total health means that our BEHAVIOR matters to our health and to our happiness. It means that we are not just bodies, attacked by germs and waiting for medicines. We are body, mind, and spirit, and that we cannot be truly healthy or truly happy unless we follow the laws of God who made us.

Susan Boe, I congratulate you, and your artist too! The greater part of this book is a simple guide to bodily health, but it is all in the context of right relationships and healthful behavior. That again is seen in the context of God's love and concern for the way we choose to live. God bless this book, and may parents, school teachers and principals recognize it for what it is — a great guide and foundation for TOTAL HEALTH for us and our children.

Dr. Paul Brand

Paul Brand is a physician, teacher and author of seven books including co-author with Philip Yancey of *Fearfully and Wonderfully Made*, *In His Image*, *Healing*, and *Pain: The Gift Nobody Wants*.

He is the author of a tape series for high schools called *You Are Wonderful*, produced by Norlynn Audio Media.

Paul and his wife Margaret travel around the world to teach, preach and serve.

Preface

Morality is a healthy basis for life and a very necessary part of health and health education, even for those who do not follow any particular religion. In my years of teaching health education I found it difficult to teach the physical, mental, and social aspects of health without bringing in the spiritual dimension. I wanted to help my students understand that the condition of their spiritual health was the key to finding fulfillment in all areas of life.

From a child I always loved God and had a deep hunger to know more about Him. To my peers I seemed very "religious." However, I never quite understood how to relate personally with such a "big" God. In junior high school my simple life became more complicated. My body was sending me confusing messages and my emotions were always changing. I found that my tendency toward perfectionism was driving me crazy — I could never be perfect! When I heard that God's unconditional love was for *me*, I decided to get personal with God. That was the beginning of my experience with total health; body, mind and *spirit*.

It was not always easy finding the balance. My lifestyle went from one extreme to another. When I attended a university to study physical education and participate in competitive athletics, it seemed even more difficult to find balance in my life. Today, I am married and have two small children and I am still trying to "practice what I preach."

Much of what I have to say in this book comes from the expertise and knowledge of those who are professionals in the area of health and health education. The spiritual dimension of the book is the combined efforts of many who have experienced God's faithfulness in their lives. I bring to it a personal style and a heart that desires to see young people excited about serving a "big" God.

As I wrote this book, I imagined myself standing before my students. Therefore, it is written in a conversational style. It is full of true, personal testimonies and tributes to show that life is real, with real problems, real temptations, and real solutions. My goal in being so personal in the approach of this book is to encourage students to expect God to help them in their daily trials. Living the Christian life is not "uncool" — it is living a powerful life!

The information presented in *Total Health* is natural yet spiritual, practical yet inspirational. It is a blend of practical knowledge, common-sense and godly principles. It was written to provide a sound, inspirational guide to good health. It is not a book meant to lay condemnation on young people, but to show that it is possible, even with personal weaknesses, to tap into the love and grace of God and find fulfillment in serving a living King.

I present this book with no apology for the spiritual and moral truths that are its foundation, nor do I apologize for presenting the human body as a beautiful creation designed by God. Educators, as well as parents, don't always agree on what should and should not be taught in schools. This "difference of opinion" reinforces the fact that God has made everyone different with different perspectives. I have not deleted those issues that may concern physical maturity, abstinence, peer pressure, dating, marriage, and drugs and alcohol. I have presented them in a way that I feel is appropriate and God-glorifying.

Students, I hope you find in the pages of this book encouragement to face the unique pressure of today and the motivation to lead the Christian life — leaning on Him as your strength.

Teachers and parents, I hope you find the tools for instruction and the resources you need to build up and strengthen the sheep that God has placed in your care.

Finally, I want to say a special thank you to those who I feel have been very instrumental in my life:

To my mom and dad, Barbara and George Mackin. Thank you for showing me how to make wise choices and for teaching me respect for God and others. Dad, your provision in my life goes beyond the natural. Mom, your commitment to your children and your sacrificial love is a continual example for me.

To my husband, Scott. Thank you for encouraging me to finish this project even when it took over the house. I know your prayers enabled me to have the strength over these four years to stick with it. As your name so rightly means, you are my "loyal one." I am excited for what the Lord will continue to do in our lives together.

To my siblings, David, Tom, Kathy and Ann. Thank you for teaching me what it means to be the youngest of five! You each have been instrumental in my life. I hope the tributes and stories in this book make you realize how much I love and respect each one of you.

To the staff and students at Bible Temple Christian School. Thank you for believing that this book could go beyond the walls of our school and could meet the needs of others. Thank you for being the pilot school and for accepting each chapter in its unedited form. Janice Dorszynski, I just have to let you know you are the best! Your encouragement has gone past the administrative duties you hold. Your inspiration and insight has helped make this book complete. A ton of thanks to you, my friend!

To my illustrator, layout designer and friend, Lisa Million. I am thankful that after ten years out of high school, God brought us back together to tackle this book. Your gifts and callings in the Lord are evident. Thank you for keeping that vision in front of me and saying, "Sooney, we will get this finished." That goes for you too, Greg!

To my editor and friend, Barbara Wright. What can I say? Your hard work and dedication is a great example to me. It reminds me of the saying, "If you want to get something done, give it to a busy person." Thank you for taking on another project.

Thank you for letting me write the book in a style that is personal for me even when it may not have been the "best" style. Thank you for believing that the heart of God can penetrate the pages of paper to encourage and bring life. You are a joy to know and my phone bill knows it too!

May God Bless you all with total health; body, mind and spirit!

Table of Contents

Acknowledgements vii

Credits ix

Art Credits xi

Foreword xiii

Preface xvii

Introduction: A Higher Goal 1

Physical Health 11

1   Welcome To The Human Body 13
    1-1   The Awesome Power of Creation 13
    1-2   Introduction to Anatomy and Physiology 14
    1-3   The Organization of the Human Body 17

2   Eleven Systems: One Body 27
    2-1   Circulatory and Respiratory Systems 27
    2-2   Skeletal and Muscular Systems 32
    2-3   Digestive and Excretory Systems 39
    2-4   Integumentary and Immune Systems 46
    2-5   Nervous, Endocrine and Reproductive Systems ... 51

3   Nutrition 61
    3-1   Back to Basics 61
    3-2   God in the Doctor's Office 66
    3-3   The Role of Vitamins and Minerals 79
    3-4   The Diet Dilemma 84

UNIT 1

4 Fitness and Exercise **97**
   4-1   What is Fitness? 97
   4-2   Facing the Facts 100
   4-3   Principles of Exercise 103
   4-4   Choosing the Right Program 108
   4-5   Preventing Injuries 113
   4-6   Fatigue and Sleep 116

5 Infectious Disease **125**
   5-1   The Cause of Infectious Disease 125
   5-2   The Process of Infectious Disease 128
   5-3   The Battle Against Infectious Diseases.......131
   5-4   Fighting Common Infectious Diseases 136
   5-5   Sexually Transmitted Diseases 140

6 Noninfectious Disease **153**
   6-1   The Cause of Noninfectious Disease 153
   6-2   Fighting Noninfectious Diseases.................159

Mental Health 179

7 Stress and Anxiety **181**
   7-1   What Is Mental Health? 181
   7-2   What Is Stress? 183
   7-3   Coping With Stress 188
   7-4   Choose Life 192

8 L.I.F.E. Management **201**
   8-1   Managing your Lifestyle 201
   8-2   Managing your Influences 208
   8-3   Managing your Friendships 212
   8-4   Managing your Earthquakes 215

9 Made In His Image **227**
   9-1   "It's All in My Head" 227
   9-2   "But I am Comfortable Being Miserable" 231
   9-3   "I am Made in Whose Image?" 234

UNIT 2

Social Health 239

10 Head to Toes 241
   10-1 A Shining Light 241
   10-2 Fragile, Handle with Care 242
   10-3 Protecting your Eyes and Ears 252
   10-4 A Healthy Smile 258
   10-5 Standing Tall 262

11 Risky Business 271
   11-1 Taking a Risk 271
   11-2 Safety First 275
   11-3 Basic First Aid 283
   11-4 Emergency! 288

12 What's Your Responsibility? 299
   12-1 It's in the Attitude 299
   12-2 Responsibility as a Christian 300
   12-3 Responsibility as a Person 304
   12-4 Responsibility as a Citizen 308

13 Maturity: What's it All About? 325
   13-1 "Volumes" of Choices 325
   13-2 More than Just Saying "No" 333

14 Changing Relationships 359
   14-1 When Friendships Become Relationships............359
   14-2 When Two Become One 367
   14-3 When Two Become a Family 371
   14-4 When Death Means Life 375

UNIT 4

Spiritual Health **387**

15 Building Your Spiritual Muscles **389**
  15-1 Keys to Spiritual Fitness 389
  15-2 Keys to Consistency 402

16 Reaching Your Potential..**411**
  16-1 In Hot Pursuit 411
  16-2 Seeing Through the Darkness................................ 415
  16-3 In My Father's House 421

Epilogue..**429**

Notes 431
Bibliography..435
Glossary 439
Index 453

Introduction: A Higher Goal

Colored flags wave in the wind. The feeling of anticipation spreads throughout the stadium as the time draws near for the first event. The sick feeling of anxiety fills my stomach. My coach notices my nervousness and gives me one last piece of advice, "just do your best." The starter gives the first command to enter our starting blocks. I glance at my competitors; they look so strong, so together, so confident. I wonder what they think of me....

I adjust my feet in my blocks and carefully place my hands behind the line. I look ahead and all I see are hurdles — obstacles I must overcome to reach the finish line. Although only seconds pass as I wait for the start, it seems like forever. I find myself distracted by the movements of the other athletes. I must concentrate on my start and the steps to my first hurdle. "Lord, please don't let me fall." "Set," the command is given, my heart is pounding. "Go!" With the sound of the gun, I am off....

A HIGHER GOAL

I press on toward the goal for the prize of the upward call
of God in Christ Jesus.
Philippians 3:14 (NAS)

Have you ever thought of life as a race? It begins when you are born and ends when you die, with many hurdles to overcome along the way. You do not get a choice of what event to enter. Your only choice is how you are going to handle each obstacle or hurdle you will face. Every day you make choices that determine your success. Are you prepared to win the race? To win in a race you first must have a competitor. In life there is not one opponent that you can face and defeat — your competition is life itself. The key to victory is not in being "perfect." The key to a winning lifestyle is in striving to live a life pleasing to God; physically, mentally, socially and spiritually.

Some days you will face the opponent of laziness or the enemy of depression. On other days your competitor may hide himself in an attitude or reveal himself in a temptation. Whatever challenges you face you must try to do your best. What if you fall, do you have the strength and determination to get up? Although not everyone falls in an athletic event, everyone falls sometime in the race of life. The key is deciding to make the right choices to avoid making the same errors.

Do you have a purpose to your race? The Apostle Paul did and he encourages us to have a purpose also (I Corinthians 9:25–26).

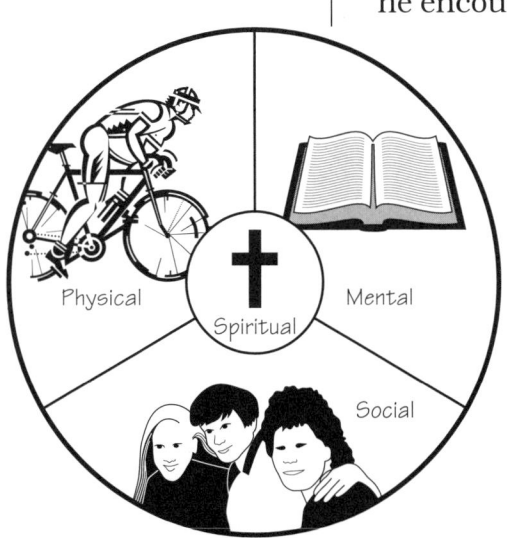

When an athlete competes in a race he sets his eyes ahead of him. This drive to the finish is what keeps the athlete on track. If you allow yourself to lose sight of why you are running in this life you will be sidetracked. As a result, you may not reach your God-given potential.

God's desire is that you experience an abundant life (John 10:10), but that quality of life is *not* guaranteed. *The decisions you make today, as a teenager, will directly affect your life, tomorrow, as an adult.* You may be asking yourself, "what does this have to do with my health?" There are many factors that affect your health. The state of your physical health may not affect whether you enter the Kingdom of Heaven, but it can directly affect the productivity and quality of life along the way. Your health is a multidimensional measure of the quality of your life. **Total health** therefore is: physical, mental, social and spiritual wellness.

If your only goal is to live long and have fun, then you may concentrate on your physical, mental and social well-being. However, your spiritual health is the link to an *abundant life.* The condition of your spiritual health takes you down another road. This road may seem more difficult but it leads you on a more meaningful journey to reach a higher goal.

GOOD HEALTH? DON'T BUY THE LIE!

What would be your definition of good health? Through advertisement, television, the media and fashion, our society portrays an individual who is not the same as the person portrayed in the Bible. Our society places great emphasis on a person's physical condition. Good health is often measured by a person's outer appearance and is based on whatever society thinks is important at a given point. For example, because of skin cancer, a tan is not considered as "healthy" as it once was. Even ideal weight has changed with the fitness craze. Those female models you see sporting an ultra thin body are not necessarily considered healthy. The athletes who use steroids to look "fit" and to enhance their performance may not truly be healthy.

The Christian's view of good health includes

The Secular View	The Christian's View
Physical: Outer appearance and physique	Physical: Inner beauty and countenance
Mental: Concerned with self	Mental: Concerned with others
Social: Popular with many no matter what the cost	Social: Clear conscience with those you relate to
Spiritual: Freedom of choice	Spiritual: Strong relationship with God

the spiritual dimension. It begins with inner qualities and is based on what the Bible says is important. Your appearance or countenance (your face as an indication of mood, emotion or character), is enhanced by being fit physically, mentally, socially, and spiritually. Webster's dictionary defines health as: "freedom from disease; good condition, normal and efficient functioning." When you feel stress over an exam at school, are you healthy? When you feel depressed because you lack quality friendships, are you healthy? It is difficult to come up with one definition of good health that includes all aspects of a person. Take a moment to consider your own personal definition of good health.

YOU *CAN* MAKE GOOD CHOICES

Do you ever wonder if you are living up to the potential God has intended for your life? Imagine yourself in heaven, face to face with God. He pulls out a chart of your life to show you your life's accomplishments. As you view the chart you think to yourself, "I could have done much more." Although God is not in the business of keeping charts, the choices that you make will eventually determine how close you come to reaching your God-given potential.

Being in good health allows you to live up to your potential. You are continually changing and so is your state of health. You are not at the same level of wellness today as you were yesterday and will be tomorrow. Each aspect of your total health is affected daily. Ken Malmin describes the human body as a wheel, traveling on the road of life. Your spiritual condition is in the center, while the other three aspects, physical, mental/emotional, and social are on the outer wheel.

Do you ever wonder if you are living up to the potential God has intended for your life?

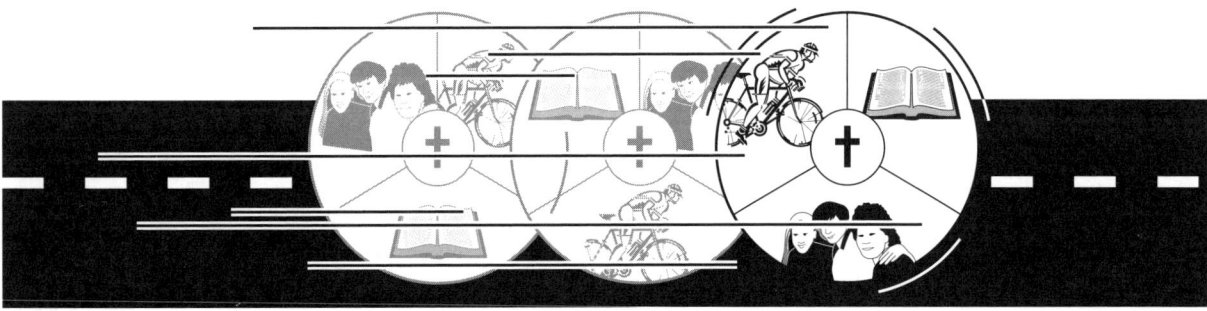

Life is one of seasons. Sometimes you involve yourself in one area and you let the other areas slip. The key to maintaining wellness in each area of your life is *balance.* Problems occur when you become so out of balance that your responsibilities are affected for a long period of time. Can you think of some examples in your own life when your responsibilities have been out of balance?

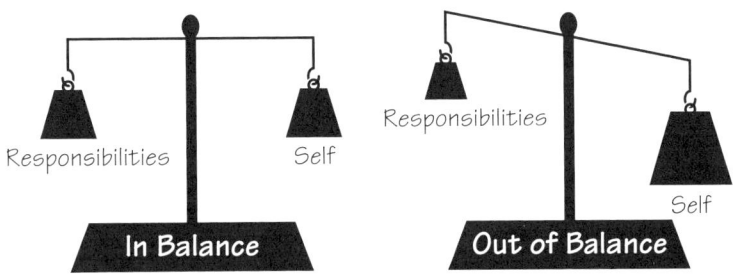

One day you may be experiencing stress over an exam at school. This feeling may affect the way you eat or the amount of sleep you receive. You may choose to eat junk food and sleep only three hours. As a result, your body gets rundown and you physically get sick. Because of being sick you are unable attend a social gathering with your friends and you sink into depression. This cycle is one example of how the choices you make in *one* area affect the others.

Emphasizing one aspect of your health over another is an example of the *cycle* you may experience. Consider the following example: You have decided to go out for a sport at school. Throughout the season you must practice after school for several hours. This commitment limits the time you have to study for school and your grades begin to drop. When your parents see your report card for the quarter, they decide you are involved in too many activities so they limit the time you get to spend with your friends. The homework is building up and you decide you cannot attend your church activities because you are too busy. Although you enjoy your involvement in the sport and the extra exercise, the sports commitment has affected other aspects of your total health.

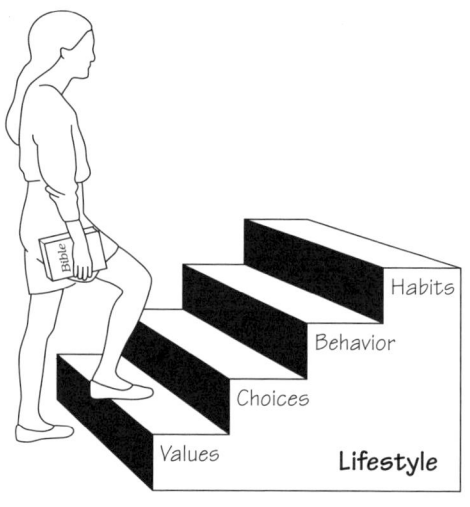

Many factors determine your state of health. Those health conditions you inherit are generally out of your control. However, your *behavior* throughout your life will affect your total health condition. You determine much of your health by your *decisions,* and you base your decisions on those *values* that you believe deep inside. When you "set" your value upon something, you are determining its relative importance to you. Certain values change with age or experiences; but for a Christian, basic values or convictions should never change.

You face *choices* everyday. Will you stay up late, eat a good breakfast, fasten your seatbelt, brush your teeth, go jogging or watch television? You make choices that are good for you and bad for you. Although you may not see the results immediately, the *habits* begin to form that will continue the rest of your life.

Habit is one of the most powerful friends we can have, as well as our most potent enemy when our habits are wrong. Since so much of life flows from habit, special attention needs to be given to building godly habits based on biblical convictions.[1]
Jerry White

You may do things without even thinking, or you may do things just because you are not aware of the *consequences.* Sometimes you may make choices knowing full well the negative consequences of your decisions. Adopting good habits is often easier than changing bad habits. For example, refuse to start smoking rather than give up the habit. Why do you think people do things that are bad for them? What does God think of these decisions?

Although many things influence your behavior, your concern for your health is *not* the most powerful influence. Let's consider some of these influences:

Culture: Culture is the general way of life of any group of people. The customs, language, arts, religion, and even the food is cultural. Have you ever visited another culture? Did it change your life?

Religion: Your faith will influence your behavior in many ways. Not only in the activities you choose to be involved in, but also the way you handle difficulties you face. Your faith may determine how you respond to your parents, peers and adults. It is the basic foundation of the choices you make.

People you admire or respect: The type of people you choose to model will affect your choices and decisions in life. These role models may have a positive or negative affect on your life. Can you give some examples of both positive and negative role models? Who are the people you respect or admire?

Peers: Those who are of the same age group as yourself are your peers. The influence of your peers can become a very strong factor in determining your behavior. Although the desire to be accepted by your peers is a normal feeling, it can be detrimental when you compromise your own standards to please an individual or a group. As you learn to handle peer pressure at a young age, you will be better able to handle the peer pressure you will face as an adult.

School: In school you may learn specific things that may influence your health behavior, such as proper nutrition in a health class, the hazards in the environment, and safety in and out of doors.

Media: The media involves television, radio, and printed material. The information that you see and/or hear may be misleading. Their influence may be positive and negative.

Organizations: Clubs, athletics, church organizations are some examples of groups that can influence your health behavior.

Family: During the early years of your life, the most powerful influence on your health behavior is your family. The values that you learn, the food you eat, the sleeping patterns that you develop, the activities you are involved in as a family and even the products that your family buys, all affect your own health decisions.

Self-Inventory of Family Patterns

Eating patterns begin with the family and help shape your future eating habits.

1. What do I notice about my family's attitude toward food?
2. Any specific family eating habits? (positive and/or negative)
3. What do I notice about my family's attitude toward exercise?
4. How does my family handle stress?
5. Does my family eat out at restaurants or fast food restaurants regularly? How often?
6. How often does my family eat meals together?
7. Do I notice anyone in my family eating breakfast regularly? Do I eat breakfast regularly?

Values: Values are your personal standards for what is important or has worth. Developing your values is a process throughout your life. They may change due to certain circumstances or influences you meet. Your values are the key to how you choose to live. Professor Colleen Hacker from Pacific Lutheran University states the connection between your actions and values in a powerful "one-liner":

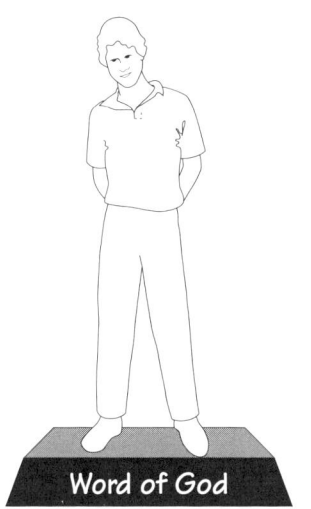

Word of God

"Your actions reflect your values."

The factors that influence your values are endless, but *the foundation upon which you base your values should be the Word of God.*

Developing positive health habits brings great benefits. When you feel good physically, you experience more energy and avoid illness. When you experience good social health, you enjoy the company of others and you have a more positive self-image. Being mentally healthy helps you have a clear mind for learning and decision making. The results of a healthy lifestyle reach beyond yourself. You not only affect your own personal happiness, but the happiness of those around you.

The greatest benefit of being *totally healthy* is living a life that is pleasing to God. The scripture says: "I press toward the goal for the prize...." To "press on" means to pursue, to make every effort to press forward in a race. Although each area of life is important to God, there is a bigger picture than what you see here on earth. Make the right choices for a winning lifestyle. Run the Christian course without taking unnecessary detours and without losing the vision of the higher goal.

Do you not know that those who run in a race all run, but one receives the prize? Run in such a way that you may obtain it. And everyone who competes for the prize is temperate in all things. Now they do it to obtain a perishable crown, but we for an imperishable crown.
I Corinthians 9:24,25

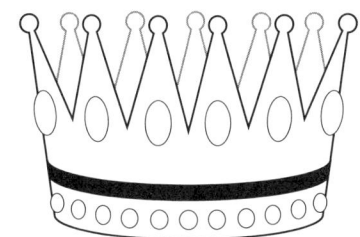

PHYSICAL HEALTH

For Thou didst form my inward parts;
Thou didst weave me in my mother's womb.
I will give thanks to Thee,
for I am fearfully and wonderfully made…
Psalm 139:13-14 (NAS)

CHAPTER 1   WELCOME TO THE HUMAN BODY

CHAPTER 2   ELEVEN SYSTEMS: ONE BODY

CHAPTER 3   NUTRITION

CHAPTER 4   FITNESS AND EXERCISE

CHAPTER 5   INFECTIOUS DISEASE

CHAPTER 6   NONINFECTIOUS DISEASE

Unit 1

1 Welcome To The Human Body 13
   1-1   The Awesome Power of Creation.............................13
   1-2   Introduction to Anatomy and Physiology.............14
   1-3   The Organization of the Human Body 17

2 Eleven Systems: One Body 27
   2-1   Circulatory and Respiratory Systems...................27
   2-2   Skeletal and Muscular Systems 32
   2-3   Digestive and Excretory Systems 39
   2-4   Integumentary and Immune Systems 46
   2-5   Nervous, Endocrine and Reproductive Systems...51

3 Nutrition 61
   3-1   Back to Basics 61
   3-2   God in the Doctor's Office 66
   3-3   The Role of Vitamins and Minerals 79
   3-4   The Diet Dilemma 84

4 Fitness and Exercise 97
   4-1   What is Fitness?...97
   4-2   Facing the Facts...100
   4-3   Principles of Exercise 103
   4-4   Choosing the Right Program 108
   4-5   Preventing Injuries 113
   4-6   Fatigue and Sleep..116

5 Infectious Disease 125
   5-1   The Cause of Infectious Disease 125
   5-2   The Process of Infectious Disease 128
   5-3   The Battle Against Infectious Diseases...............131
   5-4   Fighting Common Infectious Diseases 136
   5-5   Sexually Transmitted Diseases 140

6 Noninfectious Disease 153
   6-1   The Cause of Noninfectious Disease 153
   6-2   Fighting Noninfectious Diseases............................159

Welcome To The Human Body

1-1   THE AWESOME POWER OF CREATION
1-2   INTRODUCTION TO ANATOMY AND PHYSIOLOGY
1-3   THE ORGANIZATION OF THE HUMAN BODY

1-1   THE AWESOME POWER OF CREATION

And the Lord God formed man of the dust of the ground, and breathed into his nostrils the breath of life; and man became a living being.
Genesis 2:7

Do you remember a school assignment when you were asked to create something? Maybe it was an art or science project, or a written essay. Most likely you were encouraged to do it on your own. The teacher may have said, "be creative," "use your imagination." It can be very difficult and frustrating to try to think of something without the help of someone else. Webster defines creation as *"the act of inventing or producing; an original work of art."*

Have you ever thought of God as an artist? He had a blank canvas, and out of His own thoughts and imagination, without the ideas of someone else, He created the heavens and the earth. What an awesome art project! When God created man, and breathed life into him, God had an original work of art.

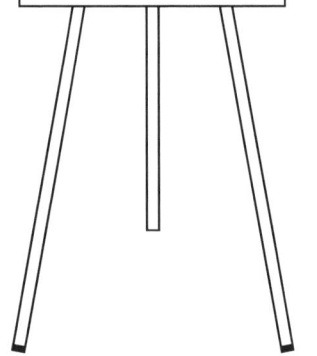

Have you ever thought of God as an artist?

Men go abroad to wonder at the height of mountains, at the huge waves of the sea, at the long courses of the rivers, at the vast compass of the ocean, at the circular motion of the stars; and they pass by themselves without wondering.
Saint Augustine

Let yourself wonder for a moment. Close your eyes and concentrate. Do you hear your breathing, can you feel the beat of your heart? These are obvious clues that you are alive. Now concentrate on the inside of your body. Do you feel your cells multiplying, your organs functioning, your intestines digesting your last meal or your hairs in your ears moving so you could hear the slightest sound? These are daily functions that are often taken for granted. Your body is full of remarkable functions and abilities that scientists are learning more about everyday.

Have you ever noticed how a small child can find the simplest things amazing? An adult may look past a flower, but a child may stop and examine it very closely. A child's faith and gratitude is simple and uncomplicated. That is one reason Jesus had such a special place for children in His heart (Matthew 18).

David expresses his appreciation to God in Psalm 139:13–14. "For Thou didst form my inward parts; Thou didst weave me in my mother's womb. I will give thanks to Thee, for I am fearfully and wonderfully made; Wonderful are Thy works, and my soul knows it very well" (NAS). If you recognize God as the creator of all things, then you can give your gratitude toward God. David said, "I will give thanks to *Thee*...." God created you special, in His image, and He said it was *very good*.

God created you special, in His image, and he said it was very good.

1-2   INTRODUCTION TO ANATOMY AND PHYSIOLOGY

The study of the human body goes back many years, but until the discovery of the microscope scientists did not have the knowledge needed to understand the nature of the body. In 1674 Anton van Leeuwenhoek, a man who ground lenses as a hobby and used them to study small objects, opened the doors to the invisible world when he invented the microscope. Researchers use the microscope as the basis for scientific development.

The microscope has brought scientists closer to the wonders of the human body and allowed scientists to branch out into numerous specialties. There are doctors who specialize in the study and treatment of the heart (cardiologists), those who specialize in the eyes (ophthamologists), infants and children (pediatricians) and many more. A person who studies the *structure* of body parts, their forms and arrangements, are called *Anatomists*. This field of study is called **Anatomy.** *Physiologists*, on the other hand, are concerned about the *function* of the body parts, what they do and how they do it. This field of study is called **Physiology**. Anatomy and Physiology are closely related and are often discussed together. It is difficult to separate the structure of body parts from their function.

THE PURPOSE OF THE HUMAN BODY'S STRUCTURE AND FUNCTION

Ask someone this question: why is the human body built the way it is? Can anyone tell you exactly why the human body is formed the way it is? Why don't humans have eyes in the back of their heads; it would be helpful sometimes. Or why don't humans have four arms and hands instead of only two. This too would come in "handy." No one can tell you why God formed mankind into the structure that He did.

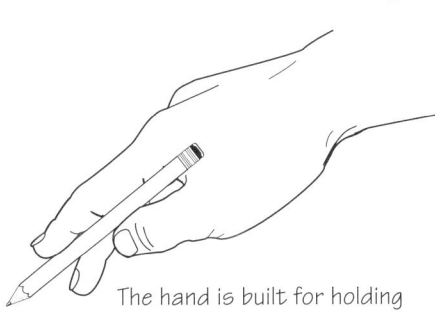

The hand is built for holding

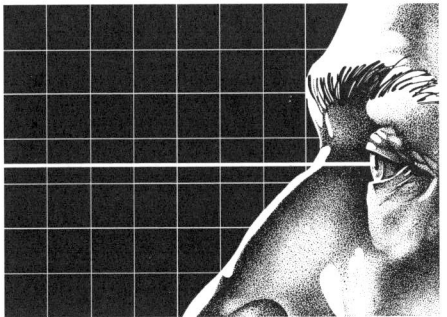

The eye is built for seeing

The physical body is magnificently formed. The structure and function of all body parts are focused on achieving one goal — maintaining life. The reproductive system is the only system that has a separate function from the total human body; its primary function is to reproduce. **Homeostasis** is the condition of

It is difficult to separate the structure of body parts from their function.

SOMETHING TO **THINK** ABOUT

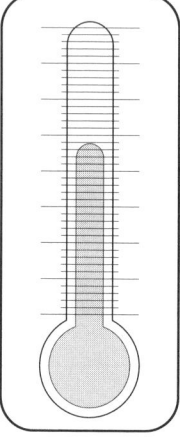

To better understand the body's ability to maintain a stable internal environment, imagine a room equipped with both a heater and an air conditioner. If the room temperature was to remain at 68°F the thermostat would be set at 68°F. Once the outside environment caused the room temperature to rise above the 68° set temperature, the furnace would automatically shut off and the air conditioner would turn on. With this system working properly, the room should stay at a relatively constant temperature.

The body's internal thermostat is set at 98.6°F. If factors cause this temperature to drop, the body automatically triggers the brain to generate heat, and the body may begin to shiver. If the body is too hot, the brain may turn on the body's natural cooling system and the body begins to sweat.[1]

a stable internal environment. When the environment outside your body changes, changes in temperature or oxygen for example, the conditions within your body must remain stable. This constant need for balance is one of the body's primary functions.

The Needs of the Human Body

Although you may like to think of yourself as being very independent, you are very dependent. The human body depends upon certain factors for its survival.

1. **Water:** water is the most abundant substance in the human body.
2. **Food:** food is a source of energy, nourishment for growth, and the regulation of bodily functions.
3. **Oxygen:** oxygen is the gas that releases energy from food and supplies the body with what is needed for all functions of the body.
4. **Heat:** heat is also a form of energy. Heat is produced from the body's metabolism.
5. **Pressure:** pressure is necessary for bodily functions such as breathing.

This list does not mention the emotional and social needs of the human body. Researchers, however, will agree that the human body needs affection and love from others to fully develop both physically and emotionally. God says that He knows your needs and that He is able to provide for you.

Therefore I say to you, do not worry about your life, what you will eat or what you will drink; nor about your body, what you will put on. Is not life more than food and the body more than clothing?...For your heavenly Father knows that you need all these things. But seek first the kingdom of God and His righteousness, and all these things shall be added to you.
Matthew 6:25,32–33

1-3 THE ORGANIZATION OF THE HUMAN BODY

As God designed the human body, He did not randomly throw some materials together to form the basic frame. Out of the dust of the ground God formed a dynamic, highly organized, living organism. Although the body is made up of basic physical elements that are found in the earth, the composition of these elements is uniquely arranged. In your biology classes you will learn more about the specific elements that make up the human body.

God created the body as a composition of parts within parts, each varying in its purpose, but each very important in the proper function of the whole. The human body is designed to *move* (internally and externally), to *respond* (reacting to internal and external changes), to *grow*, to *regulate* its own functions, and to *heal* itself. Most importantly, it is designed to *reproduce*. God thought His idea was so good He wanted it to continue. He gave man and woman a great role in the creation of another human being, the miracle of conception and birth.

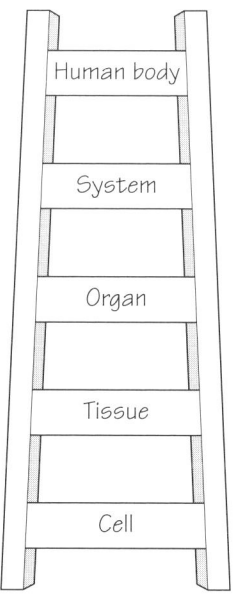

He gave man and woman a great role in the creation of another human being, the miracle of conception and birth.

THE CELL

Scientists have found the human body to be organized into four levels, with the cell being the smallest living unit. The human body is made up entirely of cells. **Cells** are the basic building blocks from which all larger parts are formed. Cells are combinations of other elements such as water, oxygen, carbon, hydrogen and other trace elements.

Characteristics of a Cell:
1. Cells are alive
2. Cells have the power to move
3. Cells are sensitive
4. Cells take in oxygen (breathe)
5. Cells take in food and water
6. Cells get rid of waste
7. Cells grow
8. Cells can reproduce

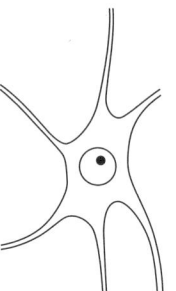

The different sizes and shapes that cells have closely relate to their individual function. For example, muscle cells look different than nerve cells, thus they have a very different function. Interestingly, cells know their function and do not try to do something they were not originally designed to do. Life begins with the union of two cells, the sperm cell and the egg cell, not a bone cell and a muscle cell. Two specific, separate, living cells in the body join to create one living human being.

Although you do not see the cell in its individual form, you see and are aware of the combinations of cells everyday. Cells are responsible for the shape, organization, and construction of the body as well as for keeping the body in a living state. Cells reproduce to provide new cells needed for growth and to replace injured cells with healthy ones.

The next time you get the opportunity to view a slide of cells under the microscope, notice the life in each individual cell and marvel at the thought that your body is made up of trillions of these, in various shapes and combinations.

> Cells are the basic building blocks from which all larger parts are formed.

Paul Brand expresses his thoughts concerning the cell in his book, *Fearfully and Wonderfully Made.*

I have closed my eyes. My shoes are kicked off, and I am wiggling the small bones in my right foot. Exposed, they are half the width of a pencil, and yet they support my weight in walking. I cup my hand over my ear and hear the familiar seashell phenomenon, actually the sound of blood cells rushing through the capillaries in my head. I stretch out my left arm and try to imagine the millions of muscle cells eagerly expanding and contracting in concert. I rub my finger across my arm and feel the stimulation of touch cells, 450 of them in each one-inch-square patch of skin.

Inside, my stomach, spleen, liver, pancreas, and kidneys, each packed with millions of loyal cells, are working so efficiently I have no way of perceiving their presence. Fine hairs in my inner ear are monitoring a swishing fluid, ready to alert me if I suddenly tilt off balance.

When my cells work well, I'm hardly conscious of their individual presences. What I feel is the composite of their activity known as Paul Brand. My body, composed of many parts, is one.[2]

> My body, composed of many parts, is one.
>
> Paul Brand

THE TISSUES

Tissues are made up of similar cells that are specialized to carry on particular functions in the body. Although cells are the basic living structure of the human body, their activity becomes much more specialized when they are organized into groups or layers called tissues. The human body is organized into four

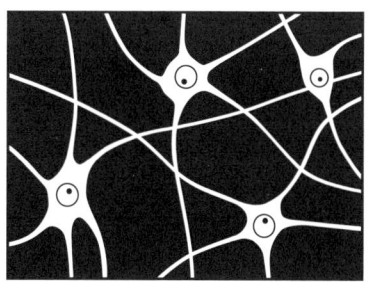

primary types of tissues: epithelial tissues, connective tissues, muscle tissues, and nerve tissues. The study of these individual tissues can be very complicated, but the following is a general overview for each.

Epithelial Tissue

Epithelial tissues are like sheets that cover all body surfaces — inside and out. They form the most obvious protective layer, the skin, as well as the inner lining of the body cavities such as the stomach and the intestines. Epithelial tissues can reproduce quickly in case cells are damaged or injured. For example, your skin heals quickly when you have a cut because the epithelial tissues replace the injured cells rapidly.

These important tissues also provide protection. The cells of the mouth and skin are a good example of this function. Other functions of these specialized tissues are absorption of nutrients from food (in the intestines), the secretion of hormones in the glands, saliva in the mouth, perspiration in the skin, and enzymes in digestion.

Connective Tissue

Connective tissues are in all parts of the body. They bind structures together, provide support and protection. Some stronger types of connective tissue include tendons, ligaments, bone and cartilage. Other types of this specialized tissue store fat (adipose tissue), produce blood cells (vascular tissue) and destroy bacteria (reticuloendothelial tissue).

> The human body is organized into four primary types of tissues...

Muscle Tissue

You are probably most familiar with **muscle tissue**. Their primary function is to contract, becoming shorter or thicker and cause body parts to move. The three types of muscle tissue are skeletal muscle, smooth muscle, and cardiac muscle.

The skeletal muscles can be controlled by you, thus they are said to be voluntary. These tissues are responsible for major body movements such as the arms, legs, trunk and head. Your facial muscles are also voluntary. Smooth muscle tissue is found in the walls of hollow internal organs such as the stomach, intestines, bladder and blood vessels. Unlike the skeletal muscles, smooth muscle tissue is involuntary; you do not have conscious control over their function. The cardiac muscle tissue is found only in the heart. Its specialization is very important in the continual function of the heart muscle. Like the smooth muscle tissue the cardiac tissue is involuntary — you cannot control the beating of your heart.

Nerve Tissue

The basic cells that make up the nerve tissue are called neurons and of all the body cells, neurons seem to be the most specialized. Nerve cells can be as long as six feet. Think of all the specific impulses that the nerve tissue must send in order to keep the body functioning. **Nerve tissues** are sensitive to changes, receive and transmit impulses to various parts of the body. These highly complex structures are located in the brain, spinal cord and nerves.

THE ORGANS

Moving up the ladder of complexity you reach the category of the organs. Did you know that your skin is an organ of your integumentary system, or that every separate bone in your body can be called an organ? An **organ** can be defined as two or more tissues grouped together and performing specialized functions.

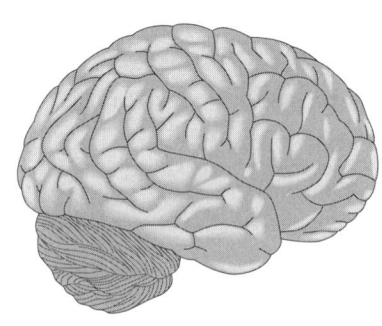

As the body increases in complexity, the body becomes more dependent on each functioning part. The body is like a team. Each one of its members needs to be functioning the way it was designed so the whole body can accomplish its task. If the heart decided it was not necessary and stopped beating, the lungs would soon stop functioning. If your intestines were rebelling and decided not to absorb nutrients from foods, then the whole body would soon suffer. Every organ of your body needs to be healthy and functioning to ensure the health of the eleven systems of your body.

THE SYSTEMS

The following chapter will give you a general overview of the systems of the body. This knowledge will help you understand the relationship between each system.

Related organs make up the **systems of your body**. The systems are often listed in various categories but this book lists 11 systems of the body:

1. Circulatory System
2. Respiratory System
3. Skeletal System
4. Muscular System
5. Digestive System
6. Excretory System
7. Integumentary (skin) System

As the body increases in complexity, the body becomes more dependent on each functioning part.

8. Endocrine System
9. Nervous System
10. Immune System
11. Reproductive System

While you are learning about the various systems do not be confused when certain organs belong to more than one system or if one system interacts directly with another. The purpose of this unit is to give you a general introduction to anatomy and physiology. As you are learning, remember, God created man and woman in His image. He designed the body to work together as a marvelous physical and spiritual being.

CHAPTER REVIEW

DEFINE

Anatomy

Physiology

Homeostasis

Cells

Tissues

Epithelial tissue

Connective tissues

Muscle tissue

Nerve tissue

Organs

Systems of the body

EXPLAIN

1. Explain why the microscope changed the course of scientific research.
2. Explain why anatomy and physiology are often discussed together.
3. Explain the goal of all bodily structures and functions.
4. Explain why homeostasis is so important in the body.
5. Explain the factors that the body depends on for survival.
6. Explain the characteristics of all cells.
7. List the four primary types of tissues in the body and explain their general function.
8. Explain the unique relationship between the organs in your body and the systems in your body.

DISCUSS

1. How might having a grateful heart affect your attitude and the way you live?
2. How is the function and structure of body parts closely related?
3. Even though you may like to think of yourself as being very independent, discuss the ways in which you are really dependent on certain other factors. What are those factors? Discuss things that may not be listed in this chapter.
4. What is meant by Matthew 6:25–33, and how might it affect the way you live?

SUGGESTED ACTIVITIES

1. **Key Concepts:** Outline the chapter and make a study guide for yourself. You can work in groups and let each student be responsible for a section in the chapter.

2. **Digging Deeper:** Take one or two concepts in this chapter (for example the cell, or one system of the body, the microscope, etc.) and write an indepth report researching the topic. Share the report with the class; don't forget to include some interesting illustrations.

3. **The Miracle of the Microscope:** Get a microscope from the biology lab, learn how to properly make a slide and then scrape some cells from your body (inside the cheek, under the armpit, etc.) view them under the slide, draw pictures of what you see, label them and put them up in the class for others to see.

4. **Uniquely Designed:** Interview several people and ask them why they think God designed the human body the way He did. Then ask them what life would be like if we were formed differently (four arms, four eyes, etc). Then draw a picture of yourself (or bring a few photos) and post the interviews next to your picture and put it up in the classroom. This is a fun way to learn to appreciate the way the human body is uniquely designed.

5. **Levels of Organization:** Choose a system of the body. Draw a general picture of the system, then draw an organ found in that system, then draw a tissue belonging to that organ, and lastly draw a picture of the human cell. This will show the levels of complexity of the human body. Use your biology book or an Anatomy and Physiology book from the library to find your illustrations. This can be done in a group where each student has something different to draw. Post these in the classroom.

Eleven Systems: One Body

2-1   CIRCULATORY AND RESPIRATORY SYSTEMS
2-2   SKELETAL AND MUSCULAR SYSTEMS
2-3   DIGESTIVE AND EXCRETORY SYSTEMS
2-4   INTEGUMENTARY AND IMMUNE SYSTEMS
2-5   NERVOUS, ENDOCRINE AND REPRODUCTIVE SYSTEMS

2-1   CIRCULATORY AND RESPIRATORY SYSTEMS

THE CIRCULATORY SYSTEM

The **circulatory system** can best be understood as your body's transportation system and defined as the group of body parts that transports the blood throughout the body to keep the body functioning properly. This system has four main functions: to transport fuel to the body, to transport wastes to the liver and kidneys to be eliminated, to transport cells to fight disease and to transport hormones throughout the body. The organs of the circulatory sytem include the heart, arteries, veins and capillaries.

Heart: Known as the muscular pump. With every beat, blood is being pumped to the rest of the body.

Arteries: The largest blood vessels that carry oxygenated blood away from the heart. The arteries are very strong due to the high pressure of blood flowing through them.

Veins: Take blood from the body back to the heart. Veins have thinner walls than the arteries due to the lower pressure of blood flowing through them. They also have valves to direct the blood flow.

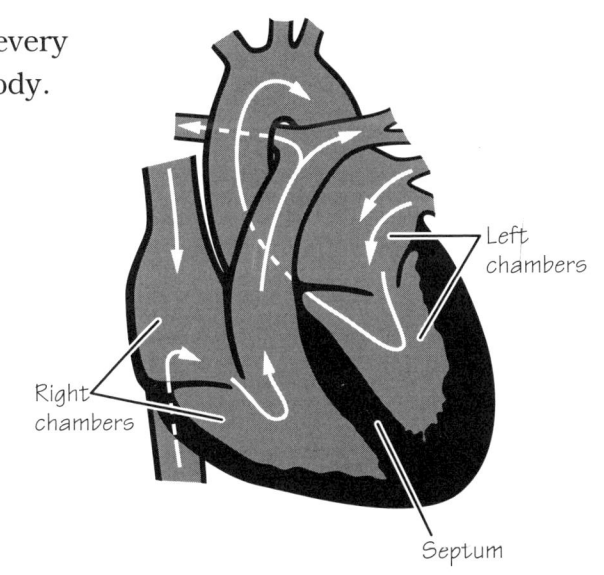

Left chambers

Right chambers

Septum

The Circulatory System

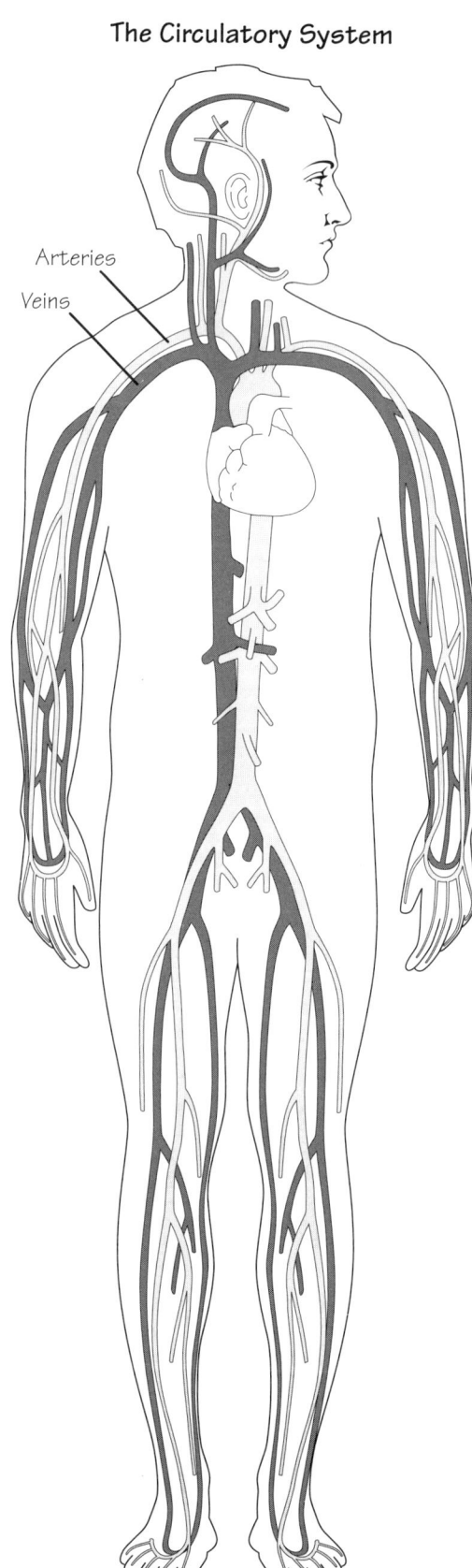

Arteries

Veins

Capillaries: The smallest blood vessels that carry blood from the arteries to the body's cells and from those cells to the veins. The capillaries have semipermeable walls so that nutrients, gases, and wastes are exchanged between blood and tissues.

It is extremely important that your heart functions efficiently to allow your body to adjust to changes. For example, your heart beat increases as you exercise so that more blood can be pumped to your muscles and your lungs. When you are frightened, a hormone called adrenaline causes your heart to beat faster to provide more oxygenated blood to your muscles and your brain. In the average individual, the heart may beat 60–80 times a minute. The number of beats per minute is called your pulse. The condition of your blood and your body's ability to circulate it efficiently is closely related to your overall health.

Your *kidneys* have a dual role. These organs function as the cleansers of the blood as well as the regulators of your body's fluid content. It is amazing that these two bean shaped organs process and cleanse the total amount of blood in your body every 50 minutes (about 1,800 quarts of blood per day!). Your kidneys are essential for survival. If your kidneys failed, a dialysis machine would have to do their job.

Your body has about 100,000 miles of blood vessels and men have more blood in their circulatory system than women. Men also have more red blood cells than women. The exception is during pregnancy when a woman's blood supply will increase with approximately 3–4 pounds of added blood.

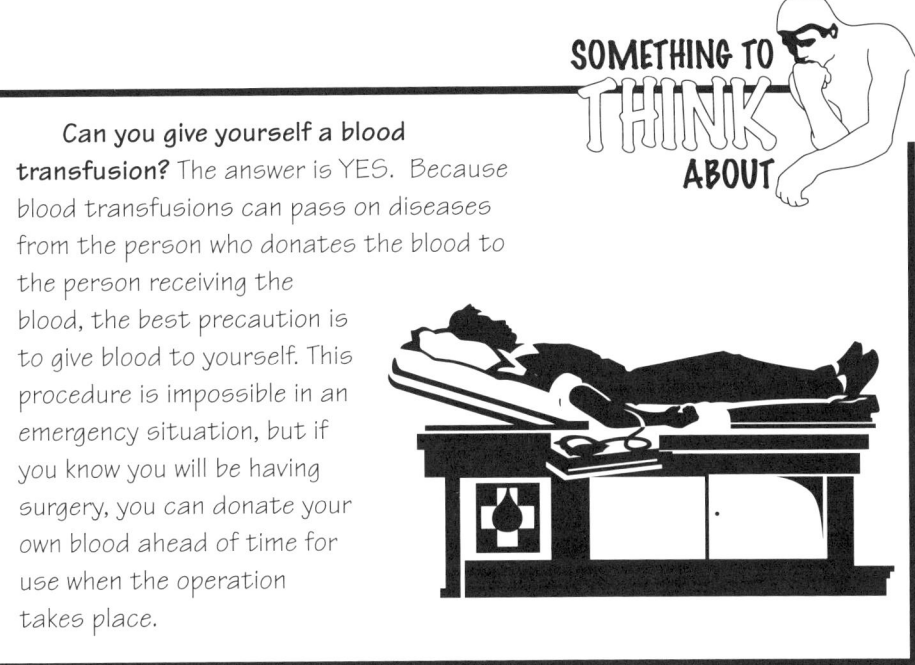

SOMETHING TO THINK ABOUT

Can you give yourself a blood transfusion? The answer is YES. Because blood transfusions can pass on diseases from the person who donates the blood to the person receiving the blood, the best precaution is to give blood to yourself. This procedure is impossible in an emergency situation, but if you know you will be having surgery, you can donate your own blood ahead of time for use when the operation takes place.

Problems In The Circulatory System

1. Anemia: **Anemia** is a condition characterized by a shortage of or an inadequate number of red blood cells. There are many causes and types. One of the more common causes of anemia results from an inadequate amount of iron in the diet.

2. Leukemia: **Leukemia** is a form of cancer characterized by an uncontrolled or abnormal production of white blood cells. The white blood cells do not function properly and cause a lowering of resistance to infection. There are many types of leukemia as well as many types of treatment.

3. Hemophilia: **Hemophilia** is a disease in which the blood is lacking one or more of the elements (clotting factors) that cause the blood to clot. This results in very little, if any, blood clotting in response to injury. A medicine that allows the blood to clot is available to those who have hemophilia.

4. Arteriosclerosis: **Arteriosclerosis** is a disease where certain arteries become hardened and obstructed, eventually limiting or stopping the flow of blood to certain organs of the body. It is a problem that people usually don't know they have for a long time. It is very common in Western societies like America. Heart attacks are an example of the results of this disease.

5. Stroke: A **stroke** occurs when the blood flow to one part of the brain is severely restricted or cut off. Common causes

of strokes are blood clots, arteriosclerosis, and untreated high blood pressure.

6. **High blood pressure:** High blood pressure (**hypertension**) is also a very common condition in Western societies. Lifestyle can influence blood pressure. Medication is also effective in controlling this condition.

THE RESPIRATORY SYSTEM

Breathing is a natural function of the body. It seems so simple but it actually involves several organs which are divided into two

parts: the upper respiratory tract (throat and nose) and the lower respiratory tract (the lungs). The **respiratory system** is the group of passages that exchanges gases in order for the body to function properly.

The *lungs* are the main organs of the respiratory system. Without healthy lungs a person's breathing is impaired and the oxygen flow to the rest of the body is deficient. The lungs are large, soft, cone-shaped organs, one on each side of your heart. Within the lungs are air passages called the bronchial tree. At the ends of the bronchial tree are millions of tiny air sacs called *alveoli*. The main function of the alveoli is to exchange gases with the blood.

The terms *inspiration (inhalation)* and *expiration (exhalation)* are used to describe the action of breathing. You could not survive without both inspiration and expiration. With inspiration, air is carried into the alveoli where the oxygen in the air passes through the alveoli into veins that carry it to the heart. At the same time carbon dioxide (a waste product) passes from the blood into the alveoli. During expiration, carbon dioxide is carried up the airways and out of the body.

SOMETHING TO THINK ABOUT

The lungs contain millions of air sacs. If the walls of the air sacs were stretched out, they would cover a tennis court.

Notice for a moment your breathing pattern. Sit quietly and concentrate on your breathing. You inhale air through your nose or mouth and your chest rises slightly. As you exhale your chest returns to its normal position. For this movement to occur, a group of muscles called your intercostal muscles as well as your diaphragm are used. The *diaphragm* is a large muscle that separates the chest from the abdomen.

Problems In The Respiratory System

1. **The common cold:** This is the one of most the most common illnesses that affects primarily the respiratory system. Depending upon the virus that you get, it may affect only your upper respiratory system with signs such as a runny nose, itchy, watery eyes, and a sore throat, or it may affect your lower respiratory system by giving you a cough.

2. **Pneumonia:** A more serious illness that can affect your respiratory system. **Pneumonia** is an infection of the lungs and causes difficulty breathing. Medication can help certain kinds of pneumonia.

3. **Bronchitis: Bronchitis** is a swelling or inflammation of the bronchi. A serious cough, a general feeling of fatigue and a fever usually comes with bronchitis. Medications can help but it usually lasts several weeks.

4. **Asthma: Asthma** is a fairly common condition that can make breathing difficult. Attacks of asthma can be mild to very severe and even life threatening. In this condition, the air passages in the bronchial tree swell and constrict. It can be trig-

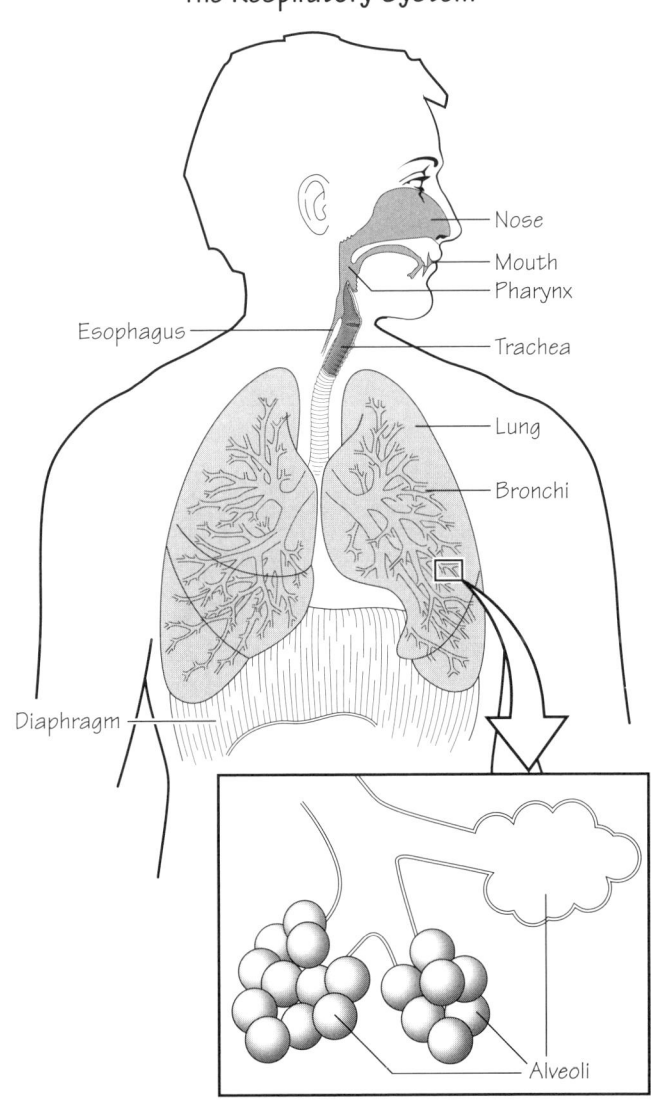

The Respiratory System

Nose
Mouth
Pharynx
Esophagus
Trachea
Lung
Bronchi
Diaphragm
Alveoli

gered by an allergic reaction to something, by exercise or by psychological factors such as intense fear or nervousness. Asthma cannot be cured but it can be treated with certain drugs. Some people grow out of their asthmatic condition.

5. *Emphysema:* When a person suffers from **emphysema**, air sacs in his lungs become enlarged and lose their elasticity. The main cause of emphysema is breathing in smoke. Symptoms include shortness of breath, wheezing, bluish skin and a chronic, painful cough. There is no cure for emphysema but if the person stops smoking the disease will not progress. Emphysema usually leads to further complications of the heart and lungs.

6. *Cancer:* Lung cancer was a rare disease before the increase in air pollution and the rise in smoking. **Lung cancer** occurs when the cancer cells grow out of control and destroy the air sacs in the lungs. Radiation and chemicals are used to treat the disease. Sometimes a lung or portion of a lung must be removed.

2-2   SKELETAL AND MUSCULAR SYSTEMS

Bones do not burden us; they free us.[1]
Dr. Paul Brand

THE SKELETAL SYSTEM

Have you ever been by a construction site? Once the foundation is ready for the structure, the framework begins. Workers carefully nail boards and beams together in a specially-organized design. Each day you come by the site the structure takes on a new dimension. If you were to talk to a building engineer he/she would say that the way the framework is built is one of the keys to a quality building. The rest of the existing structure must be supported

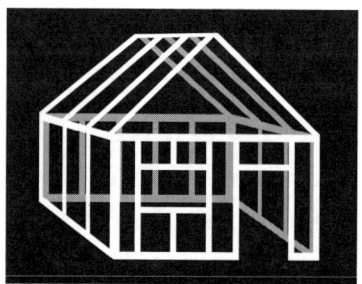

The rest of the existing structure must be supported and maintained by the frame even though, by itself, the frame is not a beautiful sight.

and maintained by the frame even though, by itself, the frame is not a beautiful sight.

Your skeletal system is like the framework for your body. Your **skeletal system** can be defined as the combination of your joints and connecting tissues. Each of your 206 bones has a particular function in your body's unique design, but the combination of all of your bones provides support and protection. Your bones must hold your body upright for hours, with no rest. Even when you sleep, your bones are still providing support for your organs and muscles.

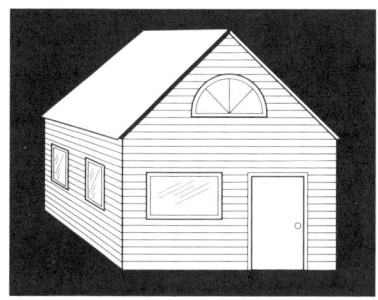

Now, go back to that house at the construction site. It is now finished, it is painted a beautiful color, the new windows reflect the sunlight and the finished product looks perfect. As you walk through the house you quickly forget the bare, wooden scaffolding you saw just days before. You admire the color and design of this exciting new home. If there are any flaws in the framework, you probably do not notice them, they are success-fully hidden...until the stress of age begins to expose them.

You may think that your bones are just a white mass of hard substance, but actually your bones have three uniquely designed layers. If you were to cut a bone, you would notice the first layer called the *periosteum*. This membrane of outer skin is filled with nerves and blood vessels and helps in the formation and repair of bone tissue.

The next layer you would notice is the solid, strong, and dense bone called the *compact bone*. This portion of the bone is so hard that surgeons must use a saw to cut through it rather than a knife. The third layer inside the bone is the *spongy bone*. It looks somewhat like a honeycomb with thousands of tiny holes which are passageways for nerves and blood vessels. It is in this inner area of the bone that the bone marrow exists.

If there are any flaws in the framework, you probably do not notice them, they are successfully hidden...until the stress of age begins to expose them.

Your bones provide your body with protection. They also work with your muscles and joints and act like levers to provide you with movement. The marrow in your bones produces blood cells and your bones also store substances needed for your body. Although your bones themselves are very rigid and resist movement, they are linked together with a very unique design of tissues. These fibrous connective tissues are cartilage, joints and ligaments. Working together, they provide you with the flexibility you need everyday to make your movements fluid and graceful.

Bone's strength is quiet, dependable. It serves us well, without fanfare, and comes to our attention only when we encounter a rude, fracturing stress that exceeds its own high tolerance.[2]
Dr. Paul Brand

Problems In The Skeletal System

The most important and yet the most unique feature of bone is its hardness. Although it can withstand a great amount of stress upon it, it is not without its limitations. Some complications of the skeletal system are caused by accident, unnecessary risk taking, deficiencies in the body, or disease.

- Scoliosis: Sometimes the vertebral column develops an abnormal curvature, so that one hip or shoulder is lower than the other. This condition is called **scoliosis** and is most common in young adolescent girls. There is no known cause for this condition, and the only treatment is to wear a brace that corrects the curvature.
- Bursitis: Bursae are commonly located between the skin and the bone. They help in the movement of the tendons that pass over these areas. **Bursitis** is the inflammation of a bursa and is usually due to excessive stress on the joint. Tennis elbow is an example of bursitis. The shoulder and the knee are also common areas where bursitis can occur.
- Arthritis: **Arthritis** is inflammation of a joint or joints. Pain and/or swelling of the joint is often noted. There are many types and causes of arthritis. Some types cannot be cured. The treatment goals are to reduce pain and to restore or preserve movement of the affected joint as much as possible.

- **Osteoporosis:** A loss of bone tissue. The spaces and canals within the bones become filled with soft tissue. As a result, the bones become weaker and are more easily fractured and broken. A lack of good diet and exercise can contribute to the development of this disorder. This disease most commonly affects women after menopause, but elderly men can also be affected. Calcium supplements and estrogen replacement after menopause may help to slow down this disease in women.

Injuries

It is obvious that you cannot live your life in a safety net. Your body is built to be active and energetic. Accidents happen and they are often out of your control. Examples of injuries that are not easily avoided are: hurting your knee while playing basketball, jamming your finger while playing volleyball, and twisting your ankle as you are walking down some stairs. Unnecessary risks can be avoided by following a few safety precautions. You may have already experienced any of the following injuries, but while you are actively enjoying life, try not to push your body past its own limitations. Play carefully!

- **Fractures:** A fracture can be defined as a break in a bone. There are six different types of fractures, each named according to its cause and degree of break. The treatment of a broken bone depends upon its severity. A cast is usually used to help in the natural healing of the bone.
- **Dislocation:** A dislocation occurs when the end of a bone is pushed out of its joint. It is usually the result of vigorous physical activity or a fall. The bone must be placed back into its joint and kept still until the area heals. This should be done by someone who has knowledge in this area.
- **Sprain:** Sprains are the result of stretching or tearing the ligaments at a joint. This can be very painful and should be

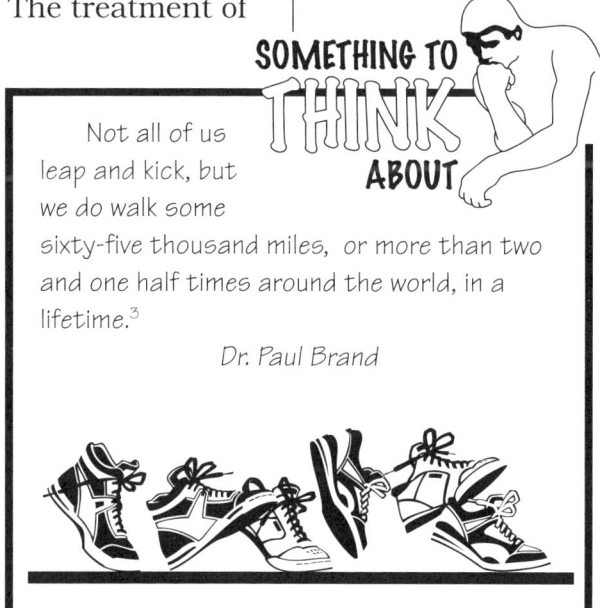

SOMETHING TO THINK ABOUT

Not all of us leap and kick, but we do walk some sixty-five thousand miles, or more than two and one half times around the world, in a lifetime.[3]

Dr. Paul Brand

treated with cold packs on the injury as soon as possible to keep the swelling down. Sprains are usually caused by unusually twisting a joint.

THE MUSCULAR SYSTEM

In the absence of any other proof, the thumb alone would convince me of God's existence.[4]
Isaac Newton

As you are reading this book you may not be thinking of the complex muscles needed to enable you to read the words and turn the pages. Think for a moment of the millions of movements your body makes every day, even life-or-death functions, that you may take for granted.

Nearly half of the body weight of a human is made up of the muscles. People often associate the muscles of the body with strong or skilled athletes. As you watch an ice skater gracefully glide across the ice, or a muscle bound weight lifter win a competition, you do not often think about the hard work the athlete had to endure to train the body to perform such amazing feats. It is not only the trained athlete that has a complex system of muscular strength, but your body is built for specific movements and strength as well.

Seventy separate muscles are needed to allow you the wide variety of movement in your hands.

Did you know that you use 17 muscles to smile, and 43 muscles to frown? It actually takes less thought and energy to smile than it does to frown!

The next time you sit down to practice the piano or other fine instrument, take a close look at your hands and fingers. Seventy separate muscles are needed to allow you the wide variety of movement in your hands. Dr. Paul Brand states: *"I could fill a room with surgery manuals suggesting various ways to repair hands that have been injured. But in forty years of study I have never read a technique that has succeeded in improving a normal, healthy hand."* [5]

SOMETHING TO THINK ABOUT

Fun facts:

Your muscles produce large amounts of heat. One estimate says enough heat is produced to boil a quart of water for an hour! Did you know that your muscles are so strong that if all the muscles in your body pulled together in one direction they could lift 25 tons!

Your **muscular system** can be defined as the group of tissues that makes body parts move. There are three types of muscle tissue in the body: the skeletal muscle, smooth muscle, and cardiac muscle. A muscle tissue is either *voluntary* (you control its movement) or *involuntary* (you do not control its movement). The cardiac muscle, the heart, is an example of an involuntary muscle. You have no conscious control over its pumping. Your skeletal muscles, however, are an example of the voluntary muscles in your body. You can make your hand move or your leg move at your own will. Can you think of other examples of muscles that are involuntary?

With every movement of a muscle there is another muscle working as well.

Your body has over 600 major muscles that need energy from food to produce all the movements your body makes. Although your muscles produce different movements, they all work the same way: they *contract, or shorten,* and they *extend, or lengthen.*

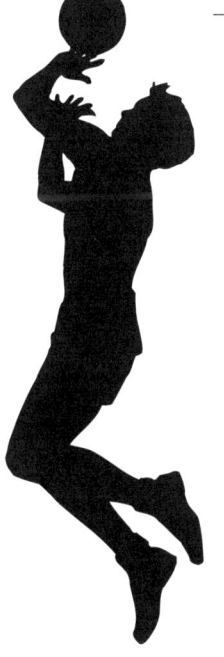

Have you ever been involved in sports? Consider the movement of shooting a basketball. As you bring the ball into proper position, your bicep muscle is shortened but your tricep muscle is lengthened. As you shoot the ball, your bicep muscle extends and your tricep muscle is shortened. This kind of action is an example of how your skeletal muscles work in pairs. With every movement of a muscle there is another muscle working as well. It's a balancing act. Try to remember this concept this way: *with every action, there is an equal and opposite reaction.*

Consider the sport of skiing. If you were weight training to improve your lower body strength, you would want to strengthen both your quadriceps (front of your thigh) and your hamstring (back of your thigh). If you only strengthened your quadriceps you would not have the balance of power that is needed for this activity. As a result of this imbalance of strength, injuries may occur. Can you think of other muscles that work together this way? Did you know that your abdominal muscles and your back muscles both need to be strengthened in order for you to have good posture and to stand erect?

Problems In The Muscular System

Most problems associated with the muscles are related to injury. No matter how well you take care of your muscular system, there remains the risk of injury. Your muscles have their limitations, and it is your responsibility to stay within your own personal limits.

1. **Strain:** A strain is caused by overworking a muscle or group of muscles and may have several degrees of severity. The treatment for a strain is rest and application of heat.
2. **Cramp:** A muscular cramp results when a muscle does not relax. Relaxation and applying heat to the area should relieve the cramp.
3. **Bruise:** When a muscle is injured, blood vessels are broken in the area and can create a hematoma, or bruise. A bruise can be caused by a direct blow to the area or may appear in the area of a more serious injury.
4. **Pulled or torn muscle:** A muscle that is overused or did not get adequate warm-up or stretching can result in the muscle pulling away from the bone. This can be a serious injury and needs medical attention.
5. **Muscular fatigue:** Muscle fatigue is not an injury in itself but may put you at greater risk for injury. When your muscles are tired or overworked they are more susceptible to an injury.

2-3 DIGESTIVE AND EXCRETORY SYSTEMS

Your body is the house in which you live. By analogy, it is just like the building in which you make your home. Your home needs, at the very least, periodical attention, otherwise the roof may leak, the plumbing may get out of order and clog up, termites will drill through the floors and the walls, and other innumerable cases of deterioration will make their appearance. Such is the case with your physical body. Every function and activity of your system, day and night, physical, mental, and spiritual, is dependent on the attention you give it.[6]
Norman W. Walker, D. Sc., Ph.D.

THE DIGESTIVE SYSTEM

The **digestive system** can be defined as the organs that take in food and break it down into a chemical form that can be absorbed by the body. This process by which food is broken down is called **digestion**. The digestive system consists of a long muscular tube called the alimentary canal that extends from the mouth to the anus. The *alimentary canal* measures about 30 feet in length. Although different sections of the canal are designed for specific purposes, the structure, and the way it moves food are similar throughout the length of the organ. The alimentary canal does not work alone. Other organs that are not considered part of the canal such as the salivary glands, pancreas, gallbladder, and liver are also needed in the process of digestion.

The food you eat is broken down by digestive juices into small, absorbable nutrients that generate the energy required to maintain life, replace the cells that are constantly dying, and keep you functioning.[7]

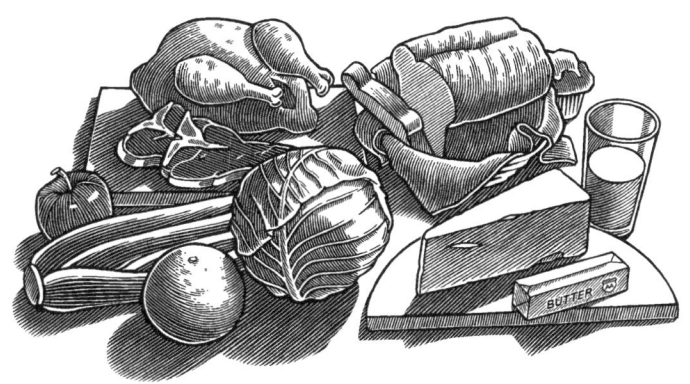

Every function and activity of your system, day and night, physical, mental, and spiritual, is dependent on the attention you give it.

Norman W. Walker, D. Sc., Ph.D.

The gallbladder is a pear-shaped sac which lies underneath the liver. Bile that is produced by the liver passes to the gallbladder. This bile is stored and then released into the duodenum, the first part of the small intestine, where the bile breaks down fats contained in food. The liver is the largest and one of the most important internal organs. It lies beneath the diaphragm and has numerous functions.

The Digestive System

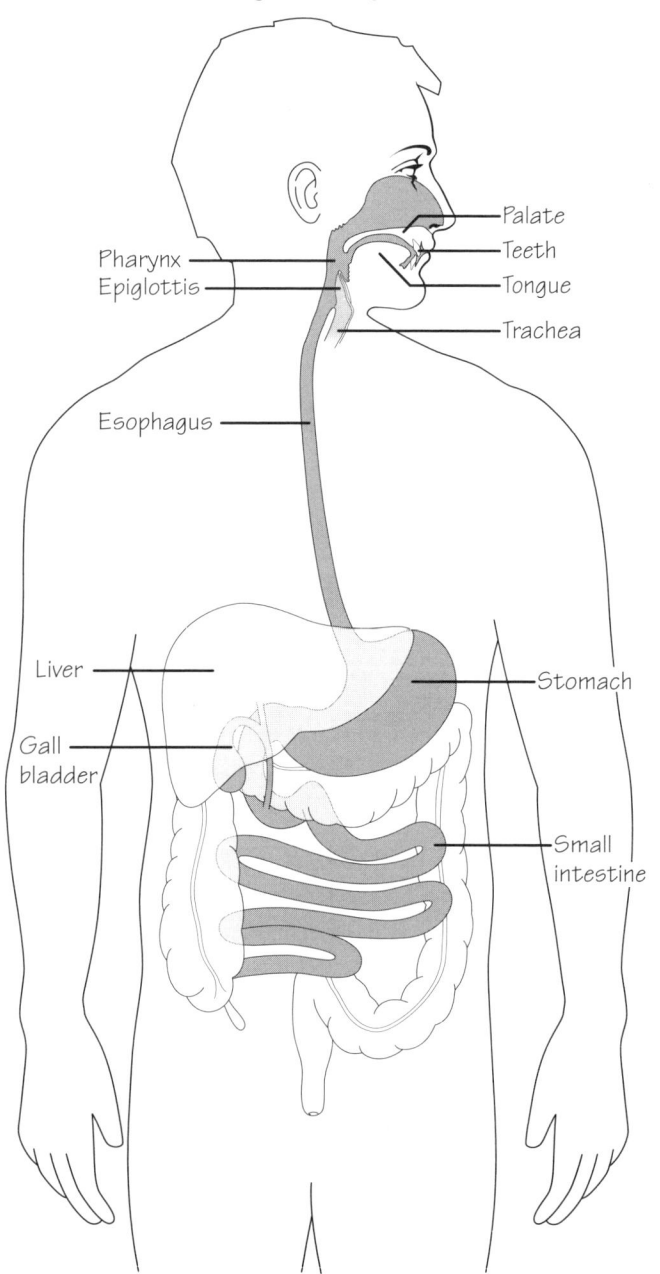

Palate
Teeth
Tongue
Trachea
Pharynx
Epiglottis
Esophagus
Liver
Gall bladder
Stomach
Small intestine

Digestion begins in your mouth where certain enzymes begin the process of digestion before the food reaches the stomach and small intestines. Your teeth and tongue help prepare the food for digestion. *Saliva* is a liquid that is 99% water, and is released by the salivary glands to moisten food and begin the digestion of starches. Saliva not only helps you eat your food, but keeps your mouth moist so you can speak and helps to keep your mouth clean of harmful bacteria. The four primary tastes are salty, sweet, sour, and bitter. They are easy to recognize when the source of the taste is strong.

The *esophagus* is a straight tube that is about 10 inches long and functions as a passageway for food from the mouth to the stomach. *Peristalsis* is the wave like movement of the esophagus that moves food down into the stomach. The action of swallowing is often so quick and natural that you do not even notice what is happening. Sometimes you may try to do too much while you are eating. Talking, laughing or placing too much food in your mouth at once can keep you from swallowing correctly and you may choke.

Once the food enters the stomach it is mixed with chemicals to continue the breakdown of the food. The main function of the stomach is to store food before the food moves on to the small intestine. The small intestine is a long tube measuring 18–23 feet in length and is about one to 1.5 inches wide. The main function of the small intestine is absorption of nutrients into the bloodstream. Millions of villi line the intestinal wall and act like fingers to grab the absorbable nutrients.

Throughout your small and large intestines you have an abundance of bacteria — both good and bad bacteria can thrive here. It is important to have a nutrition-rich diet to help your intestines stay healthy and promote good absorption of the nutrients that fuel your body.

Problems In The Digestive System

Like other systems in your body, your digestive system may encounter problems. The following is a list of common problems you or someone you know might experience. Remember, when you are facing health problems, your body is built to restore itself. While you are feeling healthy, remind yourself that *prevention is the best medicine!*

1. **Indigestion and heartburn:** Indigestion occurs when food is not totally digested. It is caused by overeating, eating too fast, or eating while you are upset. Heartburn occurs when the stomach acid flows back into the esophagus. It is caused by the muscular valve called the cardiac sphincter not closing.

2. **Nausea and vomiting:** Nausea is an ill feeling in your stomach often accompanied by a headache or body aches. The vomiting center in your brain is triggered by various things such as motion, certain drugs, contamination in foods, strong emotions or a virus or bacteria that the body is trying to cleanse.

SOMETHING TO **THINK** ABOUT

Everyday the small intestines process about 2.5 gallons of food, liquids, and secretions. The absorption area of the small intestine is three times the entire surface area of the human body.

The digestive system takes about 24 hours to digest a meal. Depending on the food you have eaten, food may be in your stomach from 1 to 8 hours, in the small intestine 4 hours and then 10–15 hours in your large intestine before being expelled from your body as waste.

While you are feeling healthy, remind yourself that prevention is the best medicine!

3. **Ulcers:** An ulcer can occur in the stomach or in the small intestine. An **ulcer** is an open sore in the membrane lining the stomach and the small intestine. It is thought to be aggravated by a person's diet, level of stress, and the use of tobacco and alcohol. More recent studies indicate that some ulcers are caused by a bacteria present in the stomach and small intestine. Ulcers can be treated with medication.

4. **Gallstones: Gallstones** are formed when the bile stored in the gallbladder hardens into small crystals. These pebble-like solids may block the flow of bile into the small intestine and cause a great amount of pain. The stones are removed and often the gallbladder itself is removed. Unlike the liver, you can live without your gallbladder.

5. **Cirrhosis of the liver:** Cirrhosis of the liver is a condition where enough of the liver cells have been damaged or destroyed that the liver no longer functions adequately. Common causes of cirrhosis are hepatitis, excessive alcohol consumption and exposure to certain poisons or toxins.

6. **Halitosis or bad breath:** A person can have either a mild case of bad breath or a horrible ongoing problem. Halitosis can be caused by not only what you just finished eating such as onions or garlic, but from poor nutrition. When halitosis is caused by the immediate affects of strong food, mints or mouth wash can help. But when a person has consistent and offending bad breath the diet is often the main cause.

SOMETHING TO THINK ABOUT

Food poisoning

Food poisoning may come on suddenly or it may take up to 24 hours to manifest the symptoms. Food often contains bacteria that does not affect you, but certain bacteria can attack your system with a vengeance. Food poisoning may cause damage to your liver and even cause death. You can help avoid food poisoning by following a few guidelines:

1. Do not eat foods from cans that are dented or are bulging.
2. Do not eat foods that have not been kept refrigerated or stored properly.
3. Do not eat any food that has an unusual discoloration or odor.
4. Do not eat foods that have not been cooked thoroughly (poultry, beef, pork).

THE EXCRETORY SYSTEM

The elimination of undigested food and other waste products is equally as important as the proper digestion and assimilation of food.[8]
Norman W. Walker, D.Sc., Ph.D.

The very purpose of your **excretory system** is to provide ways for waste to be excreted from the body. There are several ways your body rids itself of waste. Your lungs expel carbon dioxide, your large intestine expels semi-solid waste, your sweat glands expel water and salt and your **urinary tract** expels waste in the form of urine.

The Large Intestine (The Colon)

The *colon* is the organ of the excretory system whose whole purpose is to expel waste from the body. The remaining, unused portion of food is passed into the large intestine (colon) where nearly all the water will be absorbed. What remains is semi-solid waste that is passed out of the body. If waste matter is not expelled the substances that accumulate over time become toxic to the body — poisonous!

> ### SOMETHING TO THINK ABOUT
>
> **Do you still have your appendix?**
>
> The veriform appendix is a pouchlike structure that hangs off the lower side of the cecum. There are many theories concerning the function of the appendix; however, no known purpose has been found. The appendix extends about three inches in length and contains lymphatic tissue that may serve as some resistance to infection. When the appendix becomes enlarged and infected, it causes a condition called appendicitis. A person who has appendicitis may experience extreme pain in the lower right hand side of the abdomen and feel nauseated. The treatment for appendicitis is surgery to remove the appendix.

When compared to the small intestine, the large intestine is only larger in the diameter, not in length. The large intestine is about 2.5 inches in diameter and five feet in length. It begins in the lower right side of the abdomen and travels upward forming a kind of border around the small intestine.

The large intestine is made up of the cecum, colon, rectum and anal canal. You will notice on the diagram how waste moves through the large intestine finally reaching the anus where it is expelled. The primary function of the first half of

The Large Intestine

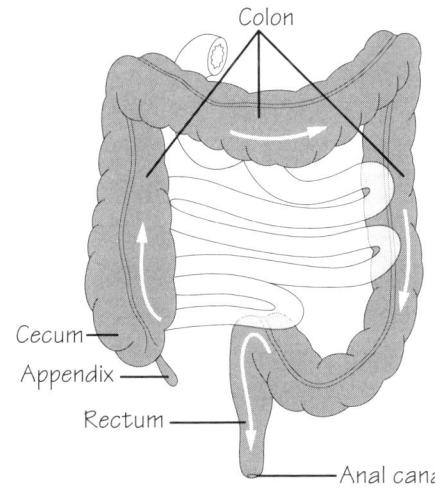

Colon

Cecum

Appendix

Rectum

Anal canal

the colon is the absorption of liquids; the second half is storage and excreting the waste.

The very best of diets can be no better than the very worst, if the sewage system of the colon is clogged with a collection of waste and corruption.[9]
N.W. Walker, D.Sc., Ph.D.

The Kidneys (Urinary Tract)

The Urinary Tract

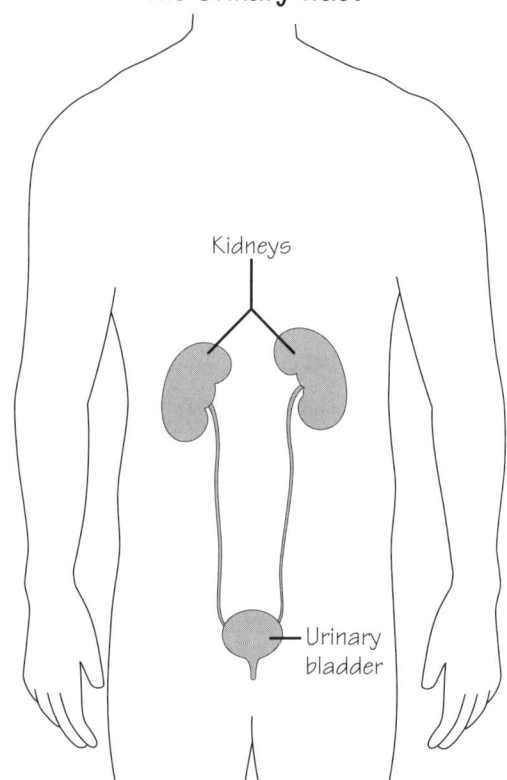
Kidneys

Urinary bladder

The kidneys are located on either side of the spinal column. They are kidney bean in shape and are reddish brown in color. Although the main job of the kidneys is to cleanse the blood of impurities, the kidneys play a vital role in the regulation of water and electrolytes (salts) within your body.

Although water is the major component of urine, the amount depends on your state of health and the amount of food, water, and other liquids you consume. The amount of exercise you do also contributes to the concentration of water in your urine. It is interesting to note that your body maintains a fairly constant balance of fluid. Your kidneys will draw liquid from other sources of your body (other organs and tissues) to keep you hydrated (proper fluid balance). As a result, you will eliminate the same amount of fluid that you take in.

Problems In The Excretory System

Most of the complications you may encounter with your excretory system are common and not serious. However, being knowledgeable about your body and taking responsibility for your health may keep you from a more serious and life-threatening problem.

1. **Constipation:** Constipation occurs when the feces are hard and dry making a bowel movement very difficult. Some of the causes include: poor diet, no or little exercise, ignoring the urge to use the bathroom, lack of water in your diet,

and the use of laxatives that cause your body to lose its natural ability to eliminate waste. It is important to use natural means to take care of constipation. Avoiding over-eating and unnecessary snacking in addition to making wise food choices will help keep your system healthy.

2. **Diarrhea:** Diarrhea is the opposite of constipation. There is too much water in the bowels causing loose feces that are passed often. Some of the causes of diarrhea include: a bacteria or virus, a change in diet, food poisoning or strong emotions. The danger in diarrhea is becoming dehydrated.

3. **Flatulence or gas:** A certain amount of gas in the stomach or intestine is normal. Some causes include: a diet includ-ing gas-producing foods, or foods that your body is particularly sensitive to. Other causes include eating too fast, or extra bacteria in the intestines and bowels.

4. **Kidney stones:** The kidneys can develop stones that are composed mostly of calcium. They may be very small and pass out with the urine or they may be larger and block the passageway. Kidney stones are very painful but can be removed with surgery or by sound waves that break up the stones and allow them to pass. Kidney stones can be pre-vented by drinking large quantities of water. Some medications can help prevent the formation of kidney stones.

5. **Urinary tract infections:** Infections can occur in the urinary system. A common type of urinary tract infection is infec-tion of the bladder. This specific infection is called cystitis. It is an inflammation of the bladder. The main cause of these infections is the presence of a bacteria. The symp-toms include frequent need to urinate even when you pass small amounts of urine and pain while urinating. Notify your doctor if any of these symptoms appear. Antibiotics are used to clear up the infection. Drinking large amounts of water can help also.

6. **Cancer:** Colon cancer has been on the rise, but you can make some dietary changes to help prevent it. Increase your fiber and eat a healthy diet to keep your system run-ning clean. See your doctor if you have any unusual symptoms such as bleeding in your stools.

2-4 INTEGUMENTARY AND IMMUNE SYSTEMS

THE INTEGUMENTARY SYSTEM

Each morning you are greeted in the mirror by the same image. Your face and body form the package that you will present to others. Just imagine if you did not have the organ of the skin. What would bind you together? How could you feel the sun on your face or the wind in your hair? Your skin is an organ like no other and on it holds the unique blueprint of who you are.

Your **integumentary system** includes not only the skin but the hair, nails, sweat glands and oil glands. The skin is the largest organ of the body. It weighs between six and ten pounds. If the skin were spread out flat it would cover an area about three feet to seven feet. The skin is made up of two distinct layers of tissues. The outer layer is called the *epidermis* and the inner is called the *dermis*. The organ of the skin has several important functions, all of which play an important role in daily living.

Protection: one of the most important functions of the skin is protection. The skin protects you from water (it is waterproof), and germs. Infection can occur if the skin is cut or broken. That is why prompt first aid is necessary.

Regulation of body temperature: the integumentary system plays a key role in the heating and cooling of your body. The skin protects your internal organs and body temperature from extreme cold and heat. The integumentary system has several mechanisms that enable it to function as a natural heating and cooling system.

What is it, then, this seamless body stocking, some two yards square, this our casing, our facade, that flushes, pales, perspires, glistens, glows, furrows, tingles, crawls, itches, pleasures and pains us all our days, at once keeper of the organs within, and sensitive probe, adventurer into the world outside?[10]
Richard Selzer

46

Sensitivity: your skin is your connection with the outside world. Without the specialized sensory receptors throughout your skin, you could not feel the sensations of pressure, touch, heat, cold, and pain.

Problems With The Skin

Most of the complications of the skin are only a little more than annoying and uncomfortable. There are things you can do to lessen the effects of these common conditions. In most cases time takes care of the situation. You will learn more about common problems of the skin, hair and nails in the chapter on personal hygiene.

SOMETHING TO THINK ABOUT

There is no one like you... and your skin proves it!

The pattern created by the ridges and grooves of your fingers prove that there is no one like you. Even the fingerprints of identical twins are not exactly alike. Did you know that if you seriously injured the skin of your  fingers, the same pattern would grow back? God has uniquely designed you and not only does He know the number of hairs on your head (Matthew 10:30) but the fingerprints on your fingers!

1. **Warts:** Warts are small growths on the skin caused by a virus. Warts seem to be harmless unless they are on the bottom of your feet or are numerous and bothersome. They can be removed at a doctor's office or can be treated with a doctor-recommended wart remover. Do not try to cut out warts yourself; the result could be an infection of the area or the growth of more warts. Often warts disappear by themselves. If you notice any unusual changes in a wart, contact your doctor.

2. **Calluses and corns:** Although calluses and corns seem similar, they are slightly different. Calluses are a build up of thickened skin usually caused by pressure or friction on the feet. Corns may be soft or hard but in both cases the result is pain when pressure is applied. People who develop corns have a difficult time wearing shoes and may wear a soft pad on the corn to keep it from recurring. Do not try to cut off a corn or callus. Using a pumice stone to gently rub the area after a shower or bath may help to decrease the thickness of skin.

3. **Cold sores or fever blisters:** Some people are more prone to develop cold sores or fever blisters. Most often they are

Your skin is an organ like no other and on it holds the unique blueprint of who you are.

caused by the Herpes Simplex I virus. If you have ever had one you know how annoying one can be. Usually a cold sore or fever blister appears as a small sore on or near the lips. The blister may become irritated and be painful. The sore usually clears up in 10–14 days. Some over-the-counter medications may help decrease the pain and help to keep the virus from spreading.

4. *Skin Cancer:* There are three types of skin cancer: basal cell carcinoma, squamous cell carcinoma, and malignant melanoma. Basal cell and squamous cell carcinoma are the most common and the least dangerous of the three cancers. Excessive sun exposure increases the risk of skin cancer and accelerates the aging process especially in fair-skinned people. Malignant melanoma is more serious and may spread to other parts of the body. Malignant melanoma requires early detection and treatment if the patient is to have a good chance of survival. The next time someone tells you to stay out of the sun or to use a good sunscreen, remember, it is to protect you from the dangerous effects (such as skin cancer) of the sun on the skin.

THE IMMUNE SYSTEM

If your body was not created with natural defenses to guard against foreign invasion, you would be sick continually and at high risk for life-threatening diseases. Your lymphatic system and your **immune system** work together to fight off intruders. The function of the immune system will be briefly discussed here to shed more light on the body's natural defenses.

Defense Mechanisms

Your body is equipped with a variety of defense mechanisms that help protect you from unfriendly invaders. Your skin is your first line of defense, but once a pathogen (a germ that invades a person) enters your body, other defenses must go into action. Your body has within itself two main types of defense mechanisms: natural and acquired immunity.

Natural or Inborn Immunity

Your body has an inborn resistance to certain diseases. This is called **natural immunity**. For example, humans are susceptible to some diseases that other species are not. For example, certain microorganisms may cause diseases in certain birds but not in humans. The reverse may also be true. This difference in resistance is called species resistance.

Another form of inborn resistance includes the natural barriers the body has as protection against general diseases. The skin and the mucous membranes of the body are examples of physical barriers that guard you. Certain enzymes such as the gastric juices in your stomach help you resist infection.

Have you ever wondered what is happening at the site of a cut or injury to your body? Resistance begins immediately as your body tries to protect itself from infection. Swelling, redness and general inflammation are signs that the process of healing has begun. The whole healing process is another example of the body's unique ability to rebuild and repair itself.

Acquired Immunity

Part of the mystery of the human body includes the ability it has to resist specific diseases. The body adapts to respond to certain invaders and then can remember who the intruders were so next time they are ready to attack. This ability is called **acquired immunity**. *Immunity* is the body's resistance to specific foreign intruders. Lymphocytes play an important role in recognizing certain invaders. The two kinds of lymphocytes are the B-cells and the T-cells, each with their own unique function. Immunizations are also used to give the human body an acquired immunity to a specific disease.

Repeat bouts with colds or flu viruses, continual fatigue, increased allergic reactions, incomplete recovery from a sickness and poor response to treatment are some of the symptoms you may experience when your immune system is not functioning effectively. As you grow older you will notice changes in your body,

The whole healing process is another example of the body's unique ability to rebuild and repair itself.

some positive and some negative. As you get to know what is "normal" for your body you will become more aware when there is an unusual change. You should always contact your doctor when you sense something out of the ordinary.

Immunodeficiency disorders result in the body's failure to fight infection and tumors. The immune system is weakened or malfunctioning for some reason. This is often caused by an inherited or congenital defect that interferes with the normal development of the immune system. A disease can also damage the immune system to the point that it cannot function effectively. When the defense system is weakened certain infections (opportunistic infections) can take advantage of the situation and cause more serious complications. Opportunistic infections are caused by microorganisms that don't normally cause infection when the immune system is healthy.

1. **Allergies:** Allergic reactions are related to the immune system. A person who suffers from an allergy has become hypersensitive to the allergen (the object that causes the abnormal response). If you are allergic to something, it is likely that someone in your family experiences allergy problems as well. Common antigens that may produce allergic reactions are: plant pollens, house dust, animal hair and certain foods. Common symptoms include itchy and watery eyes, runny nose, skin rashes as well as gastric and intestinal upsets. Allergic reactions can usually be controlled by avoiding the allergen and the symptoms can be relieved with some medications suggested by your doctor.

2. HIV: **HIV** is the virus that causes AIDS (Acquired Immunodeficiency Syndrome). It causes illness by weakening the body's ability to fight off infections and to resist tumor growth. A simple cold could cause a life-threatening case of pneumonia. Opportunistic infections develop and common minor infections can be much more serious in the presence of this condition.

SOMETHING TO THINK ABOUT

Do you still have your tonsils?

Your tonsils are located in the back of your mouth, on either side of the tongue. They are made up of lymphatic tissue that can protect your body against infection. However, the tonsils are often a source of infection and can cause continual problems in some people. The swelling and soreness that accompanies tonsillitis may result in having the tonsils removed.

Autoimmune diseases differ from immunodeficiency disorders. Your immune system is designed to attack foreign intruders. However, when your body's immune system mistakes its own cells and tissues for possible antigens, the condition is called **autoimmune disease**. Examples of diseases thought to be autoimmune in origin are rheumatic fever, rheumatoid arthritis and lupus erythematosis.

2-5 NERVOUS, ENDOCRINE AND REPRODUCTIVE SYSTEMS

THE NERVOUS SYSTEM

The single goal of your **central nervous system** is to maintain homeostasis (a stable internal environment.) This complex system accomplishes this goal by controlling and coordinating all the body parts so that they work as one flowing unit and respond to changes appropriately.

Right now as you are reading this page you may not realize how your body is functioning in other complex ways. Your nervous system is controlling your internal organs, your movements, your perceptions, your thoughts and your emotions.

Your brain and spinal cord are the main organs of your central nervous system. The *peripheral nerves*, which connect the central nervous system to other body parts make up the peripheral nervous system. Your ability to sense and respond to things from the outside environment such as sight, smell, taste and hearing are controlled by the sensory nerves of your somatic nervous system. Your internal environment which is involuntary (without your conscious effort) is being controlled by the portion of your nervous system called the autonomic nervous system.

Masses of neurons, or nerve cells, in the brain and spinal cord are specialized to react to physical and chemical changes in your body. When you experience a strong emotion such as fear, adrenaline released in your body may cause you to run away from the situation. If you were to touch something hot, your sensory nerves would tell your brain "pain" and then your brain would cause you to pull your hand away quickly from the source of pain. All these reactions can occur in a fraction of a second. Impulses can travel through your nervous system at a rate of 350 feet per second!

Problems In The Nervous System

1. **Pinched nerve:** When one part of the spine becomes displaced, a nerve or group of nerves can become pinched or squeezed. This can be very painful and is usually caused by an injury.
2. **Infections:** Polio and rabies are infections that directly affect the nervous system.
3. **Epilepsy:** **Epilepsy** is a brain disorder that results from a sudden burst of nerve action. Some medicines can control seizures caused by this disorder.
4. **Tumors:** The central nervous system, especially the brain, can be affected by tumors that originate from the central nervous system itself or spread there from other places such as the lungs. Some can be removed surgically, others may be treated by radiation or chemicals.
5. **Cerebral Palsy:** **Cerebral Palsy** is a condition in which the cerebrum of the brain is damaged. It can cause muscular spasms, poor balance, or problems with seeing, hearing and talking. There is no cure for Cerebral Palsy, but therapy

Impulses can travel through your nervous system at a rate of 350 feet per second!

is used to help the individual cope with the condition.

6. Multiple Sclerosis: **Multiple Sclerosis (MS)** is a disease in which the outer coating that protects some nerves is destroyed. As a result, the individual has no control over certain body movements. It can also affect a person's speaking and hearing. Although some medicine and therapy may help, there is no cure for MS.

THE ENDOCRINE SYSTEM

Although your endocrine system works closely with your nervous system to maintain that vital internal balance in your body, they accomplish their tasks in different ways. While the nervous system sends messages to muscles and glands via nerve impulses, the glands of the **endocrine system** secrete hormones to send messages to the cells in the body via the blood.

The chemicals secreted by the glands of the endocrine system are called *hormones* or chemical messengers. Hormones have many functions which help regulate the body such as energy control, sugar and insulin balance, as well as water and salt balance. Certain hormones produce changes over a long period of time; for example, a child's growth and sexual maturity. Other hormones control rythmic changes such as the menstruation cycle in a female. Hormones send a chemical message to an organ to either speed up or to slow down. They have the ability to cause dramatic responses in your body and also affect your emotions such as fear, anger, joy and sadness.

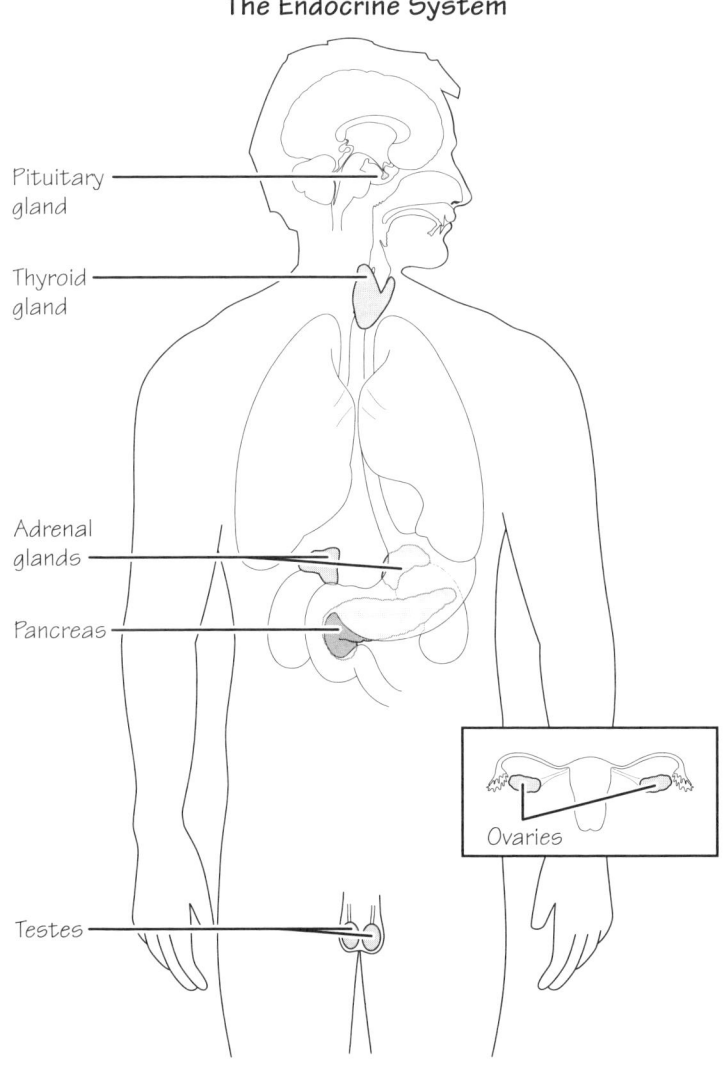

The Endocrine System

Pituitary gland

Thyroid gland

Adrenal glands

Pancreas

Ovaries

Testes

A healthy endocrine system is important to your overall health. When one or more of your glands is not functioning properly it can affect other systems in your body. The following are some of the problems that can occur in your endocrine system.

1. **The pituitary gland:** This gland is responsible for releasing your growth hormone. If too much or too little is released the individual's size will be negatively affected.
2. **The thyroid gland:** When the thyroid gland is not functioning properly a person experiences different symptoms. If too little hormone is produced hypothyroidism occurs. If too much is produced hyperthyroidism occurs. A blood test at your doctor's office can determine the health of your thyroid.
3. **Diabetes: Diabetes** is an example of a disease where the body cannot properly utilize the glucose (sugar) that it needs. This disorder has to do with the release and use of the hormone insulin. A careful diet or insulin shots might be needed to control this condition.

THE REPRODUCTIVE SYSTEM

Your **reproductive system** is the system responsible for the continuation of the human race. When God created Adam and Eve He thought that it was so good He wanted the human race to continue. God gave man and woman the ability to be involved in this miraculous process. Your reproductive system is unique in that its function is not necessary for your own survival. In other words, you could live without the organs of your reproductive system. Its vital function is to bring new life into the world.

Your knowledge of your reproductive system has much to do with your perspective on your sexuality. God made man and woman in His image, each individual unique and special. Your reproductive system, like the other systems of your body, is functioning the way God designed it to function. It is common to feel uneasy when discussing the organs and functions of the reproductive systems. God has given all of mankind an inborn, godly modesty. This feeling of uneasiness causes people to respect other's privacy. As you are learning about both the male and female reproductive systems, try to see a greater purpose behind all the scientific information: God designed man and woman to be involved in the miracle of life.

The male reproductive system includes: the prostate gland, the testes, the scrotum and the penis. The *prostate gland* produces the seminal fluid (fluid which is added to the sperm to produce semen). The *testes* are the glands that produce the sperm. The *scrotum* is the sac that surrounds the testes. The *penis* is the organ that is used for urination and reproduction. Unlike the female reproductive system, the organs of the male system lie *outside* the male body. Both the male and female systems are influenced by the production of hormones in the endocrine system.

The female reproductive system includes the ovaries, the uterus and the vagina. These structures lie *inside* the body. The *ovaries* are the organs that store the egg cells. One ovary lies on either side of the body, and each holds a certain number of eggs at birth. As a young girl matures the eggs begin to mature and are then released by the ovaries one at a time every month. This release of an egg is called *ovulation*. This is the time of the month that *fertilization* (the joining of a sperm and an egg) may take place if a sperm cell is present. The female *uterus* (womb) is the muscular sac in the mother's abdomen that provides a place for the fertilized egg to grow and develop into a mature baby. The *vagina* is the canal for the birth of a baby.

Every month the uterus prepares to support a fertilized egg and sperm. The lining of the uterus begins to thicken with blood to prepare for ovulation. When fertilization does not take place the lining of the uterus breaks down and passes out of the female body. This process is called *menstruation*. If fertilization took place

SOMETHING TO THINK ABOUT

The male sperm cell is one of the smallest of all human cells, yet it carries the father's full legacy to the child. The female egg is much larger in comparison to the sperm, and it carries the mother's full legacy to the child. Millions of sperm are released at one time, and while they all try to swim vigorously toward one egg, only one sperm will successfully penetrate and fertilize the egg. When a sperm has penetrated the egg, the egg hardens and does not allow any other sperm to enter.

during ovulation, the lining of the uterus would be used to supply nourishment to the growing fetus.

The amount of blood that is passed and the length of time of menstruation is different for many females, but when all the tissue and blood is gone from the uterus, the ovaries begin to release another egg. The time from one menstruation to the next is called the *menstruation cycle*. This cycle is vital for reproduction. Many females experience discomfort during this time. This discomfort associated with the menstrual cycle is called premenstrual syndrome (PMS).

We should not be ashamed to discuss what God was not ashamed to create.[11]

Dennis Rainey

God sees both the male and female reproductive systems as beautiful. He has designed them to function the way they do.

Male Reproductive Problems

1. **Testicular Cancer:** This type of cancer can be a common disease in men. Seeing your doctor regularly can help to catch this cancer in its early stages.
2. **Inguinal Hernia:** This happens when a hole opens in the abdomen wall and a piece of intestine pushes through into the scrotum. Lifting heavy objects can cause a hernia.

Female Reproductive Problems

1. **Premenstrual Syndrome:** PMS is a common occurrence in females. The symptoms are different for many, but it is still an uncomfortable condition. Some symptoms include headache, moodiness, cramps, tension and depression.
2. **Vaginitis:** *Vaginitis* is an infection in the vagina. It can cause itching and irritation. See your doctor if you have these symptoms.
3. **Cancer of the female organs:** Like other cancers, early detection is important. Be aware of any unusual changes in your reproductive system or your menstrual cycle. See your doctor regularly.

CHAPTER REVIEW

DEFINE

Circulatory system

Anemia

Leukemia

Hemophilia

Arteriosclerosis

Stroke

Hypertension

Respiratory system

Pneumonia

Bronchitis

Asthma

Emphysema

Lung cancer

Skeletal system

Scoliosis

Bursitis

Arthritis

Osteoporosis

Muscular system

Digestive system

Digestion

Ulcer

Gallstone

Excretory system

Urinary tract

Integumentary system

Immune system

Natural immunity

Acquired immunity

HIV

Autoimmune disease

Central nervous system

Epilepsy

Cerebral palsy

Multiple sclerosis

Endocrine system

Diabetes

Reproductive system

EXPLAIN

1. Explain the primary function of each system of the body.
2. Explain one health problem from each of the eleven systems.
3. Explain the parts of the upper respiratory system and the lower respiratory system.
4. Explain how the air you breathe is being filtered of dirt and harmful particles.
5. Explain the effects of exercise on the bones.
6. Explain what is meant by the term atrophy and what might be the cause.
7. Explain why it is important to thoroughly chew your food.
8. Explain why it is important to eat plenty of fiber and why this is important to your excretory system.
9. Explain how your reproductive system is unique from the other systems of your body.

10. Explain the functions of the hormones in your body.

DISCUSS

1. Discuss what you might tell a friend if he/she started smoking cigarettes.
2. Discuss why exercise is so important for the health of your muscular system and tell how you might include exercise into your schedule.
3. Your brother Mark leaves the house without any breakfast. He eats a candy bar at school for a snack and at lunch he has a soda and a bag of chips. After sports practice he comes home and eats a large dinner. Discuss what you might say to Mark concerning his eating habits.
4. Discuss why people generally feel uneasy when discussing the male and female reproductive systems. How can this feeling be positive and how can it be negative?
5. Discuss the importance of respecting each other's sexuality and privacy.

SUGGESTED ACTIVITIES

1. **What type are YOU?** Find out your blood type and bring the information to class. Everyone tries to figure out who could donate blood and who could receive blood. Divide up into groups according to blood type and Rh factor. Try to make several matches and write down the names of those possible donors for you. You will need to do research on blood typing.

2. **Key concepts:** Outline the chapter and make a study guide for yourself. You can work in groups and each student be responsible for one system of the body.

3. **Let me inform you:** Choose one disease from one system of the body and write a full report on it. Share it with the class.

4. **All systems GO!** Draw a detailed picture of the circulatory system or the respiratory system. You may work in groups and make them life-size or you may work on it alone. Put it up in the classroom.

5. **Growing up:** Write a report on the physical results of growing older. Concentrate on the systems of the body and what can happen to the systems as you age. Do not forget to include what you can do to prevent the effects of aging on your body.

6. **Lever action:** Skeletal bones provide shape and support for the body, but they also act as levers that give the body movement. Find information on the three types of lever actions in the body. Use a biology book, anatomy book or exercise physiology book to provide you with information. Use illustrations to help describe the three levers. For example: The first-class lever is like a seesaw at a play ground. When the arm is straightened at the elbow it is an example of a first-class lever.

7. **Wanted: A career in the health field:** There are certain careers that are specifically designed to one or more systems of the body. Pick one or two systems and find out what careers these would include and what the qualifications and preparation would be to get a job in this area. For example: A sports trainer or sports medicine doctor. Try to find at least five different jobs for your selected systems.

8. **Help me understand:** To better understand the diseases that can afflict the body, do a report on one or more diseases that may affect a system (such as Diabetes, Epilepsy, Scoliosis, or Arthritis). Try to interview someone who has the disease and share your findings with the class.

9. **I Think I am going crazy!** Make a list of questions you have concerning your reproductive system and present them to one or both of your parents. If you feel uncomfortable discussing them with your parents, ask your teacher or youth pastor. If the questions are too personal do not write them down, but get an appointment with someone whom you trust. Avoid asking your peers; they may not have the correct answer for you.

10. **Learn to respect:** Do a report on respect. What does it mean to respect God, your parents, others and yourself? How can you show respect to your peers and how might this influence your actions and attitudes dealing with personal subjects such as sexuality? Are you showing respect if you ask personal questions of others? Or if you talk behind someone's back?

Nutrition

3

3-1   BACK TO BASICS
3-2   GOD IN THE DOCTOR'S OFFICE
3-3   THE ROLE OF VITAMINS AND MINERALS
3-4   THE DIET DILEMMA

3-1   BACK TO BASICS

If you do not smoke or drink excessively, your diet can influence your long-term health prospects more than any other action you might take.
C. Everett Koop M.D.

As manufacturers come up with new cereals, snack crackers and cookies, making healthy food choices becomes more difficult. Eating well is still possible, but the decision of what to eat has become somewhat complicated. People who understand the importance of good nutrition are more likely to make wise food choices and are also more likely to be selective of the foods they eat.

Food is the fuel that keeps the body alive. Eating can be one of the great pleasures of living. To eat for good health does not mean you must miss out on the pleasure of eating. You may notice that as you eat healthier your body craves more nutritious food that satisfies the body. Eating healthy food can improve your whole outlook on life. Scientists have identified many nutrients that your body needs. There are six main kinds of nutrients: *proteins, carbohydrates, fats, vitamins, minerals, and water*. The combination of these nutrients provide the following for the body:

- fuel for energy
- the basic building blocks for growth and maintenance
- substances that act to control body processes

> To eat for good health does not mean you must miss out on the pleasure of eating.

Vitamins, minerals, and water have no calories and do not provide energy, but they are an essential part of your nutritional needs.

Making wise food choices daily can be very difficult not only because of the prevelance of unhealthy food, but because researchers are continually finding new information concerning healthy food choices. For example, the consumption of generous quantities of red meat has been accepted as an ideal source of protein. Nutritionists now believe, however, that with the protein comes more animal fat than the body needs. Red meat is a source of high protein but today people are encouraged to eat more vegetable protein and cut back on the animal fat. Until recently dairy products have been a safe "good-for-you" food. No one would dispute the good food value of dairy products, but with high consumption comes high levels of animal fat.

Another change in society is the role of the fast food industry. Some of the changes and additions are good, but others are not. For example, some of the so-called "healthy" chicken items served at fast food restaurants are as bad as burgers and fries. To be able to eat a good diet today requires more knowledge than ever before and the ability to read labels carefully. It requires a knowledge and a discernment as to how foods are prepared, as well as commitment and discipline. With the explosive growth of the fast food industry, the number of choices available to the consumer has become bewildering, and at times confusing as to the "healthyness" of the choices. It is still necessary to make the personal dietary changes that are best for you and your family.

PROTEINS

Protein is an essential part of every cell in your body — the largest portion existing in the muscle tissue. You supply protein to your body cells by eating foods that contain protein. **Protein** is the only source your body has for nitrogen, which is needed for building new tissue. The chief component of every protein is a string of **amino acids.** The body extracts the amino acids from the proteins you eat and rearranges them into new proteins. These

Protein

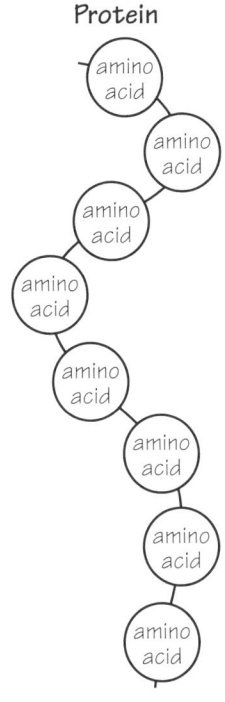

new proteins are then used by the body for growth and maintenance of body cells. The human body needs about 22 amino acids to make these strings or links. Your body can convert some of these amino acids from other amino acids. Others are called **essential amino acids** because they must come as they are from the foods you eat.

Complete proteins, those that contain all the amino acids, come from animal sources such as meat, poultry, fish, cheese, and eggs. You do not have to eat animal protein to be healthy; however, a vegetarian diet (one that typically excludes animal products) must be arranged very carefully to ensure that the proper nutritional requirements are met. Vegetable proteins, however, are incomplete. That is, no single vegetable source contains all the amino acids. To obtain all the amino acids from vegetable sources, it therefore is necessary to combine at least two sources, such as grains with legumes, seeds, nuts and vegetables in the same meal to provide the right combinations of amino acids for the body. Animal sources of protein are not necessary for a healthy diet.

Carbohydrates are energy producers for the body.

CARBOHYDRATES

Carbohydrates are energy producers for the body. The main carbohydrates in foods are sugars and starches. Carbohydrates are very important for:

- providing energy for the body
- helping to control the breakdown of protein
- protecting the body against toxins

Once eaten, the body responds to carbohydrates by turning them into a type of sugar called **glucose.** This glucose is fuel for the body. All carbohydrates are made of links or strings of sugar. These strings are either simple or complex

in nature. *Monosaccharides* are the single molecule sugars known as simple sugars. Glucose is a monosaccharide.

Complex carbohydrates or *polysaccharides*, are starches composed of many monosaccharide molecules and are broken down by the body into two or more sugars. Your body stores some glucose for emergencies, which is called glycogen. When your glucose and glycogen reserves are gone, you should eat. Otherwise, your body will begin turning some of your protein into glucose for energy. Complex carbohydrates have a higher nutritive value than simple sugars, and supply more fiber which helps food and waste move through the intestines. Food sources high in complex carbohydrates often provide good sources of vitamins, minerals and protein as well. These starches take more time to digest so the feeling of being full or satisfied lasts longer. Milk, dried fruit, fruit juices, honey, candy, some cookies and sweet desserts are high in sugar content. Good sources of starches or complex carbohydrates are grains, beans, peas, and potatoes. Your diet should include a good amount of complex carbohydrates, while avoiding large or excessive amounts of simple carbohydrates.

FATS

As carbohydrates are chains of glucose and proteins are chains of amino acids, a **fat** is a chain of fatty acids, long molecules of carbon, hydrogen, and oxygen. In the body, fats provide a concentrated source of energy. They can provide more than twice as much energy as carbohydrates. Fats are an essential part of the diet. The body needs fat for:

- growth and repair
- maintaining body temperature
- cushioning vital organs
- insulation of the body through the stored fat in tissues
- keeping the skin from becoming dry and flaky
- manufacture of certain hormones

Most Americans eat far more fat than the body needs. A very important characteristic of fat is the degree of *saturation.*

Saturated fat tends to increase blood cholesterol levels, which increases the risk of heart disease. The body does not need any saturated fat in its diet. It can manufacture all it needs from the other fats. High levels of saturated fats are found in red meats, pork products, egg yolks, butter, hard margarines, most (but not all, read the labels carefully) cheeses and dairy products. Certain vegetable oils known as tropical oils (coconut, palm and palm kernel) as well as any oil that has been hydrogenated or used for frying are all high in saturated fat.

Unsaturated fats do not tend to elevate cholesterol levels. They are usually liquid at room temperature. Corn, safflower, cottonseed and canola oils are examples of unsaturated fats. Even though these oils are low in saturated fat, if they are used for frying or deep frying (for example, french fries, fried chicken, do-nuts, etc.) the frying process changes the unsaturated fat to saturated fat, and soaks the product in this fat.

CHOLESTEROL

Do you know that your body needs a small amount of cholesterol? However, as with saturated fat, the body does not need any cholesterol from the diet. The liver can manufacture all it needs from other fats. Cholesterol is needed to:

- make vitamin D useful to the body
- make hormones
- build cell structure by forming cell membranes
- make bile acids to help digest fats
- build nerve tissue

Cholesterol is a waxy substance that is carried around the body in the bloodstream by lipoproteins, proteins to which fats are attached. Most of the cholesterol in the blood is carried throughout the body on two different lipoproteins. These lipoproteins are known as **low density lipoproteins (LDL)** and **high density lipoproteins (HDL)**. The LDL is also called bad cholesterol because it is the cholesterol that tends to be deposited in the arteries. The higher the amount of LDL in the blood,

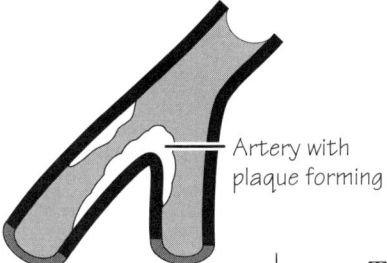

Artery with plaque forming

the greater the risk of heart disease by the formation of *plaque* or clog in the arteries. The HDL cholesterol is also called good cholesterol because it is the form of cholesterol that is being removed from circulation and transported to the liver to be eliminated.

The aim of your diet should be to lower the LDL cholesterol and raise your HDL cholesterol. In some cases regular exercise can help to increase your HDL just as a low cholesterol, low fat diet can help to lower your LDL cholesterol. The typical American consumes 400–500 milligrams of cholesterol a day, but the American Heart Association recommends 300 milligrams a day or less. However, ideally the consumption of cholesterol should be reduced to no more than 100–200 milligrams daily.

Controlling your cholesterol and the fat intake in your diet does not have to be a complicated chore. Becoming informed about the cholesterol and saturated fat content of foods can help give you some of the tools you need to make wise dietary choices. Remember that your blood cholesterol level is strongly influenced by both the amount of cholesterol and saturated fat that you eat in your diet. It is often a good idea to have your cholesterol checked even if you think you are eating well. This is especially true if there is a history of heart disease in your family.

Beware of how foods are advertised and described. For example, labels that read cholesterol free and 95% fat free, etc. can sometimes be very misleading.

3-2 GOD IN THE DOCTOR'S OFFICE

And the Lord commanded us to observe all these statutes, to fear the Lord our God, for our good always, that He might preserve us alive, as it is this day. Then it will be righteousness for us, if we are careful to observe all these commandments before the Lord our God, as He has commanded us.
Deuteronomy 6:24–25

The commandments of the Lord throughout the Bible help people live a life pleasing to God. Although there is no list of commandments for healthy eating etched in stone, God has given us guidance through research related to diet and nutrition. Imagine yourself getting a check-up and God was in the doctor's office! What kind of prescription for good nutrition would He write? If God were to write you out a personal prescription, would you follow it? Educating yourself is a key to making wise food choices. The following are ten statements to remember when making your food choices.

Prescription for Good Nutrition

1. Eat a variety of foods
2. Maintain ideal weight
3. Use exercise to keep your metabolism high
4. Increase dietary fiber to 25–35 grams a day
5. Eat less sugar
6. Eat less sodium
7. Eat less fat
8. Avoid alcohol and smoking
9. Drink plenty of water
10. Avoid eating while under stress

1. EAT A VARIETY OF FOODS

To be healthy you need to eat foods from many different sources. A diet that is very limited may result in your body being low in the essential nutrients, vitamins, minerals, proteins, and fats it needs for good health.

The Department of Agriculture has changed dietary guidelines over the years as research points toward a more healthy food balance. The *Food Guide Pyramid* (shown on the following page) given by the United States Department of Agriculture can help you make healthy food choices. Notice that some groups allow more daily servings than other groups.

Breads, Cereals, Rice and Pasta

This is the largest group in the food pyramid, with 6–11 servings a day. Although a person may not eat 11 servings of grains a day, the important point is that the foods in this group should be

If God were to write you out a personal prescription, would you follow it?

Food Guide Pyramid

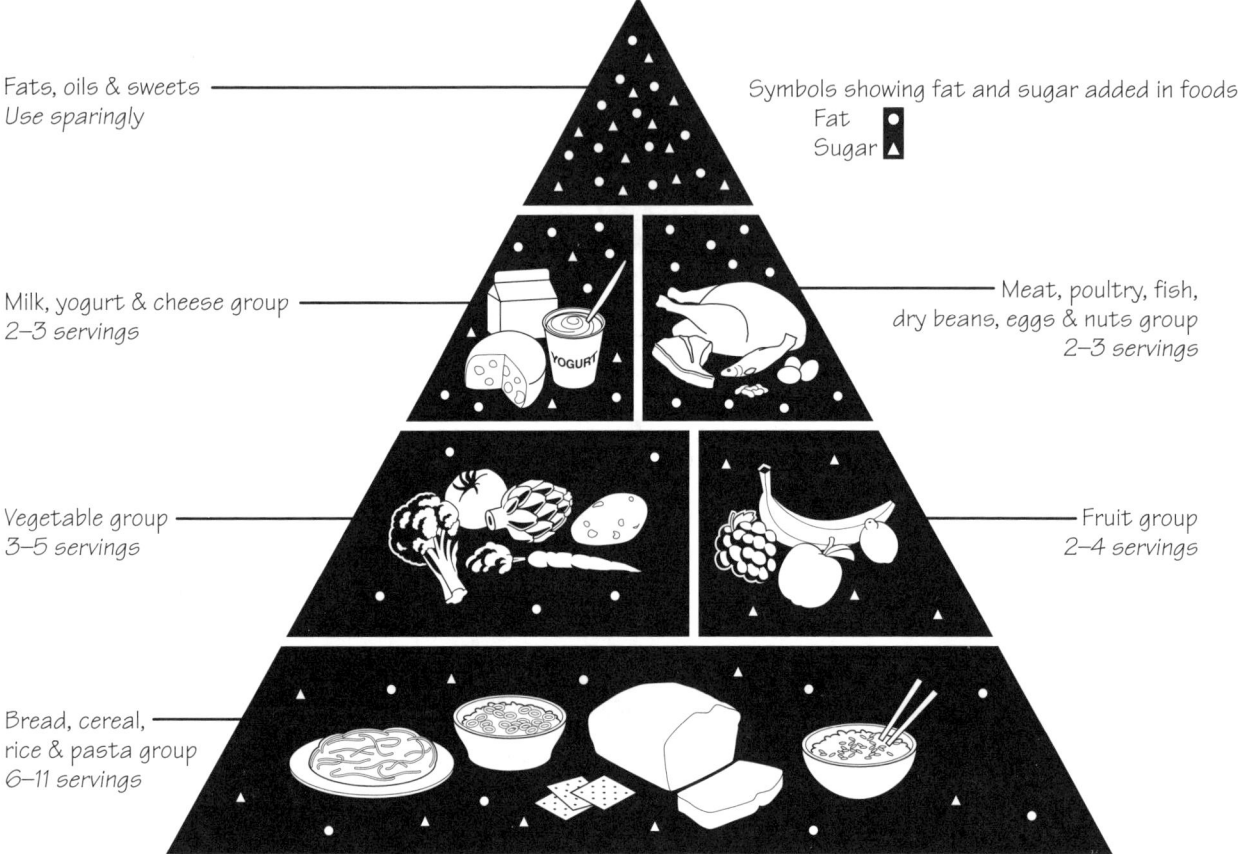

Fats, oils & sweets
Use sparingly

Symbols showing fat and sugar added in foods
Fat ●
Sugar ▲

Milk, yogurt & cheese group
2–3 servings

Meat, poultry, fish,
dry beans, eggs & nuts group
2–3 servings

Vegetable group
3–5 servings

Fruit group
2–4 servings

Bread, cereal,
rice & pasta group
6–11 servings

Source: U.S. Departments of Agriculture and Health and Human Services

the foundation in the diet. These foods provide B vitamins and iron. They also provide fiber, magnesium, zinc, and folic acid, as well as help to maintain a low-fat diet. Remember, it is the condiments you may add to these foods that increase the calories, and often add considerable fat to a meal.

Vegetables and Fruits

The American diet is changing. Meals are becoming more creative, including a variety of vegetables and fruits to please the palate as well as the waistline. With the recommendation of *2–4 fruit* servings, and *3–5 vegetable servings a day*, people must change their attitude toward these groups of food.

Dark green and yellow vegetables add folic acid, magnesium, zinc, and fiber to the diet. The starchy vegetables add fiber, carbohydrates, vitamin C, B_6, iron and magnesium. Fruits are known to be good sources of vitamin C, especially the citrus fruits. Fruits also provide folic acid, potassium and some fiber. Vegetables and fruit are becoming the customers' choice because they carry a nutritious punch while being low in calories, sodium, and fat.

Dairy (Milk, yogurt, and cheese)

There are various opinions about the value of the dairy group. Although this group is the primary source of calcium, some people cannot tolerate the lactose that milk and milk products contain. Today there are milk substitutes or lactose-free products which are still high in calcium. The foods in this group also provide protein and vitamins A, riboflavin (B_2), B_6, and B_{12}. If you are trying to cut back on your fat intake, then go lightly in this group by choosing low fat products.

Meat, Poultry, Fish, Dry Beans, Eggs, and Nuts

A meal that was traditionally built around red meat, fish or poultry can now be built around dry beans or legumes. By selecting less fatty meats (such as fish and poultry), as well as removing visible fat and skin from poultry, and by avoiding egg yolks, a person can lower his/her fat consumption. The foods contained in this group are good sources of protein, phosphorus and niacin. Iron, zinc, vitamins B_6 and B_{12}, as well as trace minerals are provided from this group. By being careful in your choices from this group, you will help to eliminate unnecessary fat and calories from your diet. Certainly 2–3 servings of meat and eggs is unnecessary. All the cholesterol and fat is in the yolk of the egg. For example, substitute two egg whites for each egg required.

Fats, Oils, and Sweets

Although fats are important for your diet, and a small amount of sweets will not put you on your death bed, Americans consume more from this group than they would like to believe. The problem is the "hidden" fats and sugars that are in foods. People must learn to read labels and consider fats and sweets as a treat rather than a regular part of the diet.

What is a Serving?

When you have your bowl of cereal in the morning, do you read the label regarding the suggested serving size? When you are drinking a tall glass of milk or juice, are you aware of the suggested serving size? The following is a list of serving sizes to correspond to the Food Pyramid's suggested daily servings.

Breads, cereals, rice and pasta group
One serving equals:
- 1 slice of bread or 1 small roll or muffin.
- ½–¾ cup hot cereal, or 1 oz. ready-to-eat cereal.
- ½ cup of cooked pasta or rice.

Vegetables and fruit group
One serving equals:
- 1 small salad or ½ cup cooked vegetable
- ¾ cup (6 oz.) fruit or vegetable juice
- 1 medium fruit or 1 cup of fruit.

Meats, poultry, fish, eggs and nuts group
One serving equals
- 2-3 oz. in serving size.
- 1 egg is equal to 1 oz. of meat
- 1 cup cooked dry beans equals 2 oz. of lean meat, poultry or fish.

Dairy group
One serving equals:
- 8 fluid oz. of milk, or 1–2 oz. of cheese or 6–8 oz. of yogurt.

When you have your bowl of cereal in the morning, do you read the label regarding the suggested serving size?

Fats and sweets
- Use sparingly!

For young children serving sizes may vary. The American Dietetic Association (ADA) recommends that serving sizes should start at 1 tablespoon and increase by 1 tablespoon a year for kids between ages 3 and 5.

How to get your 5 a day — Sample menu for 1 day:

Breakfast: 6 ounce glass of orange juice = 1 serving fruit; no fat
2 ounces cold cereal = 2 servings bread; check label for fat content
1 cup 2 percent milk = 1 serving milk; 5 grams of fat
Banana on top of cereal = 1 serving fruit; no fat
English muffin = 2 servings bread; 2 grams of fat

Lunch: Turkey Sandwich
3 ounces white turkey = 2 servings meat (protein); 6 grams of fat
2 slices bread = 2 servings bread; 2 grams of fat
Lettuce, tomato = 1/2 serving vegetable; no fat
1 medium apple = 1 serving fruit; no fat
Plain non-fat yogurt, 1 cup = 1 serving milk, no fat

Dinner: 3 ounces white fish = 1 serving meat (protein); 6 grams of fat
2 cups green salad = 2 servings vegetable; no fat
1 tablespoon lowfat dressing = 7 grams of fat (check label for content)
1 cup brown rice = 2 servings bread; no fat
1 cup broccoli = 2 servings vegetable; no fat
1 cup 2 percent milk = 1 serving milk; 5 grams of fat

Total: Bread, cereal group: 8 servings
Vegetable group: 4 1/2 servings
Fruit group: 3 servings
Milk, Dairy: 3 servings
Meat, poultry, fish: 2 servings
Fats: 33 grams

2. MAINTAIN YOUR IDEAL WEIGHT

The saying that an ounce of prevention is worth a pound of cure is certainly true in the area of controlling your weight. For some, how much they weigh is a secret even to themselves. The emotional as well as physical stress put on a body from continued dieting can be a lifelong struggle. For the purpose of nutrition, knowing and maintaining your ideal weight as best you can will help motivate you to make wise food choices. Heart disease, cancer, high blood pressure and diabetes are some of the health problems that are linked to obesity.

Although being overweight or normal weight as a child does not always correlate with the presence or absence of obesity as an adult; being overweight at any age is unhealthy. In addition, many lifestyle choices including eating habits are established in childhood. Furthermore, it is easier to change poor eating habits at a young age. If a child by the age of eight has developed healthy eating habits, those positive habits are more likely to carry into adulthood.

3. USE EXERCISE TO KEEP YOUR METABOLISM HIGH

Have you ever noticed how some individuals are able to eat a lot but never gain a pound, while others eat very little and gain weight anyway? This ability to use energy at a higher rate when your body is *at rest* is called your **basal metabolism**. Your metabolism is the sum of all the chemical activities in the body. The energy for the function of your metabolism is provided by the foods you eat. When a person burns energy at a high rate they are said to have a fast metabolism and those who burn energy at a low rate have a slow metabolism.

Although being overweight or normal weight as a child does not always correlate with the presence or absence of obesity as an adult; being overweight at any age is unhealthy.

Basal metabolic rate (BMR) varies with age, sex, body size and shape. It changes as you get older, generally slowing down after the age of 28–30. Men have a tendency to have a higher BMR due to the amount of lean muscle they have. A person with more muscle will burn energy at a higher rate. Both exercise and eating habits can influence the metabolic rate.

A **calorie** is the name given to a unit of heat the body uses for energy. Foods that are high in calories have a higher energy value. Typically, people refer to calories when they are trying to lose excess fat. Exercising *and* decreasing your total calorie consumption must go hand-in-hand when losing fat. While exercising, you increase your need for energy (metabolic rate) causing your body to burn more calories. Staying on a consistent exercise program can raise your BMR so you are burning more calories while resting.

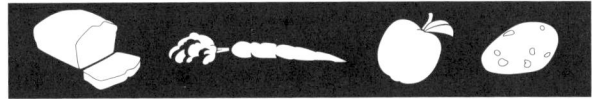

4. INCREASE DIETARY FIBER TO 25–35 GRAMS A DAY

Most Americans eat about 10–20 grams of fiber a day. This is far below the recommendation from the National Cancer Institute of 25–35 grams. Fiber comes from the foods you eat, typically, complex carbohydrates: fruits, vegetables and whole grain products. Fiber cannot be totally digested in the stomach or the intestines. Although **fiber** is not a nutrient, it passes through the intestines and acts like a broom carrying with it unwanted waste. When a person has too little fiber in his diet, the body holds the waste in the intestines for a long period of time, often resulting in constipation. Suffering from constipation is not only uncomfortable but very unhealthy. As the waste material remains in your intestines, toxins, or poisons begin to build up causing various symptoms. Scientists believe fiber may have a role in preventing certain digestive diseases and cancers.

Although fiber is not a nutrient, it passes through the intestines and acts like a broom carrying with it unwanted waste.

5. EAT LESS SUGAR

Imagine sitting down to eat a bowl containing a third of a pound of white sugar! This is the amount the average American eats in one day, about 130 pounds a year. It is not all in the form of table sugar, but also in "hidden" sugars and sweeteners in a variety of foods. Next time you pick up a box of cereal, a can of soup, a jar of peanut butter, or a can of soda, read the label and look for words such as: glucose, sucrose, dextrose, fructose, maltose, lactose, syrup and "other sweeteners." These are all forms of sugar. Often the sweets people eat also have lots of fat and are low in healthy nutrients. Foods containing natural sugars, such as fruits, also contain other healthy nutrients for the body.

The body responds to sugar, as with other carbohydrates, by releasing the hormone **insulin** from the pancreas to regulate the sugar. The more sugar you eat, the more insulin your body needs to release. Everyone's body responds differently to the increase in blood sugar. Dentists will also tell you that sweets promote tooth decay. No matter what, everyone should keep their intake of sugars low.

A word about artificial sweeteners. Saccharin was once the leading artificial sweetener until they found it may have caused cancer in laboratory animals. Now Nutra Sweet® leads the sweetener category. Scientists do not really know how the body responds to these artificial ingredients. A good suggestion is to avoid consuming large quantities of artificial sweeteners.

6. EAT LESS SODIUM

Salt and sodium are not the same. Table salt is sodium chloride, which is about 40% sodium. **Sodium** is an essential mineral in our daily diet, and is found naturally in many of the foods you

74

eat. The Recommended Daily Allowance for a safe amount of salt in your diet is 1,100–3,300 milligrams (or 1–3 grams) a day; however, it is not uncommon for people to consume 7,000 milligrams in a day. The processing of food today can add unwanted sodium to your food. As you learn to read labels faithfully, be aware of the following high sodium items:

- Monosodium glutamate (MSG), a flavor enhancer
- Sodium nitrite, a preservative
- Sodium bicarbonate, a raising agent
- Sodium phosphate, a wetting agent
- Sodium benzoate, a preservative
- The sodium salts of saccharin, propionate, and ascorbate
- Brine and pickling juices
- Soy sauce

The easiest way to cut back on your intake of salt is to reach for the salt shaker less often. Try also to avoid eating processed foods such as sandwich meats (especially ham), hot-dogs, canned soups, and salty restaurant foods. If you cut back on your salt, you will be surprised just how quickly you will get used to the real taste of your food.

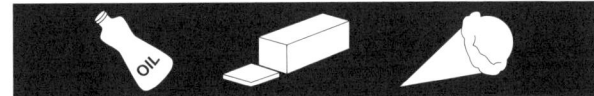

7. EAT LESS FAT

A menu that is very low in fat is the challenge of the day. The American Heart Association, the American Cancer Society, and the National Cancer Institute all recommend that a person should not consume more than 30% of one day's calories from fat. Ideally the fat content should not be more than 20% of total calories and even less for individuals with high cholesterol levels, heart disease and other metabolic diseases. Those who are trying to lose weight should consume a much lower percentage. With the knowledge you have learned already concerning fat, and the information you will read in the text, you will be on your way to a healthier lifestyle and a healthier heart.

8. AVOID ALCOHOL AND SMOKING

Alcohol is a depressant to your central nervous system including your brain. It is also an addictive substance, affecting your eating habits and your emotional well being. People drink alcohol for different reasons and in various amounts. For many people, regular or excessive alcohol use indicates a deeper issue that needs attention. Young people who try drinking often do so for acceptance or approval from their peers. If the drinking persists, it may become a way of coping with or escaping from the stresses in life. The Bible tells us that there is a way out of every temptation. If you find yourself struggling with alcohol, or even the temptation to try it, look for a safe adult with whom you can talk.

Nicotine is a very powerful addictive drug. Tobacco smoke not only contains nicotine, but also carbon monoxide, tars, and poisonous substances that are dangerous to the body. Even those who inhale the smoke of others (second-hand smoke) can suffer from the same illnesses as the smoker. Every cigarette you smoke can shorten your life by an average of five and a half minutes. This in itself is enough reason not to start the smoking habit. Smoking also affects your ability to taste food. Many times people smoke instead of eating, depriving the body of its nutrients.

9. DRINK PLENTY OF WATER

Are you drinking enough water? When was the last time you drank some water? A normal adult is about 60–70% water. Although you could go without food for quite some time, you could only survive a few days without water. Usually your body tells you when you are hungry, but when your body tells you that you are thirsty, you may have already been walking around in a dehydrated state.

Usually your body tells you when you are hungry, but when your body tells you that you are thirsty, you may have already been walking around in a dehydrated state.

The consumption of water helps keep your body's fluid in balance. Drinking water can help you lose weight, aid in your digestion, help keep constipation at bay, and keep your skin from becoming dry. Water is also found in the foods you eat. By eating fruits and vegetables, you are consuming the highest amount of water other than by drinking it.

Generally, your body needs seven to ten 8 oz. glasses of fluid a day (in addition to the foods you eat) to stay in balance. If you are one who regularly exercises then you need to drink more.

Your food choices can affect your fluid balance. Although you may lose a few pounds of body water while on a diet, water weight is quickly regained. Drinks containing alcohol or caffeine, such as coffee, tea, and some sodas act as diuretics and make the kidneys expel extra fluid from the body. These dietary choices can lead to dehydration and stress on the body systems including the heart and blood vessels. Like nicotine, caffeine is also an addictive substance.

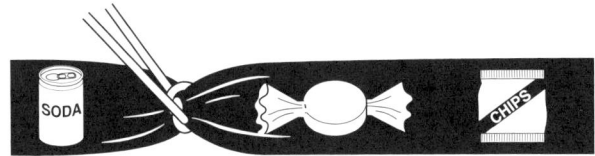

10. AVOID "STRESS" EATING

Some people handle the stress in their lives by eating. This often results in poor food choices and overeating. If you notice yourself eating the wrong foods and/or more foods, especially when you do so when you are upset or under stress, try to recognize the factors causing this response.

While eating "on-the-run" can seem to be a normal part of your lifestyle, it is not a very healthy part. When you eat fast, your digestive juices do not have adequate time to break down the food. Eating a meal while you are emotionally upset is not wise. Your stomach is in a state of being all "tied up" and is not in the best condition to handle the digestion of food. Often you make poor food choices based on your emotional state and this only aggravates the situation. The next time you find yourself in that "hurried" condition, stop what you are doing and reach for the door knob. Take a walk rather than reach for that candy bar or soda pop.

Healthy Snacks

Fruits: Any fruits such as: bananas, oranges, apple slices, apricots, grapes, fruit juices, no added sugar.

Vegetables: Any raw vegetables such as: carrot and celery sticks, sliced tomatoes, cooked artichokes.

Breads and Cereal: Slice of whole wheat bread, or rolls, toast with no butter, tortillas (corn or wheat), cup of oatmeal, whole-wheat crackers, popcorn without the butter.

Dairy: nonfat yogurt, cottage cheese, cheese cubes.

Nuts and meat: Peanut butter in moderation (high in total fat and calories, however), almonds, sunflower seeds, tuna fish (water packed without mayonnaise), slice of lean ham or turkey.

Combinations: Any combinations including healthy foods may be eaten as a snack.

A Word About Heart Disease

- Every minute three Americans have a heart attack
- 1.5 million deaths from heart attack each year. That equals the number of Americans who died in 10 Vietnam wars.
- By age 60, one in five men and one in 17 women in the U.S. will have a heart attack.
- If six 747s crashed in one day the media would shout "2,200 dead." Yet that is the number lost each day to heart attacks.

- Your chance of contracting AIDS (if heterosexual and non IV drug user) = 1 in 1,000,000.
- Your chance of being murdered = 1 in 10,000.
- Your chance of dying in auto wreck = 1 in 5,000.
- Your chance of dying from a heart attack = 1 in 2.

Coronary mortality rates:

1963————————————————1982
(1.2 million)   (500,000)

Why the drop? The Harvard Study states that the number of lives saved from heart attack has improved with medical advances.

39.5% from by-pass surgery, better high blood pressure treatment, more hospitals with coronary units.

54% from reducing smoking and cholesterol in the diet.

3-3   THE ROLE OF VITAMINS AND MINERALS

VITAMINS

Vitamins are organic substances the body needs to help regulate and coordinate functions of the body. Vitamins are essential for maintaining a healthy balance in the body systems. The best source of vitamins comes from the foods you eat. A healthy diet including foods eaten in their natural state, as well as foods that are stored and cooked properly, can provide much of your vitamin needs. However, each individual's needs are different. Age, sex, heredity, illness, diet, stress, as well as the amount you exercise, all contribute to your body composition and needs. The **RDA** or Recommended Dietary Allowance is an assumed percent for the average non-pregnant, adult. It is a broad-based

If six 747s crashed in one day the media would shout "2,200 dead." Yet that is the number lost each day to heart attacks.

Vitamin	Function	Source	RDA
A (Retinol)	Helps resist infections. Helps maintain skin, hair and body membranes.	Liver, eggs, milk, green and yellow vegetables.	1 milligram
Thiamin (Vitamin B_1)	Helps the body burn carbohydrates for energy.	Meats, esp. pork; liver; nuts, peas, whole grains, beans, vegetables.	1.0–1.4 milligram
Riboflavin (Vitamin B_2)	Helps maintain skin, eyes, nerves. Needed by all cells for energy release and repair.	Liver, milk, green vegetables, cheese, eggs, poultry.	1.2–1.7 milligram
Pyridoxine (Vitamin B_6)	Needed by red blood cells and nerves for proper functioning.	Liver, lean meat, whole grains, milk, eggs.	2 milligrams
B_{12}	Needed for red blood cell production in bone marrow, and needed for nervous system.	Eggs, meat, dairy products.	3 micrograms
Folic Acid	Needed to produce red blood cells, and to produce RNA, DNA.	Liver, green leafy vegetables, poultry, fish.	400 micrograms
Niacin	Needed by cells for proper use of fuel and oxygen.	Whole grains, enriched wheat flour, cereals, liver, poultry, lean meats.	13–19 milligrams
Pantothenic Acid	Helps in metabolism of carbohydrates, fats, protein.	Egg yolk, meat, nuts, whole grains.	4–7 milligrams
Biotin	Needed by skin and circulatory system.	Liver, kidney, egg yolk, nuts, legumes, fresh vegetables.	100–200 milligrams
C (Ascorbic Acid)	Needed by bones and teeth. Aids in healing wounds and aids in resisting infection.	All citrus fruits, tomatoes, raw cabbage, potatoes, strawberries, green leafy vegetables.	60 milligrams
D	Helps build strong bones and teeth.	Fish, fish-liver oil, dairy products.	5–10 micrograms
E	Prevents damage to cell membranes, helps tissues handle fatty substances.	Vegetable oils, whole grains, cereals, vegetables.	8–10 milligrams
K	Needed for normal blood clotting.	Green leafy vegetables, peas, grains.	70–140 micrograms

percentage to help guide you in your dietary choices.

The two main classifications of vitamins are water-soluble and fat soluble. Water-soluble vitamins are those that can be excreted from the body, therefore you need to replace them daily. Fat-soluble vitamins are those that can be stored in the body for weeks. The C and B-complex vitamins are water soluble; vitamins A, D, K, and E, are fat soluble. Study the chart to learn the best sources of the essential vitamins.

MINERALS

Minerals are inorganic substances essential for your body. Minerals help the body form bones, teeth, and blood cells. They help regulate the body's fluids and aid in the chemical reactions of cells. Your body cannot manufacture the essential minerals, therefore you must get them from the foods you eat. Although everyone needs minerals, there are certain times when your needs will change. During periods of growth, as well as during pregnancy, minerals are vital to the proper development of the body. Study the chart to see if you are eating foods rich in essential minerals.

ARE SUPPLEMENTS NECESSARY?

Vitamin and mineral supplements may be necessary if you are not eating a balanced and varied diet. However, supplements are not a replacement for eating the right foods. Infants and young children may need certain vitamins or minerals added to their diet. Doctors prescribe supplements for women who are having children to help them during, and sometimes after, pregnancy. Most importantly, if you are going to take vitamin and mineral supplements, talk to your doctor and take them sensibly. Mega doses of either vitamins or minerals can cause serious health problems. If you are concerned that your diet needs a supplement, a good multivitamin, multimineral product may be your best choice. Read the labels carefully and check with your doctor or nutritional expert.

Vitamin supplements are not a replacement for eating the right foods.

Mineral	Function	Source	RDA
Calcium	Builds and maintains strong teeth and bones. Helps blood clot. Helps nerves and muscles function.	Dairy products, green vegetables.	800 milligrams (more during growth spurts)
Phosphorus	Helps nerves and muscles function. Key to cell reactions.	Meat, dairy products, beans, peas, cereals.	800 milligrams (more during growth spurts)
Potassium	Needed for fluid balance and cell reactions.	Avocados, bananas, apricots, potatoes.	not established
Magnesium	Activates many enzyme reactions. Helps make proteins.	Beans, peas, nuts, cereals, green leafy vegetables.	300–350 milligrams
Iodine	Needed by the thyroid gland to regulate the rate at which foods are burned.	Seafood, iodized salt.	0.1 milligrams
Iron	Needed to make hemoglobin, and aids in growth of muscles, glands, and nerves.	Liver, meat, eggs, enriched cereals, green leafy vegetables.	10–18 milligrams
Fluorine Copper Zinc	Helps protect teeth from decay. Needed by cells to use oxygen. Needed in the structure of cell enzymes.	Water, fluoride toothpaste, liver, seafood, meat, whole wheat, beans, peas, nuts.	1.5–15 milligrams
Chromium Selenium Molybdenum Manganese	Minor roles in body chemistry.	Trace elements in many foods.	minute amounts
Sodium	Builds fluid balance, muscle contraction, and nerve reaction.	Most foods except fruit.	1,100–3,300 milligrams

Researchers continue to study the positive role of vitamins and minerals in your diet. Vitamins C, E, and A are thought to be antioxidants, aiding in the prevention of cancer. They have also learned that the increased doses of calcium and vitamin D are slowing down osteoporosis, bone degeneration. The B vitamins have been known to help women with PMS (premenstrual syndrome). Vitamin B$_6$ often helps those who suffer from bronchial asthma. The research concerning the value of vitamins and minerals will continue; but, in any case, you must first make sure you are feeding your body proper nutrients in the foods you choose. What can you do? Eat whole foods (those foods closest to their natural condition) as much as possible. Adding cheese, sauces, or butter/margarine adds fats, so it is best to eat fruits and vegetables plain and fresh.

WHAT ABOUT ENRICHED AND FORTIFIED FOODS?

Enriched and fortified foods are foods that have vitamins and minerals added to them. You may see on a label **"fortified"** with essential vitamins. This means that the product has added vitamins above what it would have had naturally. **Enriched** is when vitamins or minerals are added to the product after some of the nutrients have been removed during processing. For example, enriched white flour has added iron, riboflavin, niacin, and thiamin after processing.

WHAT ABOUT ADDITIVES AND PRESERVATIVES?

Both positive and negative points can be made about additives and preservatives in food. Ideally, eating foods as close to their natural state as possible would be the most beneficial to the body. Much of the food industry relies on preservatives to help food stay fresh from the farm to the market to your kitchen. The best advice is to become an educated consumer. Read the labels and if you do not know what is in the food you are eating, don't buy it. If you are making an effort to eat more fresh fruits and vegetables, you will automatically cut back on the amount of additives and preservatives in your diet.

3-4   THE DIET DILEMMA

Diet is a word that carries with it a powerful message. When you hear the word diet what comes to mind — starvation? sacrifice? failing? splurging? The phrase, "I am going on a diet" is spoken everyday, not only by teenagers and adults but unfortunately by young children. Ideally, a "diet" should not be some program you need to go on and when you reach your goal, you go off of it. Try to change your thinking of the terms *diet* and *food*. Food is not your enemy, but a source of nutrition and strength to your body. It is possible to enjoy food that is good for you and to remain at your ideal weight throughout your life.

The diet dilemma is in your mind before it is in your mouth. Think of your diet as a commitment to adopt new habits for a lifetime. As a result, you will lose unwanted pounds as well as gain a healthier body. People are consumed by the thoughts that surround body image and eating. According to a 1990 Gallop poll, 52% of all Americans want to lose weight. Americans spend more that 33 billion dollars each year on weight-loss products. Of the 44% of Americans who go on a diet each year, 95% will regain the weight. Changing your physical body, as well as your body image, takes time and effort.

NO MORE DIETS

Instant weight loss programs do not change bad eating habits and losing those extra pounds does not guarantee permanent results. Losing weight does not have to be a complicated program that wears you down both mentally and physically. The principles of weight loss are straightforward — calories in, calories out. If you take in more calories than you are putting out (burning up) then the excess will be stored as fat. If you burn up more calories than you take in, then the excess fat will be used up as fuel. Temporarily cutting calories for the purpose of losing weight will not produce long-lasting results. Furthermore, yo-yo dieting (losing and gaining

> The diet dilemma is in your mind before it is in your mouth.

> "If you do not take time for health today, you will have to take time for sickness tomorrow."

84

weight repeatedly) is known to reduce your metabolic rate (the speed at which your body burns calories). This puts added stress on the systems of the body (most importantly the cardiovascular system).

Research shows that diets do not work. When you begin to restrict your caloric intake, your body thinks it is starving and begins to guard its fat stores. Your metabolism slows down while your body stores more fat. When the diet is "over" and you slightly increase your calories, your body stores more fat to protect itself against the next famine or starvation. As a result of the dieting cycle, you gain more weight than before you began the diet. The **Set Point Theory** indicates that your body maintains a certain comfort zone, a weight that seems difficult to break. This setpoint of weight is actually a protection for your own existence. The way to break your natural setpoint is to feed your body wholesome food while increasing its metabolism through exercise.

Losing the weight is only part of the success; keeping the weight off is the true victory. Today's healthy eating plan stresses *what* you eat, rather than *how much* you eat, and stresses an active lifestyle rather than a sedentary one. There are many tantalizing diet programs on the market. Be suspicious of the programs that claim promises too good to be true, and of those fad diets that suggest you limit your calories to 800 or less. Beware of the diets that only allow you to eat one type of food a day for an extended period of time. Avoid using appetite suppressants which can cause a false sense of security for you. Studies have shown the success

SOMETHING TO THINK ABOUT

A change in history

Have you ever thought of the changes that have occurred in society. Prior to World War II much of the United States was a blue collar society. People worked manual labor and as a result burned more calories. With the automobile and the television, and the change from physical labor to mental labor, society has become a basically sedentary one. Now people spend much of their time sitting in the office, sitting in the car, and sitting in front of the TV. Think of your lifestyle. Drive to school, sit at school, drive home, sit in front of the TV, sit and do homework, go to bed. And all the time you are consuming more than 30% of your calories from fat. No wonder there has been an explosion in obesity in society!

Today's healthy eating plan stresses what you eat, rather than how much you eat, and stresses an active lifestyle rather than a sedentary one.

of such programs is not long lasting. If you want to lose weight, don't diet. Going on a diet causes you to think only short-term. To lose weight for the long-term and keep your body healthy, you must make a commitment to change your lifestyle.

EATING FOR GOOD HEALTH

The Four Sources of Calories	
Source	Calories per gram
Carbohydrate	4
Protein	4
Fat	9
Alcohol	7

The key to controlling your calorie intake is to control your calorie sources. Although any excess of calories consumed, regardless the source, will be stored as fat, fat calories are stored more efficiently than those from other sources. There are calories, and then there are **fat calories**.

Remember that your body burns calories for energy 24 hours a day. By eating a balanced and varied diet you can receive enough calories to give your body the fuel it needs. The amount of energy the body needs to function normally (your BMR) is approximately 1,200 calories a day for a woman and 1,500 a day for a man. It takes about 3,500 stored calories to make one pound of fat. Although this seems like a lot of calories to consume, pounds of fat can accumulate quickly if you are not paying close attention to the quality of foods you are eating. The American Heart Association as well as the National Cancer Institute have agreed that *a diet for most Americans should obtain no more than 30 percent of its calories from fat, and ideally about 20% or less.*

Reading Labels

A good way to control the amount of fat, sodium, and sugar in your diet is to read product labels. The Federal Drug Administration (FDA) is requiring manufacturers to supply more nutritional information on their labels to help consumers make wise choices. Avoid products that only list ingredients. When reading labels remember that the list of ingredients is in order of weight, from highest to lowest. So if glucose is listed first, sugar is the highest ingredient in the product.

The key to controlling your calorie intake is to control your calorie sources.

Reading labels is a three-step process. The *first* step is not to be swayed by the packaging and the claims that products are "lite" or "light." Although they may be reduced in calories, the labelling says nothing about the amount of salt, sugar, or fat.

The *second* step is to see if the actual amounts of fat and cholesterol are listed. Choose products that contain the least amount of fat and cholesterol. When doing this, compare products of the same type by reading them while you are standing in the store. For example, you are choosing a type of cold cereal where two products claim to be "high fiber, low fat" cereals. Hold both cereals together and compare serving size with calories, grams of fiber, sodium, and the amount of fat per serving.

The *third* step is to be aware of the types of oils contained in the product. Companies may say that a particular product contains "one or more of the following" ingredients. If the list that follows contains both coconut oil and safflower oil, you do not know the amount of each. As a result you cannot make an educated choice. It is wise however, to avoid tropical oils such as coconut oil, palm and palm kernel oil which contain high concentrations of saturated fat.

A mystery term often listed on products is "hydrogenated" or "partially hydrogenated" oil. Hydrogenation is a chemical process used to make an unsaturated fat more saturated or a liquid fat hard at room temperature. This method also extends the shelf life in many products. The hydrogenation process produces something called trans fatty acids, which have been shown to raise the LDL (bad) cholesterol levels.

If the label does not list the fat calories, or the percentage of calories from fat, you can figure this out from the information listed. Through recent regulations, food products will include the number of calories the food contains, the number of grams of carbohydrate, protein, and fat. From the total calories and grams of fat, you can calculate the percentage of calories that come from fat for a single serving.

Consider the comparison of calories from fat from the labels of both 1% and 2% milk:

2% milkfat Vitamin A & D Lowfat milk	1% milkfat Vitamin A & D Lowfat milk
Nutrition information per serving	Nutrition information per serving
serving size .... 1 cup	serving size .... 1 cup
servings per container 4	servings per container 4
calories 120	**calories** 110
protein 8g	protein 10g
carbohydrate 11g	carbohydrate 13g
fat **5g**	**fat** **2g**
sodium 130mg	sodium 130mg
<u>% of calories from fat:</u>	<u>% of calories from fat:</u>
5g of fat x 9 calories/g = 45 calories	2g of fat x 9 calories/g = 18 calories
45 ÷ 120 calories/serving = .38	18 ÷ 110 calories/serving = .16
.38 x 100 = 38% of calories from fat	.16 x 100 = 16% of calories from fat

You can see from the example that fat calories are sometimes hidden calories. You can avoid these extra calories by reading labels and making wise choices. If you've been pushing aside the bread at the salad bar and reaching for that creamy salad dressing, make a change. Eat the bread but avoid butter or margarine and skip the creamy salad dressing.

KEEPING A FOOD JOURNAL

A food journal is a diary of all the food and beverages you consume. The result is an honest evaluation of your diet. The journal can be kept for one week or for an indefinite period of time. You may be quite surprised by what you learn from your own personal food journal. The keys to an effective food journal are:

1. Be totally honest with yourself. Write down everything!
2. Be as exact as possible. Instead of saying "I ate a few crackers," count the crackers and say, "I ate ten crackers."
3. Make no dietary changes when beginning your journal.

You may be quite surprised by what you learn from your own personal food journal.

4. Write down the time of day you eat or drink something.
5. Be accountable to someone. Trust someone to look over your journal or to ask you if you are keeping up on it.

My Daily Food Journal

	Sun.	Mon.	Tues.	Wed.	Thurs.	Fri.	Sat.
Date:							
Breakfast							
Snack							
Lunch							
Snack							
Dinner							
Snack							
Comments:							

A food journal may have several different purposes. At first, you may only want to see what times of the day you make poor food choices. For example, do you tend to eat more when you get home from school, or after dinner before bed? Do you skip breakfast? If so, how often? After you have consistently kept your food journal for a week, and critically evaluated it, you are ready to make some changes. This is not the time to stop keeping the food journal. Continue monitoring your food and beverages to make sure you are eating a balanced and varied diet. Don't forget to monitor your intake of water.

As you continue to monitor your changes, set realistic goals for yourself. If you forget to drink water, make a goal that each time you pass a water fountain you will take a drink for the count of ten seconds. Another goal might be to avoid eating anything past 7:00 pm. Whenever you feel your diet has been slipping, go back to the food journal to keep yourself on the healthy diet track.

EATING DISORDERS

It is normal to go through different seasons in your life where your eating habits are a bit unbalanced. It is when these seasons become extreme that an eating disorder may develop.

Three eating disorders that can cause both mental and physical problems are anorexia nervosa, bulimia and chronic overeating. **Anorexia** is a self-induced starvation resulting in extreme weight loss and characterized by an intense fear of gaining weight and becoming fat.

Bulimia is a pattern of bingeing (eating large amounts of food) followed by self-induced vomiting or laxative abuse with or without weight loss. In both conditions, there is a severe struggle with self image and self acceptance, as well as the concept of unconditional love. These people usually have a deep need for personal healing and unconditional acceptance and usually require professional help. God has made you in His image, and you are loved and accepted.

Chronic overeating as an eating disorder is far more common than anorexia or bulimia. The habits of chronic overeating begin in childhood and especially the teenage years.

There is not one single cause of developing an eating disorder. An individual's personal battles can trigger a depression that may result in this dangerous eating pattern. The most profound similarity in people who suffer from an eating disorder is a sense of insecurity. That individual suffers from an obsession with or about his body, and feels as if he cannot live up to others' expectations.

Just as there is not one simple cause for an eating disorder, there is also no simple or single cure. Many things can lead a person to develop an eating disorder and often it takes a professional with considerable expertise in this area to determine what these are. If you know of someone who may be exhibiting consistent unusual eating behavior, do not try to counsel or nag her about the food she should or should not be eating. Let the person know that you are her friend and you have a concern for her. Consider talking to the parents and above all support her in her efforts to get professional help.

If you find yourself struggling with any of the things that have been mentioned, you are not meant to handle it on your own. In all trials and difficulties God is there to strengthen and comfort you. Having been both God and man, Christ can sympathize with the difficulties of living in a human body. Sharing your struggle with others and seeking appropriate help is of vital importance in gaining victory in these areas.

For we do not have a High Priest who cannot sympathize with our weaknesses, but was in all points tempted as we are, yet without sin. Let us therefore come boldly to the throne of grace, that we may obtain mercy and find grace to help in time of need.
Hebrews 4:15-16

One Girl's Story
by Ann Finley

Eating a balanced diet wasn't always easy for me. I would find myself upset about something — my family, my friends, boys, or even my weight — and it would affect my eating. At first I just wanted to lose a few pounds to look slimmer, but as the weight came off I decided I liked the way I was feeling and the way my clothes began to fit. I continued to exercise heavily and this made the weight loss even greater.

When my parents and family began to notice my eating habits and my weight loss they tried to make me eat, which only made me more determined not to eat. There seemed to be nothing anyone could say or do to make me change. When I looked into the mirror I did not see myself as the thin rail I was becoming, but still pudgy and overweight with just "a few" more pounds to lose. My friends at school began to act differently around me. At lunch hour, while I was eating my apple and Rye Krisp cracker, they would turn the other way to eat their sandwiches and chips.

I began to feel weaker and weaker. When I could not even keep my hands up long enough to wash my hair in the shower and when I could not make it up my stairs at home, I knew I was not healthy. Finally, my eighth-grade teacher informed my parents that I would not be allowed to stay at school for the full day due to my condition. Then my mom took me to our doctor.

Somehow by the grace of God I managed to pull myself together. Now at the age of 34, I still do not know what caused my unusual eating behavior. Today they would call it anorexia nervosa, but back then I just called it a diet.

CHAPTER REVIEW

DEFINE

Protein

Amino acids

Essential amino acids

Complete protein

Carbohydrate

Glucose

Complex carbohydrate

Fat

Saturated fat

Unsaturated fat

Cholesterol

LDL

HDL

Basal metabolism

Calorie

Fiber

Insulin

Sodium

Vitamins

RDA

Minerals

Fortified

Enriched

Set Point Theory

Fat calorie

Anorexia

Bulimia

EXPLAIN

1. Explain what is meant by the phrase "your actions reflect your values."
2. Explain what the guidelines are on the Daily Food Pyramid.
3. Explain why God cares about what you eat.
4. Explain what the purpose is for using a food journal.
5. Explain why Americans are so prone to heart disease.
6. Explain the three steps to reading labels.
7. Explain what really motivates people to make positive health changes.
8. Explain why it is important to eat a diet high in complex carbohydrates.
9. List and briefly explain the prescription for good nutrition.
10. Explain some of the problems associated with trying to gain or lose weight by going on fad diets.

DISCUSS

1. Discuss why many teenagers have poor eating habits.
2. Imagine you have a close friend whom you think might have an eating disorder. Discuss how would you try to help him/her?
3. Discuss how this chapter on nutrition may change your personal eating habits. Discuss why exercise plays such a vital role in weight loss.
4. Discuss what role stress has in your eating habits.

SUGGESTED ACTIVITIES

1. **Keep a food journal:** For one week keep a food journal and evaluate your eating habits.

2. **Write an editorial:** Write an editorial for your local newspaper (you may or may not send it) on one of these subjects: fast foods, snacks, commercial weight loss programs, processed foods, health foods, vitamin and mineral supplements, food labeling and packaging, and eating disorders. You may come up with more ideas. Remember there are two sides to each issue.

3. **Plan a menu:** Take a field trip to your local grocery store. You must plan two days worth of cooking for your family. Make a list of all your food purchases, menus for each meal, and why you have chosen such items. Read labels. You must be specific on the items you are pretending to purchase. For example, for breakfast you must say what brand of cereal and why you have chosen it.

4. **Media madness:** The media is only one source, but a very strong influence, on your food choices. Keep a log of the food advertisements you see on billboards, signs, magazines, and television. After two to three days, share the results with the class and discuss what foods were predominately advertised and why. What does this say about how the media influences your food choices?

5. **Make a portrait:** Cut out pictures, words, colors, etc. that you feel represents your likes and dislikes. Pictures could be of foods, activities, or influences (no indiscreet pictures or foul language). The collage may be in the form of a body or of a favorite food. Decorate the classroom at the beginning of the nutrition unit with the collages. At the end of the unit evaluate if your portrait may have changed.

6. **Key concepts:** Outline the chapter and make a study guide for yourself. You can work in groups and each student in the group be responsible for one section of the chapter.

7. **Be grateful:** Write a brief outline of your future plans, (or goals) where you want to be in five, ten, etc. years. Then make a list of all the assumptions you made in outlining your future plans (examples: money, ability to get a job). The one assumption that you made above all others was your *good health* (physical, mental, social, spiritual). People often take for granted their good health, but some people are not as fortunate as others (they are paralyzed, have a disease such as epilepsy, etc.)

Fitness and Exercise

4-1   WHAT IS FITNESS?
4-2   FACING THE FACTS
4-3   PRINCIPLES OF EXERCISE
4-4   CHOOSING THE RIGHT PROGRAM
4-5   PREVENTING INJURIES
4-6   FATIGUE AND SLEEP

4-1   WHAT IS FITNESS?

Most people would think of themselves as being fit if they were in a general state of good health. Until you really know the condition of your physical body, you will be ignorant concerning your health. Fitness is more than being without sickness. **Fitness** is the ability of the whole body to work together to the highest level possible. Your physical fitness includes *cardiovascular fitness, muscular strength, flexibility,* and your *body's fat-versus-lean relationship.*

CARDIOVASCULAR FITNESS

The most important measurement of your fitness is the condition of your heart, your **cardiovascular fitness**. Your heart is a muscle that never gets a rest. Although it may beat slowly or seem nonexistent, it is the most vital organ in your body. With each contraction of the heart, life-giving blood is being pumped to the rest of the body. To function properly the heart needs the constant supply of oxygen that the lungs supply. Thus, the heart and the lungs work together.

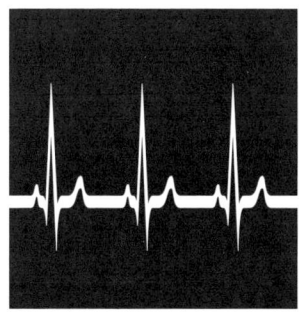

Like any other muscle, the heart needs exercise. The daily functioning of the heart is not enough to keep it in top shape.

The daily functioning of the heart is not enough to keep it in top shape.

97

When you exercise, your muscles actually change in their physical composition and the heart is no exception. Exercise increases your heart's efficiency.

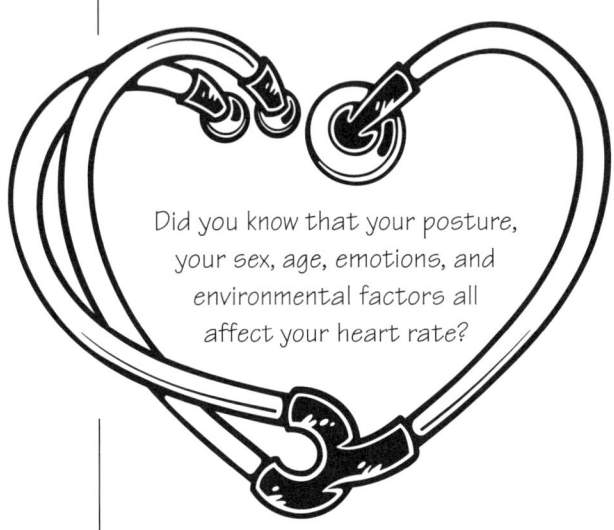

Did you know that your posture, your sex, age, emotions, and environmental factors all affect your heart rate?

As your level of fitness increases, your **resting pulse rate** (taken in the morning as you wake-up) and the rate at which your heart beats during exercise will decrease. These are signs that your heart is improving its performance. **Cardiac output** (the volume of blood pumped by the heart in one minute) and **stroke volume** (the volume of blood the heart pumps at each stroke) both improve with consistent exercise.

A healthy heart is better able to resist the number one killer in America, cardiovascular disease. By controlling your **blood pressure** (the measure of the resistance to blood flow in the vessels and the efficiency of circulation) and cholesterol levels through aerobic exercise, you can increase your chances of living a longer and more active life.

MUSCULAR STRENGTH

You will burn more calories at rest if you increase your muscular strength.

The muscles in your body are made up of a fixed group of fibers. Each muscle works by contracting its individual fibers. A contraction is a shortening or pulling of the muscle that causes movement to occur.

Muscles are made up of two types of fiber, slow and fast twitch fibers. Slow twitch fibers are those that respond relatively slowly when responding to a stimulus. Persons who have predominately slow twitch muscle fibers seem to be better suited for endurance exercise while those with more fast twitch fibers, are better suited for fast bursts of movement or sprinting.

With consistent exercise your muscles will become adapted to the added stress. They will become more efficient in their use of energy (stored glucose), stronger in their ability to support weight and able to endure longer periods of training. Another added benefit of increasing your lean muscle mass is that muscles burn more calories than fat. You will burn more calories at rest if you increase your muscular strength. This will improve your appearance as well as make you feel great.

FLEXIBILITY

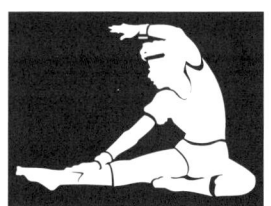

The importance of flexibility of the muscles, tendons and joints is often overlooked. Many people seem naturally flexible. There are those who can do the splits without really trying, or who can touch their palms to the floor while you struggle to touch your ankles. No doubt about it! Flexibility takes consistent effort but the effort is well worth it. Flexibility not only helps keep you agile in relation to sport and skill, but it can help keep you from injury.

FAT VS. LEAN BODY WEIGHT

The relationship between your fat and **lean body weight** is vital to your fitness level. It is not how much you weigh that is the key, but how much "muscle weight" and "fat weight" you are carrying. Muscle weighs more than fat, so an obese individual carrying 35% body fat may  weigh less than an individual with 25% body fat. If the scale in your bathroom has been getting you down, toss it out. With a change in diet and exercise, you can decrease your percentage of body fat and increase your muscular fitness.

It is not how much you weigh that is the key, but how much "muscle weight" and "fat weight" you are carrying.

4-2 FACING THE FACTS

HOW FIT ARE YOU?

Many people have an unrealistic opinion of their fitness level. Most often, people believe they are in better physical shape than they are. They engage in activities that are too stressful on their body. How should you approach your physical fitness? An important part of being responsible for your health is being informed about your true state of fitness.

Fitness testing is useful for two reasons. First it can determine if you are at risk for any physical ailment (such as heart attack or asthma). Second, with any exercise program, you must know your own physical limitations. Consider the following measurements of your physical fitness.

Self-Tests

1. **Look in the mirror!** Are you pleased with the image that looks back at you. Are you overweight? Do you have toned muscles, good posture, and a "light" countenance? Do you look depressed? An exercise program can help all these areas.

2. **Fat-skin fold measurements:** Can you pinch an inch or more? If so, you may need to lose a few extra pounds. Have someone who is experienced in the area of fitness measure your body fat using fat calipers. General areas of measurement should be taken from the right side of the body. For men and women the areas of measurement are: back of arm (triceps), bicep (the front of the upper arm), back (subscapula: under the shoulder blade), waist (suprailiac) right above the hip bone on the side of the waist. From the sum of these four skinfold measurements, you can accurately determine your total percentage of body fat.

3. **Body Composition:** Are you large, medium, or small boned? There is a correlation between your bone size and your frame size. There is a proper range for your height and frame size. Wrist and ankle circumference and shoulder, elbow and knee width are used to determine frame size. A

Chapter 4 Fitness and Exercise

simple illustration is using your wrist. By using your middle finger and your thumb, measure the distance around the boney part of your wrist. If you cannot touch your fingers, you may be large boned. If your fingers just touch, you are medium boned. If your fingers overlap, you may be small boned. Most height and weight charts include a frame size.

4. **Flexibility:** Can you touch your toes? Sit with your legs straight out in front of you, and reach for your toes. How close can you come to touching your toes?

5. **Cardiovascular Test:** Step test (measures heart rate and recovery time). An experienced physical educator can administer this test. Step 24 times for three minutes onto a bench. Stop, take your pulse. After resting 30 seconds, take your pulse again and see the change. Repeat this after a few weeks of aerobic exercise and see the difference.

6. **Muscular Strength:** Maximum lift test (should only be taken when supervised by an experienced trainer). You may do the sit-up test; how many sit-ups can you do in one minute?

7. **Resting Heart Rate:** Take your pulse first thing in the morning before you get out of bed. Count beats per minute by counting for 10 seconds and multiply this number by six. Take this for three consecutive days and take the average reading. This measurement will help monitor your progress.

Underwater Weighing

This test can only be administered in a laboratory setting. The results can by very accurate; however, the skin-fold measurement test, when done correctly is known to be very accurate as well.

Doctor's Physical Exam

Most teenagers do not need an in-depth physical exam before embarking on an exercise program. If you are concerned for your health and are interested in knowing your level of fitness, a doctor's physical would include the following: A treadmill test with an

101

EKG (electrocardiogram: recording the electrical impulses set off by the heart), blood pressure readings, lung capacity test, and any history of heart disease. Pre-season physicals, if done correctly, will help you determine if it is safe for you to participate in sports.

SKILL-RELATED VS. HEALTH-RELATED FITNESS

Before getting involved in your personalized fitness program, it is important to distinguish between fitness that is related to your health and fitness that is skill-related. Health fitness focuses on the development of good health while the skill-related aspects of fitness are not vital to good health. However, improved skill will most likely enhance your enjoyment of health fitness activities.
Dr. Gary Chase, Exercise Physiologist
Pacific Lutheran University

You may be involved in sports activities that seem to keep you in good physical condition. However, if you analyze the workouts your sport requires, you will notice a variety of activities revolving primarily around improving your skill. Although endurance conditioning is also important, the main concern is not your health, but your skill at the sport. Examples of skills related to fitness are: agility, balance, coordination, power, reaction time, and speed. You may be surprised to find that at the end of a sport season you are not in as good of condition as you had thought. Covert Bailey, one of the leading nutritionists on the subject of exercise shares one of his experiences.

"When I was in college I played a lot of hard squash and thought I was in great shape. Occasionally I played with a dentist friend who did a lot of running. He usually lost but seemed to have a lot of endurance on the squash court. One day he talked me into taking a long, slow run with him. After about half a mile, I had to stop and vomit." [1]

Your fitness level is not measured by how far or how fast you can run. Running is an example of one test of muscular and cardiovascular strength. Some individuals are better suited for running than others. Furthermore, it takes both skill and health fitness to enhance your athletic performance. When you choose to concentrate on your health fitness, it is important to choose an activity that you enjoy. **Lifetime sports** are those activities that you can participate in throughout your life. Team

sports are often difficult to continue because you need to find a recreational league you can join. For instance, having great skill in basketball does nothing for your health unless you can participate in the sport consistently.

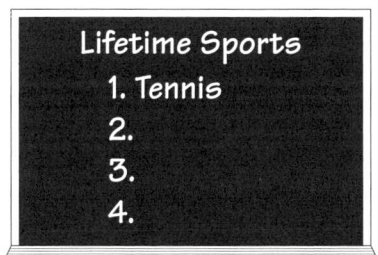

Lifetime Sports
1. Tennis
2.
3.
4.

4-3 PRINCIPLES OF EXERCISE

AEROBIC VS. ANAEROBIC

Covert Bailey changed his view of exercise when he realized that running put his friend in shape to play squash, but that squash failed to put him in shape for running. This realization helped Bailey develop an interest in steady, uninterrupted exercises known as aerobics. Aerobics is not just a class to attend at a health club or an exercise video to do in your living room. Aerobics is a principle of exercise.

The word aerobic means "oxygen." Every minute of every day your body needs oxygen to produce energy. When your muscles demand more oxygen than normal, the activity is called **aerobic**. Aerobic exercise is a main ingredient for overall good health. Some of the benefits include improved cardiovascular system, (including lungs and circulation), weight loss, improved mental outlook, and a longer life expectancy. Every exercise program should include some consistent aerobic activity.

Aerobics is not just a class to attend at a health club or an exercise video to do in your living room. Aerobics is a principle of exercise.

In contrast to aerobic activity, **anaerobic** exercise is short bursts of energy, without the use of oxygen, such as sprinting or weight training. The benefits to anaerobic activity are not as great as those from aerobic. Improved muscular strength is the main benefit from anaerobic exercise and this can be an important ingredient in your personal exercise program.

OVERLOAD, PROGRESSION AND SPECIFICITY

To improve your health through exercise, you need the principles of overload, progression, and specificity. **Overload** simply means to gradually do more than normal to improve your performance. For example, Jim is on the swim team and he wants to

improve his time in the 800 meter race. To do this, Jim's coach has him swimming longer distances to increase his endurance. During the season, Jim has some hard practices and some easier ones to help him improve his time. Jim always tells his coach if he is experiencing pain during those hard workouts, because pain is his body telling him something is wrong. The saying "No pain, no gain" is not a safe motto.

Progression is an important principle in exercise. Starting with a little and adding to it regularly as you improve is known as **progression**. When you improve in various aspects of your program, you can increase the time, weight or speed at which you train. For example, Amy joined the track team and has potential in the mile competition. Her coach has her start out with slow easy runs, working mainly on endurance. As her endurance improves, Amy gradually increases her distance and her speed.

104

Setting goals in fitness is an important part of exercise. Along with goal setting come specificity training. **Specificity** is the principle of exercise that you must do specific kinds of exercise to develop certain parts of the body. For example, Sue is a member of the volleyball team. Her vertical jump is weak so her coach put her on a specific weight program to increase her leg strength. When Sue improves her jumping ability, her hitting skill will increase and her overall game will improve.

Cross training is a term used for those who want to vary their exercise routine. It is important to work different muscles in your body to gain balanced strength. Jim, Amy, and Sue could use cross training to improve their fitness as well as to enhance their sport.

EXERCISE AND WEIGHT CONTROL

Fitness experts will agree, there is no diet that will make you healthier unless it is combined with an aerobic exercise program. If your goal is to gain weight, the best kind of weight for your body is muscle. A healthy diet and a consistent exercise program will help you put on the pounds you need.

The result of a diet without exercise will be temporary and your body will not reach its optimal level of fitness. Exercise increases your metabolism so that calories are burned, not only during the workout but for hours afterward. Regular exercise increases your lean muscle mass and since muscle burns more calories than fat, you will be burning calories more efficiently. As a result of a personal exercise program your body will look toned and fit, and you will feel physical and emotional improvement. You may notice a

SOMETHING TO THINK ABOUT

Six ways to burn
300 calories a day[2]

1. 60 minutes of moderate-paced walking
2. 45 minutes of brisk walking
3. Three 20-minute walks
4. 35 minutes of hill-trail walking
5. 30 minutes of aerobic dancing and a 30 minute walk
6. 18 holes of continuous golf (without a cart)

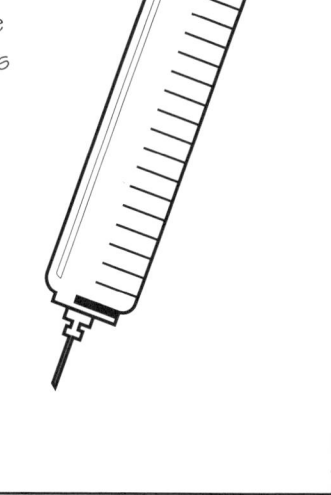

Winning isn't Everything!

An **Ergogenic Aid** is something that improves physical work performance.

Anything from a strict diet to anabolic steroids have been used to help athletes feel they have a edge over the competition. Steroids are synthetic forms of the male hormone testosterone. The negative consequences of excessive use of these steroids outweigh any improvement in performance or appearance.

The negative side effects include: stunted growth, liver damage, strokes, heart disease, and possible infertility. In women, steroids may result in a disruption of the menstrual cycle and may lead to an increase in masculine physical features. If you are ever tempted to use unnatural ergogenic aids, turn them down and pursue wholesome fitness.

slight increase in your weight because muscle weighs more than fat. But take heart, your clothes will fit better as you lose inches instead of pounds. Consider taking body measurements (upper arm, chest, waist, hips, derriere and thigh) at different times throughout your program to monitor your progress.

SOME MISCONCEPTIONS CONCERNING EXERCISE

You can find an excuse for everything. Here is a list of common excuses that may be keeping you from an exercise program. Consider the following misconceptions.

Exercise will make me hungry.

True   False

Actually exercise can be a good hunger depressant. When your BMR increases after exercise you may feel hungry. But because you are burning more calories, your body may need more.

If I weight train I will build bulky muscles.

True   False

Different weight training programs produce different results. Women who want to gain muscle definition and strength can do light weights with many repetitions. Men who want to gain muscle mass will concentrate on heavy weights with fewer repetitions. Generally speaking, men develop more "bulk" muscles because they have a greater amount of the male hormone testosterone to increase their muscle size.

It doesn't matter what I do as long as it is aerobic exercise.

True   False

This is false because the activity you choose must be safe for your body and your present level of fitness. You would not advise someone to go run a marathon if he just started a jogging program, or tell someone to begin running if she suffered from knee problems.

I have to be good at a sport to be involved in exercise.

True   False

As you have learned, being involved in sports does not guarantee you are fit. Furthermore, a personal exercise program is just that, personal. It is designed with you in mind to create a program that best suits your strengths and weaknesses.

Everyone at my age is able to do more than me, so I must be out of shape.

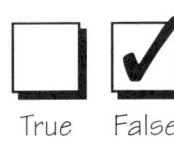

True   False

This is a false statement as well as a comparison trap. Do not compare your level of fitness with your peers because everyone has different abilities and fitness levels. Start with what you can do and try to improve yourself to be the best you can be.

> Do not compare your level of fitness with your peers because everyone has different abilities and fitness levels.

Exercise takes too much time.

True   False

Consider the amount of time thirty minutes of exercise will add to your life. Keep a chart for one week on how you spend your time. Evaluate the time spent and see where exercise can best fit in. Try it, it will work. After experiencing the benefits of exercise, you will make it a priority in your daily schedule.

4-4   CHOOSING THE RIGHT PROGRAM

What Are Your Personal Needs?

There are several factors to consider when choosing your exercise program. The first to consider is "what are my fitness goals?" *Realistic goals* are goals that fit you personally. Your current fitness level, your diet, your ability to handle stress, your health history, your lifestyle (home life, school schedule, work, leisure time, and emotional and spiritual life) all influence your exercise choices.

Goals are things you work to achieve. Once you reach them, you set new ones. You never stop setting fitness goals. Once you stop setting goals, you start the fast decline of becoming unfit. Your final fitness goal may be to *maintain* your desired level of fitness. The following are examples of some goals you might consider:

1. Muscular strength
2. Weight loss or gain
3. Inches lost or gained
4. Competition
5. Overall physical well being
6. Improve specific health problems or injuries

Once you stop setting goals, you start the fast decline of becoming unfit.

COMPONENTS OF EVERY EXERCISE PROGRAM

Every exercise program should include six basic components: type of activity, intensity, duration, frequency, maintenance, and motivation.

Type of Activity: "What should I do?"

The type of activity you choose is determined by several factors. If your schedule is such that time is a problem, then you may only want to go for a brisk walk outdoors, or use an exercise video in your own home. If you have the finances and time to belong to a health club, then you have more options from which to choose. You may want to invest in home exercise equipment to use at your convenience. Another consideration may be to add variety to your sport workout by doing extra jogging, walking or exercises after your practice.

"Do I enjoy the activity?" Maybe not, but if you can vary your program to include different activities (cross training) you may endure the ones you do not enjoy to reach your fitness goals. Cross training also helps to avoid overstress injuries caused by doing the same action repeatedly.

Intensity: "How hard should I work?"

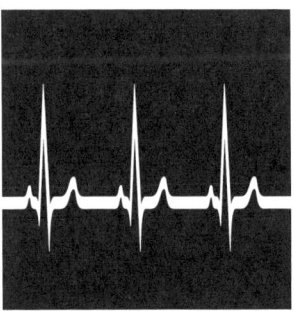

To answer this question you need to know at what fitness level you are starting your program. Consider your resting pulse rate, have a physical if necessary, and be sure to start at a beginner's level. Finding your **target heart rate** will help you to monitor your workout intensity during exercise. Use the following formula to figure your own target heart rate: 220 – (subtract) your age = your maximum heart rate (DANGER ZONE). Take 80% of your maximum =

your higher limit. Take 60% of your maximum = your lower limit. For example, if you are 15 years old:

- 220 - 15 = 205 (your maximum heart rate or danger zone)
- Take 80% of 205 (.80 x 205) = 164 (your higher limit)
- Take 60% of 205 (.60 x 205) = 123 (your lower limit)

Using the example, you can see that this 15 year old should stay between 123 and 164 beats per minute while working out or by using a quicker measurement, between 12 and 16 beats per six seconds.

Checking your pulse rate is a good monitor of your level of intensity. As you continue to workout, you will also be able to use a mental chart to determine how hard you are working. Ask yourself this question while you are exercising: "how hard am I working?"

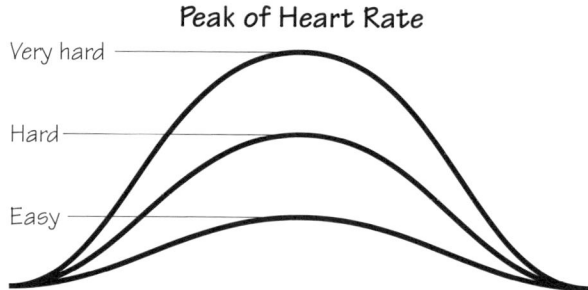

Peak of Heart Rate

Very hard

Hard

Easy

You may experience this progression several times during a workout session and your intensity may change with how you are feeling on that day. Do not compare your intensity level with another person. For example, exercising at 80% of your ability for 30 minutes may wipe you out if you are just beginning, but a marathoner can run at 80% for two to four hours. To reach a comfortable level during your workout, you must alternate periods of higher intensity with lower intensity.

Ask yourself this question while you are exercising: "how hard am I working?"

Duration: "How long should I work out?"

To get the maximum benefits from your exercise, you should work out between 15–60 minutes per session. This varies with the type of exercise you are doing. Start out slowly. Even with walking you will begin to see a difference in the amount of time you are able to exercise. Aim for at least 30 minutes per workout.

Frequency: "How often should I work out?"

How often you work out depends in part on the duration and intensity of the sessions. Three to five times per week is a good guide — three times per week to maintain your level of fitness and more often to improve. If you are not suffering from an injury, your work-

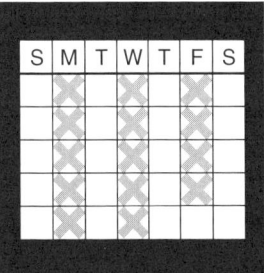

out schedule should allow no more than three days between sessions. Not only does your fitness level slowly begin to drop with long lapses, but your motivation fades.

When a long period of time goes between workouts, **atrophy** may occur. When a muscle is not used, the muscle decreases in size and loses its strength. An example of atrophy is when a person has a broken arm and it is in a cast for a period of time. When the cast is removed, the arm is much smaller than before the injury.

Maintenance: "How long will I keep up my program?"

If you have made a decision to change your lifestyle to a more healthy one, then your goal is to maintain your program indefinitely. Although the type of activity may change, you will want to continue making exercise an important part of your life. It is

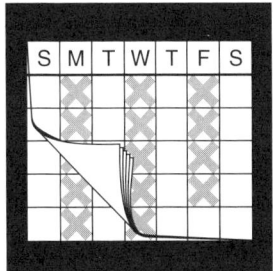

fine to change your activity with the seasons, but watch out for seasonal exercise. For example, only exercising in the spring because summer is just around the corner may not produce your

If you have made a decision to change your lifestyle to a more healthy one, then your goal is to maintain your program indefinitely.

desired fitness results.

Staying motivated is a vital part of your maintenance. Follow some of the suggestions and you will begin to look forward to your exercise program.

Motivation: "How can I stay motivated?"

Exercising can be just as frustrating as yo-yo dieting. That on-and-off, start-and-stop routine is physically as well as emotionally damaging. The best thing for your health is a consistent program of good eating and moderate exercise. Keeping an exercise journal can help monitor your progress. When designing your journal include the following information: the date, the distance (if relevant to the activity), the total amount of time you exercised, and a place for any comments to describe how you were feeling. There are times when you allow yourself to a sweet treat and times when you miss your exercise session, but overall do your best to stick to your goals. A good motivator will be experiencing the benefits of exercise for yourself.

---

10 Ideas to Keep You Motivated

1. Keep an exercise journal. Just as a food journal is good for keeping track of your eating habits, an exercise journal can help keep you motivated. You can evaluate your rate of progress and be encouraged by the level of fitness you are attaining.
2. Make and evaluate your goals continually.
3. Plan a regular program and follow it.
4. Add music or speaking tapes to your workout.
5. Enter a competition or fun walk/run.
6. Train with a friend.
7. Join a club or group or take lessons.
8. Be accountable to a friend or family member.
9. Reward yourself when you have reached a goal.
10. Add fun activities to your program (bike trip, hike, aerobics tape)

The Benefits of Exercise

1. Increases strength and stamina.
2. Reduces stress and tension and helps you handle the "unexpected."
3. Improves your mental alertness and concentration.
4. Helps relieve depression.
5. Helps you lose excess fat, weight.
6. Increases your BMR.
7. Helps give you a more restful sleep.
8. Helps regulate your body temperature by improving circulation.
9. Helps to relieve pain, such as backache and menstrual pain.
10. Increases body flexibility.
11. Helps delay signs of aging, such as osteoporosis.
12. Improves your digestive and excretory systems.
13. Helps your body adjust to climate changes.
14. Improves the functioning of your nervous system.
15. Improves your cardiovascular and circulatory system.
16. Improves your social outlook. You're more apt to participate in social activities.
17. Improves your spiritual outlook. Your perspective about life improves.
18. Improves your countenance.
19. Improves your general health — less illness, more time for work and play.
20. Improves your relationships because you are less concerned about yourself.

Exercise makes the whole body more efficient — body, mind, and spirit!

4-5 PREVENTING INJURIES

The keys to preventing injuries are first, start your program in good condition; and second, choose a program that best suits your level of fitness. It is better to start out easy and increase than to start out hard and get injured.

STRENGTH TRAINING FOR INJURY PREVENTION

Weight training is one precaution that you can take to help prevent injuries. It improves your muscles, ligaments, tendons, and even your bones. There are several strength training programs

It is better to start out easy and increase than to start out hard and get injured.

offered through home gyms, health clubs, and school classes, but it is important for you to choose the program that is appropriate for your age, level of fitness and fitness goal. Your method and the intensity at which you work will determine your improvement.

1. **Isometric:** Muscle contraction but no movement involved. Example: pressing against the wall, contraction of the muscle but no shortening.

2. **Isotonic:** Muscle contraction against a fixed resistance. Example: free weights, universal gym, Soloflex®, Nautilus® equipment. Full range of motion for the muscle.

3. **Isokinetic:** Combination of isometric and isotonic. Muscle contraction with the resistance changing with the amount of force applied to it. Full range of motion for the muscle.

Tips for the prevention of injuries

1. Choose a realistic and appropriate program for yourself.
2. Begin the program slowly.
3. Use quality equipment, including shoes.
4. Make sure you know proper form for the activity.
5. Always have a warm-up no matter how little time you have.
6. Always have a warm-down no matter how little time you have.
7. STOP when you feel faint, dizzy or pain.
8. Vary your activity by cross training to avoid stress injuries.

RICE

For the immediate treatment of injuries, follow the acronym RICE.

- Rest the injured area
- Ice the injured area with ice in a towel to prevent swelling
- Compress the injured area if possible with a towel or bandage to prevent swelling.
- Elevate the injured area above the level of the heart to help drain fluid that might collect at the injury.

You should always consult a doctor if you get a serious injury.

For milder injuries, see a doctor if the condition does not improve after a few days.

With the variety of weight systems to choose from, it is good to ask for some professional advice. The safest sort of strength training equipment is that in which the weights are fixed rather than free. Training with free weights demands more control and skill. No matter what weight system you decide to use, you need instruction and supervision on how to use the equipment properly.

114

Hot or Cold?

Exercising in heat or cold may pose special problems.
Note the following safety precautions:

Heat:
- Make sure you have a light warm-up and a thorough cool-down.
- Wear a sunscreen if you plan to work out outdoors.
- Work out during the coolest time of the day (early morning or later evening).
- Wear loose, cotton clothing. Often sweating causes the skin to rub which will result in a rash. Carry a petroleum jelly to help protect those areas (between legs, armpits, arms).
- Drink plenty of water prior to the workout, 15-30 minutes before depending on the intensity and form of activity.
- Drink water during the activity. If you wait until you feel thirsty, it is too late.
- After the workout, replenish your fluids with water and/or electrolyte drink to balance your fluids.
- Effects of exercising in the heat may be: Dehydration, heat cramps, heat exhaustion, and heat stroke.

Cold:
- Make sure you have a proper warm-up and cool-down
- Wear thin layers of clothing rather than one or two thick pieces of clothing.
- Always wear a hat to maintain your body temperature.
- Use a cotton bandanna or sock around your neck to place over your nose and mouth if the air is freezing. This will help warm the air before breathing into your lungs.
- Be careful exercising where there is snow, ice, rain or uneven ground. Injuries may occur more often when a person is distracted by the extreme weather.
- Although you do not feel like you need much liquid, make sure you drink plenty of fluids.

The Warm-Up

Preparing your muscles for activity is the purpose of a warm-up. A warm-up includes very light stretching of major muscle groups, followed by some activity to raise your body temperature, jogging, fast walking, etc. Only after your body is warm do you stretch slowly and thoroughly. The warm-up should last anywhere between eight to fifteen minutes. This activity will help prepare the body for the workout to follow.

The Warm-Down

A proper warm-down is often overlooked. After a strenuous work-out, your muscles have lactic acid build-up but a period of cooling down provides time for your muscles to release this lactic acid slowly. Stretching and movement of large muscle groups including your back, arms and legs helps to prevent stiffness and injury.

4-6 FATIGUE AND SLEEP

"I don't know why, but I am always tired; even when I get up in the morning I feel tired. It doesn't matter how many hours of sleep I get, I am still tired."

D o you know anyone who sounds like this? Maybe it is you. Besides headaches, fatigue is the most frequent health complaint. Fatigue may be defined as: weariness from physical or mental exertion. The state of being fatigued lowers your ability to work, play, exercise, and even to think clearly. To combat fatigue people need to rest. Resting can mean different things to different people. To some, resting is reading a good book, going for a walk or even a run. Any change in activity can provide rest. The Bible tells us in Genesis that God rested on the seventh day of creation. How God rested we do not know, but he ceased from all His work.

Then God blessed the seventh day and sanctified it, because in it He rested from all His work which God had created and made.
Genesis 2:3

God knows that your body needs rest from the responsibilities in life. He set aside the Sabbath, once a week, to provide a time of rest and worship.

TYPES OF FATIGUE

After a physically demanding activity, you may experience **physical fatigue**. Your muscles become exhausted from the work they have had to perform. When you exercise your muscles, carbon dioxide and lactic acid are produced. These wastes cause the muscles to stop responding and often cramping or stiffness occurs. It is important to replace the missing fluids that your body needs after a difficult workout or activity.

Physical fatigue may also result from inadequate sleep or diet. Your muscles need rest and good nutrition to keep them functioning properly. For example, failing to eat breakfast may cause fatigue until you give your body adequate food. The best cure for physical fatigue is giving the body proper rest and nourishment.

Imagine a day like this: John sleeps through his alarm and skips breakfast because he is late for school. When he arrives at school he gets in trouble for being late. Because he was in such a hurry to get to school he forgot his finished homework on the kitchen table. John tries to explain this to his teacher but she doesn't accept his excuse. By mid-morning his stomach is growling from starvation. In class, John gets back a test and finds a red F on the top of the paper. Finally lunch rolls around and he rushes to his locker only to find that his locker partner jammed the door and John cannot get his lunch out. By this time he is so stressed he feels like going home. Finally when the last bell rings for school to be dismissed, John heads out the door only to be handed a note from the office stating: "your mother cannot pick you up today, you must find another way home." At reading this, John drops his books and buries his head in his arms. John is a candidate for emotional fatigue.

You do not have to have a day like John's to experience **emotional fatigue**. Tension, stress, frustration, fear and even boredom can cause you to become

Tension, stress, frustration, fear and even boredom can cause you to become emotionally tired.

emotionally tired. It is common to feel tired when your emotions are working overtime. It is when you feel depressed and exhausted all the time that you may need to consult your physician. Talking to someone about the problems you face may help give you the tools to cope with the stress.

The best cure for emotional fatigue is to change the activity that you are doing. If you are bored, you should work on a project or go for a walk. If you have been under stress at school or home, exercise is a great stress reliever. If you are continually exhausted, you need to evaluate your daily routine. Are you doing more than you can handle? Make a change in your schedule and do not expect too much from yourself. Another hint might be to do some fun activity to break up the monotony of your responsibilities. Having something to look forward to will help lighten your spirit.

Fatigue due to illness is expected when your body is fighting a sickness. Colds cause a feeling of overall sleepiness. More serious illnesses can result in an overwhelming feeling of fatigue. One symptom of Mononucleosis is an extreme exhaustion. When you are sick, your body is telling you it needs rest to repair itself. Learn to listen to your body and give it what it needs to recover. It is important to see a doctor if extreme fatigue persists.

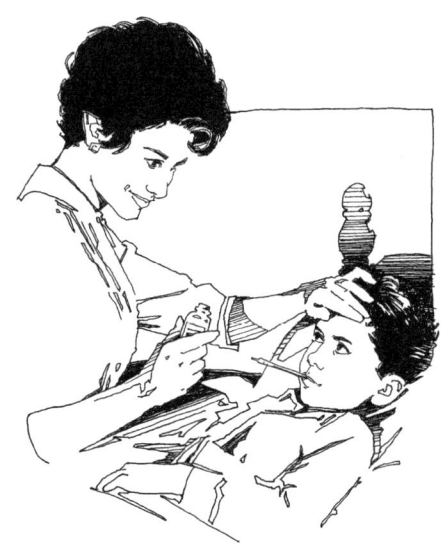

SLEEP

Sleeping is the body's natural state of rest. Sleep is a necessary part of your physical existence. No matter how hard you try to stay awake the body's demand for sleep causes you to give-in. Have you ever experienced such a great desire to sleep that it almost "hurts" if you do not nod off?

Have you ever experienced such a great desire to sleep that it almost "hurts" if you do not nod off?

One third of your life, or approximately twenty-three years is spent sleeping. It must be important for your body to demand so much time in a sleeping state. Sleep regulates body growth, stimulates tissue growth, speeds healing and lowers blood cholesterol. In general, sleep is a time when the body can restore itself. Not everyone needs the same amount of sleep. Infants and small children need more sleep because they are growing rapidly. Some adults can manage with as little as five hours of sleep while others need eight or nine. Can anyone get too much sleep? Yes, too much sleep can cause people to be just as irritable and uncomfortable as too little sleep. Scientists believe it is not how long a person sleeps but the quality of sleep that is important.

Through research, scientists found that people experience two kinds of sleep. One kind is characterized by rapid eye movements (REM stage), while the other is called the state of relaxation. During this state your body may go through four stages and then enter the REM state.

Stage I: Occurs just after you fall asleep. Everything slows down, and you could be easily awakened. Some may experience muscle spasms just before falling asleep due to bursts of brain activity.

Stage II: Brain waves in quick bursts. Eyes roll slowly from side to side. You still could be awakened.

Stage III: Deep calm sleep. Brain waves are long and slow. Muscles are relaxed, heart rate slows, temperature and blood pressure drops.

Stage IV: Deepest level of sleep. Large slow brain waves. Breathing is even. If an alarm went off during this stage you may not hear it. Most nightmares and walking in your sleep occurs during this stage.

REM: After stage IV, your brain moves into REM state. Eyes dart back and forth and much of the dreaming takes place during this state. The body is almost in a paralyzed state while breathing and heartbeat are irregular.

After experiencing the REM stage of sleep, your body drifts back to the beginning with stage I. The first REM stage may occur about 60 to 90 minutes after you have fallen asleep, and you may go through this cycle four or five times a night.

It is important for your body to experience all the stages of sleep, but most importantly the REM stage. Through dreaming your body releases anxiety and stress that you have in your conscious and subconscious. Loss of stages III, IV, and REM state result in feelings of fatigue and frustration the following day. Consistent loss of sleep can affect your ability to even fall asleep. It is best to have a regular schedule for sleeping, for instance, going to bed by 10:00 pm and rising at the same time each morning by 7:00 am. This regular schedule helps your body cope with the stress of everyday living. Having irregular sleeping times actually puts an added stress on your body. Researchers also believe the best hours of sleep for your body are before midnight. You will not wake as refreshed if you sleep from midnight to 10:00 am as you would sleeping from 10:00 pm to 8:00 am although you are getting the same number of hours of sleep.

Hints for getting a better night's sleep

1. Have a winding down time.
2. Get exercise regularly.
3. Eat a balanced diet.
4. Get up earlier (do not sleep until noon even if you are exhausted).
5. Have a consistent bed time.
6. Avoid eating right before going to sleep.
7. Avoid alcohol and caffeine.
8. Give your cares and worries to God.
9. Avoid sleeping pills to sleep or substances to keep you awake.
10. Avoid heavy exercise right before going to bed.

Insomnia is the inability to go to sleep. It is not uncommon to experience some difficulty in falling asleep, but if you have a persistent problem with insomnia, you need to find out what may be causing it. Sleep seems to be one of the first things teenagers go without. If you would put sleep as a top priority, you would feel an improvement in your ability to concentrate, in the amount of energy you feel, in your ability to cope, and in your overall attitude about life.

Resting in God

Come to Me, all you who labor and are heavy laden, and I will give you rest.
Take My yoke upon you and learn from Me, for I am gentle and lowly in heart,
and you will find rest for your souls.
For My yoke is easy and My burden is light.
Matthew 11:28-30

CHAPTER REVIEW

DEFINE

Fitness

Cardiovascular fitness

Resting pulse rate

Cardiac output

Stroke volume

Blood pressure

Lean body weight

EKK

Lifetime sport

Aerobic activity

Anaerobic activity

Overload

Progression

Specificity

Cross training

Ergogenic aids

Target heart rate

Atrophy

Isometric

Isotonic

Isokenetic

Physical fatigue

Emotional fatigue

Fatigue due to illness

Insomnia

EXPLAIN

1. Explain the importance of cardiovascular fitness and explain what a person must do to achieve it.
2. Explain why it is important to have fitness testing.
3. Explain the difference between aerobic and anaerobic exercise; give examples of each.
4. Explain why exercise is so important in weight control.
5. Explain why it is important to set realistic goals for your exercise program.
6. List the six basic components to every exercise program and briefly explain each.
7. Figure out your target heart rate and explain how it might be used in an exercise program.
8. List and explain five of the benefits of exercise.
9. Explain how strength training helps prevent injuries.
10. Explain the meaning of the acronym RICE.
11. Explain what physical fatigue is and how a person may deal with it.
12. Explain how you might help someone who is experiencing emotional fatigue.
13. Explain why it is important for your body to experience REM stage of sleep.

DISCUSS

1. Discuss why your cardiovascular health is the most important measure of your fitness. How can you achieve cardiovascular fitness?

2. Discuss why consistent exercise is one of the hardest things to put into your lifestyle. How might teenagers place exercise as an important part of their schedule?

3. Discuss the difference between "muscle weight" and "fat weight." Why is your muscle weight more important?

4. Discuss the difference between fitness that is related to your health and fitness that is skill-related. Are both important? How might each level of fitness affect the other as well as affect your choice of exercise activity?

5. Discuss the important role that exercise has in weight control. How might an active teenager benefit from consistent exercise and how might this affect his/her adult lifestyle?

6. Discuss the positive and negative affects of using anabolic steroids. What might you tell a friend who was thinking of using them to enhance his/her performance?

7. Discuss the importance of getting enough sleep. Discuss the different kinds of fatigue and how each may affect a teenager.

8. Discuss ways that a teenager can get a better night's sleep. What are some of the most common complaints that teens make about being tired and about rest?

9. Discuss some of the reasons why teenagers may experience insomnia. Are these reasons different than reasons why an adult may experience insomnia? Why or why not?

10. Discuss Matthew 11:28–30. How does this scripture relate to you?

SUGGESTED ACTIVITIES

1. **Keep an exercise journal:** This activity may be done as a class project or as an individual assignment. Design a model for an exercise journal. Include the components of exercise, a space for comments, and anything else that may be significant.

2. **Plan an exercise program:** Plan an exercise program for a friend, family member or for yourself. Make sure it includes all the components to an exercise program. Don't forget goal setting.

3. **Make a portrait:** Cut out pictures, words, colors, etc. that you feel represents your likes and dislikes. Pictures could be of activities, sports, etc. (no indiscreet pictures or offensive language can be used). The collage may be in the form of a body or sports equipment.

4. **Evaluate your sleep habits:** Keep a personal log of your sleeping habits. Include what activities or routine you have before getting to bed, what time you go to bed, how long you think it takes you to fall asleep, and what time you get up. Keep a log for one week and share your findings with the class.

5. **Interview:** Interview a person in your community who appears to be in very good shape. Ask him/her how his/her eating and exercise habits have helped him/her. Share your findings with the class.

6. **Have a laugh:** Create skits to show the importance of exercise and/or sleep. Share these skits with the class or student body. Make sure each skit has a main theme.

7. **Take a chance:** The teacher will hand out 3 x 5 cards on which a problem has been written. You randomly pick a card and must either write a one-page report dealing with the problem or come up with a skit dealing with the issue written on the card.

8. **Helpful books to fitness:** Check out a book at the library or buy a book at the bookstore dealing with the issues of exercise or sport. It may be fiction or nonfiction. Write a book report and give it orally to the class. Check with your teacher on your selection of reading material before beginning the project.

Infectious Disease

5-1 THE CAUSE OF INFECTIOUS DISEASE
5-2 THE PROCESS OF INFECTIOUS DISEASE
5-3 THE BATTLE AGAINST INFECTIOUS DISEASES
5-4 FIGHTING COMMON INFECTIOUS DISEASES
5-5 SEXUALLY TRANSMITTED DISEASES

5-1 THE CAUSE OF INFECTIOUS DISEASE

Infirmities that afflict the body, although unpleasant, are a reminder of the weakness of the human body. From the common cold to the mystery of cancer, God will comfort those who are sick. He is Jehovah Rophe, the God who heals you (Exodus 15:26). A person can experience great peace even in the midst of illness. The Bible is full of stories of God's faithfulness to the sick and suffering, but sometimes the result of sickness is pain, grief, and death.

If you have ever been sick with a cold you probably did not consider yourself suffering from a disease. However, the degree of seriousness does not determine if an illness can be called a disease. Generally, the word **disease** can be used to describe any condition that negatively affects the normal functioning of the mind or body.

SOMETHING TO THINK ABOUT

Ring around the rosy,
A pocket full of posies,
Ashes, ashes,
All fall down…

Ring Around the Rosy, a familiar children's nursery rhyme with an unfamiliar historical truth.

"*Ashes, ashes,*" used to be read "*achoo, achoo,*" a sneeze from someone who was suffering from the bubonic plague. In medieval days, people did not know exactly what caused diseases. A common remedy was chanting or sprinkling perfumed water in the air. Today with the great medical advances scientists have made, people are better able to prevent and control many diseases.

TYPES OF PATHOGENS

In the mid-1800's Louis Pasteur founded the idea that germs cause disease. This became known as the *germ theory* of disease. All diseases that are caused by the spread of germs are called **infectious diseases,** also known as **communicable diseases.** These diseases can be passed on from one person to another. **Pathogens** or germs are microorganisms that cause disease: *bacteria, viruses, fungi,* and *tiny animals* are pathogens.

Bacteria

Bacteria are one-celled tiny organisms that come in many shapes, rodlike (bacillus), round (coccus), and spiral (spirochete). Bacteria grow everywhere. Not all bacteria are harmful. For example, your body produces a bacteria that lives in your intestines and helps with digestion. These good or harmless bacteria are called *resident bacteria.*

Because bacteria are living organisms, they need food for energy and they produce waste. Disease-bearing bacteria produce poisonous wastes that are harmful to the body. Some diseases that are caused by bacteria are: cholera, pneumonia, tuberculosis, certain venereal diseases (such as gonorrhea), strep and staph infections. It is a wonder how such tiny organisms can make you feel so sick. Some bacteria, if left untreated, can even cause death. Botulism bacteria is so potent that even a fraction of an ounce can kill millions of people. Your body's defenses work to stop the growth of these bacteria and to neutralize any toxins they produce. When the growth of the bacteria is under control, your body eliminates the poisons and you recover.

A person can experience great peace even in the midst of illness.

126

Viruses

When you suffer from a cold you are suffering from a virus and not a bacteria. **Viruses** are responsible for more infections than any other pathogen. They are much smaller in size than bacteria. Hundreds of viruses have been identified but scientists have not found a cure for all of them.

While bacteria produce toxins in the body, viruses attack individual cells. The virus chooses the tissue it wants to damage and then invades the cells of the tissue. For example, viruses that cause polio invade cells of the nervous system, viruses that cause cold sores invade the skin, and flu viruses attack the cells of the respiratory system. Viruses are also responsible for mumps, measles, chicken pox, smallpox, rabies and most cases of hepatitis and AIDS. Scientists are still researching the possibility that viruses cause certain cancers such as leukemia, but this does not mean that cancer is contagious.

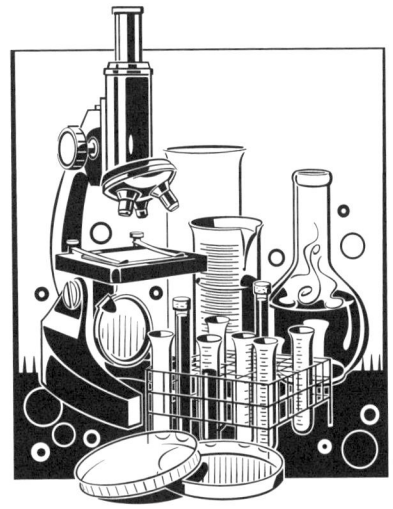

After a virus invades a cell, the damage to the cell begins. The virus is able to multiply within the cell, then moves on to attack another cell. When the damaged cells cannot function properly, your body develops symptoms to let you know it is fighting an "intruder." Your body is working overtime to fight the virus and as a result becomes tired and rundown. During this time, listen to your body. Give it strength through proper nutrition and rest.

Fungi

Fungi are organisms that usually cause diseases of the skin such as ringworm and athlete's foot. Although not as common, fungi can penetrate the deeper tissues of the skin and cause symptoms similar to a virus. Fungal infections can also be caused by spores that enter the body through the air.

> When the damaged cells cannot function properly, your body develops symptoms to let you know it is fighting an "intruder."

Tiny Animals

One-celled organisms called the amoeba can penetrate the human body and cause problems in the lining of the membranes of the intestines. A person who is carrying an amoeba pathogen may not know it but may still infect others. For example, people who handle food in restaurants may unintentionally infect customers.

Some infectious animals are called parasites. If a person carries too many parasites in the body, it can interfere with the individual's ability to digest food and absorb nutrients. Roundworm and tapeworm are examples of parasites. Rickettsia, a type of parasitic microorganism causes diseases such as Rocky Mountain spotted fever, Q fever, and forms of typhus.

5-2   THE PROCESS OF INFECTIOUS DISEASE

To fully understand and fight against infectious disease, researchers must research the path that all communicable diseases will take. The *infectious disease process* includes four factors: the pathogen, the source of the pathogen, the spread of the pathogen, and the new host. To defeat the enemy, the pathogen must be destroyed during the infectious disease process or the sickness will continue to spread.

The Process of Infection

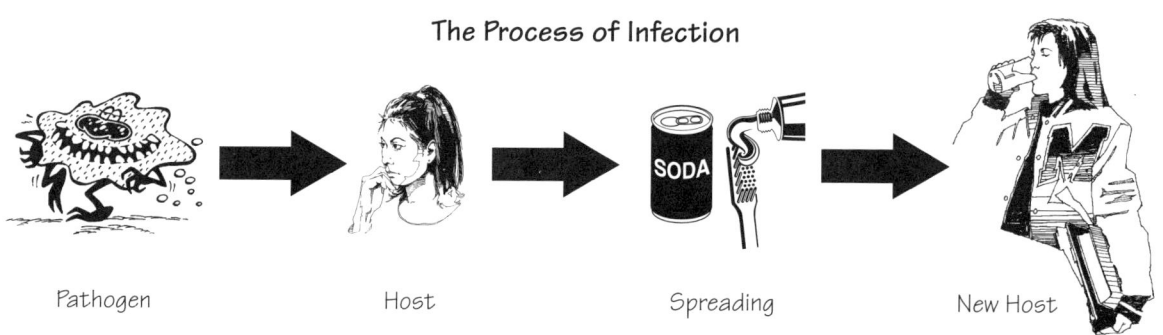

Pathogen   Host   Spreading   New Host

The Pathogen

The germ that invades a person is called the *pathogen*. If the pathogen can be destroyed at this stage, the chain is broken and the disease process ends. For example, penicillin is used to destroy some bacteria at this early stage.

The Source of the Pathogen (host)

The germ must live somewhere before it can infect an otherwise healthy individual. The best living arrangement for a germ is an animal or a human, but plants, soil and water are also homes to many pathogens.

The Way the Pathogen is Spread

The germ's primary concern is getting to a new host or person to infect. Germs use two main ways to escape from their existing host. One is the respiratory tract by way of coughing and sneezing and the other is the intestinal tract by way of feces. Germs travel through the air by way of droplets and usually live in warm and moist environments.

Germs can be spread in the following ways: *Direct contact* with the person infected, for example, sexually transmitted diseases; *contact with animals* such as bites from various insects; and *contact with objects* by touching things that an infected person has handled, by sharing towels, drinking glasses or toothburshes, for example. A food handler who does not wash after using the bathroom may pass on germs to the customers as he/she prepares food. Food that has spoiled and then is eaten will result in the pathogen infecting the individual eating the food.

The **incubation period** is the period of time from which a person becomes infected with a microorganism to the time when they actually have symptoms allowing them to recognize the disease. The incubation period is the most infectious time of the disease (contagious period) and is often difficult to pinpoint because it is usually during the early stages of the disease. An individual who is infected may not even realize he/she is spreading the disease.

The New Host

The pathogen usually enters the new host the same way it escaped from its previous one. Once it invades its new host the disease cycle continues. However, if the new host has a strong resistance to the germ, it can fight it and may only suffer a slight illness from the pathogen.

People respond differently to the same pathogens. A person who is carrying the germ but does not seem to be suffering from the illness is called a **carrier.** Carriers can still infect others with the disease. Your **resistance**, or ability to fight the invading germ, has much to do with the symptoms you will experience. Building up your immune system through proper nutrition, exercise and rest will help you resist the invasion of the enemy. If you are infected, you become the new home for the pathogen and the battle continues.

ACUTE VS. CHRONIC ILLNESS

Acute diseases are those that develop suddenly with symptoms that are often severe. The sickness takes its course and the symptoms subside as the pathogen weakens and the body recovers. Infectious diseases are usually acute diseases. A cold and the flu are examples of acute illnesses. Another example of an acute illness is appendicitis. It may come on suddenly and after emergency surgery, the patient almost always recovers.

Chronic diseases develop gradually and may persist for years. Malaria is a chronic disease because after a time of sickness the individual may have symptom-free times alternating with times of illness. If left untreated, some acute illnesses may become chronic. For example, syphilis, a venereal disease, and hepatitis, a viral illness, may have symptoms that recur throughout a person's life.

Building up your immune system through proper nutrition, exercise and rest will help you resist the invasion of the enemy.

130

5-3 THE BATTLE AGAINST INFECTIOUS DISEASES

And Jesus went about all Galilee...healing all kinds of sickness and all kinds of disease among the people. Then His fame went throughout all Syria; and they brought to Him all sick people who were afflicted with various diseases and torments...epileptics, and paralytics; and He healed them.
Matthew 4: 23, 24

In the battle against infectious, as well as noninfectious, diseases there are two lines of defense. One is not more important than the other; both defenses play vital roles in the fight against disease and in the healing process. The two defenses you have available are *physical* and *spiritual*.

YOUR PHYSICAL DEFENSES

The human body is a remarkable, yet complex, creation. God designed your body with its own physical armor to battle in the war against sickness. Your *skin* is your first physical protection against the attack of the enemy, the pathogen.

With the exception of such substances as poison ivy and certain caustic chemicals and irritants, most substances and microorganisms cannot penetrate your unbroken skin. When pathogens make their way into the body through the few openings in the body, like the mouth, nose or eyes, the tissues are protected by a soft skinlike layer called the *mucous membrane.* Its job is to stop invading bacteria by secreting mucous. Mucous is a thick, slimy fluid that moistens, lubricates and protects areas of the body. The hair on your skin, in your nose and ears, the blinking reflex of your eyes along with your eyelashes are all forms of protection.

Your nose and mouth secrete mucous to help stop the progression of a virus or bacteria. Congestion in your nose or chest is a sign that your body is fighting against a pathogen. A good example of this reaction is *allergies*. An **allergen** is a substance to which your body is particu-

God designed your body with its own physical armor to battle in the war against sickness.

SOMETHING TO THINK ABOUT

A horse does not have a vomiting reflex. If a horse eats a large amount of a poisonous weed such as tansy, the horse could die because its body could not rid itself of the poison.

131

larly sensitive. Common allergic reactions are watery eyes, runny nose, and a rash on the skin.

Once a virus or bacteria has made its way past the skin into your system, your body is designed to continue to fight it. Vomiting and diarrhea are defenses your body often uses to get rid of poisonous substances or bacteria from your stomach and intestine. Although this reflex is far from pleasant, without it your body might not be able to fight off the poison and you could suffer serious physical complications and even death.

The Immune System

The **immune system** is the body's natural resistance. A healthy body is a strong defense against invasion. Scientists are learning more about the body's defense system and how to use it to attack specific diseases.

A healthy body is a strong defense against invasion.

Have you ever heard the phrase "something is going around the school." It just seems like everyone in your school is getting sick with the same illness. Doctors call times like these flu seasons. This occurs when people are together in close quarters and remain indoors much of the time due to the weather. After being around individuals who are carrying germs, students carry these "bugs" home to their families where the illness "goes around" the family members.

Have you ever wondered why some people never got sick during the flu season? It also seems that mothers never get the sicknesses their children bring home from school. People who don't seem to "catch" the bugs may have developed an immunity in their bodies to that bacteria or virus. The development of this acquired immunity is called the *immune response.* When the body is invaded by a foreign substance, the lymphocytes are triggered to produce special proteins called **antibodies.** If the body's resistance is strong enough, the antibodies eventually destroy the pathogen. From that time on, your lymphocytes have made a mental note of the germ and can destroy it quickly if it reappears in the body.

Antibodies instinctively know to attack viruses and bacteria but *not* to attack your body's healthy cells. If a germ has found its way into a body cell, antibodies will not fight against it. Therefore, your cells must take care of themselves. If invaded, a cell produces *interferon.* Interferon is like an inside communication system for your cells. The release of this chemical informs the other cells to prepare to fight the virus. If the virus cannot enter these cells, the infection is stopped.

A *fever* is another way your body reacts to a potentially harmful invasion. A higher temperature may destroy some germs. Also with the presence of a fever, the body releases more germ-killing cells. You may wonder if a fever is good or bad for your body. If you have a low grade fever, it is good to allow the fever to run its course. If your temperature is very high and accompanied by body aches and pains, a non-aspirin medication can be taken to keep you more comfortable until the fever is broken.

The Lymphatic Network

A complicated, yet vital part of the war on disease is your lymphatic system. When a pathogen gets by your first line of defense of the skin and membranes, a second line of defense goes into action. The **lymphatic network** includes vessels that circulate a special body fluid called lymph. Lymphatic vessels lead to specialized organs called lymph nodes. One function of lymph nodes is to manufacture white blood cells called **lymphocytes** which travel through the lymphatic system fighting off germs. The two kinds of lymphocytes are the B-cells, and the T-cells.

Lymphocytes that make antibodies that attack germ cells are called **B-cells**. These white blood cells and antibodies act like warriors for your body by de-

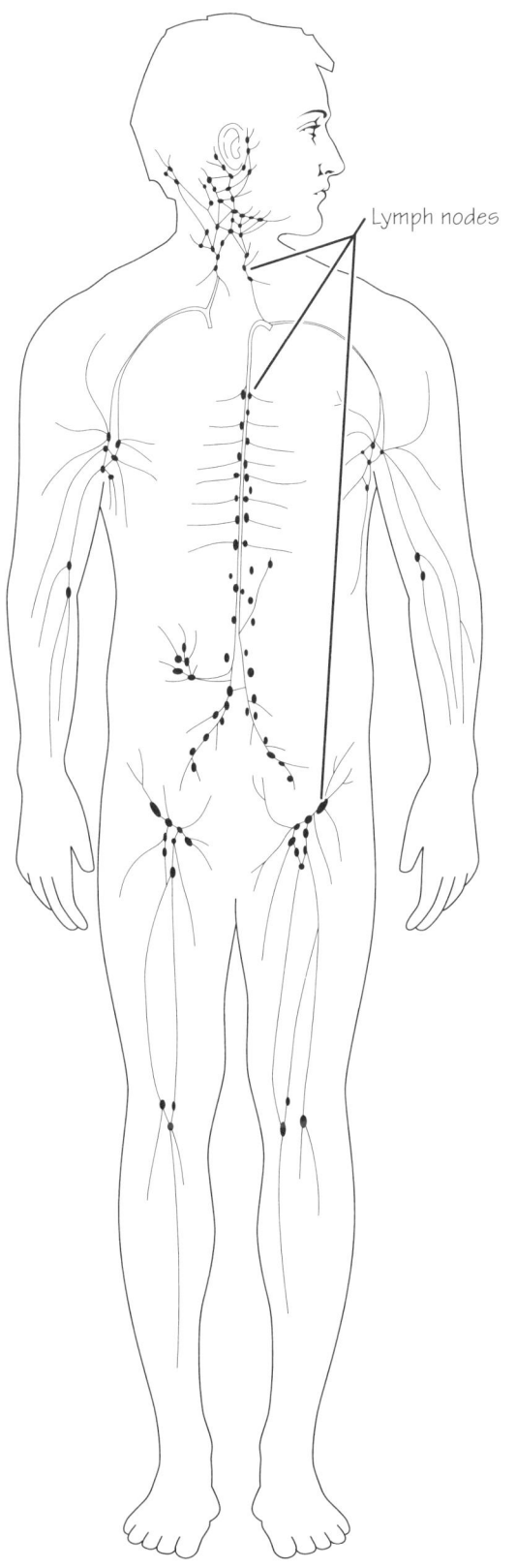

The Lymphatic Network

Lymph nodes

stroying individual germ cells and help the body organize an attack against groups of germ cells. B-cells are made in the lymph nodes, the tonsils, the appendix, the intestines, and the spleen. **T-cells** have a different job than the B-cells. The body produces a matching T-cell to specifically fight a disease, then it makes four new T-cells. One kind of T-cell helps the B-cells, another kills off the body cells that have been wounded or damaged by the disease, the third kind gives the order to stop when the second T-cells have finished their job so they do not kill all the body cells. The fourth T-cell makes the mental picture of the attacking disease so if it ever tries to enter the body again the body will be prepared to fight it quickly.

The *spleen* is an organ that works closely with the lymphatic system. It manufactures and stores white blood cells. If the numbers of pathogens in the body are too great, the spleen helps by releasing stored white blood cells to destroy pathogens.

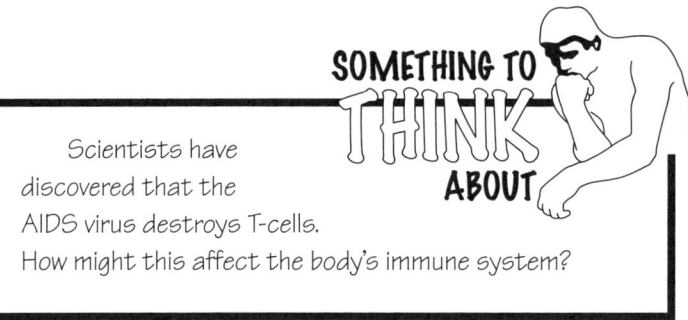

SOMETHING TO **THINK** ABOUT

Scientists have discovered that the AIDS virus destroys T-cells. How might this affect the body's immune system?

Vaccination

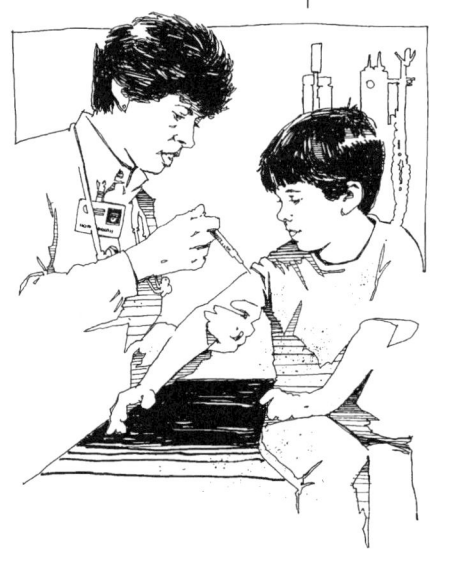

God designed the body's defense strategy to work against attack; however, sometimes your body needs help from supporting forces. God has given scientists the knowledge to help understand the body's intricate design. Over the years scientists have found that a **vaccine**, a mixture of weakened or killed germ cells, will cause the body to produce enough antibodies for that particular disease. Vaccines are given orally or through an injection or shot. As a result of the vaccine, the body is prepared to fight the disease when exposed to it. A doctor should be notified if a person experiences unusual side effects as a result of the vaccine. In some cases the immunity to a disease wears off and booster shots are needed.

God protects the newborn from certain diseases through a natural short-term immunity. Antibodies pass from the mother's bloodstream to the developing fetus. Although this immunity only protects the infant for its first few months of life, it allows time for the child's own immunity to develop. Doctors also believe that if a mother is able to nurse her baby, continued immunity is given to the infant through the nourishment of breast milk.

YOUR SPIRITUAL DEFENSES

In all things the battle here on earth is not only a physical struggle against flesh and blood, but a spiritual one as well. Life is not always "fair." Sickness, disease and death affect you and those you love. There is no definite answer to the question of why difficult situations occur. Consider the story of Job in the Bible. In the midst of his suffering he said, "Shall we indeed accept good from God, and shall we not accept adversity?" (Job 2:10 NAS).

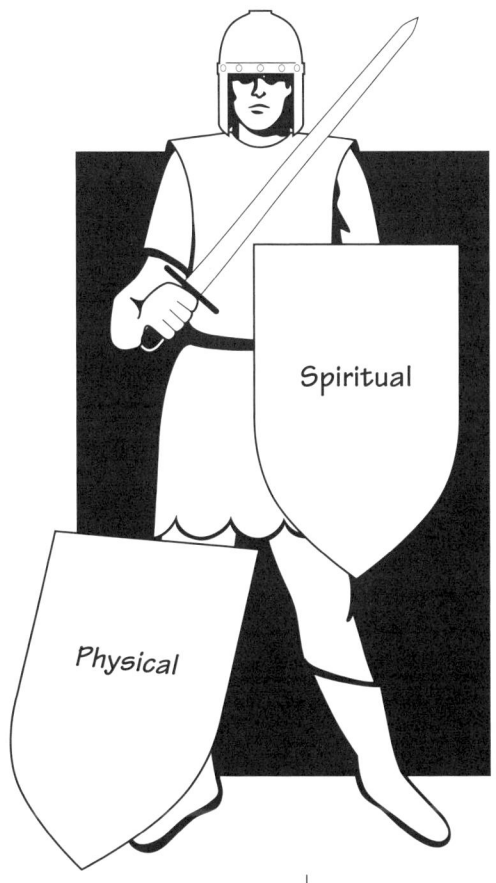

It is important to use your spiritual defenses to battle disease. You are not called to be the healer of those who are sick, but God does call you to pray. When you pray, in faith, believing in the Word of God, your spirit is encouraged even in the midst of physical adversity.

- Pray for healing
- Meditate on the Word of God
- Keep an attitude of faith.

FINDING PEACE IN THE MIDST OF THE BATTLE

The garden of Eden was a place of peace, harmony between man and the animals, man and God, and man and his own flesh. When Adam and Eve stepped out of the boundaries that the Lord had established for them, the peace they once experienced changed forever. When you deviate from what God intended for your life, both a spiritual and physical battle takes place. Satan would like to do to you what he successfully did to Eve — deceive her and lead her into disobedience. He wanted to destroy Adam and Eve spiritually as well as physically. Thousands of years later, his motives and tactics are still the same.

No matter how hard scientists study the human body, they will never fully understand the intricate workings that God so uniquely designed. God created the body's own healing process. When you follow godly health habits your body is built to regenerate itself. Random House Dictionary defines *regenerate* as: *to renew or restore, made over in a better form, born again spiritually.*

Your body strives for balance and inner peace. The American Medical Association explains that the process by which the body maintains a constant internal environment despite the external changes is called **homeostasis.** Simply stated, your body strives to maintain a healthy balance. Today, society has become a physically and spiritually toxic place to live. Your challenge is to help your body, mind, and spirit, live as close to God's laws as possible.

5-4 FIGHTING COMMON INFECTIOUS DISEASES

THE COMMON COLD

When you come up against the common cold, you may think you are battling against only one virus. However, cold symptoms may be caused by many different viruses. Similar symptoms that people experience may be caused by 200 different viruses. This is why scientists are unable to find a cure for this annoying and widespread infection.

No matter how hard scientists study the human body, they will never fully understand the intricate workings that God so uniquely designed.

The cold is spread through air, water, and contact with someone who is infected. When the cold virus first enters your body it produces no **symptoms** (the changes in the body that signal that a particular disease is present). It is difficult to say exactly how long a cold lasts, but if you begin counting the days from the time the first symptoms appear to the day it finally clears up, a cold typically lasts seven days. Everyone responds to cold viruses differently, so this time frame may vary.

The typical symptoms of a cold virus include runny nose, itchy and watery eyes, sneezing, a cough, throat irritation, a headache, body aches, and a mild fever. Any combination of the symptoms may appear with a greater degree in one or more areas. If your symptoms worsen, and you suffer from a high fever, contact your physician, for you may be suffering from something other than the common cold.

Fighting the Common Cold

1. **Eat well:** Eating a balanced diet including foods that are naturally high in vitamins and minerals will build your strength. If you regularly skip meals, you are more likely to weaken your body and become susceptible to catching a cold. Also drink plenty of liquids, preferably water, to help keep your body cleansed and in proper balance.

2. **Get plenty of sleep:** No matter how little sleep you think you need, a growing teenager needs eight hours of sleep a night. The hours before midnight are the best sleep for your body.

3. **Exercise regularly:** Exercise keeps your resistance against infection strong and also helps relieve stress that can contribute to a run-down condition.

4. **Keep the stress in your life in balance:** Continual stress in your life can weaken your body's resistance to infection.

5. **Avoid smoking:** Due to the upper respiratory condition of smokers, their chances of getting a cold are much higher than those who do not smoke. Also, smokers have a more difficult time getting over colds.

Preventing Colds

Strengthening your immune system is the way to combat the attack of any of the cold viruses. Although you may not completely prevent yourself from catching a cold, keeping your body strong will help strengthen your resitance to the virus, and lessen the degree to which you suffer from its symptoms.

Treating Colds

When you take medication for a cold, you are not treating the virus itself, only relieving the symptoms of the cold. The best way to treat a cold is to help your body fight it. Drink plenty of water to help your mucous membranes wash out the virus, get pleny of sleep so your body has the strength to fight the virus, and eat light, nutritious meals that are easily digested. Warm chicken soup has always been a favorite when people suffer from colds. The warm steam helps clear the nasal passages and the chicken broth may help you feel better. If you take medications, you may feel better but you are still contagious and you may find yourself unwelcome in school or around your friends.

PNEUMONIA

Pneumonia is a serious disease affecting the lungs. It can be caused by either a bacteria or a virus. The air sacs of the lungs fill with fluid and the individual has difficulty breathing. Pneumonia is a common cause of death especially in elderly people or those who have other chronic diseases. Today, doctors prescribe medication for those who suffer from pneumonia caused by a bacteria. For pneumonia that is caused by a virus, the treatment is limited. The person's body must overcome the pneumonia and heal itself.

MONONUCLEOSIS

Mononucleosis is a viral infection that is common to young people around the ages of 15–25. Mono results in a high number of white blood cells in the body. The first symptoms are similar to the flu; fever, headache, sore throat, and general exhaustion.

> When you take medication for a cold, you are not treating the virus itself, only relieving the symptoms of the cold.

Symptoms that clearly indicate the presence of the virus are swollen lymph glands, and enlarged liver and/or spleen. A blood test will show if there are any unusual blood cells present.

Mononucleosis has been called "the kissing disease" because it may be spread through direct contact. The treatment for someone suffering from mono is complete bed rest to allow the body's immune system to destroy the virus. Although the person may recover within four to six weeks, recurrent bouts with fatigue may continue for up to a year.

HEPATITIS

Most cases of hepatitis (inflammation of the liver) are due to infection. There are three kinds of hepatitis; Type A, type B, and non-A, non-B type.

Hepatitis A is caused by a virus that is spread through fecally-contaminated food, water, or objects. The symptoms do not appear until three to four weeks after the person has been infected. The symptoms include loss of appetite, weakness, possible vomiting and yellowish coloring of the eyes and skin. Although Hepatitis A can make one very sick, most people will recover with no long-term consequences.

If a person has come into contact with a person who has hepatitis, he/she can get a shot of protein called **gamma globulin** that gives protection against the disease. This shot must be given within the first week of possible infection.

Hepatitis B can cause extensive liver damage in a person suffering from the infection. Type B is spread through direct contact with the infected person or through infected needles. Although Hepatitis B is much more dangerous than Type A, the symptoms and treatment are much the same — bed rest with good nutrition and plenty of liquids.

Hepatitis non-A, non-B was discovered in 1975. It has this unusual name because neither type A or type B was found in the virus. This type of virus is spread through sexual contact and through contact with infected blood. The symptoms and treatment are similar to the other types of hepatitis and it is also known to lead to liver damage.

5-5 SEXUALLY TRANSMITTED DISEASES

TYPES OF STDS

Sexually transmitted diseases are a major health problem around the world. Researchers have found a number of STDs, but the most serious are *chlamydia, gonorrhea, syphilis, herpes simplex II*, and *HIV* that causes AIDS.

Chlamydia

Chlamydia is the most common of the STDs in the United States. While it is the most difficult to discover, it can cause great damage to the reproductive system, especially in women. If untreated, this disease can cause **sterility** (incapable of producing offspring) in both men and women. Some of the other problems include *pelvic inflammatory disease (PID)* in females. This is a painful disease of the female reproductive organs. In males, the result of Chlamydia can be an inflamed urethra.

Although Chlamydia can be treated with an antibiotic, early detection is important in stopping its progression in the body. There is no natural immunity to Chlamydia, so a person can be infected a number of times. Newborn babies can become infected with the disease as the baby passes through the mother's birth canal. The signs of Chlamydia include frequent desire to urinate, painful urination, unusual discharge from penis or vagina, and pain in the pelvic area.

Gonorrhea

Gonorrhea is the next most common STD after chlamydia. Statistics show that there are two million cases of gonorrhea reported each year in the United States. Gonorrhea is often called the "preventer of life" because it can cause sterility in both males and females. Often a person shows no symptoms of infection. When viewing a slide of body tissue, a doctor can detect the disease and if found early, gonorrhea can be treated with antibiotics.

If left untreated, gonorrhea can cause damage to body joints, the heart, and other organs. In females PID can occur just as with chlamydia. The signs and symptoms of gonorrhea are somewhat similar to those of chlamydia, so without a lab test from a medical professional the diagnosis can be inaccurate.

If you would like more information concerning STDs, the VD hotline number is 1-800-227-8922. The AIDS hotline number is 1-800-342-AIDS.

Syphilis

Syphilis is an STD that has been called "the great imitator" because it looks like so many other diseases. This characteristic however, does not make it less harmful. Syphilis is the least common but one of the most dangerous. Three stages in the infection with signs and symptoms for each make this STD unique to the others. In the first stage a reddish sore apprears where the infection entered the body. After developing symptoms in the first stage of the infection, the person may feel fine and believe that he/she is well. The time between stages varies with each individual case, but even if the symptoms disappear, the disease is still present.

About four to eight weeks after the sore develops the second stage of symptoms appear. A rash develops covering the whole body and the person may feel generally sick with a sore throat and body aches. In the third stage of the disease damage may occur to the heart, brain, blood vessels, liver, kidneys, reproductive organs and may even cause death.

Syphilis can be treated with antibiotics, but if left untreated it can cause blindness and insanity. Untreated syphilis can be passed on to an unborn child. If the child does not die from the disease before or after birth, it will still suffer physical difficulties. Syphilis can be diagnosed through a blood test, but once the damage has been done from the infection, it cannot be repaired. Like all STDs, early treatment is extremely important.

Herpes Simplex II

The herpes virus has many forms, but **herpes simplex II** is the STD that causes a painful rash on the genitals (reproductive organs). Once infected with the disease, it remains in the body. Although there is no cure, the symptoms may disappear and never return, or a person may experience recurring bouts with the virus. Herpes can be passed on to an infant during delivery if the mother has herpes simplex II.

Herpes simplex I is a virus that produces cold sores or blisters around the mouth. It is generally considered less serious but it is contagious and there is no cure. Both herpes simplex I and II can seem very similar but when it is transmitted through sexual contact, it is considered an STD.

FIGHTING SEXUALLY TRANSMITTED DISEASES

If you diligently heed the voice of the Lord your God and do what is right in His sight, give ear to His commandments and keep all His statutes, I will put none of the diseases on you which I have brought on the Egyptians. For I am the Lord who heals you.
Exodus 15:26

Nowhere is the need to use your spiritual armor more important than in the battle against Sexually Transmitted Diseases (STDs). Prevention is the *only* medicine to fight the spread of these illnesses. **STDs or Venereal Diseases (VDs)** are diseases that pass from one person to another through sexual contact.

> Nowhere is the need to use your spiritual armor more important than in the battle against Sexually Transmitted Diseases (STDs).

Sexual intimacy is a wonderful gift from God intended to be experienced in the bond of marriage. You may feel that temptation, peer pressure, and your own curiosity are too much to handle. Find an adult you can trust to discuss your concerns. You are not alone in the battle and God gives you strength over your mind and your body. You can make the wise choice and practice abstinence until marriage.

No temptation has overtaken you except such as is common to man; but God is faithful, who will not allow you to be tempted beyond what you are able, but with the temptation will also make the way of escape, that you may be able to bear it.
I Corinthians 10:13

What are the Consequences?

Life is full of consequences; the results of an action can be either good or bad. If a person chooses to drink heavily through-out his/her life, the possible consequences are liver damage, emotional and relational problems, problems with the law and even early death. If an individual chooses to experiment with a harmful drug, the consequences will be physically as well as emotionally harmful.

Throughout your life you will face the consequences of your choices. The power to make wise choices is in your own hands. The choice to be sexually active may not be of concern to you today, but if you do not make a stand now, when the temptation arises you may not have the proper perspective to make a good decision. The result may be to compromise and do something you really did not want to do. Learning about the possible physi-cal consequences of becoming sexually active may help shape your convictions.

A myth about being a teenager is that you are indestructible.

If you believe that having an STD won't happen to you, then you are setting yourself up for a harmful disease. The term "safe sex" is a myth. The *only* way to be sure that STDs will not directly affect you is to say *"NO" to sex.*

Your protection from this enemy starts *before* you are confronted with a decision. Make a commitment to yourself and to God that you will keep yourself pure and follow God's commandments. Physical disease is not the only consequence to breaking the commandments of God. The emotional and spiritual consequences of sex before marriage are often overlooked. In disobeying God's laws, you lose much more than your virginity!

With eyes wide open to the mercies of God, I beg you, my brothers, as an act of intelligent worship, to give him your bodies, as a living sacrifice, consecrated to him and acceptable by him. Don't let the world around you squeeze you into its mould, but let God re-make you so that your whole attitude of mind is changed. Thus you will prove in practice that the will of God is good, acceptable to him and perfect.
Romans 12:1,2 (Phillips translation)

The emotional and spiritual consequences of sex before marriage are often overlooked.

AIDS

What is AIDS? You have probably heard a lot about AIDS in the news, from your friends, family or teachers. The information concerning this disease is changing as researchers are discovering more about the virus. As a result of changing information, this section will deal with important vocabulary and the most recent information available. For more information, the AIDS hotline number is: 1-800-342-AIDS.

AIDS stands for acquired immunodeficiency syndrome. AIDS in itself is not a disease but a result of **HIV (human immunodeficiency virus).** Discussing this virus brings out more fear and frustration than any of the known STDs. Two undisputed facts stand out in all the research concerning AIDS:

SOMETHING TO THINK ABOUT

290,000 cases of AIDS have been reported in the United States.
The first cases of AIDS were reported in 1981. By the end of 1992, more than 250,000 Americans had developed AIDS and more than 170,000 had died – nearly three times more Americans than those who died in the Vietnam War.[1]

1. AIDS is fatal, there is no cure.
2. AIDS can be prevented.

History of AIDS

In 1981, the Centers for Disease Control received some reports of an unusual lung infection in normally healthy adults. The lung infection was found to be pneumocystis Carinii, an organism that had caused pneumonia only in patients with weakened immune systems.

An increase in the number of illnesses linked to weakened immune systems alerted research from both French and American scientists. In 1984, both French and American researchers identified the virus, and in 1986 the virus was named HIV.

The virus that causes AIDS is a kind of germ called a *retrovirus*. The particular retrovirus is called *human immunodeficiency virus, or HIV*. A person is said to be HIV-positive when tests show that the person's body is producing antibodies to the retrovirus. An infected person may be symptom free for weeks, months or years because the virus may not progress quickly. When the symptoms appear, the individual is then said to have AIDS.

What the Virus Does to the Body

The virus attacks the body's immune system, leaving it open for deadly infection and disease. You have learned that the body's immune system produces different white blood cells that attack intruders. When the AIDS virus enters the body, it infects one of the four T-cells. When the T-cells begin to multiply they do not make more T-cells to help the body, they make more AIDS virus cells.

The AIDS virus shuts down the ability of the T-cells to signal other white blood cells to fight off germs. As a result, the body's defense against *any* germ is weakened.

> **SOMETHING TO THINK ABOUT**
>
> The Department of Health and Human Services reports that one in every 250 Americans now has the AIDS virus, and the current rate of infection is one new case every 13 minutes.[2]

Discussing this virus (AIDS) brings out more fear and frustration than any of the known STDs.

Opportunistic infections are those diseases that do not normally affect a person with a healthy immune system, but do take advantage of a person with AIDS. Three common opportunistic diseases are: a form of pneumonia, a rare form of cancer and a disease of the brain and nervous system called AIDS dementia.

How Do You Get AIDS?

Although it is listed as a sexually transmitted disease, HIV can also be spread by using infected IV needles, such as dirty needles used in drug use, shooting steroids, ear piercing, or tattooing. Receiving infected blood products or being born to an infected mother are also ways of infection. HIV has been found in blood, semen, saliva, tears, nervous system tissue, breast milk, and fluids from the vagina. However, to this date, only semen and blood have been a proven means of infection.

For infection to take place, there must be a mixing of body fluid from an infected person into an uninfected person either by way of a mucous membrane, or directly from blood to blood.

You cannot get AIDS through casual contact such as shaking hands, embracing, kissing on the cheek or sharing utensils with someone who is infected with HIV. Since 1985, receiving blood donations has become an unlikely source of infection, except in third world countries where there is inadequate screening of blood supplies. Nonetheless, the Red Cross recommends that if you are having surgery, donate your own blood (autologous donation), prior to your surgery. Giving blood is risk-free because only sterile, disposable needles are used.

SOMETHING TO THINK ABOUT

What about a cure for AIDS?

In the late 1980s, C. Everett Koop (the Surgeon General at the time) predicted that a vaccine for AIDS would not be found until after the year 2000 and that a cure for AIDS would never be found.

You can get AIDS from:
- sexual contact with an infected person.
- using an infected needle.
- infected blood.

Prevention

Being informed about AIDS is not enough to make sure you do not get infected. Making a habit of wise decisions is the best form of prevention. *The only true safe sex is no sex.* That is why abstaining from sexual intercourse until marriage is not only pleasing to God, but a wise health decision. Many pastors today may also encourage both partners to get blood tests for STDs and AIDS before marriage. Many states are requiring premarital blood testing to include the test for AIDS. Faithfulness after marriage will continue to prevent STDs and AIDS.

Abstaining from sexual intercourse until marriage is not only pleasing to God, but a wise health decision.

CHAPTER REVIEW

DEFINE

Disease	B-cells
Infectious disease	T-cells
Communicable disease	Vaccine
Pathogens	Homeostasis
Bacteria	Symptoms
Virus	Hepatitis A
Fungi	Gamma globulin
Incubation period	Hepatitis B
Carrier	Chlamydia
Resistance	Sterility
Acute disease	Gonorrhea
Chronic disease	Syphilis
Allergen	Herpes simplex II
Immune system	STD
Antibodies	AIDS
Lymphatic network	HIV
Lymphocytes	Opportunistic infections

EXPLAIN

1. Explain the Infectious Disease Process.
2. Explain the difference between Acute and Chronic disease.
3. Explain the two defenses against disease.
4. Explain why vomiting and diarrhea are necessary defenses for your body.
5. Explain why the Lymphatic System is such an important part in the body's ability to fight disease.
6. Explain why some people do not get sick when a virus may be going around your school or home.
7. Explain when a fever may be helpful and when a fever may be harmful.
8. Explain how a vaccine works to protect you against a disease.
9. Explain why scientists have not been able to find a cure for the common cold.
10 Explain how you can strengthen your immune system.

11. Explain the emotional and spiritual consequences that may occur from having sex before marriage.

DISCUSS

1. Look up I Corinthians 10:13 and discuss the meaning of the scripture and how it may help in time of any temptation.
2. Discuss the consequences of your daily decisions and then discuss the possible reasons a teenager may engage in sexual activity before marriage.
3. Discuss why it is important to set standards concerning your sexual behavior *before* you are confronted with a decision.
4. Discuss the meaning of Romans 12:1,2 and how it relates to you and your friends.
5. Imagine someone who is close to you has been diagnosed with AIDS. Discuss how you would treat this individual and how you would help other people better understand the disease.

SUGGESTED ACTIVITIES

1. **What's the Problem and What's the Solution?** Write an essay discussing why there is still a problem with STDs and what could be the solution to stop the spread of the diseases. What is the role of teenagers in the solution to the problem?

2. **Make a Call:** Have several students call the STD hotline and the AIDS hotline with a list of 10 questions concerning the diseases. Write down the answers and share your results with the class. Did everyone get the same answers to the questions? This will help to illustrate that information is always changing concerning the spread of diseases.

3. **Myth or Fact?** Make up a list of statements concerning STDs and AIDS and pass them out to the other students in the school or to your parents. See how much they really know about sexually transmitted diseases. Make it a True or False questionnaire.

4. **Key Concepts:** Outline the chapter and make a study guide for yourself. You can work in groups. Each student in the group will be responsible for one or more sections of the chapter.

5. **Write an Editorial:** Study the samples of editorials from your local newspaper. Write an editorial for your newspaper on one of the following subjects. Teenagers say NO to sex. Making wise choices: the consequences of your decisions. (Come up with some more titles based on the information in this chapter).

6. **Medical Detective:** Interview members of your family. Ask them at least ten questions concerning their health. For example, do you have any allergies? If so, what are your symptoms, and what are you doing for it? When was the last time you had a cold or flu? What were your symptoms and what did you do for it? How many days of work/or school did you miss last year due to illness? Summarize your findings in a paragraph explaining any family patterns and what might be ways to help your family be healthier.

7. **The Doctor is IN:** Interview your family doctor or have a doctor visit your classroom. Have him/her talk on communicable or non-communicable diseases, what is a typical check-up?, and the importance of knowing your family health history.

8. **Declaring War on the Cold:** Make a list of all the ways you can prevent the spread of the common cold. Place it on your refrigerator at home, in your classroom or school health room to remind everyone. Some examples might be: cover your mouth and nose when you sneeze or cough, wash your hands after sneezing or coughing and always before you eat.

9. **Make a Poster:** Make a poster in the shape of a shield of scriptures dealing with sickness, healing and/or disease. Decorate it to place in your classroom or school health room to remind people of their spiritual defenses. A poster in the shape of a shield listing the physical defenses can also be made to go along with the spiritual defenses poster.

10. **Let Me Inform You:** Make a group or individual report to the class on one of the subjects dealing with infectious disease. Try to relate it to the class by dealing with things teenagers commonly experience. For example, strep throat, mononucleosis, flu, colds, the role of stress in illness, the importance of sleep, etc.

Noninfectious Disease

6

6-1   THE CAUSE OF NONINFECTIOUS DISEASE

6-2   FIGHTING NONINFECTIOUS DISEASES

6-1   THE CAUSE OF NONINFECTIOUS DISEASE

DEGENERATION

Physical and Spiritual Degeneration

Although the human body is the most wonderful creation of all living things, it is not without its weaknesses. No matter how hard people may try to produce a perfect body through physical and mental training, the inner workings of the body are imperfect — there is no perfect "10"!

When Adam and Eve sinned in the Garden of Eden, the process of spiritual and physical degeneration began. Webster defines **degeneration** as: *a lowering of effective power, vitality, or essential quality to a worsened kind or state; to pass from a higher to a lower type or condition.* As the result of sin, Adam and Eve's relationship with God changed as did their mental and physical conditions.

And the Lord God commanded the man, saying, "Of every tree of the garden you may freely eat; but of the tree of the knowledge of good and evil you shall not eat, for in the day that you eat of it you shall surely die."
Genesis 2:16–17

> No matter how hard people may try to produce a perfect body through physical and mental training ...there is no perfect "10"!

153

What kind of death was the Lord talking about when He said "...for in the day that you eat of it you shall surely *die*"? Adam and Eve did not fall over and die physically when they ate the fruit, but physical and spiritual degeneration did begin then. What was once meant to be a perfect living situation in the garden now became imperfect. Adam and Eve's inner spirits died and so affected all of mankind.

> For as by one man's disobedience many were made sinners, so also by one Man's obedience many will be made righteous.
> Romans 5:19

It took Jesus Christ to come to earth and die to restore man's spiritual state. However, the physical body continues to decline and disease becomes an accepted part of the human condition.

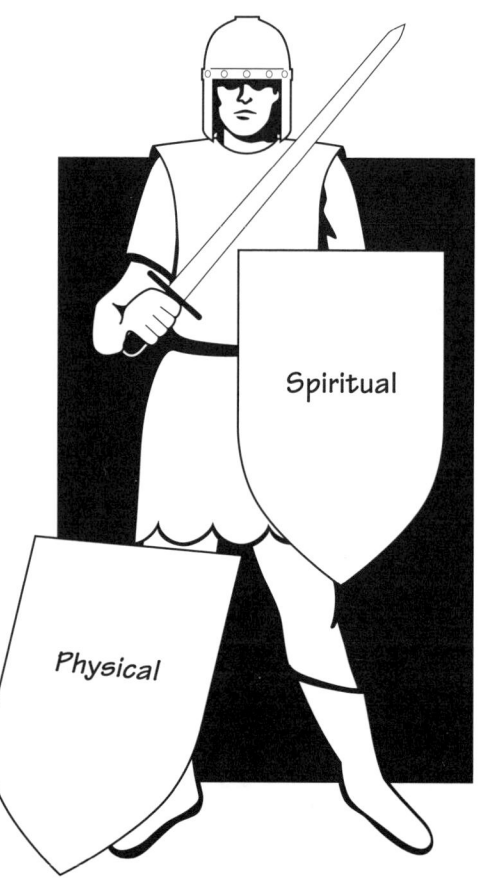

Your spiritual defenses are in order here, just as they are with other illnesses and diseases. Keeping an attitude of faith and belief in God's Word gives strength even when the circumstances seem too much to bear.

Scientists study noninfectious (noncommunicable) diseases to try to *prevent* them from occurring. Unlike infectious diseases (those that are caused by germs that spread from one person to another), **noninfectious diseases** are caused by *heredity*, the *environment*, and a person's *lifestyle* and are *not* passed on from one person to another. Noninfectious diseases are said to be **degenerative diseases** because the body's tissues break down and do not grow or function properly. For example, arthritis is a degenerative disease where the joints become swollen and painful.

Although the symptoms of a noninfectious disease may show up suddenly, the disease itself may have been developing over a long period of time. Most noninfectious diseases are called chronic because these illnesses can last a long time. For this reason, *prevention* is very important in fighting degenerative diseases.

There are times when modern medicine needs to step in to help the body fight degenerative disease. Along with the gifted physicians that help us today, God has made the human body with wonderful restorative powers, the ability of the body to - **regenerate:** *to renew or restore.* Your body wants to take care of itself and with your help you can keep it functioning efficiently.

HEREDITY (GENETIC DISEASES)

The development of any disease is an unfortunate situation, but one of the most difficult to understand is genetic disorders that affect a newborn child. A baby is an innocent victim of disease. He/she is born into a fallen world where sickness does not discriminate or play favorites.

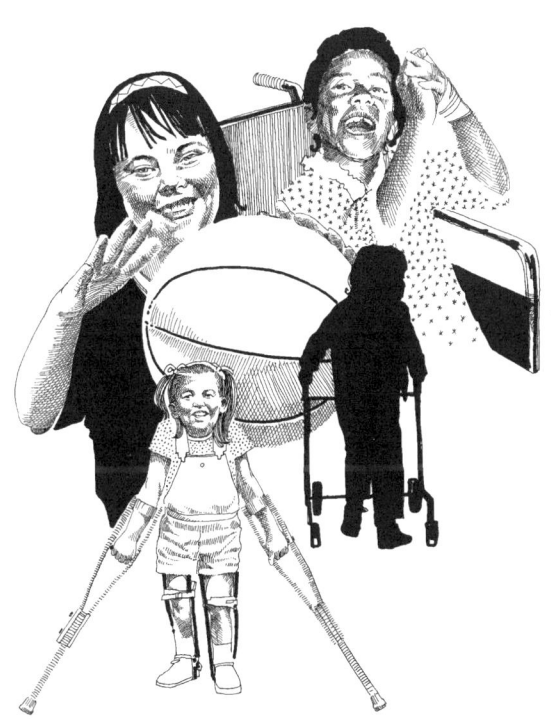

However, in the midst of sickness it is important to remember that God is sovereign *(all power and authority)* and full of grace *(unmerited favor and love).* Life on earth is only a blink in time when you consider the bigger picture — eternal life.

Genetic disorders and birth defects are two causes of infant diseases. A **Genetic disorder** is a disease or condition caused primarily by a defect or defects in the inherited, genetic material within a person's genes. Diseases caused by genetic disorders cannot be prevented. Genetic disorders that are evident at birth are called **congenital**. However, many genetic

Life on earth is only a blink in time when you consider the bigger picture — eternal life.

disorders do not show up until many years after birth. For example, a heart defect that a doctor can detect from birth is congenital, where some forms of muscular dystrophy do not show up until years later.

Birth defects are abnormalities obvious at birth or detectable early in infancy. Birth defects are called congenital and consist of both minor and major abnormalities. A birthmark is a simple birth defect where as spina bifida (a failure of the spinal column to close completely) is a serious defect.

Although there is no cure for genetic disorders and birth defects, children as well as adults can receive therapy and counseling to help deal with their limitations. Society needs to see these children and adults as Christ does. People who suffer from such disease have as much value as those individuals who do not have physical or mental limitations *(II Corinthians 5:14* and *Galatians 2:6)*.

ENVIRONMENT

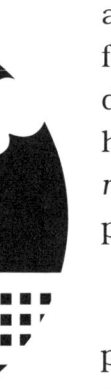

It is often difficult to determine what is the direct cause of a disease. Some people may have a history of cancer in their family, but they themselves do not necessarily acquire the disease. Others may develop the disease without any known history of cancer. Sometimes it takes the combination of *heredity, environment,* and *lifestyle* to cause the onset of a particular disease.

Doctors have found that some people are born with a predisposition (tendency) to a certain illness, but it takes something from the environment or lifestyle to trigger the disease. Heart disease, epilepsy, diabetes, cancer and arthritis are only a few examples.

This world is a physically and spiritually toxic place to live. In other words, you live in a world full of poisons that are harmful and destructive to your physical, mental and spiritual state of health. Toxins can be very obvious or almost invisible. That is why it is important for you to be alert for spiritual as well as physical poisons *(Matthew 10:16* and *Proverbs 27:12).*

Physical hazards that may cause illness may be out of your control. For example, air, water, and solid waste pollution are toxins to your body. You can be an informed and involved citizen and do your part to keep the air you breathe and the water you drink clean and safe. However, singlehandedly, you cannot control these physical hazards.

LIFESTYLE

Lifestyle diseases are those diseases caused by your health habits. Many times the results of poor choices do not show up until later in life, sometimes so much later that it is too late to reverse the damage.

You may even know someone who has continued a bad habit no matter what people, even doctors, have said to them. Tobacco, alcohol, and drugs are only a few of the poor choices many people still make after knowing the dangerous consequences of their behavior.

Risk factors are traits or habits that raise someone's chances of getting a disease. This is one reason why knowing your family history is so important in understanding your health. You can reduce your risk of developing lifestyle diseases by learning what good health habits are — and then as Nike says — "just do it!"

Habits are very difficult to break, but not impossible! If you have some poor lifestyle habits, never give up trying to break them. Building good habits while you are young is one key to making life a little easier and definitely healthier.

Remember, no one is guaranteed an *abundant life.* You must seek after it and pursue those things that are pleasing to God. Think of this: of the ten leading causes of death in the United States, seven are noninfectious diseases, and all seven are directly or indirectly affected by how you choose to live.

> Many times the results of poor choices do not show up until later in life, sometimes so much later that it is too late to reverse the damage.

A Tribute To An Old Friend
By Susan Boe

I grew up on a quiet suburban street. The kind of neighborhood that is difficult to find today. All the neighbor kids played together with no need for concern from the parents, because they knew that each home was looking out for the good of the children. At one time I recall eight families living on the street and all were close friends. They were the kind of neighbors that would do almost anything for each other.

Carol and Joe were one of the special families. Their daughter Amy grew up close to all of us. As time went on families moved in and out of the neighborhood but Carol, Joe and Amy remained faithful neighbors on the street. Joe was the big, teddy-bear type. One who seemed hard on the outside but warm and cuddly on the inside. All the kids who got to know him saw his warm, friendly side. One of Joe's weaknesses was that he would not go to a doctor for anything; he did not like check-ups. Consequently no doctor could have forewarned him of his ill health because Joe never gave him a chance.

Very suddenly, and to all of our surprise, Joe died of a heart attack. The symptoms came on quickly and the doctors could do nothing to help him — At the age of 60 he died from a lifestyle disease, leaving behind a wife and a 20 year old daughter.

Carol and Amy had a lot of support from all of their friends. My mother being one of Carol's best friends, was right there for her whenever she needed anything. As time went on Carol and Amy moved to a smaller place and although another family moved into their home, it was remembered as Carol, Joe and Amy's home.

Fifteen years later Carol found out she had lung cancer. Throughout her life she had always smoked cigarettes and had tried numerous ways to quit. Her lungs had become a weak area of her body, susceptible to lung problems. Although her symptoms came on gradually, the cancer spread quickly and the doctors could not do any more for her.

In the last remaining weeks of her life she was in a lot of pain. The old neighborhood rallied behind Amy and Carol. I remember Amy telling us that the doctor told her "this could have been prevented." Carol died at the age of 71 from a lifestyle disease.

The funeral was yesterday. As I sat with my extended family in the funeral, I looked around and noticed all of the original neighbors from the neighborhood. One boy, who is now a young man, came up to my family and said, "It is too bad we had to gather for such circumstances, but isn't it good to know the neighborhood is like a family." This really brought home to me the importance of committed and loving friendships.

We are all adults now, trying to raise our own children. We have some great memories that have shaped our lives and it would be nice to have our children experience the same. I did not write this tribute to exploit Carol, Joe, or Amy, but because I want those who are reading this to understand the impact that disease has on family and friends. Carol and Joe would want us to gain as much from their deaths as we did from their lives.

6-2 FIGHTING NONINFECTIOUS DISEASES

CARDIOVASCULAR DISEASE

Many young people take their health for granted. While you may suffer from a cold or flu once in awhile, suffering from a heart attack at your age is almost unheard of. Heart disease is something you often think of happening to older people. However, an older person may suffer from heart disease because of poor health habits that began early in life. Remember, right now you are setting the stage for future health problems. Try to see beyond today, into the future, and get a plan into action for a healthy heart.

Cardiovascular disease is the number one killer in the United States. There are different kinds of cardiovascular disease, but the most common are arteriosclerosis, high blood pressure and stroke. Keeping your heart, arteries, and blood vessels in proper working order is vital for good health.

Arteriosclerosis

Hardening of the arteries is called **arteriosclerosis.** Although several factors contribute to this disease, the most common type of arteriosclerosis is **atherosclerosis**, in which there is the buildup of fat deposits on the artery wall. This buildup of fatty deposits can involve arteries throughout the body, including the brain, and the legs, but when it directly affects the arteries that supply blood flow to the heart, the risk of a heart attack increases.

> When you pour grease, fat and oil down your kitchen sink every day,
> eventually your pipes become clogged and you have to call a
> plumber. When this happens inside your body,
> you call an ambulance.[1]
> *Michael A. Wilson, MD, Cardiology*

Many young people take their health for granted.

When the fat deposits become thicker, the arteries become narrower, and it is difficult for blood to flow through the space. Unfortunately, a person will experience no warning symptoms until the blockage is so severe that the blood flow is restricted. The symptoms that usually occur in the development of athero-sclerosis are:

Chest pain (angina): A pain or tightening in the chest. The feeling may be experienced during stress or exercise. Angina is a sign that the heart is starved for oxygen-carrying blood. This pain may cause some people to seek medical attention.

Heart attack (myocardial infarction): When blood flow to the heart is dangerously reduced, the tissues of the heart muscle lack needed oxygen and they die and the heart stops functioning.

High Blood Pressure

Your heart is a hollow muscular organ that pumps blood throughout your body by contracting and relaxing. The force of the blood on the inside walls of the main arteries is called your **blood pressure.** Your blood pressure may go up as a response to stress or during physical activity. However, when blood pressure is higher than normal for a long time, even when a person is at rest, the individual is said  to suffer from *high blood pressure* or **hypertension**. Hypertension, if left untreated, can lead to complications such as arteriosclerosis, heart attack, stroke, damage to the eyes (retinopathy), and kidney failure.

Blood pressure is measured with two numbers. During each heart beat, blood surges out of the heart and into the arteries. The peak pressure caused by this surge is known as the *systolic* pressure. When the heart relaxes blood flows into the heart and the blood pressure drops. This lower pressure is called the *diastolic* pressure. The range for normal blood pressure varies with age but in general, for adults, the upper number should be less than 140 and the lower number less than 85–90. Blood pressure readings such as 110/70 would be read as "110 over 70."

High blood pressure is often called the silent killer because there are no outward signs of the disease until it is too late. The exact cause of hypertension is unknown, but doctors do know some factors that may lead to an increase risk of developing hypertension.

- Family history of hypertension
- Obesity
- Tobacco smoking
- Eating large amounts of salt
- Extreme stress in your life
- Diabetes melitus

The Prevention and Treatment of Heart Disease

You have heard the phrase, "an ounce of prevention is worth a pound of cure." This is certainly true with the prevention of high blood pressure and heart disease. Although doctors have pinpointed several risk factors for heart disease, *prevention* is still the best medicine. Four risk factors that are out of anyone's control are: *Age* (the older the person, the more likely to develop heart disease), *sex* (up to the age of forty, males are more likely to develop heart disease), *race* (black Americans have a higher risk of developing heart disease) and a *family history of heart disease.* No matter what the circumstances, everyone can take steps to lower his/her risk of high blood pressure and heart disease. Following good health habits will help you avoid the complications associated with heart disease.

Although doctors have pinpointed several risk factors for heart disease, prevention is still the best medicine.

Preventive Measures Against Heart Disease

- **Regular Screening of Blood Pressure:** if you have a history of heart disease, regular screening of blood pressure is important for early treatment.
- **Reduce your weight:** people who are overweight are more likely to have heart disease than people who maintain their ideal weight.
- **Do not smoke:** smoking increases the risk for heart disease and stroke.
- **Reduce or stop drinking alcohol:** those who drink excessively are more likely to develop complications from heart disease than those who do not drink heavily.
- **Eat a healthy diet:** people who eat a healthy diet that is low in sodium, fats, and cholesterol and high in fiber can reduce their risk of heart disease.
- **Exercise regularly:** exercise not only helps control weight, but also keeps the heart muscle strong.
- **Learn to manage stress:** those who learn to combat the stress in their life are less likely to develop heart disease than those who allow stress to overcome them.

Although prevention is the best medicine for heart disease, there are times when the treatment must go a step further. Doctors are continually learning about the options available for the treatment of heart disease.

The treatment of arteriosclerosis consists of changing a person's health habits, taking medication for the angina (pain) and directly treating the arteries. When the damage to the arteries is extensive doctors may do the following:

1. **Use balloons to stretch out the blocked arteries (coronary angioplasty):** This procedure has become one of the simpler procedures to open narrowed arteries. Through a small incision in the groin area, a soft wire is inserted and guided up to the artery. The balloon is then inflated until the narrowed artery is stretched open. After the balloon is re-

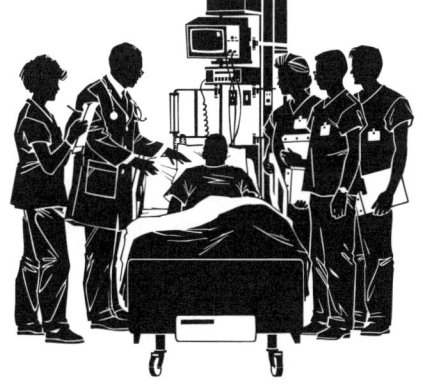

moved, the artery will usually stay open, at least for a time.

2. **Cut out the plaque ("roto-rooter"):** As with the angioplasty, a balloon is inserted into the patient. However, instead of the balloon only stretching the artery, a rotating blade inside the balloon chamber shaves off the plaque and then the plaque is removed.

3. **Dissolving clots with a laser:** This procedure uses laser energy to dissolve blood clots.

4. **Surgery:** In *bypass surgery* doctors create new paths for blood flow by using healthy veins from the patient's leg, then attaching them above and below the blocked area so that the blood goes around the blockage. When a patient's heart is badly damaged or is not able to function properly, a *heart transplant* may be necessary. In this procedure, a patient's heart is removed and then replaced with another heart from a donor.

By combining strong preventive programs with new technologies to open arteries, doctors are giving individuals with heart disease a second chance to live longer, healthier, more productive lives.[2]
Dr. Michael A. Wilson

SOMETHING TO THINK ABOUT

Pacemakers are battery-operated devices that send electrical impulses to the heart muscle to make it beat regularly. People who have irregular or weak heartbeats may need a pacemaker. Pacemakers run on batteries, but don't worry, new models use batteries that never run out!!

STROKE

A stroke may result when damage to part of the brain has been caused by blockage of blood supply or leakage of blood outside of the artery wall. There are three main causes of a stroke: blockage by a clot that has built up on the wall of a brain artery, blockage by a clot that drifts into an artery in the brain, and rupture of a blood vessel and bleeding within the brain area.

There are several factors that increase the risk of having a stroke, but the two most important are hypertension (high blood pressure) and atherosclerosis (hardening of the arteries). The effects of a stroke vary from almost no noticeable side affects to death. The more common effects are weakness or paralysis on one side of the body. The part of the body controlled by the damaged area of the brain cannot function properly as a result of the stroke. There is no "cure" for the effects of a stroke, but through physical therapy and speech therapy some patients can improve.

CANCER

A tumor is called benign if its effect is fairly localized and it stays within membrane boundaries. But the most traumatizing condition in the body occurs when disloyal cells defy inhibition. They multiply without any checks on growth, spreading rapidly throughout the body, choking out normal cells. White cells, armed against foreign invaders, will not attack the body's own mutinous cells. Physicians fear no other malfunction more deeply: it is called cancer. For still mysterious reasons, these cells — and they may be cells from the brain, liver, kidney, bone, blood, skin, or other tissues — grow wild, out of control. Each is a healthy, functioning cell, but disloyal, no longer acting in regard for the rest of the body.[3]
Dr. Paul Brand

Think about this for a moment. When was the last time you heard someone talk of cancer? Do you know anyone personally who has cancer or who has died as a result of cancer? How did you feel when the word *cancer* was spoken? When you hear the word cancer, it is not uncommon to feel fear and an overpowering sense of dread. It may be interesting to note that cancer is not a new disease. Researchers have found signs of bone cancer in some ancient Egyptian skeletons. Scientists know more about cancer today than ever before, but even with all the research it is still somewhat of a mystery.

Although cancer is a complicated disease, the definition is simple. **Cancer** is caused by abnormal cells growing without control. The human body is made up of billions of cells; many die each minute and are being replaced constantly with new cells. Some cells are unhealthy and are destroyed by the body. The body is a place of constant activity and growth. God made every cell in the human body to serve a purpose, but at times the cells become abnormal and begin to rebel.

God made every cell in the human body to serve a purpose, but at times the cells become abnormal and begin to rebel.

Cause of Cancer: Mutiny in the Body

Dr. Paul Brand and Philip Yancey in their book *Fearfully and Wonderfully Made* describe the human cell as follows:

…though a hand or foot or ear cannot have a life separate from the body, a cell does have that potential. It can be part of the body as a loyalist, or it can cling to its own life. Some cells do choose to live in the body, sharing its benefits while maintaining complete independence — they become parasites or cancer cells.[4]

Groups of abnormal cells grow quickly and may form masses of cells called **tumors**. Tumors can be either **benign** (not cancerous) or **malignant** (cancerous). Malignant tumors have a horrible characteristic and bedside manner. Once a group of cells become malignant they divide more rapidly and spread throughout the body. These malignant cells no longer contribute positively to the body (they no longer function the way they were meant to) yet they still consume nutrients from the body. **Metastasis** is the name given to tumors that spread to other parts of the body through the blood stream or lymphatic system.

Although scientists have found over 200 different kinds of cancers that can attack the body, the most common develop in major organs such as the lungs, breasts, intestines, skin, stomach and reproductive organs. Cancer can also develop in the bone

---

Breast Self-Examination from the American Cancer Society

You, as a female, should do this simple three-step procedure that could save your life by finding breast cancer early when it is most curable. Follow this same procedure once a month about a week after your period, when breasts are usually not swollen or tender.

1. In the shower; examine your breasts. Feel for any possible lumps, hard knots or thickening. Press the flat part of the fingers on the outer edge of the breast and move around in circles and slowly move closer to the nipple.

2. Look in the mirror; a change in the size or shape of a breast, a swelling, skin changes or discharge from the nipple.

3. Lying Down; while lying on your back, place a pillow or towel under right shoulder, place right hand behind your head. With left hand examine your right breast as you would in the shower, moving your hand in a circular motion noticing how your breast feels. Finally squeeze your nipple gently, any discharge should be reported to your doctor. Do this same procedure on your left breast.

marrow (leukemia) and lymphatic system.

The specific cause of cancer is not known. However, there are certain factors that researchers believe increase a person's chances of developing cancer:

Factors contributing to the development of cancer
1. A person's genetic makeup (inherited).
2. Lifestyle habits.
3. Environmental factors.
4. Occupational hazards.
5. Body's reaction to a virus.

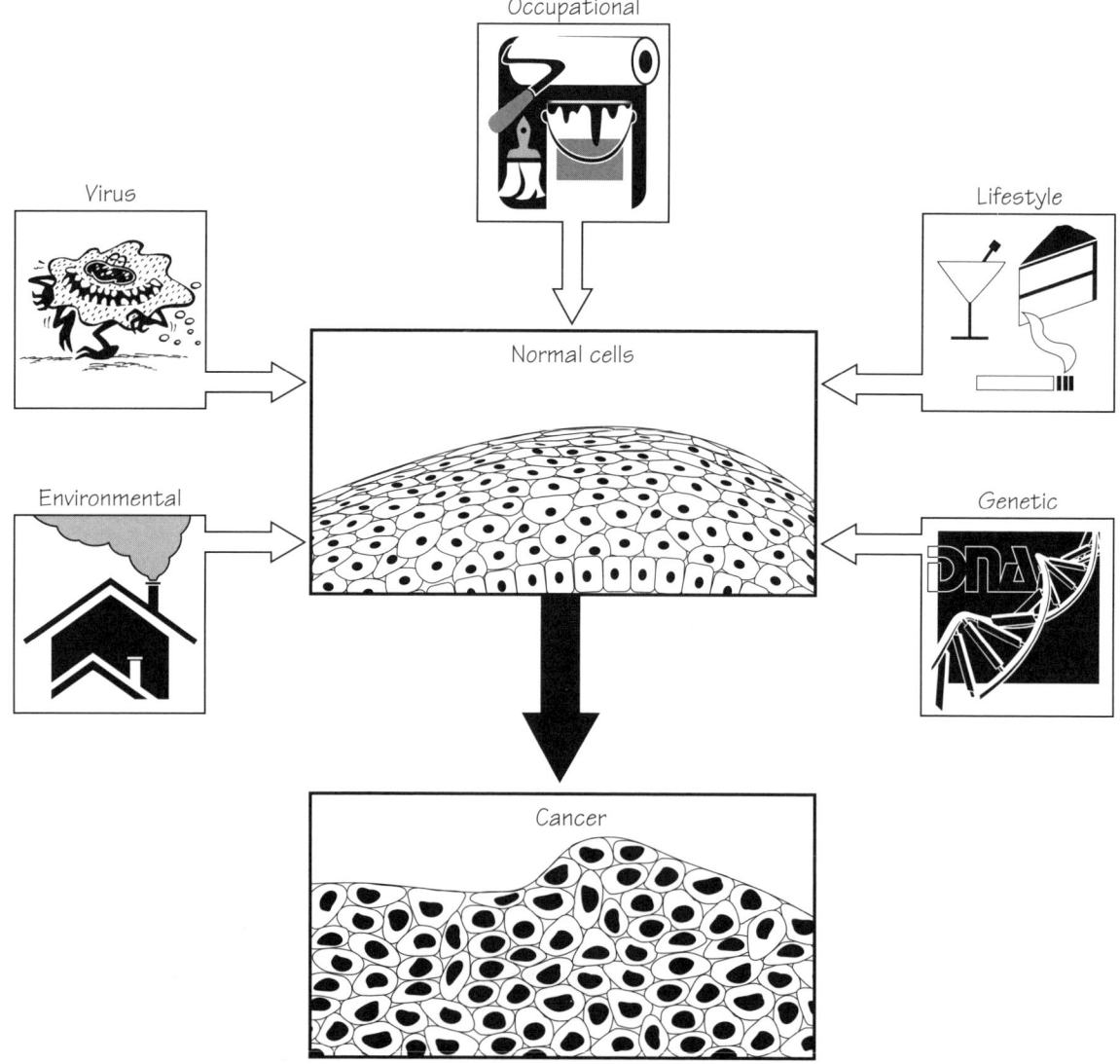

The substances around you that cause cancer are called **carcinogens.** Today scientists are learning more about the substances that are found in nature, such as the sun, and those substances that are man-made, such as pollutants from factories, or smoke from tobacco that can cause cancer. Even saccharine, a widely used substitute for sugar was found to cause cancer if eaten in large quantities.

What you can do in the fight against cancer

☑ Eat a diet rich in fruits (especially rich in vitamin C), vegetables and fiber, and low in fat.

☑ Eat vegetables rich in beta carotene (broccoli, cantaloupe, carrots, spinach, squash).

☑ Eat a diet rich in calcium (low-fat dairy products).

☑ Eat fewer salty and highly processed foods.

☑ Limit your consumption of alcohol.

☑ Say "NO" to tobacco in any form.

☑ Always use sun-blocking protection on exposed areas of your skin.

☑ See your doctor regularly for complete physicals.

☑ Males and females should properly do self-exams for testicular and breast cancer.

The Prevention of Cancer

The way a person chooses to live has become a great concern to cancer researchers today. A person's diet, scientists say, may have much to do with an individual's susceptibility to cancer.

According to the American Cancer Society the vitamin A found in dark green and deep yellow fruits and vegetables may reduce the risk of lung, esophagus and larynx cancer. Vitamin C prevents nitrites from combining with proteins, which can form cancer-promoting chemicals, which in turn increases the risk of stomach, esophagus and larynx cancer. The research on the role of diet in the prevention of disease has shown that people who eat a plant-rich diet suffer lower rates of cancer than do those who eat meats. Natural antioxidants in foods "clean-up" free radicals (cancer-causing agents).

A person's diet, scientists say, may have much to do with an individual's susceptibility to cancer.

Testicular Self-Examination from the American Cancer Society

Two or three times a month, you, as a male, should check yourself for possible signs of testicular cancer. The test is simply a matter of feeling each testicle for any hard lumps. It can be done during the shower. If anything feels unusual, you should notify your doctor.

The Treatment of Cancer

The earlier a cancer is found, the better the chance of a cure. Knowing the warning signs of cancer is very important. The American Cancer Society identifies seven warning signs of cancer.

Warning Signs of Cancer...
spell CAUTION!!!

Change in bowel or bladder habits
A sore that does not heal
Unusual bleeding or discharge
Thickening or lump in the breast or elsewhere
Indigestion or difficulty swallowing
Obvious change in a wart or mole
Nagging cough or hoarseness

Once the diagnosis of cancer has been determined through various tests, the treatment may begin. For most cancers, tests are usually performed after the appearance of symptoms. Although various tests are used to diagnosis cancer, the cancer is confirmed by a microscopic examination of tissue cells obtained by a **biopsy** (cancer cells look different from normal cells).

The treatment of cancers is primarily surgical with the combination of radiation therapy and anticancer drugs. The purpose of

---

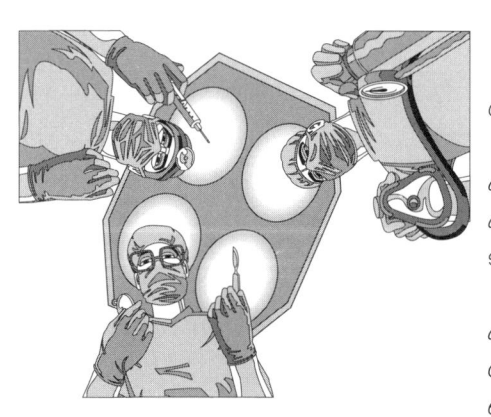

The Treatment of Cancer

Surgery: remove the cancer cells that have not spread throughout the body. Localized tumors are the easiest to remove.

Chemotherapy: anticancer drug treatments, use chemicals to destroy cancer cells. There are some negative side effects of these drugs. They are often used in the treatment of cancers that have spread throughout the body, such as leukemia.

Radiation: the use of x-rays or some other radiation are aimed directly at the cancerous tumor. The purpose is to destroy the cancerous cells while avoiding healthy cells. There are some negative side effects of radiation because it can damage healthy cells as well.

these treatments is to remove the tumor and to stop the growth of the cancerous cells that may be left after surgery.

Today the word "cancer" is not synonymous with death. Both the cure and survival rates of cancer victims continue to improve. The most important thing is early diagnosis.

DIABETES MELLITUS

Diabetes mellitus results when the pancreas does not produce adequate amounts of insulin. It is a noninfectious disease that prevents the body from efficiently utilizing sugar to make energy.

The Cause and Treatment of Diabetes

You have learned that the food you eat is changed into a sugar called glucose your body can use as energy. Insulin is a hormone produced by your pancreas to control how your body uses this sugar for energy. If more sugar is present in your blood, then more insulin is released to regulate the sugar. There are typically three conditions related to blood sugar regulation. Hypoglycemia, Diabetes I, and Diabetes II. **Hypoglycemia** is an abnormally low level of sugar in the blood. In this case, low blood sugar can often be regulated by eating more frequently.

The causes of diabetes are not totally understood. There are various factors that researchers have found that contribute to the development of the disease: a family history of diabetes, obesity, and being older. The two kinds of diabetes are determined by how much insulin is being produced by the pancreas. Those who suffer from **Diabetes Type I** (insulin dependent) produce little or no insulin. This more severe form of the disease usually appears in young people between the age of 10 and 16 but may also develop up to the age of 35. 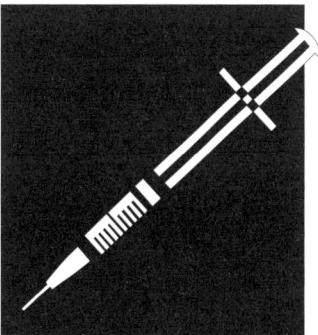 Without the treatment of regular injections of insulin the individual who has diabetes type I could die.

The Symptoms of Type I Diabetes
- Urinating often and feeling very thirsty.
- Increased appetite.
- Unexplained loss of weight.
- Vomiting and nausea.
- Weakness and fatigue.

Diabetes Type II (non-insulin-dependent) usually appears gradually in people over the age of 40. In this case, some insulin is produced by the pancreas but not enough to meet the body's needs, or the body cannot use it correctly. Diabetes type II can most often be treated by weight control, diet, exercise and some oral medications.

The Symptoms of Type II Diabetes
- Tingling and numbness in hands and feet.
- Blurred vision.
- Lack of energy.
- Skin abrasions that heal slowly.
- Itching.

The primary concern of someone who has diabetes is to keep the blood sugar level in balance. The most accurate way to measure this is through a blood test. A person who has diabetes learns how to test her own blood sugar levels. Although diabetes cannot be cured, a person with diabetes can live a fairly normal life by learning to control his diabetes by the use of insulin or oral medication and a proper diet.

If a person with Type I diabetes gives herself too much insulin, insulin shock may result. The person will feel dizzy, irritable and may be sweaty and can even become unconcious. To treat insulin shock the individual must eat some food high in glucose, such as a piece of candy or a small amount of fruit juice. If a person with Type I diabetes takes too little insulin, high blood sugar will result. The person will feel thirsty, urinate often, vomit and have flushed skin. If the reaction is severe enough, they may go into a diabetic coma and die. In any of these situations the person needs medical attention immediately.

ARTHRITIS

Arthritis is characterized by pain, swelling, stiffness, and redness in the joints. It is not a single disease but the name given to over 100 conditions of the joints. Arthritis may affect one joint or many, and can vary in degree from slight stiffness to extreme pain and even deformity of the joint. Arthritis is not an "old person's" disease; it can affect people of any age. Two types of arthritis are the most common. They are osteoarthritis and rheumatoid arthritis.

Osteoarthritis

This degenerative arthritis is the most common of the two types of arthritis. It typically affects older people and is a result of wear and tear on the joints. The hips, spine and knee joints are the areas affected most because they carry most of the body weight, as well as finger joints because they are used so often.

The first stage of osteoarthritis occurs when the cartilage in and around a joint wears down and the body does not replace it. The second stage of osteoarthritis consists of a grinding at the joint because there is no longer enough cartilage for a smooth movement. Finally after much irritation, the end of the bone produces a bone spur, a small knob that ultimately causes the joint to be deformed.

Doctors treat osteoarthritis with medications such as ibuprofen and aspirin to help the pain. Special exercises may help the joint from getting too stiff. If the damage is too great, doctors may operate to replace the joint with a mechanical one.

Arthritis is not an "old person's" disease; it can affect people of any age.

Rheumatoid Arthritis

This is the most severe type of arthritis. Doctors believe that the body's own immune system attacks the tissues surrounding the joints. The joints that are affected the most are the joints of the wrists, knuckles, hips, legs, and feet. As a result of the swollen tissues around the joints, the bone and cartilage begin to disintegrate and the joint becomes severely deformed and stiff.

The cause of rheumatoid arthritis is unknown, but scientists believe that having a family history of the disease greatly increases the chance of developing the disease.

The treatment of rheumatoid arthritis is not to cure the patient but to relieve the pain and prevent further joint damage. A wide variety of medications are used to help the swelling and pain. Exercise and therapy are used to help keep the joints working properly. Surgery may be done in some cases if the damage to the joint is extensive.

CYSTIC FIBROSIS, MUSCULAR DYSTROPHY AND MULTIPLE SCLEROSIS

Although the following diseases may not affect you directly, it is important to have the knowledge to better understand those who suffer from them. For example, when you look at someone who is afflicted with MS, you may only see a body of distorted muscles, but when you can understand the disease, you can better understand the person on the inside. You may know of someone who is afflicted with a disease, or you may find you have a history of one of them in your family. Whatever the situation, compassion for those who suffer from any noninfectious disease is important.

Cystic Fibrosis

An inherited disease present at birth, cystic fibrosis was a fatal disease in the 1930's before any antibiotic treatment was found. CF is caused by a defective recessive gene. The disease is characterized by a tendency toward chronic lung infections and the inability to absorb nutrients from food. A child may show symptoms of the disease early in life by persistent bronchial prob-

Whatever the situation, compassion for those who suffer from any noninfectious disease is important.

172

lems as well as difficulty growing.

Early diagnosis is important in the treatment of CF. Antibiotics for the chest infections and dietary changes may help the person suffering from CF have a much better quality of life.

Muscular Dystrophy

An inherited muscle disorder, muscular dystrophy has no known cause and is characterized by progressive degeneration of the muscle fibers. The different forms of muscular dystrophy are classified according to the age at which the symptoms appear, the rate at which the disease progresses, and the way in which it was inherited.

Although muscular dystrophy is rare, there is no effective treatment. Children who are afflicted with the disease should use their muscles as much as possible to keep them in healthy condition.

Multiple Sclerosis

A progressive disease of the central nervous system, MS is the most common acquired disease of the nervous system in young adults. There is no known cause of MS but scientists believe that the body's own immune system may attack the myelin (the protective covering of nerve fibers) in the central nervous system. Because of the damage done to the nervous system, a person suffering from MS experiences symptoms of numbness to paralysis. The symptoms vary with the degree of damage done to the body. The symptoms may last from several weeks to several months. Relapse may occur due to an injury or stress in life.

Doctors also believe there is a higher incidence of MS in persons who have a family history of the disease. While researchers are looking for a cure, patients are encouraged to lead as active a life as possible. Certain drugs may be prescribed for the pain and physical therapy may help strengthen the muscles.

ALZHEIMER'S DISEASE

Alzheimer's disease is a progressive condition in which nerve cells in the brain degenerate and the brain loses its ability to function. Research into Alzheimer's has increased because people are living longer. This degenerative disease of the brain affects people over the age of 65 and is the leading cause of dementia (insanity).

Scientists do not know the cause of Alzheimer's but many theories have been made. The symptoms of the disease begin with forgetfulness of little things to total memory loss, especially for recent events. People who suffer from Alzheimer's become severely confused and may become paranoid.

There is no treatment for Alzheimer's disease. Caring for the patient and keeping him active helps to lessen the anxiety. The families who care for those suffering from Alzheimer's need counseling and support for the situation. Do you know of anyone or any family that is dealing with Alzheimer's? What could you do to help people have a better understanding of the disease?

SOMETHING TO THINK ABOUT

Do your health homework!

One of the most important things you can do to help avoid certain diseases is to know your medical history. You need to know what kind of health background your birth parents and relatives had. Ask your parents or guardian if they have any health records that you may look at. Do you know if your grandparents had heart disease, cancer, diabetes, asthma or other genetic disorders? As you grow older keep a health record of yourself so that when your children ask you for a health history you have done your homework!

Medical Records

CHAPTER REVIEW

DEFINE

Degeneration	Cancer
Noninfectious disease	Tumor
Degenerative disease	Benign
Regenerate	Malignant
Genetic disorder	Metastasis
Congenital	Carcinogens
Birth defects	Biopsy
Lifestyle diseases	Diabetes mellitus
Risk factors	Hypoglycemia
Arteriosclerosis	Diabetes type I
Atherosclerosis	Diabetes type II
Blood pressure	Arthritis
Hypertension	Alzheimer's disease

EXPLAIN

1. Explain what is meant by spiritual and physical degeneration.
2. Explain why noninfectious diseases are said to be degenerative diseases.
3. Explain what the role is of heredity, environment and lifestyle on degenerative diseases.
4. Explain why hypertension (high blood pressure) can be dangerous to your health.
5. Explain why heart disease is called the "silent killer."
6. Explain why Dr. Paul Brand describe cancer as a "mutiny in the body."
7. Explain what is the primary concern of someone who has diabetes.

DISCUSS

1. Discuss how you might talk to someone who has a close relative who was diagnosed with cancer.
2. Discuss how teenagers can begin to make the positive choices to help them in the prevention of heart disease.

3. Read "A Tribute to an Old Friend" in this chapter and discuss its contents. Write a summary of how it made you feel.

4. Discuss some of the risks that teenagers take that increase their risk of degenerative diseases.

5. If the physical body is destined to die, discuss why people should have hope.

6. Discuss the meaning of Romans 5:19 and how it relates to you.

7. Discuss how you might encourage someone who has a relative or friend who is suffering from Alzheimer's disease.

SUGGESTED ACTIVITIES

1. **Health History Family Tree:** Interview your parents, grandparents and any relatives who can help you make a health history family tree. List any significant illnesses and all the known causes of death of those relatives who have passed away. Make it more interesting by putting it in the shape of a real tree with the names of your relatives and their diseases on the branches of the tree. Don't forget to include yourself!

2. **A Tribute to a Friend:** Write your own tribute to a friend or relative who has passed away. Describe how his/her life and death affected you and how you dealt with it.

3. **Key Concepts:** Outline the chapter and make a study guide for yourself. You can work in groups and each student be responsible for one or more of the sections.

4. **Let Me Inform You:** Write a full report on one noninfectious disease. Make an oral report to the class.

5. **Plan of Action:** Now that you know the importance of lifestyle and diseases, hopefully you would like to make some changes to better your chances of avoiding certain diseases. Choose one or two poor health habits you have and want to change. Write a plan of action to help you accomplish your goal. Include what the habit is you are trying to change, list all the negative factors, both personal and scientific, that make quitting or starting seem worthwhile. Then develop your own plan to change your negative health habit to a positive one. When you are finished, you may be asked to share it with the class.

6. **Did You Know?** Make a creative poster showing the connection to lifestyle and degenerative diseases. Use pictures, interesting facts, and words to get the point across. You may choose one disease and one poor habit (for example, heart disease and smoking) and create your poster focused

on that one issue. Put these up in your classroom or in your school to help the students understand the concepts you are learning.

7. **Help Me Understand:** To better understand diabetes, interview someone who suffers from the disease. Ask them what it is like to deal daily with the challenges that come with having diabetes. Share your findings with the class.

MENTAL HEALTH

*Finally, brethren, whatever is true,
whatever is honorable, whatever is right,
whatever is pure, whatever is lovely,
whatever is of good repute, if there is any
excellence and if anything worthy of praise,
let your mind dwell on these things.
Philippians 4:8 (NAS)*

CHAPTER 7   **STRESS AND ANXIETY**

CHAPTER 8   **L.I.F.E. MANAGEMENT**

CHAPTER 9   **MADE IN HIS IMAGE**

7   Stress and Anxiety **181**
   7-1   What Is Mental Health? 181
   7-2   What Is Stress? 183
   7-3   Coping With Stress 188
   7-4   Choose Life 192

8   L.I.F.E. Management **201**
   8-1   Managing your Lifestyle 201
   8-2   Managing your Influences 208
   8-3   Managing your Friendships 212
   8-4   Managing your Earthquakes 215

9   Made In His Image **227**
   9-1   "It's All in My Head" 227
   9-2   "But I am Comfortable Being Miserable" 231
   9-3   "I am Made in Whose Image?" 234

Stress and Anxiety

7-1   WHAT IS MENTAL HEALTH?

7-2   WHAT IS STRESS?

7-3   COPING WITH STRESS

7-4   CHOOSE LIFE

7-1   WHAT IS MENTAL HEALTH?

With every passing year, we obtain a wider comprehension of the ability of the mind (psyche) to produce varied disturbances of the body (soma): hence the term psychosomatic. Invisible emotional tension in the mind can produce striking visible changes in the body, changes that can become serious and fatal.[1]
None of These Diseases

Research shows that the condition of your mental health has a profound effect upon your physical condition. Therefore, your mental health should not be overlooked. According to Webster, your mental state can be defined as: *of or relating to the total emotional and intellectual response of an individual to his environment.*

How can you tell if someone is emotionally and intellectually healthy? Does it mean a person must be smart or happy all the time? Some may say that having good mental health is accepting yourself just the way you are, taking charge of your life, accepting criticism, or being able to express your thoughts and feelings clearly. No matter how you may try to define good mental health, one comprehensive definition is difficult to find. An important key to understanding your mental health is in Webster's definition itself: *how well do you respond to your environment?*

How well do you respond to your environment?

181

Imagine for a moment. You live on a beautiful island. Every need you have is met. You have food, shelter and clothing. Although other people live on the island, you never encounter them and thus, you have no problem getting along with them. There are no challenges too difficult for you and you are totally satisfied with the way you live.

It is quite possible in this unique situation that you have no mental health problems. You feel at peace with yourself and your environment. However, your attitude has never been tested because everything you need or want has been provided. Something is wrong with this picture. Is it realistic to not have any challenges or trials in life? The Bible teaches that a person profits from the trials he/she faces.

...count it all joy when you fall into various trials, knowing that the testing of your faith produces patience. But let patience have its perfect work, that you may be perfect and complete, lacking nothing.
James 1:2–4

Happiness is a by-product of responding to life from God's perspective. It is not determined by your circumstances but by your attitudes or responses to them.

> Happiness is a by-product of responding to life from God's perspective. It is not determined by your circumstances but by your attitudes or responses to them.

7-2 WHAT IS STRESS?

This is Only a Test

I walked into my college Anatomy and Physiology class and seated myself in a chair a few rows from the front of the auditorium. As the other members of the class entered, I noticed that the professor had not yet arrived. This was unusual because he was always there well before the class was to begin. As we all watched the clock and waited, a general uneasiness settled over the classroom. It was a rule on the campus that if the professor did not arrive before ten minutes of class time had passed, the class was canceled and everyone could leave. Our anticipation was broken as the professor entered in the side door and walked to the podium. Instead of beginning the class with a cheerful greeting, he said: "I would like you all to place your books and notes under your chair, today we are going to have a surprise test over the material covered in class last week. You will have an hour to finish the

test and it will be worth 25% of your quarter grade." The class moaned as papers shuffled and books dropped to the floor. As the professor handed out the test my mouth began to get dry, my heart was pounding, and my mind was racing trying to recall the information discussed last week! While several students quickly walked out the back of the auditorium to avoid the test, others were complaining among themselves that this was totally unfair. When I looked over the test the questions were virtually impossible! The minutes passed slowly as the tension rose in the auditorium. Every one had received his tests, but nobody was writing any answers. After a grueling five minutes, the professor said, "This test was a joke, how do you all feel?" The class sighed in relief and the professor began his lecture on stress....

Can you relate to this story? Something happens to you and your body begins to respond with a myriad of emotional and physical changes. **Stress** is your body's response to external or internal changes. A **stressor** is the stimulus that triggers the stress. In the story you have just read, the stressor is the announcement of the surprise test, the stress would be the physical, mental and emotional responses the students experienced as a result of the announcement.

You experience the effects of stress in your life everyday. In order to function, your body needs a certain amount of stress. Stress is natural and it is unavoidable. It is also difficult to measure stress. One medical center defines stress as an "elusive monster, yet not an untameable one." The reason stress is so elusive is because the stress is not directly caused by one external event. Dr. Paul J. Rosch, clinical professor of medicine and psychiatry and president of the American Institute of Stress in Yonkers, New York, says: "Stress has to do with an individual's *perception* of that event. And because stress is different for everyone, there's no stress-reduction regimen that works for everyone."

HOW DO PEOPLE RESPOND TO STRESS?

People respond differently to the same stressor. Refer back to the story of the anatomy class. You did not know how all the students were feeling concerning the test. Maybe some students were glad for the test because they knew the material and felt confident that they would do well. Others may have had a "who cares" attitude and did not worry about it. However, you learned that others actually got up and left to avoid the stress. Instead of facing their stress, they fled.

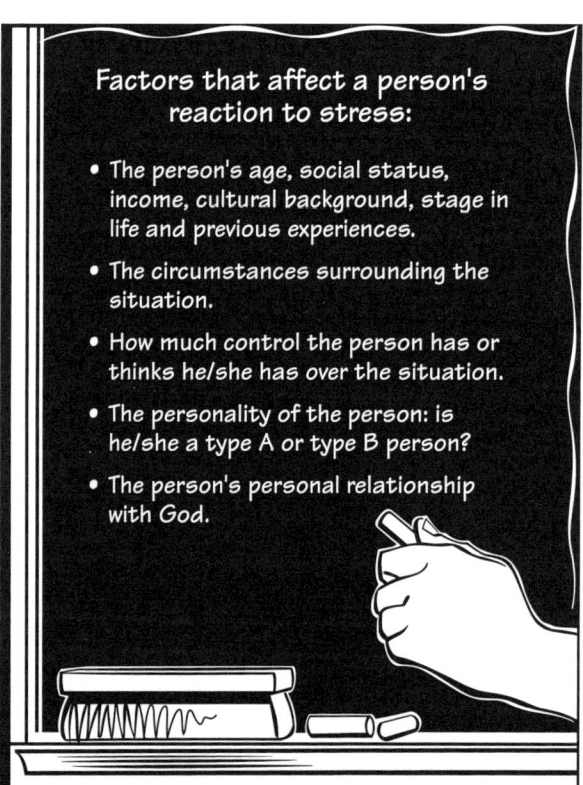

Factors that affect a person's reaction to stress:

- The person's age, social status, income, cultural background, stage in life and previous experiences.
- The circumstances surrounding the situation.
- How much control the person has or thinks he/she has over the situation.
- The personality of the person: is he/she a type A or type B person?
- The person's personal relationship with God.

To Flee, or Not to Flee

When you experience stress, your body prepares itself for a physical reaction. Your brain signals your body to send out certain "stress hormones" such as adrenaline to give you the added strength and energy to either face the stressor or to run from it. This "fight or flight" response is a natural way of dealing with the situation.

Several physical changes occur in your body as a response to a perceived threat. Your heart rate increases as does your blood pressure and rate of breathing. These changes are fine for a short amount of time, but when the stress affects you over a long period of time, your body can begin to break down, resulting in physical and mental fatigue.

Are You a Type A or a Type B Person?

The type of personality you have can greatly influence how you respond to stressful situations. Do you know someone who seems to have an intense drive, seems hurried much of the time and is extremely competitive? Maybe that someone is you. This is the description of a **type A personality.** This personality is often linked to a condition called "hurried sickness." In comparison, a **type B personality** is someone who is calmer, more patient, and less hurried. Many people are a little bit of both personalities and can react either way. It is the type A person who needs to be constantly aware of his/her intensity because of the increased health risks. A type A person can learn to change the habit of always being rushed. They can 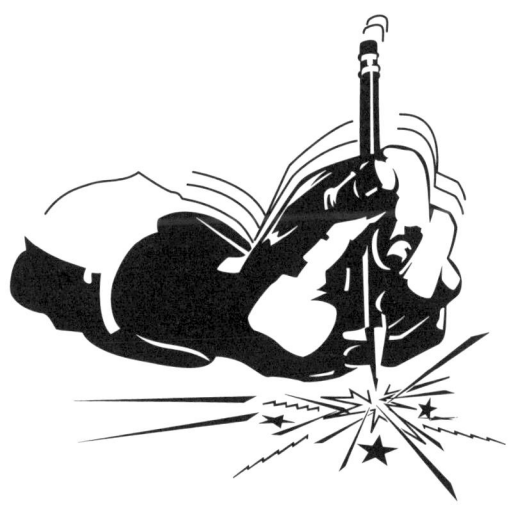 learn to live with unfinished tasks, take time to relax, and cope with daily stress in a more positive way.

RESULTS OF STRESS

Your life has both positive and negative stress. **Positive stress** causes you to be challenged enough to face daily responsibilities and to pursue your life goals. If there were no stressors in your life — for instance, the need to get out of bed to go to school — your natural tendency would be to do "whatever you feel like doing." The stress of deadlines for homework and chores helps you to manage your time and give you a feeling of accomplishment.

Chart: Stress and Performance

There is a time when positive stress turns to negative stress. Consider the chart Stress and Performance. Too little stress can negatively affect your performance whether it be an athletic event or academic test. Without stress to motivate you, your performance will be hindered. On the other hand, too much stress can lead to over stimulation and negative stress. **Distress** occurs when the stress reaches a point when the feelings of depression, confusion, and exhaustion replace the natural excitement and drive to meet a challenge. Instead of motivating you to accomplish a task, distress holds you back. When distress occurs, the results of the stress on your life can be unhealthy and even fatal.

Your total health is affected by the positive or negative stress you experience.

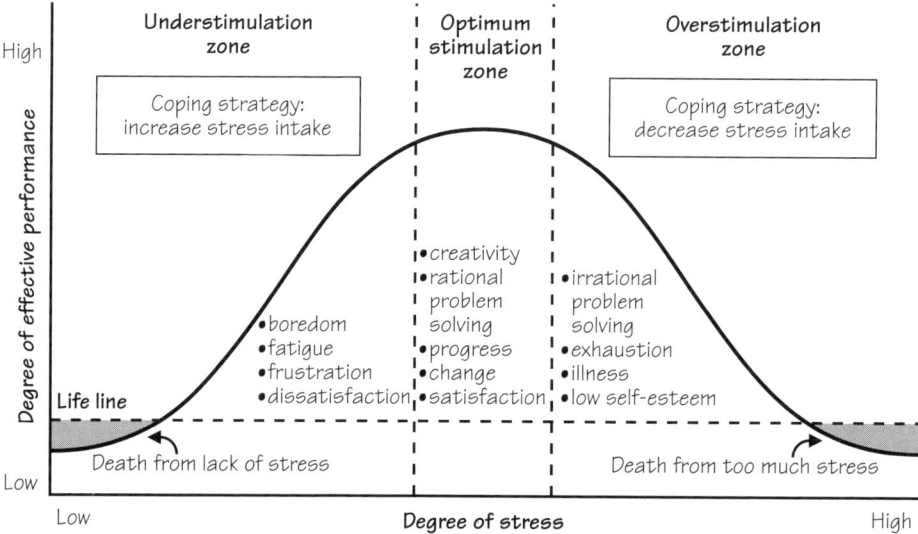

Stress and Performance

after the Forbes Continuum of Stress Chart

Your total health is affected by the positive or negative stress you experience. Stressors can take the form of activities, people, places and objects. Think for a moment about your life and the stressors that affect you. Are you experiencing positive or negative stress? Are the results of stress affecting your physical, mental, social, and spiritual life?

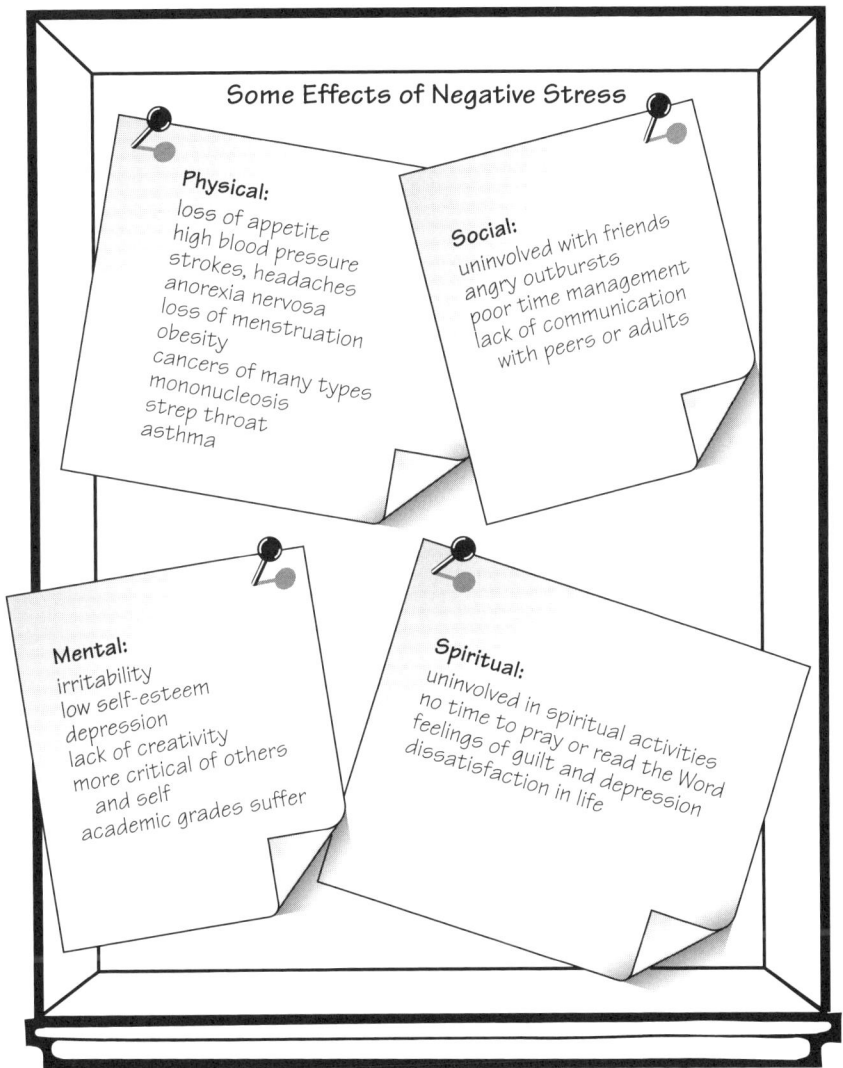

Some Effects of Negative Stress

Physical:
loss of appetite
high blood pressure
strokes, headaches
anorexia nervosa
loss of menstruation
obesity
cancers of many types
mononucleosis
strep throat
asthma

Social:
uninvolved with friends
angry outbursts
poor time management
lack of communication
with peers or adults

Mental:
irritability
low self-esteem
depression
lack of creativity
more critical of others
and self
academic grades suffer

Spiritual:
uninvolved in spiritual activities
no time to pray or read the Word
feelings of guilt and depression
dissatisfaction in life

How you perceive and handle the stress in your life will determine how it will affect you physically, mentally, socially and spiritually.

How you perceive and handle the stress in your life will determine how it will affect you physically, mentally, socially and spiritually. A proper view of stressful situations is in Romans 8:28: *"And we know that God causes all things to work together for good to those who love God, to those who are called according to His purpose"* (NAS).

7-3 COPING WITH STRESS

A man was trapped in his home during a raging storm. The water swirled up around his house until he was forced onto the roof. He was not worried, however, for God had promised him that He would rescue him. Soon a boat came by and the rescuers told him to get into the boat. But the man had faith in God and trusted Him to save him. Even when the water forced him onto the chimney this man's faith held firm, and he turned down a ride in a helicopter. This was certainly a stressful situation, but he had the assurance of God that he would be rescued. When he got to heaven, the angels were surprised to see him; for they had even sent two rescuers just to make sure that he would be saved![2]

> No matter what your religious belief, the Bible is a positive prescription for living a healthy life.

NATURAL WAYS TO COPE

Living a Christian life certainly does not guarantee a life without trials and stress. The illustration of the man in the storm is an example of how God can use several means to help you deal with the stress in your life. It is important to look at situations in a natural as well as spiritual way. In his book *None of these Diseases*, Dr. McMillen states:

Christians must realize that the Bible consistently teaches that what we do does make a difference. We are not God's pawns in some oversized chess game. We are responsible for our actions. Although God empowers and guides our actions, we still must act....Faith in God does not preclude action on our part. On the contrary, faith in God results in action.[3]

One of the most important ways to deal with stress is to prepare yourself for trouble before it actually occurs. This does not mean to be in a constant state of worry or to "borrow trouble" when it is not yours. To prepare yourself is to set your mind and heart on things that produce faith, trust and peace. Dr. McMillen calls the Bible "...God's guidebook for handling stress." No matter what your religious belief, the Bible is a positive prescription for living a healthy life.

Get Moving!

Have you ever heard the phrase "God can't guide a parked car." In other words, you must be moving in some direction to have God guide you in the proper direction. If you sit and wait for God to do something supernatural for you, you might be missing out on what God has for you. Look at your circumstances, what natural tools do you have that can help you reduce the stress in your life?

Seek out creative ideas to help motivate you to pursue your dreams and goals. Seek God for guidance and always be willing to change the direction of your life when God directs you.

Time Management

Dr. James Dobson said that one of his New Year's Resolutions was, "I will not add anything to my schedule until I take out of my schedule something that takes the equivalent amount of time." Time management became one of his natural tools to control the amount of stress that was produced by "overscheduling." Learning time management skills is only one of the ways you can reduce your stress. Ask yourself the following questions:

- Do I have difficulty completing homework assignments on time?
- Do I have trouble getting to school, church or activities on time?
- Do I feel frustrated by the lack of time I have to accomplish the things I need to?

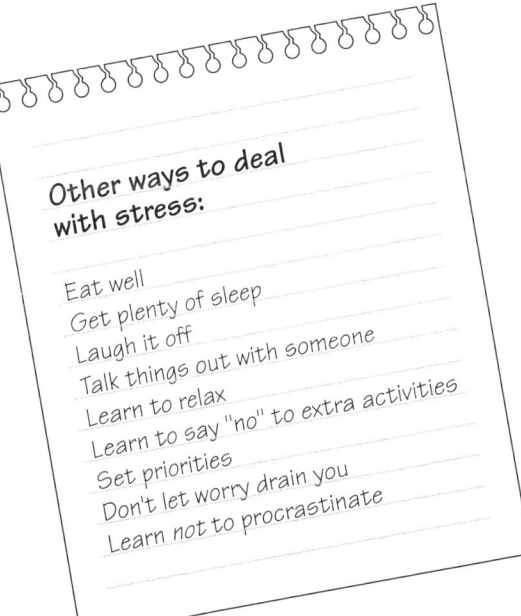

Other ways to deal with stress:

Eat well
Get plenty of sleep
Laugh it off
Talk things out with someone
Learn to relax
Learn to say "no" to extra activities
Set priorities
Don't let worry drain you
Learn not to procrastinate

- Do I feel enslaved by the lack of hours in the day?
- Do I often feel tired and sluggish because I do not get enough sleep?

Exercise

According to fitness experts, some form of exercise three times a week is enough to help you combat the effects of stress in your life. You may want to participate in some form of recreational activity or schedule in three 20-minute walks a week. The benefits of exercise are far more than you may realize; burning up that excess stress will help you physically and mentally cope with life's responsibilities.

Write it Down!

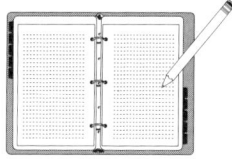

Sue was a first-year college student. She had a difficult time finding a place to be alone to pray. Her roommate always hung around their dorm room and, more than once, walked in on her while she was praying. This made for an uncomfortable living situation, so Sue decided to buy a notebook and write down her thoughts and prayers. After a few weeks of dated entries in her "prayer book," Sue found that this form of praying not only helped her devotional life but her mental life as well. The release of writing down both the good and bad of each day and adding Scriptures that encouraged her brought her a real sense of relief. Her roommate had no idea what filled the pages of her notebooks. Ten years later, Sue still keeps a journal.

ATTITUDE CHECK

Natural coping skills are important for dealing with stress, but sometimes the attitudes of the mind and heart also need adjusting. You can learn to deal with stress by controlling your thinking process. Some may call it "the principle of positive replacement" or having a "positive mental attitude." Whatever you want to call it, you must learn to take responsibility for your thoughts.

Pastor Wendell Smith writes in his book, *Roots of Character:* "when we read the message of the 'Sermon on the Mount' left to us by Jesus, we see that the emphasis He was placing on our lives was not on action but on attitude....our attitude determines our action."[4] Take the time to study Matthew 5:1–12. Can you think of examples in your life where your attitude affects your actions?

Optimist or Pessimist?

Pessimist: one who has the tendency to see what is gloomy, or anticipate the worst possible outcome.

Optimist: one who has the tendency to look on the more favorable side of happenings. To minimize adverse aspects, conditions and possibilities, or anticipate the best possible outcome; to see the worst in complete realism, but still believe in the best; a cheerful or hopeful temperament.

Frosty Westering, an influential professor, coach, author and national speaker states from Norman Vincent Peale's book *The Tough-Minded Optimist:*

"When you have what it takes to deal creatively with the harsh facts of human existence and still keep on believing in good outcomes, you are a tough-minded optimist....A tough-minded optimist is one who doesn't break apart in his/her thoughts whatever the stress and who continues hopefully and cheerfully to expect the good no matter what the apparent situation."

> Our attitude determines our action.
>
> *Pastor Wendell Smith*

THE GREATEST COMMANDMENT

Without love — that thoughtfulness and keen consideration of others — we become much more likely to perish from a variety of diseases of mind and body.[5]
None of these Diseases

Is love an attitude of mind or heart? Is it something that can be learned? How does a person love God and others? Love can be

…you shall love the Lord your God with all your heart, with all your soul, and with all your mind. This is the first and great commandment. And the second is like it: You shall love your neighbor as yourself.

Matthew 22:37-39 (NKJV)

a difficult concept to grasp. It is not some sort of feeling that comes and goes; love is making a decision to put others first. It can be expressed through good deeds towards those in need, kindness to others and an overall attitude of thoughtfulness. *"Let no one seek his own, but each one the other's well-being"* I Corinthians 10:24.

There is a close connection between the attitudes of your mind and your ability to cope with stress. You can experience an overall sense of peace in your life as you develop an attitude of faith and trust. "You will keep him in perfect peace, whose mind is stayed on You, because he trusts in You" (Isaiah 26:3).

7-4 CHOOSE LIFE

Life was given you by God…in a great big box with a wonderful ribbon on it…What we expect in there is joy, peace, contentment, and an abundance of love.

But we also find in that life, pain, despair and loneliness. They are all part of the same box called life. It's not until you dive into it and experience all of it that you will really know life. We learn from pain just as much as we learn from joy.[6]
Leo Buscaglia Author, lecturer

The beautifully wrapped box of life given to you by God is a gift. However, the gift is presented with the responsibility to respond to the challenges of life in a positive manner. Life is filled with situations that cause stress, but you always have a choice. How do you choose to respond to the challenges set before you?

DEPRESSION

If you look at the life of an adult and compare it to the life of a teenager, you will find many of the same conflicts. Adults worry about their appearance and their social acceptance. They experience problems with peer pressure, and have conflicts at work and at home. What may surprise you is that depression is not only a teenage problem, adults also experience depression. The only difference is that most adults are more emotionally mature and better equipped to deal with their feelings than teenagers. Mike Miller, a national speaker and founder for Dare to Live, compares depression to the common cold. It is like the common cold of mental disorders. "It starts with the sniffles; no one dies of the sniffles. But without proper care, a cold (or depression) can progress from the sniffles to a head cold, to a chest cold and even to pneumonia...plenty of people die of pneumonia."

Depression can be described several ways: it is that "sad and blue" feeling; it is an overwhelming feeling of hopelessness and worthlessness; it is a feeling of disappointment that leads to apathy and withdrawal. There are many possible reasons for a person feeling or being depressed. Often it is difficult to identify the specific reasons. Depression is a symptom that God gives you to help show you that something is not right or that something needs to be worked through. Whatever way you describe depression, the disorder can range from occasional to extreme. Remember that experiencing some depression is normal. Depression is also a normal part of the grieving process over any significant loss, such as the death of a loved one.

> Depression is like the common cold of mental disorders.
>
> *Mike Miller*

Definitions to Consider:

neurosis: a mild disorder that causes distress but does not interfere with a person's everyday activities.

psychosis: a severe mental disorder that prevents a person from functioning.

depression: a mental state characterized by sadness, anxiety, fatigue, underactivity, and reduced ability to relate to others.

manic-depressive illness: a mental disorder in which the sufferer alternates between extreme sadness and extreme joy.

phobia: an intense fear of an object or situation that the person knows is not dangerous.

schizophrenia: a severe form of psychosis in which the victim may have delusions, hallucinations, extreme mood changes, and paranoia.

personality disorder: a person who has trouble getting along with others or getting along in certain situations.

Causes and Signs of Depression

Many things can trigger the feeling of depression. Some people are more likely to be bothered by stress and life events than other people, but everyone has limits. Natural events in life can cause depression. For example, frustration at work or school, arguments with friends or family members, your family moving, a loss of a job, and financial problems. For most people the feeling of depression will lift after a short period of time. If you are bothered by extreme depression, you need to deal with the cause of the depression and get help from someone you can trust.

Furthermore, severe depression can result from prolonged feelings of guilt, bitterness, unresolved anger or unresolved grief. You may know someone who is always frustrated because they do not live up to the expectations of others. It is also common to find teenagers and adults who struggle with the pressure to succeed. Whatever the cause, depression can become serious and lead to thoughts of suicide.

Signs of depression:
- inability to sleep.
- decrease in appetite.
- feeling bored and unmotivated.
- losing interest in activities of life.
- inability to concentrate.
- feeling of fatigue.

SUICIDE

An estimated one million people a year in the United States alone try to take their own lives. Suicide is the second leading cause of death among adolescents (the first is accidents) with fatalities of more that 6,000 a year. Why do so many young people try to commit suicide? The answer varies with the each individual. However, an overwhelming feeling of worthlessness and hopelessness is an underlying factor. In one study, when those who had survived a suicide attempt were asked "why they tried to commit suicide," the majority answered "because nobody cares."

Very few people who attempt suicide really want to die. The overwhelming majority of those who are lucky enough to be helped... never try suicide again.[7]
Dr. Mary Griffin, Carol Feisenthal

Who Can Help Me?

People who struggle with thoughts of suicide feel that there are no solutions to their problems and that nobody cares enough to help. Even when you are confronted with a hopeless situation, you must realize that life is meaningful and people do care about you. No matter what the situation, it is important to know when and where to go for help. A good place to start is with your parents. Although you may not see it this way, the family is like a built-in support system.

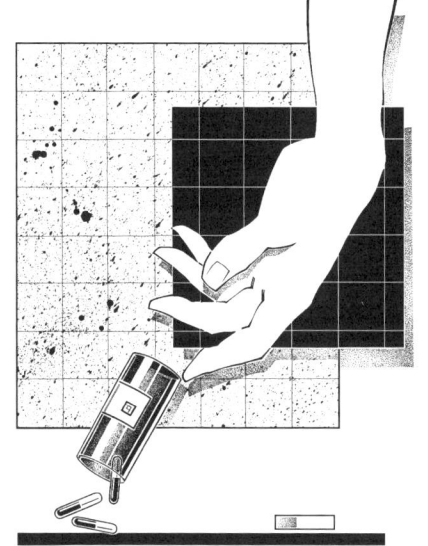

If you have an on-going relationship with a teacher, counselor, or pastor, they can help by listening and talking out your feelings with you. Sometimes you may feel that your friends are your best source of comfort and guidance. Before you expose your personal troubles to your peers, think twice. Friends mean well and often, just by talking out your problems, can make you feel better. However, your peers are going through similar situations and may not have the best advice for you. Although they may be your "friend," sometimes the personal information you share with them can "get around" and be misunderstood by others. If one of your friends came to you seeking help, how might you handle the situation? Remember one thing: never promise you will not tell anyone. If the life of one of your friends was in danger, wouldn't you want to prevent a tragedy? Offer to go with them to talk to someone who might be better able to help them.

Careers in Mental Health

psychiatrist: a physician who specializes in the treatment of mental and emotional disorders.

psychologist: a person who has a Ph.D. in psychology and who is trained to study behavior and give counseling therapy.

Don't delude yourself; if a person talks suicide, you've got to take it seriously.

Thomas P. Rossi, brother of a suicide victim

10 Warning Signs of Suicide:

1. Sudden change in behavior.

2. Signs of depression, such as apathy, crying, insomnia, loss of appetite.

3. Change of performance in school (usually poor performance).

4. Loss of interest in friends (social isolation).

5. Giving away of personal items and possessions.

6. Preoccupation with death, dying or suicide.

7. Offhand remarks such as "You may not be seeing me around much anymore," or "if anything should happen to me."

8. Loss of self-esteem, constant feelings of worthlessness, or self-hatred.

9. Excessive risk-taking.

10. Increased drug/alcohol use.

Your Faith Can Make the Difference

An ongoing personal relationship with the Lord can make the difference in your perception of your circumstances. God totally understands your feelings and wants you to see your life as He does...meaningful. Your life has purpose and God is with you in your deepest trials.

Brethren, I do not count myself to have apprehended; but one thing I do, forgetting those things which are behind and reaching forward to those things which are ahead, I press toward the goal for the prize of the upward call of God in Christ Jesus.
Philippians 3:13,14

...I will strengthen you, yes, I will help you...you were precious in My sight, you have been honored, And I have loved you....
Isaiah 41:10, 43:4

The following letter was given by Frosty Westering, the football coach at Pacific Lutheran University. As you read it, consider your place in God's kingdom — on His team.

"WHO MAKXS OUR FOOTBALL TXAM A SUCCXSS?"

Xvxn though my typxwritxr is an old modxl, it works quitx wxll xcxpt for onx kxy. I havx wishxd many timxs that it workxd pxrfxtly. It is trux that thxrx arx 41 othxr kxys that do function wxll, but just onx not working makxs a big diffxrxncx. Somxtimxs it sxxms to mx that our football txam is somxtimxs likx my old typxwritxr — not all of our txam mxmbxrs arx working. You may say to yoursxlf, "wxll, I am only onx pxrson, I won't makx or brxak a txam." But, you do makx a diffxrxncx, bxcausx a txam to bx xffxctivx nxxds activx participation of xvxry singlx individual and your xfforts arx nxxdxd. Rxmxmbxr my old typxwritxr and rxalizx that I can makx a kxy contribution to our txam.

I am only onx,
But I am onx,
I can't do xvxrything,
But I can do somxthing
And that which I can do
I ought to do,
And that which I ought to do
By God's Gracx I shall do.
Sincxrxly…Frosty

The above poem has been adapted by Frosty Westering

CHAPTER REVIEW

DEFINE

Stress

Stressor

Type A personality

Type B personality

Positive stress

Distress

Pessimist

Optimist

Depression

EXPLAIN

1. Explain what it means to be mentally healthy.
2. Explain why it is important to have some stress in your life.
3. Explain the meaning of the "fight or flight" response.
4. Explain how your personality can affect your response to stress.
5. Explain how stress can be positive.
6. Explain the meaning of the quote: *"Faith in God does not preclude action on our part. On the contrary, faith in God results in action."*
7. Explain why depression is referred to as the "common cold of mental disorders."
8. Explain why teenagers are greatly affected by depression and thoughts of suicide.
9. Explain the difference between a stressor and stress.

DISCUSS

1. Discuss the scripture in James 1:2–4. Why are you to "count it joy" when you encounter trials? How might this passage be an encouragement for you?
2. Discuss why one person's negative stress might be another person's positive stress.
3. Discuss ways to cope with negative stress.
4. Discuss why it is important to have a good attitude when dealing with stress. Include examples of the ways your attitude affects your actions.
5. Imagine you have a friend who says he is contemplating suicide. Discuss the ways you might deal with the situation.
6. Discuss ways that your faith in God can make the difference in handling stress and depression.

7. Discuss what aspects of school are the most stressful. Why? How can you cope?

8. Discuss what aspects of home life are the most stressful. Why? How can you cope?

SUGGESTED ACTIVITIES

1. **Stress Inventory:** Make a list of the ways you respond to stress. What happens to you personally? What is going on inside of you (physically and emotionally)? What are your warning signals that stress is becoming distress?

2. **Key Concepts:** Outline the chapter and make a study guide for yourself. You may work alone or in a group.

3. **Just Relax!** Do a report on the different relaxation techniques to handle stress. Present it to the class and have them try the various techniques in class (deep breathing and visualization, for example).

4. **Would Someone Please Help Me?** Create a bulletin board in your classroom. (This may be done by a group or by one person.) The board should include ways to cope with stress and depression. Include names of people (such as your youth pastor) where teens can go for help. You may want to include encouraging scriptures and quotations. Give a name to the bulletin board. Use your creativity to help your teenage friends.

5. **Interview:** Make a list of questions for other teens by asking them what causes them the most stress and ways they cope with the stress. You may want to keep the names of those interviewed annonymous if you are going to share this with the class.

6. **Keep the Faith!** Do a Bible study on the word faith. You may do it in a group in the classroom or write it yourself and share it with the class as if you were giving a sermon.

L.I.F.E. Management

8-1 LIFESTYLE
8-2 INFLUENCES
8-3 FRIENDSHIPS
8-4 EARTHQUAKES

8-1 MANAGING YOUR LIFESTYLE

Lifestyle: *An individual's whole way of living.*

MAKING THE GRADE

Although you have some control over your lifestyle now, the choices you are making as a teenager will greatly affect the lifestyle you will have as an adult. When the word "lifestyle" is discussed, it is often associated with a person's financial stability. However, your lifestyle is not only measured by how you may live financially, but more importantly, it is measured by your **conduct, character,** and **convictions**. To reach your full potential and become the best possible person you can be, you must learn to manage your lifestyle.

The choices you are making as a teenager will greatly affect the lifestyle you will have as an adult.

CONDUCT

What does self-discipline mean to you? Do you know someone whom you feel has a great amount of self-discipline? Look closely at the meaning of self-discipline in Webster's Dictionary:

self: having to do with the *entire* person of an individual: belonging to oneself;

discipline: orderly or prescribed conduct or pattern of behavior;

self-discipline: correction or regulation of oneself for the sake of improvement.

To properly manage your life, you need to develop self-discipline. It is not something you learn overnight or in a class at school. It is a character trait that requires diligence and training over a period of a lifetime. The Bible teaches that the body and the mind need to be self-disciplined.

For if you live according to the flesh you will die; but if by the Spirit you put to death the deeds of the body, you will live.
Romans 8:13

And do not be conformed to this world, but be transformed by the renewing of your mind, that you may prove what is that good and acceptable and perfect will of God.
Romans 12:2

Your **conduct** is a standard of personal behavior. It is what people see revealed in your actions and your attitudes. There is a strong connection between your thoughts and your actions. It has been said, *"Sow a thought, you reap an action; sow an action, you reap a habit: sow a habit, you reap a character: sow a character, you reap a destiny."*

The thought patterns in your life can either result in a negative or a positive lifestyle.

Self-control of your mind and your body requires you to take action. You must *put off* the old self which the Bible calls corrupt and you must *put on* the new self created in the likeness of God (Ephesians 4:22–24). You can look at this biblical principle another

Thoughts
↓
Actions
↓
Habits
↓
Lifestyle

way. Use the acronym *G.I.G.O. — Garbage In–Garbage Out* or *Good In–Good out.* What goes into your mind will eventually be revealed in your actions. Your mind is like a blank tape that records everything you see, hear, and imagine. This tape does not erase the images you allow to be recorded: you must record *over* those images with stronger, more powerful impressions. Take the advice of Jerry White, the author of *Honesty, Morality, and Conscience*:

Keep your mind active with learning new things, as well as personal and vocational development. When your mind goes into neutral, the thought life begins to crumble and questionable amusements begin to take over. Your mind is never empty. The only question is what fills it.[1]

You make choices daily that involve taking control over your thoughts and your actions. For example, when you woke up this morning did you feel like getting out of bed? Did you feel like being kind to your family? When you arrived at school, did you like taking that test? If you would have given in to your thoughts and feelings, you probably would not have chosen to behave the way you did. Can you think of other examples where your control or lack of control over your thoughts positively or negatively affected your actions? Remember that no matter the circumstances in your life, there is always a choice to respond positively or negatively. S.I. McMillen, M.D. puts it this way in his book, *None of These Diseases*:

Can a person freely choose to do something that he does not feel like doing? Yes, he can. But to do so he must consider some code or ethic to be more important than his own feelings. Our culture says, "If it feels good, do it." But this is no answer, for it enslaves us to our emotions.[2]

Your thoughts and actions will form habits that sooner or later become a lifestyle for you. It will either be a lifestyle full of positive actions or one of negative consequences. Remember — in the

> Your mind is never empty. The only question is what fills it.
>
> Jerry White

race of life, you want to run the race to win the prize (Philippians 3:13–14).

*Winners are motivated by the desire for pleasing results — losers are influenced by the desire for pleasing methods and are satisfied with the results of doing the things they like to do...The key is that **winners have strong purpose** — strong enough to make them form the habit of doing things they don't like to do in order to accomplish the purpose they want to accomplish.*
Earl Nightengale

Take time right now and do a self inventory: Do you have the self-discipline to think and act in a way that will bring about self improvement and a positive lifestyle? What is your motivation or purpose in life? Does the G.I.G.O. principle make a difference in your life?

CHARACTER

How people play the game shows some of their character; how they win it or lose it shows it all.

A much deeper yet obvious part of who you are is your character. If your thoughts and conduct have much to do with forming your lifestyle, then where does character come in? According to Webster's Dictionary, character is: *moral excellence and firmness.* **Character**, therefore, would be the underlying qualities that are revealed in your actions and attitudes that set you apart. Just like your conduct, your character can be seen as either negative or positive. Do you know someone who shows moral excellence or firmness?

God wants you to develop the character of Christ. The Bible tells us of those who had Christ-like character. Consider Job. In all of his trials, he never gave up. Or Paul. He suffered more than many could endure, yet he showed Christ-like character through it all. How do you expect to develop character? It is only through God's help that you can overcome the pressures of the world and be Christ-like. This is the grace of God at work in you, helping you, guiding you and giving you the desire and ability to become like Christ.

A person does not have to act "religious" to show character. As a matter of fact, it is true selflessness, a humble spirit, that is the foundation of character. There is no "acting" involved in true character. Consider the following chart taken from *The Roots of Character* by Wendell Smith.[3]

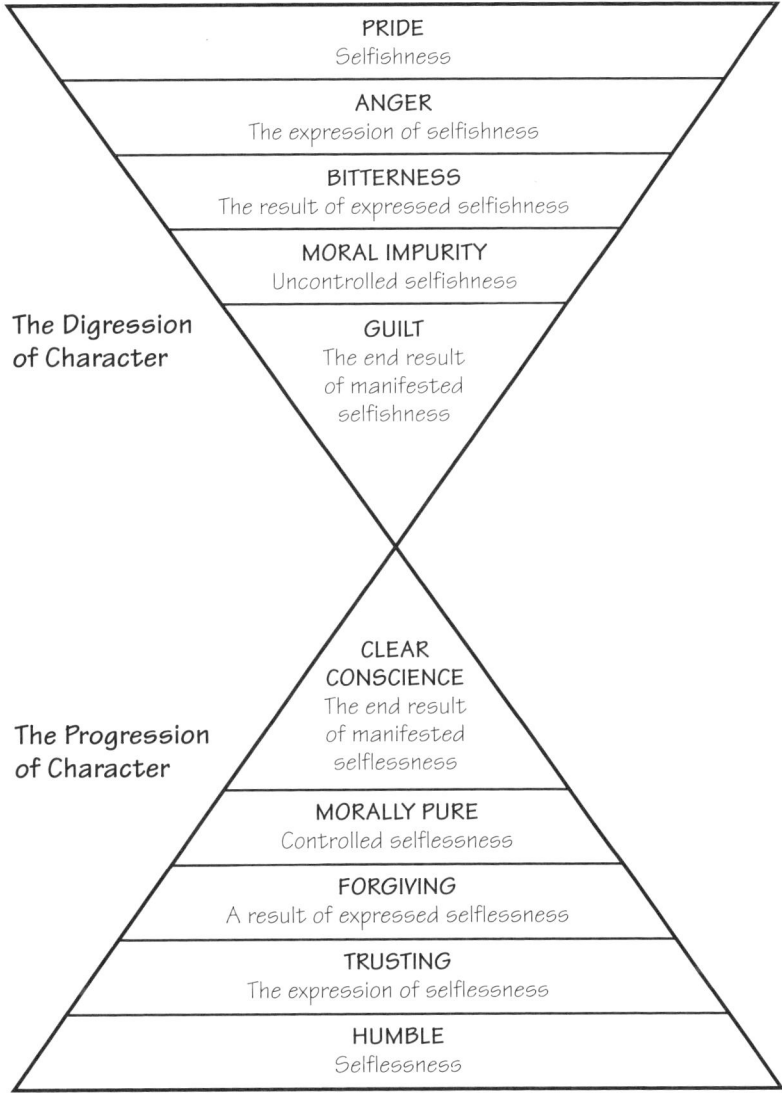

The Digression of Character

PRIDE
Selfishness

ANGER
The expression of selfishness

BITTERNESS
The result of expressed selfishness

MORAL IMPURITY
Uncontrolled selfishness

GUILT
The end result of manifested selfishness

The Progression of Character

CLEAR CONSCIENCE
The end result of manifested selflessness

MORALLY PURE
Controlled selflessness

FORGIVING
A result of expressed selflessness

TRUSTING
The expression of selflessness

HUMBLE
Selflessness

God wants you to develop the character of Christ.

Notice from the chart the progression of character and the qualities that develop. A clear conscience is the end result of manifested *selflessness* where the end result of manifested *selfishness* is guilt. If you have ever lived with the feeling of guilt, you know it is a very powerful and heavy burden. It is one that pulls you down in every area of your life. On the other hand, living with a clear conscience allows you to experience the joy of living right before God and others. It is a powerful motivator and source of strength even in the midst of the pressures of the world.

SOMETHING TO **THINK** ABOUT

Having **character** is much like having **class**. Class is having a standard of high quality that sets you apart from the crowd.
"If you have class, you don't need much of anything else. If you don't have it, no matter what else you have, it doesn't make much difference."[4]
Howard E. Ferguson

CONVICTIONS

Living By the Book

People have all kinds of convictions or strong beliefs. Some people have a conviction about saving the rain forests or being vegetarians. Although these convictions affect an individual's lifestyle, they are not the type of examples that are the basis for biblical convictions. **Biblical convictions** are like the framework that holds your Christian walk together. Convictions give structure and guidance to your lifestyle.

A **conviction** is a personal belief upon which certain actions are based. It is the motivation or reason behind the action. Also, a conviction must have a base — convictions do not emerge fully formed....Developing convictions is not an event but a process. It is a step-by-step unfolding — a developing process that leads to a conclusion....Convictions should be personal...and also biblical.[5]
Jerry White

Why Develop Convictions?

Personal convictions form the basis for your actions. In turn, your actions eventually become habits. Those habits, either good or bad, influence your lifestyle. It is important to develop strong personal, biblical convictions that will help you lead a lifestyle that is pleasing to God.

One key to managing your lifestyle is overcoming temptation. Set standards for yourself *before* you face difficult situations. This will give you the wisdom and strength to make the right choice. For example: it is wise for you to develop a conviction about the area of dating and sexual involvement *before* you are involved in a compromising relationship. Personal convictions concerning sex, drugs and alchohol must be strong personal beliefs that will affect your behavior. These convictions and others can form a hedge of protection around you that will enable you to walk securely when others are struggling with temptation.

Having strong convictions may also cause you to "stand out of the crowd." Do you have the courage to be different? The following is a list of areas that you will have to deal with in your life. Do you have a personal conviction about each area? Can you think of other areas where strong convictions are important?

- lying
- cheating
- stealing
- sexual morality
- honesty
- obeying authority
- personal devotional time
- television viewing
- reading material
- video/movie choices

How to Develop Convictions

Personal study of the Bible and prayer, as well as input from godly authority, will help you develop convictions that will have a positive and lasting effect on your life. Consider the following "formula" for many of the personal convictions you develop.

1. Does the Bible say it is wrong? (John 14:21; 1 Samuel 15:22)
2. Is it helpful to me physically, mentally, and spiritually? (I Corinthians 6:12; Philippians 4:8)

3. Does it enslave me and bring me under its power? (I Corinthians 6:12)
4. Does it hurt others or cause others to stumble? (I Corinthians 8:13; Hebrews 10:24; 1 Corinthians 8:9)
5. Does it glorify God? (1 Corinthians 10:31; Philippians 1:20)

Developing convictions is only part of the picture. The question is, "are you willing to live by these convictions?" You will be bombarded in life by temptations that will test the strength of your convictions. You must have an answer for the situation *before* it catches you in a place of indecision.

8-2   MANAGING YOUR INFLUENCES

Pressure: *a constraining or compelling force or influence.*
Random House Dictionary

PRESSURES FROM THE INSIDE AND OUT

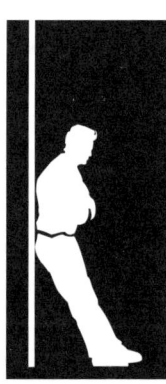

The pressures that you face daily can result from changes going on inside of your body and from those changes occuring outside your body. These pressures can be positive or negative. The key is learning to recognize and resist negative pressure while allowing positive pressure to influence you for good. Positive pressure can come from several sources. Healthy Christian friendships as well as influential adults can encourage you to live righteously. Having daily Bible reading with Scripture memorization will also help you handle the negative pressures you face.

> Developing convictions is only part of the picture. The question is, "are you willing to live by these convictions?"

I Think I'm Going Crazy!

Through your life you will feel pressure from the inside. In other words, you will feel pressure from your changing physical body that will cause you to think that something strange is happening to you. These physical changes may begin as early as nine or ten or as late as seventeen. The physical changes that begin to occur also cause you to have thoughts about the opposite sex that you may not have had before. The hormones causing your body to change rapidly are also responsible for feelings of frustration at home or school, as well as feelings of fear, inadequacy and depression. This is a good time for you to talk to someone about the way you are feeling. These changes are normal and you can make it through without compromising your values. Always keep in mind that no matter how you are feeling, the choices you make today will affect your life tomorrow.

But Everybody's Doing It!

Pressures from the outside come in many forms, some of which are easier to recognize and resist than others. Jerry White author of *Honesty, Morality and Conscience*, makes this statement:

> The influence of people on people is a powerful force, affecting everyone. Only the power of God and the innate drive for physical survival outrank it. A reasoning mind can become powerless in the face of this pressure. Even the most committed individualist conforms in some ways to the lifestyle of others.[6]

The pressure from your peers is one of the hardest influences you may face.

Other sources of outside pressure come from your peers, family, entertainment, advertisements, and society in general. The pressure from your peers, those who are your age and are similar to you in many ways, is one of the hardest influences you may face. Unfortunately this peer pressure does not stop in adulthood. There are several ways you can deal with negative peer pressure:

When you find
yourself in a
situation where
the pressure is
too great,
don't hang
around to find
out if you are
strong enough,
just get out.

2 Timothy 2:22

STOP AND THINK!

- **Develop and stand by your convictions:** *Stop and Think!* Make strong convictions before you are confronted with a decision. Ask yourself: "am I being asked to do something that will make me compromise my values and convictions?"

- **Avoid compromising situations:** *Stop and Think!* Make good decisions before you are faced with the situation. Ask yourself: "am I being asked to go somewhere or see something that I know I shouldn't?

- **Don't give in — not even once!** *Stop and Think!* Make a good decision concerning the actions you are about to take. Ask yourself: "am I going to do something that could hurt my body, mind or spiritual life now and later?" After you try something once, you are more likely to give in when faced with the same temptation.

- **Choose your friends wisely:** *Stop and Think!* Make a good decision concerning the friends you associate with. Ask yourself: "am I spending time with people who have a positive or negative influence on my life?"

- **Be a positive influence:** *Stop and Think!* Make a wise decision about your own personal influence on others. Ask yourself: "am I a positive or negative influence on my peers ?" If you are trying to be a positive influence, you are less likely to be negatively influenced by others.

- **Speak up:** *Stop and Think!* Make a good decision concerning the good of others. Ask yourself: "do I need to confront this person or this issue to help him avoid a negative situation?" Someone in the group may be just waiting for someone else to stand up for what is right.

- **Run: Don't** *Stop and Think!* When you find yourself in a situation where the pressure is too great, don't hang around to find out if you are strong enough, just get out (2 Timothy 2:22).

The standards of society are morally loose and ethically unstable. They influence people of all ages. It is up to you to hold to a higher standard (Philippians 3:16). Be aware that negative influences can enter your life by several means, television and the media being two of the strongest avenues. Money and the desire for material things can also affect your attitudes and actions. Why are people so easily influenced by what others have? And why are people so easily influenced by what others think of them? The whole issue can be summed up in the desire to conform, to be like others.

CONFORMITY

Conform: to adapt oneself to prevailing standards or customs: to be or become similar in form or character.
Webster's and Random House Dictionary

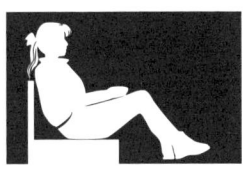 You may feel that you are not influenced to conform, but the pressure to be like everyone else can silently affect many areas of your life. Your thinking, speech, behavior and eventually your lifestyle are all affected by conformity.

The danger of conformity is that it can keep you from doing what is right. Its power is so strong that sometimes you may find yourself caught up in an activity that you never thought you would do. The scriptures warn against conforming to the world. *"And do not be conformed to this world, but be transformed by the renewing of your mind, that you may prove what the will of God is, that which is good and acceptable and perfect"* (Romans 12:2 NAS).

You have learned that the power of your mind has much to do with your attitudes and your actions. The world's influence on your mind may be very subtle and the fear of being different is a very strong emotion. The scriptures address the importance of having the mind of Christ and meditating on positive things.

> There are two kinds of failures: the man/woman who will do nothing he/she is told, and the man/woman who will do nothing else.
> Perle Thompson

"*...whatever things are true, whatever things are noble, whatever things are just, whatever things are pure, whatever things are lovely, whatever things are of good report, if there is any virtue and if there is anything praiseworthy — meditate on these things*" (Philippians 4:8). Not all conformity is negative. The Bible encourages conformity to the image of Christ (Romans 8:29 and Philippians 3:10). In other words, become as much like Christ as possible, having His influence fill each area of your life.

When the pressure to conform is so strong, how can you overcome the desire to be like everyone else? Dr. James Dobson puts it this way:

...God does not want us to follow the whims of the world around us. He expects us to say to ourselves, "I am going to control my behavior, my mind, my body, and my life....when it comes to being moral and obeying God and learning in school and keeping my body clean and healthy, then I won't let anybody tell me what to do. If they must laugh at me, then let them laugh. The joke won't be funny for very long. I'm not going to let *anything* keep me from living a Christian life. In other words, I will not conform!"[7]

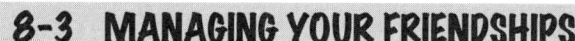

8-3 MANAGING YOUR FRIENDSHIPS

THE POWER OF FRIENDSHIPS

One of the most difficult areas of life to manage is friendships. People may try to influence your choice of friends because of the strong role friends have in your life. "*Do not be deceived: Evil company corrupts good habits*" (I Corinthians 15:33).

It is important to understand that friendships are formed on several levels, each affecting your life in a different way. You may know many people who are only *acquaintances*. You know them by name but do not spend much time with them. An example of this level of friendship may include students at your school whom you know but with whom you do not hang around. You may also find yourself having *casual* friendships. You talk to them more often but not on a personal level. An example of this level of friendship may be students in your class.

You will have fewer friends at the next level of friendship. You feel a common bond with these friends and may share interests and goals. An example of this level may be *close* friends on your sports team or close friends from your class or youth group. The last level of friendship is where you experience a mutual open flow of sharing. At this *intimate* level you may have only a handful of friends. An example of this level is a best friend or two whom you trust. It is not common to have many friends at the closest level of friendship because of the time involved. Whether a friendship moves up to a more intimate level depends on the persons involved. However, there is divine purpose in having friendships at each level. Think of the friends you have right now. Do they fit into a general level of friendship?

Four: Intimate Level

Three: Close

Two: Casual

One: Acquaintance

A Winning Combination: Love for God and Love for Others

A new commandment I give to you, that you love one another; as I have loved you, that you also love one another.
John 13:34

Friendships can bring you both happiness and heartache. This is the risk you take when you make friends. The Bible says that if you want a friend, you must show yourself friendly (Proverbs 18:24). Good, quality friendships take time and energy to develop. The winning combination for a good friendship is a love for God, and a healthy love for each other. This is not a "mushy gushy" type of love, but a love that looks out for the best interest of the other person.

Friendships change just as your life changes. Have you ever had a best friend one month and a different best friend the next month? It is a good idea to pace your friendships, that is, don't rush in. Let the relationship develop over a period of time to ensure trust. Although the level changes as you grow and change, the friendships you have throughout your life serve a purpose. Can you remember friends you had last year or several years ago, and today they are not as close a friend to you anymore? This doesn't mean that it was not a good relationship when you were friends. People change and so do friendships. This is a healthy part of relationships.

As you grow older you may notice that your friendships take on more meaning to you. Your circle of friends may become smaller and more intimate. It is common to have high school friendships, college friendships and adult friendships. Each season of your life may bring you a different group of friends, but each season of your life helps you learn and grow. Ask yourself the following questions as you think about the friends you have now:

- Is this friend a positive influence on my Christian walk?
- Is this friend loyal? Does he/she stick by me?
- Is this friend reliable? Can I count on him/her?
- Is this friend trustworthy? Can I trust him/her with the things I share?
- Is this friend sympathetic and caring? Does he/she listen to my problems and care about my well-being?

Danger Zones

It is important to recognize danger zones in your relationships. That is, be aware when the influence of the friendship is turning negative. Consider the following when evaluating your friendships:

- Is this friendship causing me to compromise my values and do things I would not do normally?
- Is this friendship demanding too much of my time?
- Is this friendship causing me to respond negatively to my parents or other significant authority?
- Is this friendship focusing on the negatives of others (gossip) and becoming criti-

Is this friend a positive influence on my Christian walk?

cal of other people?

- Is this friendship causing me to like myself more or like myself less?
- Is this friendship pleasing to God?

Remember, good friendships go both ways. It is important to have good friendships but it is just as important to be a good friend to others. Managing the friendships in your life can seem like a full time job, but by keeping your focus on God and others rather than on yourself, you will enjoy the benefits of healthy friendships.

8-4 MANAGING YOUR EARTHQUAKES

Earthquakes occur naturally and result in a shaking or trembling of the earth. Some earthquakes are devastating causing major damage, while others are no more than a tremble. You will experience your own shaking and trembling as you begin to face the natural changes that occur in life. It is how you handle these "earthquakes" that will determine the ultimate result.

EMOTIONAL EARTHQUAKES

Young people feel more strongly about everything, especially during adolescence…Little things that won't bother you later in life will bug you as a teenager. Your fears will be more frightening, your pleasures will be more exciting, your irritations will be more distressing, and your frustrations will be more intolerable. Every experience will appear king-sized…[8]
Dr. James Dobson

Many of the changes that you will experience during adolescence are closely related to your emotions. Emotions are those often unpredictable feelings that can cause you to say or do things that you may regret later. Everyone experiences the roller-coaster ride of emotions. However, it seems that a teenager's feelings

Everyone experiences the roller-coaster ride of emotions.

are much stronger. The word that best describes the strength of these emotions is...***intense!*** People have feelings about all kinds of things, but the most common emotions dealt with during adolescence have to do with your feelings about God, your parents/family, friends and the feelings you have about yourself.

Your Feelings about God

Depending upon your background and involvement in religious activities, you may be experiencing confusion concerning your own personal faith in God. This is a normal emotion during these years, but it is a good idea not to ignore it. Seek the advice of someone you trust. More importantly, seek the One who can make your faith real and powerful for you personally. Prayer and meditating on the Word of God can help you deal with the "spiritual earthquakes" you are facing and the decisions that seem so difficult right now.

Your Feelings about Your Parents and Family

Your family usually knows you the best and loves you the most.

Emotions can run high in the home as you begin to feel the need for more independence. It may be hard to communicate your feelings to your parents concerning the issues and pressures you are facing. Your family usually knows you the best and loves you the most. Try not to give in to the feeling of wanting to be alone all the time. Sometimes the best solution for this "generation gap" is to get out and do something fun with your family. Frustrations at home can be worked out and you will find that the intensity of this "family earthquake" does not last.

Your Feelings about Your Friends

You have already learned that friendships can be hard at times, but the emotions that come with changing friendships can be very difficult to handle. In the midst of your friendships remember there is One who wants to be your best friend for life. Christ is the most trusted and powerful friend you will ever have.

The most intense emotions that you will probably feel are those emotions directed toward the opposite sex. These are very real, powerful, exciting, and sometimes scary feelings. It is important that you learn how to manage these feelings. Be especially careful concerning these types of relationships. The most important thing to remember is to keep a tight handle on your emotions. In other words...keep control of this "relationship earthquake."

Your Feelings about Yourself

Your own self esteem has much to do with how you handle your changing emotions and the "earthquakes" in your life. You are growing up, becoming a man or woman in a world full of confusing messages. Your identity as a person is being molded by the many influences in your life. Someday soon you will be on your own, making decisions about your life you never thought you would have to face. Maturity and confidence does not happen overnight and the road to independence will be filled with its own shaking and trembling. Remember God created you in His image. Do not allow negative thoughts to cause a "self-esteem earthquake."

THE "NEVER ENOUGH TIME" EARTHQUAKES

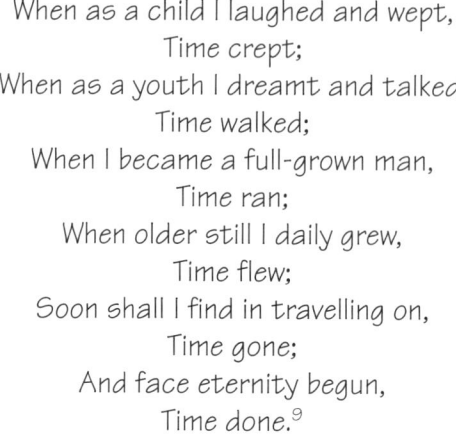

When as a child I laughed and wept,
Time crept;
When as a youth I dreamt and talked,
Time walked;
When I became a full-grown man,
Time ran;
When older still I daily grew,
Time flew;
Soon shall I find in travelling on,
Time gone;
And face eternity begun,
Time done.[9]

Today, at this very moment, you may be feeling totally frustrated with the lack of time you have. Things may seem like they can't get any worse, and they won't get any better. Your feelings and your circumstances will not change unless you begin to take control of your life. That is, speak positively to yourself and take action.

The best advice a young college student received from a professor during a review before her graduation was, "Life is like a wave, and it is ready to crash in over you. Life is controlling you, you are not controlling your life." Can you think of areas in your life that seem out of control? How about your eating and sleeping habits, or the pressure of homework and other responsibilities? Are you feeling emotionally and physically "burned out"? Are you involved in extracurricular activities that seem to take up much of your time and energy? One of the most difficult areas to control in life is *time*. Take control of the time you have and you can begin to take control of your life.

Avoiding Personal Earthquakes: Time Management and Goal Setting

Time is a unique resource given to each person — a resource waiting to be used wisely and productively. Time does not stand still nor does it "fly." Time is a constant, ongoing opportunity for you. Although you may feel time is what you need the most and have the least of, it is the same every day, every week and every year.

So teach us to number our days, that we may gain a heart of wisdom.
Psalm 90:12

See then that you walk circumspectly, not as fools but as wise,
redeeming the time, because the days evil.
Ephesians 5:15,16

Take a personal inventory evaluating your use of time. Can you account for every hour or minute of your day? Although you may have fixed responsibilities in each day, such as school, chores, job etc., it is the "in-between" minutes and hours that are often wasted. Make a copy of the Fixed Commitments Chart (on the following page). Place your fixed commitments in your personal copy. By keeping accurate record of the use of your free time, you can find the time slots that you often waste.

Responsible use of your time takes discipline and good planning. It has been said, "If you fail to plan, then you plan to fail." This is where goal setting is important. Setting a goal for yourself is like setting a course for the direction of your life. If done properly and consistently, goals can carry you from one success to another. The important lesson to learn is that you must set goals with God in the control tower. Consider the following principles to help make goal setting more practical for you.

Setting a goal for yourself is like setting a course for the direction of your life.

Fixed Commitments Chart

	Sun.	Mon.	Tues.	Wed.	Thurs.	Fri.	Sat.
6 am							
7 am							
8 am							
9 am							
10 am							
11 am							
12 pm							
1 pm							
2 pm							
3 pm							
4 pm							
5 pm							
6 pm							
7 pm							
8 pm							
9 pm							
10 pm							

Comments: _____

_____

_____

Principles for Positive Goal Setting

1. **Set goals for each area of your life:** prayerfully consider each area of your life; physical, mental, social and spiritual.

2. **Keep the goals realistic:** is it really possible for you to lose those ten pounds in a week? Or to work three jobs, go to school, and play baseball?

3. **Keep the goals positive:** don't say "I will never be late for school anymore." Say: "I will be on time for school."

4. **Make a detailed plan for accomplishing each goal...and follow the plan:** for example, if your goal is to be on time to school, then you must write out a plan explaining how you are going to do this. I will get up thirty minutes earlier, I will set my clothes and books out the night before, etc.

5. **Make long-range and short-range goals:** for example, a long range goal may be to become a teacher, or a youth pastor or to attend college. The short-range goals might be to get good grades this semester, or to study your Bible three times a week, or to begin to save money for college.

6. **Write your goals down:** making a list of your goals helps to prioritize them and allows you the pleasure of crossing them off when they are met.

7. **Keep your goals private:** you may have someone you want to share some of your goals with, but generally speaking, do not announce to everyone the goals you have in life.

8. **Re-evaluate regularly:** consider your progress but be flexible. If circumstances do not allow you to accomplish a certain goal in a certain amount of time, do not panic, adjust your goals.

9. **Do it now!** your first goal should be to begin goal setting. Plan a specific time when you will sit down and consider two to five goals for each area of your life. Then whenever you think of something you should do, don't put it off, do it now! Ask yourself, "what is the best use of my time right now?"

10. **Strive for excellence but don't become a perfectionist:** allow yourself some freedom in the area of reaching your goals. Try to keep a healthy balance in the different areas of your life. The purpose of goal setting and time management is to relieve stress, not to create it.

Ask yourself, "what is the best use of my time right now?"

THE "FEAR OF FAILURE" EARTHQUAKE

One of the biggest road blocks to your success will be the fears you face. Consider the following list of fears:

- the fear of what others think.
- the fear of the unknown.
- the fear of disappointing others.
- the fear of disappointing God.
- the fear of missing God's will.
- the fear of others being "better" than you.
- the fear of people saying "no".
- the fear of criticism.
- the fear of failure.

Fears can be so strong they can paralyze your actions. People may even mistake this "lack of motivation" for laziness. The fear of failure is one of the most common fears people face.

How can you avoid falling into the "fear of failure" trap? *First*, remember that failure is only temporary. The feeling of failure does not have to be a permanent condition. *Second*, God is not in the habit of keeping a record of all your failures. He is forgiving and gives grace and strength to you to rise up and try again. *Third*, even if you fail at something, *you* are not a failure. Do not allow negative talk from others or yourself to convince you that you are a loser. *Fourth*, failures in life can become positive learning experiences — if you let them. Learn from the mistakes you have made and make positive changes to avoid them. *Fifth*, "if at first you don't succeed, try, try again."

A Higher Goal

Life is full of goals, goals to achieve and to succeed, but when life is over the only goal that truly matters is that goal to live a life pleasing to God. Striving to live a godly life while seeking to fulfill His purpose is the ultimate in goal setting. When trying to manage all that life brings you, remember there is a higher calling and a greater reward.

Even if you fail at something you are not a failure.

CHAPTER REVIEW

DEFINE

Lifestyle
Conduct
Character
Conviction
Biblical convictions
Conform

EXPLAIN

1. Explain how the choices you make as a teenager will affect your lifestyle as an adult.
2. Explain why self-discipline is so important in managing your conduct.
3. Explain why there is a strong connection between your thoughts and your actions.
4. Explain the G.I.G.O principle and tell how it ultimately affects your actions.
5. Explain why your character is so important in managing your life.
6. Explain what is meant by the phrase "there is no acting involved in true character."
7. Explain why it is important to develop convictions *before* you are confronted with a difficult situation.
8. Explain why the desire to conform can be such a strong negative force.
9. Explain why teenagers feel so strongly about certain things. What is the best way to manage these intense feelings?
10. Explain why it is important to have friends at each level of friendship.
11. Explain how learning to take control of your time can help you take control of your life.
12. Explain why goal setting can positively affect your lifestyle.
13. Explain why most people are afraid to fail, and how people avoid the "fear of failure" trap.

DISCUSS

1. Read Romans 8:13 and Romans 12:2. Discuss the meaning of these scriptures when considering self-discipline.

2. Discuss ways of developing self-discipline as a teenager. Remember to consider all areas of your life.

3. Discuss the illustration of the brain as a blank tape that records everything you see, hear and imagine. Why can't these images be erased from your memory? How might this help you to avoid even a "little" sin in your life?

4. Frosty Westering says: "Winners form the habit of doing things that losers don't like to do." Discuss this saying and how it might influence your lifestyle.

5. God wants you to develop the character of Christ, but what does this character include? How can a person develop the character of Christ?

6. Discuss the importance of developing biblical convictions. Discuss some of the issues facing teenagers and how you might go about setting a standard for those areas. (Consider using the five-step formula for developing convictions.)

7. Read through the STOP AND THINK section of the chapter and give personal examples for how you may deal with each situation.

8. Discuss why it is important not to ignore your questions and feelings about God and religion. How can being unstable in this area negatively affect you? How can being strong in this area positively affect you?

9. Discuss why it is so important even as a teenager to learn how to manage your time. How might a teenager use his/her time wisely?

10. "Setting a goal for yourself is like setting a course for the direction of your life." Discuss the meaning of this phrase and how it directly relates to teenagers. Why is it important to remember to have God involved in the goals you set for yourself?

SUGGESTED ACTIVITIES

1. **Key Concepts:** Outline the chapter and make a study guide for yourself. You may work alone or in a group.

2. **Get a Grip:** Do a research paper on self-discipline. Include areas in which teenagers need to develop self-discipline to help manage their lives.

3. **G.I.G.O.:** Make a poster focusing on this concept. Use key pictures and phrases to show the "garbage" that you face today and the "good" that you can focus on. Consider presenting a speech to the student body about this phrase.

4. **Standing Out:** Do a skit on Christian teenagers standing out from the crowd when they follow biblical convictions. Use real life teenage problems you may face everyday.

5. **God Help Me:** Do a report or speech on peer pressure. Show how your faith in God can make a difference in your confidence level when faced with temptations. Show how conformity can be positive when you conform to the likeness of Christ and other godly examples.

6. **It's In the Book:** Get with a group of other students and pick 2–5 key scriptures to memorize. Keep each other accountable and try to recite them to each other once a week. Once you have all reached your memory goal, share with the class how it has helped you in your walk with Christ. Challenge each other to make scripture memory a regular part of your life.

7. **"But It Feels Like An Earthquake!":** Pick one of the earthquakes presented in the chapter: spiritual earthquakes, family earthquakes, relationship earthquakes, or self-esteem earthquakes. Write down your personal earthquake in this area and make a decision to take control of it and deal positively with it. You may share this with your class or just turn it into your teacher.

8. **Feeling the Crunch:** Copy and fill out the fixed commitments schedule. Keep this schedule handy in your locker, notebook and at home. See if this helps you use your time more wisely.

9. *God in the Control Tower:* Set four goals in each area of your life: physical, social, mental and spiritual. Two goals should be short term and two long term. Break down your goals so you have a plan on how to reach them. Keep God in the control tower by continually praying over these goals.

Made In His Image

9-1 "IT'S ALL IN MY HEAD"
9-2 "BUT I AM COMFORTABLE BEING MISERABLE"
9-3 "I AM MADE IN WHOSE IMAGE?"

9-1 "IT'S ALL IN MY HEAD"

THE POWER OF THE "ONE-LINER"

> ### "Girl Germs"
> #### A Personal Testimony – One Girl's Story
>
> It all started when I began school. Each year the teasing got worse. I remember walking down the hallway when all of a sudden the boys would fall down and yell "girl germs." As they ran away laughing I tried to hold back the tears. When school was out for the day I often played on the swings before my mother came to pick me up. I remember a few occasions when the boys chased me while throwing pine cones at me. Boys were not the only source of contention. Girls would make fun of the way I looked or of my performance at school. One week the girls would like me and the next they would gang up and say they hated me. It seemed if I did well in school I would be called "brain" or "teacher's pet." The peak of frustration came in junior high. My body seemed to be changing faster than the other girls. This "maturing" only gave them more reasons to tease me.
>
> We had a grade school reunion awhile back. I remember talking to some of the boys from my class. As we discussed the years we spent together they apologized for teasing me. They said it was because they really did like me. I thought to myself "what a funny way to show it." They all laughed over the thought of those years, but I didn't. Today, it is *still* all in my head.

Teasing is as common as peanut butter and jelly sandwiches. Sometimes the jokes can be humorous and fun, but most of the time the person who is the source of the teasing wishes it would all stop. Your mind is like a blank tape, taking in all the negative as well as the positive things said about you. Unfortunately, a person usually remembers more negative than positive input. After awhile, the tape plays messages back to you and you begin to develop a poor image of yourself.

The messages you receive do not just come from classmates. Have you ever been teased by an older brother or sister? Do any of these messages sound familiar to you.

- "You lost the game *again*."
- "When is the coach going to let *you* play."
- "Hey thunder thighs."
- "You are so short you cannot even reach the curb."
- "You are so fat you cannot fit through the door."
- "You didn't know that? You are so stupid."
- "Get a life."
- "You are a mistake waiting to happen."

Verbal messages from your family members, friends, teachers, and non-verbal messages from society all influence your self-image. The view you have of yourself and the way you believe you are seen by others is your **self-image**. Things people say about you and how they act toward you *reinforce* the way you see yourself. Many "one-liners" are devastating to a person's self-image. A "one-liner" that is a good motto for everyone is: "put-up or shut-up." If you don't have anything nice to say, don't say anything at all. The words you speak to others make strong impressions that can either build them up or tear them down.

Teasing is as common as peanut butter and jelly sandwiches.

But no one can tame the tongue; it is a restless evil and full of deadly poison. With it we bless our Lord and Father; and with it we curse men, who have been made in the likeness of God…
James 3:8–9 (NAS)

Your self-image is formed by all your past and present experiences. Much of the things you assume people think of you are untrue. To **assume** means to take upon yourself, take on the particular character that others are saying about you whether it is true or not. When you make assumptions about what others think of you, you actually give them power to control your attitude and behavior.

You draw conclusions about your *appearance, physical abilities* and *intelligence* not only by the input you receive from others but from your own "self-talk." Your own thoughts and words have power. *"For as he thinks within himself, so he is"* (Proverbs 23:7 (NAS). *"For by your words you shall be justified, and by your words you shall be condemned"* (Matthew 12:37 NAS).

APPEARANCE: THE CASE OF THE BIG WINDOWS

My high school was a beautiful, modern building where the main hallway circled the library and the students' lockers. Large, beautiful windows overlooking the playing fields lined this main hallway. Everyone had to walk past these windows sometime during the day to get to their classes. This area in the school became known as the *"Big Windows."* Let me tell you why the big windows became so famous. The upper classmen would sit in front of the windows and while they watched the girls pass by, they would lift up cards: "1" or "5" or "10." It would not be so bad if you were walking with a large group of students but imagine walking alone to your locker. You pass the big windows and a group of popular upper classmen hold up cards grading your appearance….They didn't have to *say* a thing to make you feel inferior.

> When you make assumptions about what others think of you, you actually give them power to control your attitude and behavior.

PHYSICAL ABILITIES: THE CASE OF THE COLORED P.E. SHORTS

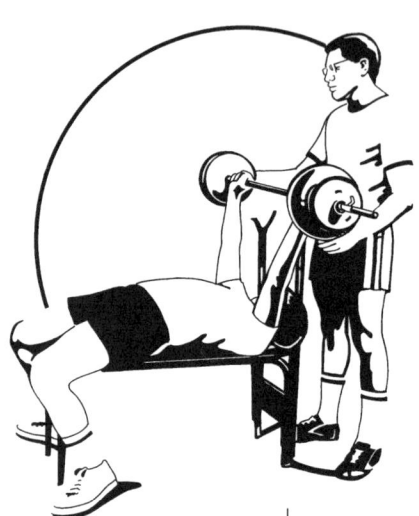

It was a common practice in my high school to assign a certain color of P.E. shorts to the boys based on the results of their physical fitness testing. The colors ranged from dark blue to white with several colors in between. Of course the boys who received the highest scores were proud to wear their dark blue shorts to P.E. class. Can you imagine what the boys felt like who had to wear the white shorts? It would be hard enough to wear them in front of the other boys, but when the girls saw what color the guys were wearing they would be devastated. Nothing had to be said to make the boys feel inferior.

INTELLIGENCE: THE CASE OF THE CLASS "BRAIN"

I remember a girl in my high school class. She was bright, cute, funny and very intelligent. "Jill" (name changed) came in as a freshman and soon became known as the "brain" of the class. If you had a question about any assignment you would go and talk to her. By the end of our sophomore year I noticed Jill was hanging around the "in" group at school (you know the group). Her behavior was changing and she wasn't spending time in the library studying like we all had known her to do. By the time we graduated from high school Jill earned a lower grade point average than what she was capable of earning. I remember asking a friend of Jill's about her surprising drop in grades. Her friend told me that Jill didn't want to be teased about being the "brain." She wanted to be ac-

cepted so bad that she didn't care anymore about her grades. Jill allowed the teasing of a small group of students to affect her future.

These three attributes, *beauty*, *physical ability*, and *intelligence* are highly valued by society and unfortunately by young people like yourself. Can you see how these values can give you an unhealthy view of yourself?

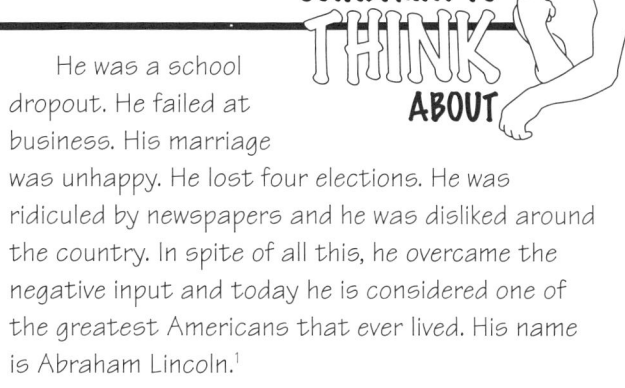

SOMETHING TO **THINK** ABOUT

He was a school dropout. He failed at business. His marriage was unhappy. He lost four elections. He was ridiculed by newspapers and he was disliked around the country. In spite of all this, he overcame the negative input and today he is considered one of the greatest Americans that ever lived. His name is Abraham Lincoln.[1]

9-2 "BUT I AM COMFORTABLE BEING MISERABLE"

GET OUT OF YOUR COMFORT ZONE

You may be thinking to yourself: "how could anyone be comfortable while feeling miserable about themselves?" Look at the definition of comfortable from Webster's dictionary: *free from stress or tension; enjoying contentment and security.* Over a period of time it is easier to remain in a state of self-pity and worthlessness than it is to shake yourself free.

A **comfort zone** is an area which a person will not go beyond. He feels secure to remain in a negative state-of-mind. It almost becomes a natural condition. The problem with staying in this comfort zone is that it will keep you from reaching your full potential. Your outlook on life will continue to look grim. *Nobody* can help you get out of your comfort zone except yourself. *You* must determine to have a positive outlook and try to overcome the negative input you receive.

DO NOT ENTER

COMFORT ZONE

Declaring War on Negative Self-talk

You cannot control what others will say about you but you can control how you respond to it. **Self-talk** is that tape running in your head, repeating all the positive or negative things you hear, see, read or imagine. These words can be about what work or activities you are involved in, or about who you are. Do you find yourself hearing that little voice inside of you saying: "I am ugly," "I will never amount to anything," "nobody likes me." These messages will only reinforce negative thoughts about yourself. When you allow yourself to believe these "untruths," your relationships and your behavior are affected. How can a person change negative self-talk to positive self-talk?

Using the Bible to overcome the negative input in your mind will help you gain a more positive outlook on life.

Overcoming Negative Self-Talk by the Power of the Word

"I will never amount to anything"

"For I know the plans that I have for you, declares the Lord, plans for welfare and not for calamity to give you a future and a hope"
Jeremiah 29:11 NAS

"I am ugly"

"For man looks at the outward appearance, but the Lord looks at the heart"
I Samuel 16:7 NAS

"Nobody likes me"

"...whatever is true, whatever is honorable, whatever is right, whatever is pure, whatever is lovely, whatever is of good repute, if there is any excellence and if anything worthy of praise, let your mind dwell on these things."
Philippians 4:8 NAS

You cannot control what others will say about you but you can control how you respond to it.

Positive self-talk focuses on truth, not on placing false or exaggerated images in your mind. The Bible warns against having a lofty view of yourself (1 Corinthians 4:6,7). Having a positive self-image means seeing yourself as God sees you; this is true humility.

You can learn to control your negative self-talk. When you hear yourself speaking falsely about yourself — STOP — and say "what does the Lord think of this?"

STAND TALL AND CONFIDENT

Most teenagers respect a guy or girl who has the courage to be his own person, even when being teased.[2]
Dr. James Dobson

Have you ever noticed tall people who slouch and short people who always wear high heels? People try to cover-up or change the things that are unchangeable. The best possible way to handle those things about yourself that are unchangeable is to accept them as part of the package. Everyone has something he does not like about himself. It may be the shape of his nose, the color of her skin, or the size of his ears. The way you feel about yourself is often portrayed by how you carry yourself, that is, how you stand, walk, and talk. Do you lack confidence in who you are? Are you consumed by what others think of you? Are you afraid of really being yourself, thinking that others may reject you? Are you spending too much time on your outer appearance and not enough time on positive inward qualities?

What really matters to the Lord are inward character qualities. What young people often overlook are those godly inward qualities that really make the best impression. Do you know that they affect the way you look *physically?* Your **countenance** (the face as an indication of mood, emotion, or character, according to Webster's Dictionary) will shine through. You can stand tall and confident. *"For we are His workmanship, created in Christ Jesus for good works, which God prepared beforehand, that we should walk in them"* (Ephesians 2:10 NAS).

Are you consumed by what others think of you?

9-3 "I AM MADE IN WHOSE IMAGE?"

And God created man in His own image, in the image of God He created him; male and female He created them.
Genesis 1:27 (NAS)

It is a difficult concept to grasp, that God, in His ultimate power and knowledge decided to create man (and woman) in *His* likeness. What does it really mean, "...in His image"? An image can be defined as: *a physical likeness or representation of a person or thing, a counter part of an object, such as is produced by reflection from a mirror* (Random House Dictionary). You are the tangible, visible representation of God. You are to be the reflection of Him, not in physical stature, talents or intelligence, but in the qualities that reflect His nature.

When God sees you, He does not see the weaknesses and faults as you see them. He sees you as a reflection of Himself, Christ in you. The key to understanding this life-changing truth is in getting to know the One who created you. The more you spend time with God, the better you will feel about your circumstances and yourself. You will begin to experience God's infinite love for you on a personal basis, not as something you read about or something someone told you. It is hard to describe with words what the presence of the Lord will do for you. Try it for yourself, and you will begin to know the power of the phrase "...in His image...."

> You are to be the reflection of Him, not in physical stature, talents or intelligence, but in the qualities that reflect His nature.

8 Ways You Can Improve Your Self-image

1. Get to know the One who made you in His image.
2. Ask for God's help in overcoming your weaknesses.
3. Thank God for the way He has made you.
4. Focus on your strengths.
5. Control your own self-talk.
6. Surround yourself with positve friendships.
7. Change those areas that are changeable.
8. Work at developing inward qualities.

Having a good self-concept gives you the power and confidence to face the challenges of life and to reach the potential God has planned for you.

CHAPTER REVIEW

DEFINE

Self-image
Assume
Comfort zone
Self-talk
Countenance

EXPLAIN

1. Explain how verbal and non-verbal input from others can influence your self-image.
2. Explain the meaning of the phrase "put-up or shut-up."
3. Explain why making assumptions about what others think of you can give them the power to influence your attitude and behavior. How can you get this power back?
4. Explain why it is much easier to remain in a "comfort zone" than to shake free from it. Why is remaining in a "comfort zone" dangerous?
5. Explain why beauty, physical ability and intelligence are valued so highly in society. Give some examples showing this is true.
6. Explain how a person can overcome a negative self-image.

DISCUSS

1. Discuss the common ways teenagers tease each other. Use specific examples to show the negative effects of "one-liners." Then discuss how teenagers can build each other up instead of tearing each other down.
2. Discuss different assumptions teenagers have about themselves. Discuss how teenagers can overcome these assumptions and take control of their self-image.
3. Discuss ways of coming out of negative "comfort zones." How can you help each other to step out of this security?
4. Discuss the difference between negative and positive self-talk. Give examples of how teenagers can overcome negative self-talk.

5. Discuss how a teenager may try to change things about him/herself that are unchangeable. Include ways a person can learn to accept these things, and learn to be content with the way God has made him/her.

6. Discuss why inward qualities are so important to develop. List some of the inward qualities that teenagers can work on developing.

7. Discuss why spending quality time in prayer and the Word can improve your self-image.

8. Discuss what is meant by the Scripture, "And God created man in His own image...." How can this Scripture affect the way you feel about yourself?

SUGGESTED ACTIVITIES

1. **Key Concepts:** Outline the chapter and make a study guide for yourself. You may work alone or in a group.

2. **The Me Nobody Knows:** Make a collage from pictures and words etc., that describes the person you are. Show your favorite music, book, color, subject in school, activity, etc. Include things that people may not know about you.

3. **It's in the Name:** Find the meaning of your name and the scripture that goes with the meaning. Add this to your collage or make a separate poster. Hang these up in the classroom and then keep it at home where you can see it.

4. **Entering the Comfort Zone:** List all the areas that you feel you cannot break free from a comfort zone. Then write a goal for each on how you plan to shake yourself from that security.

5. **Learn Contentment:** Write a paper on the word contentment. Include the meaning of the word, any scriptures that may shed light in its importance, and examples of how a person can learn to be content. Include contentment in all areas of life: physical, mental, social, and spiritual.

6. **The Altar of SELF:** Make a list of all the things you do not like about yourself. Do not show this list to anyone. During a devotional time with God, place the paper in front of you and commit these concerns to the Lord. Be honest in how you are truly feeling. Then commit yourself to accept those things that you cannot change. And ask the Lord to help you in the areas that you can change. Then write a one page report called "The altar of SELF." Define the word altar and explain how this activity made you feel.

7. **Put it to Memory:** Choose passages from the Bible that refer to your worth in God, His love for you, and the inner qualities you are to work on developing. Choose at least three scriptures and write them down, each one on separate 3 x 5 cards. Tape them to your mirror or somewhere you can see it everyday. Commit each Scripture to memory. You may recite them to the class for a class activity or extra credit.

SOCIAL HEALTH

...the fruit of the Spirit is love, joy, peace, longsuffering, kindness, goodness, faithfulness, gentleness, self-control. Against such there is no law. And those who are Christ's have crucified the flesh with its passions and desires. If we live in the Spirit, let us also walk in the Spirit.
Galatians 5:22-25

CHAPTER 10   HEAD TO TOES

CHAPTER 11   RISKY BUSINESS

CHAPTER 12   WHAT'S YOUR RESPONSIBILITY?

CHAPTER 13   MATURITY: WHAT'S IT ALL ABOUT?

CHAPTER 14   CHANGING RELATIONSHIPS

10 Head to Toes **241**
  10-1 A Shining Light... 241
  10-2 Fragile, Handle with Care.. 242
  10-3 Protecting your Eyes and Ears 252
  10-4 A Healthy Smile 258
  10-5 Standing Tall 262

11 Risky Business **271**
  11-1 Taking a Risk 271
  11-2 Safety First 275
  11-3 Basic First Aid 283
  11-4 Emergency! 288

12 What's Your Responsibility? **299**
  12-1 It's in the Attitude 299
  12-2 Responsibility as a Christian................................. 300
  12-3 Responsibility as a Person.....................................304
  12-4 Responsibility as a Citizen 308

13 Maturity: What's it All About? **325**
  13-1 "Volumes" of Choices 325
  13-2 More than Just Saying "No" 333

14 Changing Relationships **359**
  14-1 When Friendships Become Relationships............359
  14-2 When Two Become One 367
  14-3 When Two Become a Family 371
  14-4 When Death Means Life 375

Head to Toes

10-1 A SHINING LIGHT
10-2 FRAGILE, HANDLE WITH CARE
10-3 PROTECTING YOUR EYES AND EARS
10-4 A HEALTHY SMILE
10-5 STANDING TALL

10-1 A SHINING LIGHT

You are the world's light — it is impossible to hide a town built on the top of a hill. Men do not light a lamp and put it under a bucket. They put it on a lamp-stand and it gives light for everybody in the house. Let your light shine like that in the sight of men. Let them see the good things you do and praise your Father in Heaven.
Matthew 5:14–16 Phillips translation

Looking Good, Feeling Good

Have you ever noticed someone who "beamed." That is, her countenance was like a radiant light. It is often said that people can "beam with happiness." Although the light that radiates from a person comes from within, it must be portrayed through the person's physical appearance. When you care enough to keep your body clean and looking its best, you are showing respect to yourself and to others.

Feeling good about your physical appearance enhances your overall feeling about yourself. The desire to look your best is a natural desire but can become out-of-balance if too much time and energy is spent on your outward appearance. However, it is true that a person with a good self-esteem stands straighter, smiles more, and projects a sense of friendliness and confidence.

Embark on a journey to make positive changes that will enhance your natural appearance. Treat your body with respect. Take care of your outer appearance and remember that the light you reflect is naturally attractive.

What is a first impression? When you meet someone for the first time you quickly have a general feeling about that person. Has your first impression of anyone ever changed after you have gotten to know that person? There are many factors that create your image of someone. What role does personal hygiene play in making a good first impression?

10-2 FRAGILE, HANDLE WITH CARE

SKIN, HAIR AND HANDS

Skin

Because the skin is exposed to the elements it is easy to assume that it is very tough. However, the skin is a very sensitive and fragile organ. In many ways the skin takes care of itself without much attention from you. The three most important responsibilities you have in caring for your skin are: keep your skin clean, keep your skin moist and keep your skin protected.

Bathing, showering and washing with soap to keep your skin clean makes you look and feel good. The important thing to remember however, is that certain soaps can dry your skin, cause al-

lergic reactions such as itching and flaking, and cause your skin to look worn or dull. Your facial skin is the most fragile and delicate of all the skin on your body. It is also the area in which many people spend more time and money than is necessary.

The Do's and Don'ts of Skin Care

Do

1. Do use a mild cleanser on your face and body.
2. Do use a light moisturizer on your skin. Use one specifically designed for your face preferably with a sunscreen greater than SPF of 15.
3. Do use warm, not hot, water on your face and body.
4. Do finish your shower with cool water over your body.
5. Do splash your face with cool water when you finish cleansing.
6. Do use a washcloth to gently wash your face (rinse your wash-cloth thoroughly after each use to avoid unnecessary bacteria).
7. Do protect your skin from the elements. Protect your skin from cold, wind and sun.

8. Do exercise to increase your blood circulation and decrease your stress.
9. Do eat a balanced diet.
10. Do get plenty of sleep to help your overall health.

Don't

1. Don't assume expensive products mean better products.
2. Don't bake in the sun.
3. Don't smoke. Nicotine constricts your blood vessels and decreases the flow of oxygen to the skin.
4. Don't soak in hot baths or saunas for long periods of time. These can take the moisture out of your skin.
5. Don't sleep under an electric blanket that is unnecessarily hot. This will cause your skin to become dry.
6. Don't leave make-up on your face overnight.
7. Don't pull or stretch your facial skin unnecessarily.
8. Don't use abrasive soaps or scrubs on your facial skin.
9. Don't use scented soaps on your skin if you have sensitive skin.
10. Don't use heavy creams on your face.

Although some adults do suffer from breakouts, acne usually gets better or disappears altogether after your teen years.

Acne

If you have not had to deal with the problems of acne, consider yourself very fortunate. The problem of acne may begin during adolescence when your body is going through so many physical changes. Some hormones (chemicals produced in your body) cause an increase in the activity of your oil glands. As a result, an oily substance called **sebum** is made and eventually clogs the pores. **Acne** occurs when the pores of the skin become clogged with oil.

It is not very pleasant discussing the problems of acne, however learning the facts may help you take better care of your skin. There are three types of acne. The first type is called the whitehead. A **whitehead** is created when oil becomes trapped inside a pore. A pore that is plugged with oil but is exposed to the air is called a **blackhead** because of the darkened color of the pore. The third type of acne is the pimple. This condition is the most serious type of acne. Technically, a **pimple** is a clogged pore that has become infected and filled with pus.

Although some adults do suffer from breakouts, acne usually gets better or disappears altogether after your teen years. Follow the do's and don'ts of dealing with acne and you should make it through these years without causing unnecessary scars and infection on your skin.

SOMETHING TO **THINK** ABOUT

From the inside-out

Did you know that good nutrition is a good defense against skin problems?

- *Vitamin C* helps produce collagen, the substance that gives skin its elasticity.
- *Vitamin E* (an antioxidant) helps to fight against the effects of pollution and ultraviolet rays.
- *Beta-carotene* (an antioxidant) is also good in the fight against acne.
- Drinking plenty of *water* helps your skin get enough moisture and helps cleanse your body from the inside-out.

The Do's and Don'ts of Dealing with Acne

Do

1. Do wash twice a day with warm water using a mild cleanser.
2. Do use moisturizers sparingly.
3. Do check with your doctor when introducing an acne medication.
4. Do see a dermatologist (a doctor who treats skin disorders) if your condition is serious.
5. Do get plenty of rest.
6. Do exercise regularly.
7. Do eat a balanced diet.
8. Do wear make-up that is free from oils and other irritants.
9. Males who have acne should shave their face as seldom as possible and always use a sharp blade. Using a shaving cream for sensitive skin may also reduce the irritation.
10. Do understand that you are not the only one dealing with acne and the condition will get better.

Don't

1. Don't squeeze or pick at your acne. This can cause infection and spread of more pimples.
2. Don't use heavy creams or moisturizers.
3. Don't rub the areas with a towel or washcloth.
4. Don't touch your face with your fingers or hands (this can leave excess oil and dirt on your face).
5. Don't let your skin condition get you down. Don't avoid social events because of the way you think you look.

Common Skin Problems

Warts

Do you ever find yourself hiding your hands in your pockets, or worrying that someone may see or feel a wart on your hand? **Warts** are a growth on the skin caused by a virus. Generally, warts are harmless and may disappear without treatment. If your warts become irritated or unsightly, a doctor can remove them.

Be very careful when using over-the-counter medications for the removal of warts because they can burn the skin. Read the directions carefully.

Plantar warts, which develop on the bottom of the feet and toes can be very uncomfortable. You should not try to treat plantar warts yourself. A doctor can remove them surgically.

Irritated Skin

When you suffer from persistent itchy skin there may be several different causes. *Eczema* and *dermatitis* are conditions that cause the skin to be itchy, scaly, and inflamed. Dermatitis is usually caused by an irritation. For example, if your wrist develops a rash when you wear a certain watch, change the type of watch or don't wear one at all.

Psoriasis is caused by the overproduction of skin cells. The result is patches of red, scaly skin. The common areas affected by psoriasis are the elbows, knees and scalp.

Common in children and young adults is the condition called impetigo. *Impetigo* is a bacterial skin infection that causes itchy, blistering skin that forms a crust. It is highly contagious and a person who thinks they may have impetigo should see a doctor promptly.

Fungal skin infections can occur on different areas of your skin. *Jock itch* and *athlete's foot* are common examples of fungal skin infections. Some people are more prone to fungal infections than other people. Changing your shoes, socks and underwear at least once during the day will help. For athlete's foot, avoid going barefoot in public locker rooms and showers. After bathing, sprinkle a cornstarch based powder on your feet and genital areas to keep them extra dry. Try an over-the-counter medication but if the infection persists you should see a doctor.

Herpes simplex I is a virus that causes cold sores or fever blisters. They may appear on or near the lips, sometimes even inside your mouth. Herpes simplex I is very contagious if the area is scratched opening the sores. The sores are very painful but usually clear up in 10 to 14 days. A doctor may prescribe a medication if the sores spread.

Your Hair: The Frame For Your Face

You don't need to live in a beauty salon to be attractive. If you have ever changed your hair style, even slightly, you know how that can change your overall appearance. Your hair frames the most dynamic part of your presentation — your face!

No matter what a salesperson may tell you, your hair is made up of dead cells. The roots of your hair are secured in small pockets called *follicles*. When hair cells die they are forced out of the follicle and new hair cells are formed to take their place.

Have you ever known a family where each of the siblings have different types of hair? Words to describe different types of hair are: thick, thin, wavy, curly, fine, thin, straight and coarse. It is true that different hair types need different shampoos, conditioners and cuts to maximize their style.

Healthy, good-looking hair is not just a matter of inheritance. Even difficult hair can be healthy if given the proper care.

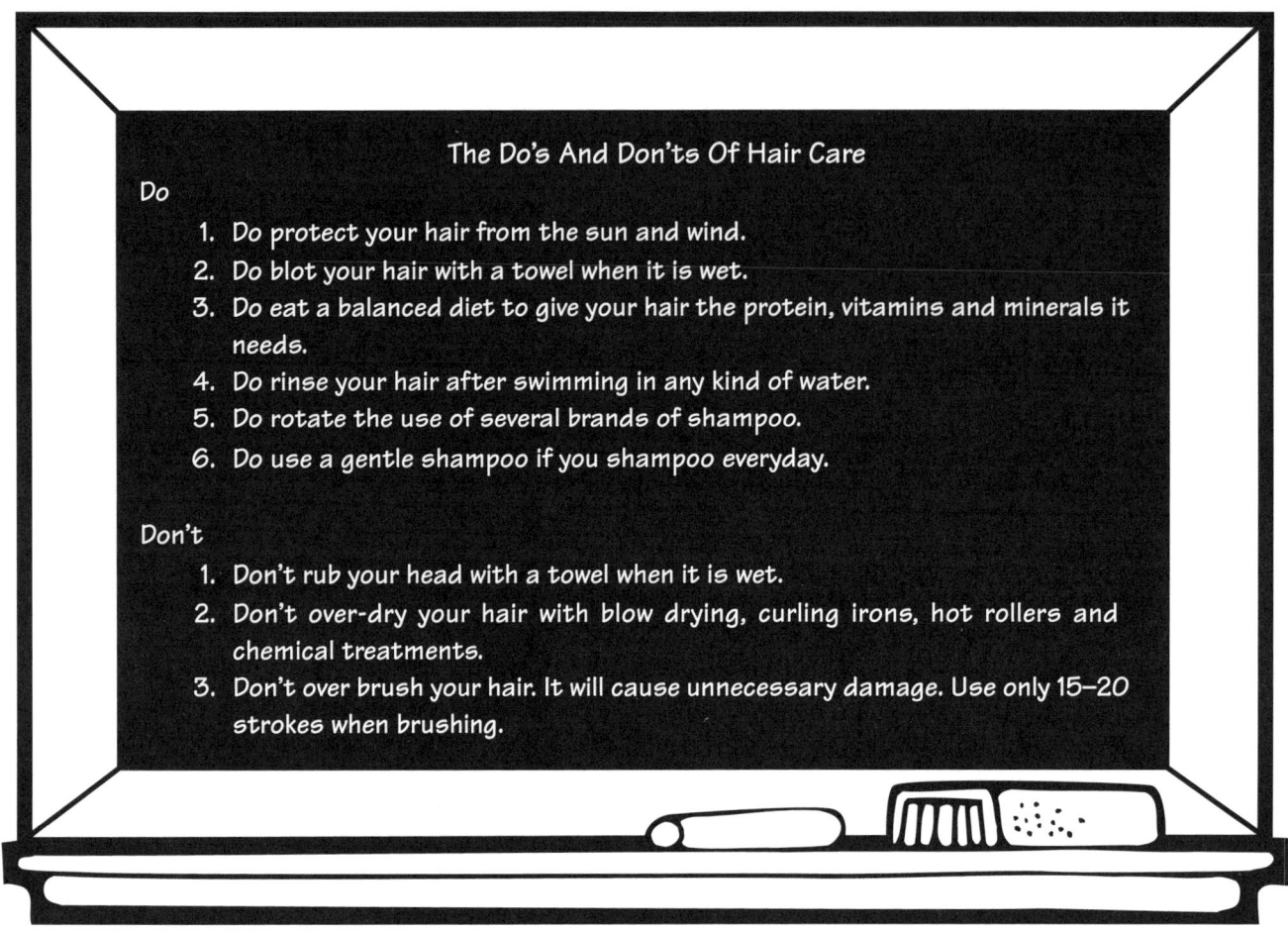

The Do's And Don'ts Of Hair Care

Do

1. Do protect your hair from the sun and wind.
2. Do blot your hair with a towel when it is wet.
3. Do eat a balanced diet to give your hair the protein, vitamins and minerals it needs.
4. Do rinse your hair after swimming in any kind of water.
5. Do rotate the use of several brands of shampoo.
6. Do use a gentle shampoo if you shampoo everyday.

Don't

1. Don't rub your head with a towel when it is wet.
2. Don't over-dry your hair with blow drying, curling irons, hot rollers and chemical treatments.
3. Don't over brush your hair. It will cause unnecessary damage. Use only 15–20 strokes when brushing.

Your personal features and type of hair determine whether a cut will look good on your face.

The Right Hairstyle For You

Hairstyles change as often as clothing styles. Each year there seems to be the "in" cut for hair. Both guys and girls have the pressure to be "in style" when it comes to their hair cut. No matter what is "in" at the time, find a style that is flattering for you. Your personal features and type of hair determine whether a cut will look good on your face. Remember, if you choose to have bangs that cover your forehead, your skin may become irritated and this may result in more acne on your forehead.

Finding a hairstylist you feel confident with is important. Your hairstylist can find a style that looks good and is practical for you. Once you find that style, don't feel pressure to make drastic changes just because it's the thing to do. Remember that if you do get a cut you do not like, your hair will grow back and you can try again!

Common Problems In Hair Care

One of the most common problems in hair care is dandruff. **Dandruff** is a flaking of the outer layer of dead skin cells. A dry and itchy scalp may also accompany the flaky skin. Using harsh or drying shampoos can aggravate the condition. Sometimes a special dandruff shampoo can control the problem.

Head lice is another condition of the scalp. Unlike dandruff, head lice is very easy to catch from someone who has it. **Head lice** are insects that can live in the hair and look much like dandruff until you examine it closely. Head lice can be controlled by using a medicated shampoo specifically designed to control lice. It is also important to wash all the bedding, towels and clothing that may have come in contact with the lice.

During adolescence your body is going through many changes. These changes often cause an increase in the production of oil in the skin and scalp. You may find that your hair becomes oily sooner than it used to. Use a shampoo for oily hair and do not use a conditioner as often. You also may need to wash your hair more frequently. If you find that your hair tends to be dry and brittle, use a mild shampoo and a conditioner. Try not to wash your hair everyday.

SOMETHING TO THINK ABOUT

Are not two sparrows sold for a copper coin? And not one of them falls to the ground apart from your Father's will. But the very hairs of your head are all numbered. Do not fear therefore; you are of more value than many sparrows.
Matthew 10:29–31

The average head of hair contains between 100,000 and 200,000 hairs. Don't try to count them. The very fact that God knows the number of hairs on your head shows you how important you are to Him.

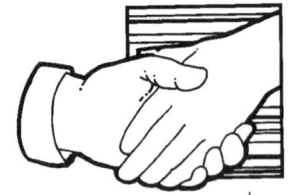

Helping Hands

People often take for granted the use of their hands and fingers. Have you ever broken your arm or hand? When you lose the use of a hand or your fingers then you begin to realize how much you use them. The skin on your hands is generally tough because it is constantly exposed to the elements and various chemicals. If you care for your hands they can be a very attractive part of your appearance.

Keeping your hands and nails looking clean is an important part of personal hygiene. Not only does it look good, but it is also good for you since you often eat with your fingers or place your fingers on your face or near your mouth. When washing your hands use a mild antibacterial soap with warm water. Rinse well and then apply a moisturizer on your hands when they are still damp. Keep a small bottle of hand lotion at each sink and after washing get into the habit of applying lotion on your hands.

If you care for your hands they can be a very attractive part of your appearance.

When the weather is cold, protect your hands from the air with gloves. Likewise in the sun, protect your hands by applying a sunscreen to your hands. When you are doing any gardening, housework, or other work that will expose your hands to chemicals wear protective gloves. You may not realize it, but chemicals can be absorbed into your body through the skin on your hands.

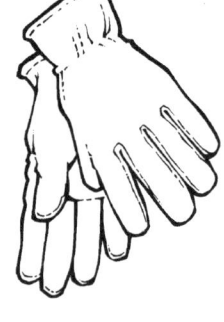

SOMETHING TO **THINK** ABOUT

STOP

"I want to stop biting my nails!"
- Make a decision to stop.
- Share that decision with a friend. Be accountable to that person.
- Take pride in the condition of your hands.
- Keep your nails trimmed and smooth so you will not be tempted to bite them off.
- Try a nail coating that has a bitter taste to keep you from biting.
- Try to find out the reason why you bite your nails. Stress? Habit?
- Treat yourself to something if you go a month without biting your nails.
- Limit your biting to one nail.

Caring for Your Nails

Your fingernails are made of a tough, dead material called **keratin.** The **cuticle** surrounds the nail and is made of nonliving skin. On the average, each fingernail can grow a half an inch every three months. If you care for your nails, they enhance your general appearance. The best care for poor nails is to keep the nails short and apply lotion to keep the cuticles moist. **Hangnails** are splits in the cuticle along the edge of the nail. These can be painful if torn. Always use clippers or nail scissors to cut the skin away.

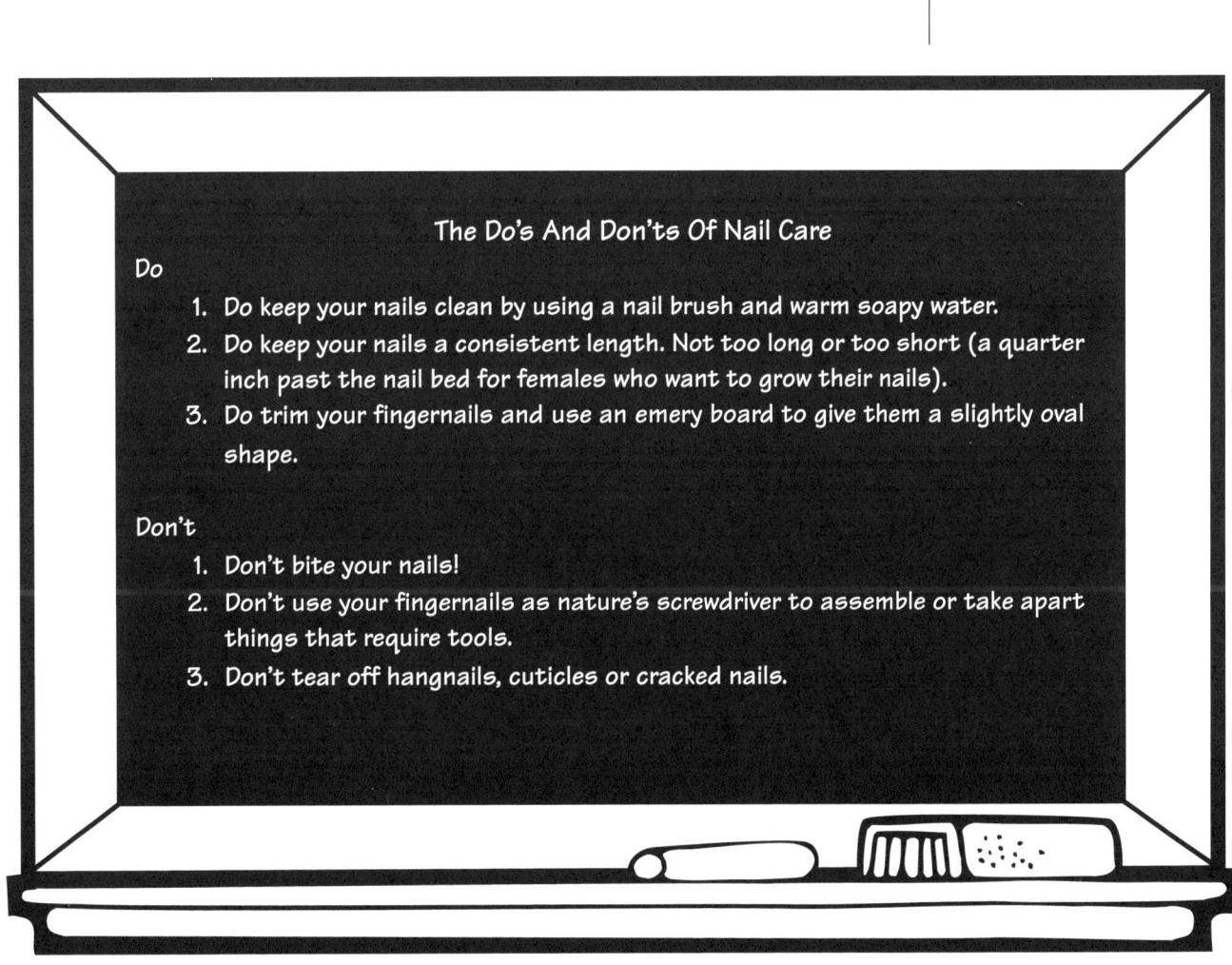

The Do's And Don'ts Of Nail Care

Do

1. Do keep your nails clean by using a nail brush and warm soapy water.
2. Do keep your nails a consistent length. Not too long or too short (a quarter inch past the nail bed for females who want to grow their nails).
3. Do trim your fingernails and use an emery board to give them a slightly oval shape.

Don't

1. Don't bite your nails!
2. Don't use your fingernails as nature's screwdriver to assemble or take apart things that require tools.
3. Don't tear off hangnails, cuticles or cracked nails.

10-3 PROTECTING YOUR EYES AND EARS

EYES

There once was a commercial on television advertising eyeglasses. The television camera takes you on a bike ride with a person who experiences blurred vision. Because the bike rider cannot see clearly, trees and shrubs keep hitting him as he is riding. Finally, corrective glasses are placed over the person's eyes just in time for him to see the tree that he is about to crash into. The commercial ends with an appeal to purchase eyeglasses.

Your eyes are the windows to the natural world around you. Even if you try to imagine what it would be like to be blind, you would not truly understand. The ability to see is often taken for granted by those who have never had problems with vision.

The Bible uses the natural illustration of the eyes to illustrate spiritual truth. It is not only important to protect your eyes from physical damage, but more importantly is protecting your eyes from the negative influences in the world.

The lamp of the body is the eye. If therefore your eye is good, your whole body will be full of light. But if your eye is bad, your whole body will be full of darkness. If therefore the light that is in you is darkness, how great is that darkness!
Matthew 6:22,23

Caring For Your Eyes

The hearing ear and the seeing eye, the Lord has made both of them.
Proverbs 20:12 (NAS)

God cares about your natural, as well as spiritual, vision. The ability to see is a gift. Your eyes need care and protection.

The hearing ear and the seeing eye, the Lord has made both of them.

Proverbs 20:12 (NAS)

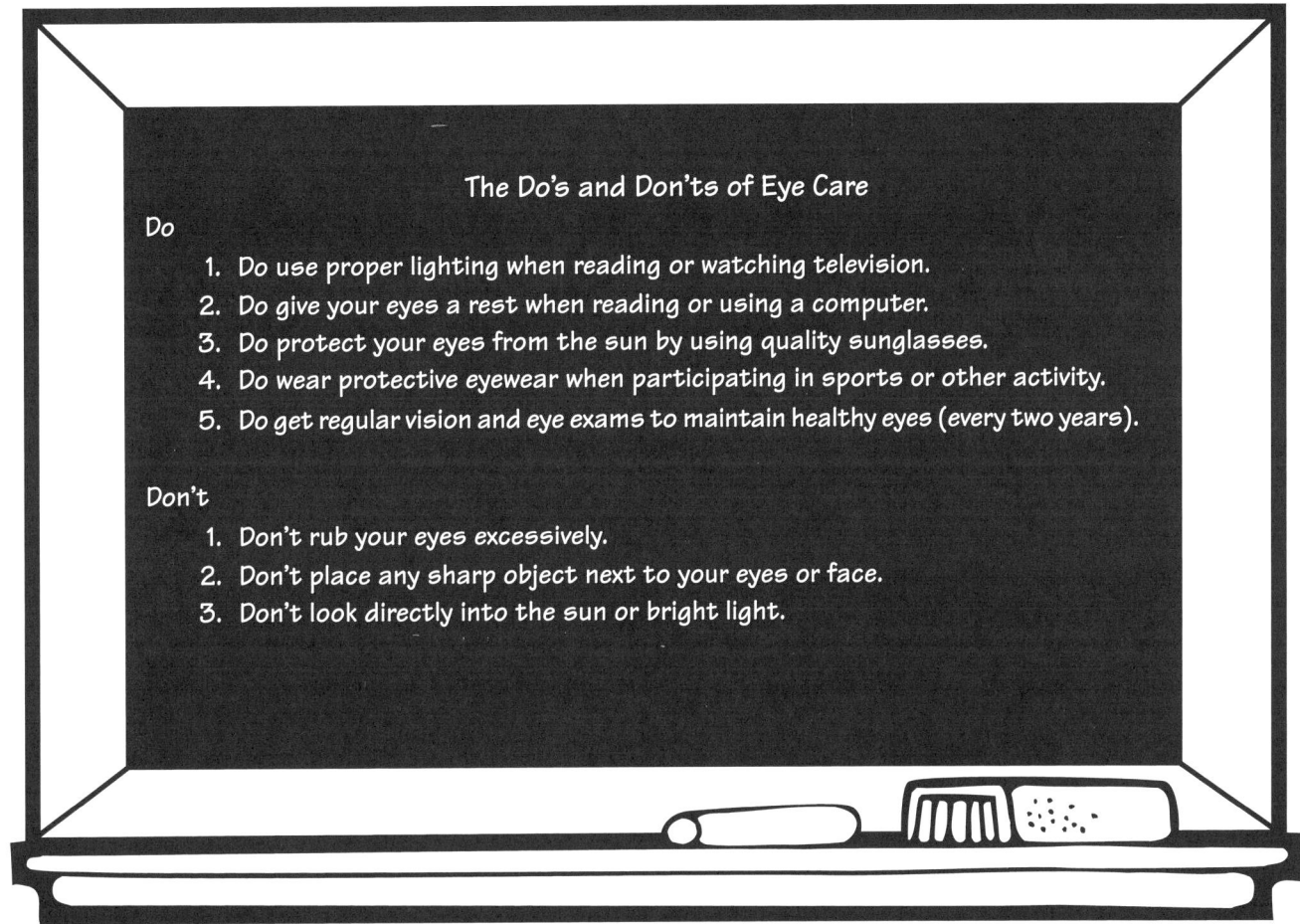

The Do's and Don'ts of Eye Care

Do

1. Do use proper lighting when reading or watching television.
2. Do give your eyes a rest when reading or using a computer.
3. Do protect your eyes from the sun by using quality sunglasses.
4. Do wear protective eyewear when participating in sports or other activity.
5. Do get regular vision and eye exams to maintain healthy eyes (every two years).

Don't

1. Don't rub your eyes excessively.
2. Don't place any sharp object next to your eyes or face.
3. Don't look directly into the sun or bright light.

Common Eye Problems

If you experience frequent headaches, squinting, reddening or watering eyes, burning or tired eyes, you may have a problem with your vision. Furthermore, if you have blurred vision when trying to read objects that are close or far away, you should see an eye specialist.

Common eye problems:

- **Farsightedness (hypermetropia):** you can see far objects clearly, but close objects appear blurred
- **Nearsightedness (myopia):** you can see close objects clearly, but distant objects appear blurred
- **Astigmatism (distorted vision):** images are distorted because the cornea or lens is an irregular shape
- **Conjunctivitis ("pinkeye"):** an infection causing inflammation of the inner surface of the eyelid. This condition is

very contagious.

- **Color Blindness:** a hereditary condition where a person cannot distinguish between certain colors. More often found in men than in women.
- *Lazy Eye (amblyopia):* a condition where normal vision has failed to develop in one eye. The healthy eye dominates the vision, thus weakens the muscles of the weaker eye.
- **Cataracts:** clouding of the lens that causes some loss of vision
- *Glaucoma:* a disease where a fluid builds up damaging the optic nerve because of the pressure. This is very serious and can lead to blindness.

Careers

- **Ophthalmologist:** a physician who specializes in care of the eyes. They conduct eye exams and may prescribe glasses and contact lenses, medication, or surgery as necessary.
- **Optician:** a person who fits, supplies, and adjusts glasses or contact lenses.
- **Optometrist:** a specialist trained to examine the eyes and to prescribe, supply and adjust glasses or contact lenses. They are not physicians, but refer patients to ophthalmologists when necessary.

EARS

It has been said: we have two ears and only one tongue that we may hear more and speak less.

Similar to the analogy of spiritual and natural sight, the Bible uses the need for natural listening and hearing to illustrate a spiritual truth. The Scriptures are full of phrases that read, "listen", "hear" and "incline your ear to Me." Just as you need to care for your physical hearing, it is also important to hear what God is saying to you in your heart.

Although you analyze sounds in a matter of seconds, physical hearing is a very complex process. Listen carefully to the noises around you. Do you hear the sound of the rain outdoors or the low hum of the heater running? Your ears are the organs of hearing and balance. There are three parts of the ear: the *outer ear*, the *middle ear* and the *inner ear*. The outer and middle ear collect and transmit the sounds. Your inner ear is responsible for carrying messages to your brain where the sounds will be interpreted. The inner ear is also responsible for keeping your balance.

CAUTION!

What about those tunes?

Headphones have several positive features but the risks are great if you do not use caution:

- using headphones can keep you inattentive to the sounds around you. For example, traffic, sirens, phone calls etc.
- using headphones can damage your hearing if they are used for extended periods of time and if the sound is too loud.

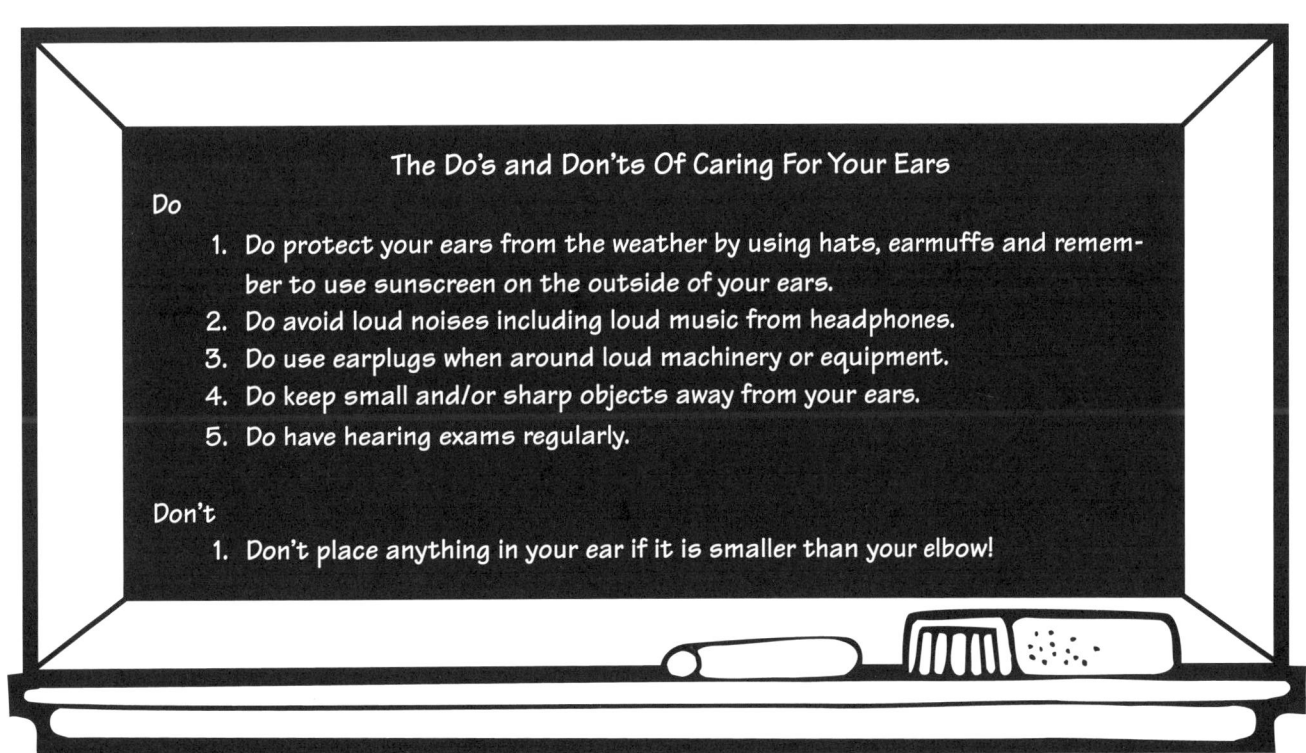

The Do's and Don'ts Of Caring For Your Ears

Do

1. Do protect your ears from the weather by using hats, earmuffs and remember to use sunscreen on the outside of your ears.
2. Do avoid loud noises including loud music from headphones.
3. Do use earplugs when around loud machinery or equipment.
4. Do keep small and/or sharp objects away from your ears.
5. Do have hearing exams regularly.

Don't

1. Don't place anything in your ear if it is smaller than your elbow!

Balance

The next time you are among your friends, have a contest. See who can stand on one foot with both eyes closed the longest.

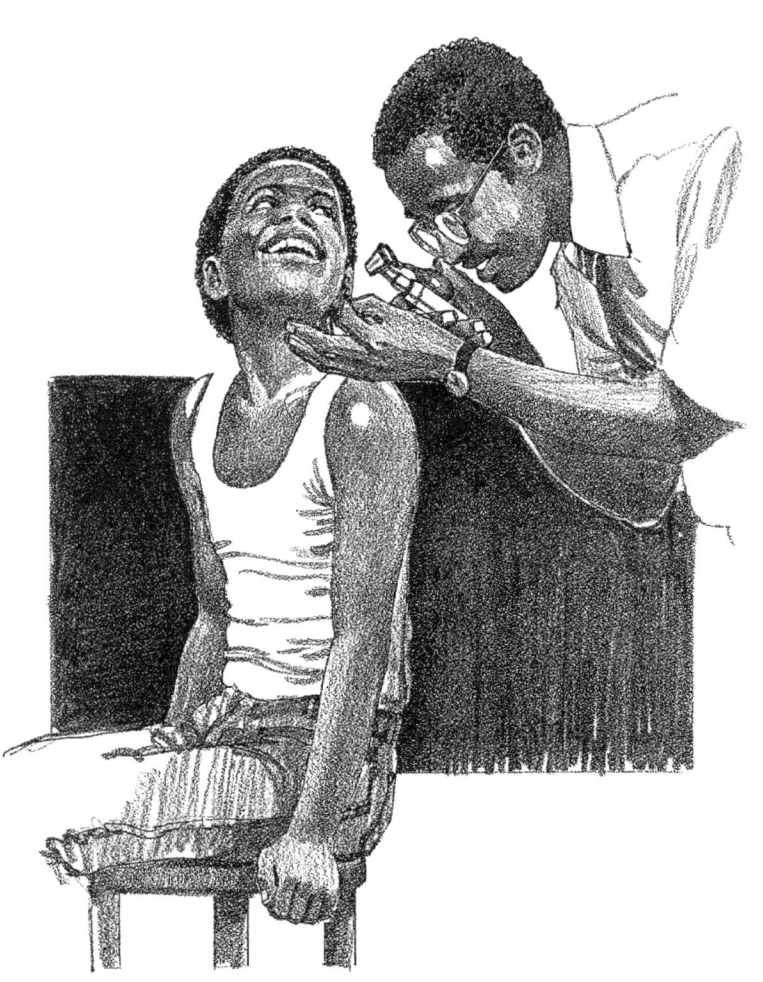

Keeping your balance is a difficult thing but the key to good balance is the condition and function of your inner ear. **Balance** or equilibrium is your ability to remain steady and in control of your body. The labyrinth in your inner ear has semicircular canals that are filled with fluid and tiny hairs. These sensory hairs are connected to your brain. When you move your head the fluid and the hairs move sending messages to your brain. Your brain responds by telling your skeletal muscles how to adjust to keep your balance.

SOMETHING TO THINK ABOUT

Is that *really* the ocean?

Did you ever believe that you could hear the sounds of the ocean if you placed the conch shell to your ear? Although the sound is similar, what you are really hearing is the echo of blood moving through your body and the sound of your own pulse.

Problems With The Ears

- **Ear infections:** The two most common causes of an earache are: an infection to the middle ear or an inflammation of the outer ear canal.
- **Earaches:** Pain in the ear caused by any infection in the nose, throat or ear.
- **Motion Sickness:** The feeling of dizziness and/or nausea while riding in a car, boat, or airplane. With the constant motion, the fluid in the ear moves around, sending messages to the brain too quickly.

As a result, the brain cannot distinguish the signals and becomes confused causing uneasiness in the individual. To deal with motion sickness some people look at the horizon, sit in the front seat of a car, or take medication that can control the uncomfortable feelings.

- **Deafness:** the loss of hearing in one or both ears. The degree of deafness can be partial or complete. People who suffer from partial hearing loss or impaired hearing can lead normal lives by using hearing aids. Those who lose total hearing often learn sign language and/or read lips to communicate.

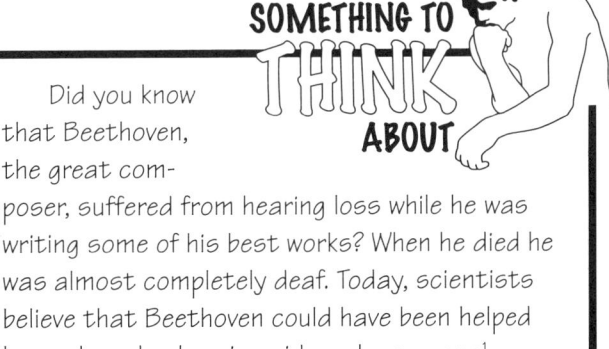

SOMETHING TO THINK ABOUT

Did you know that Beethoven, the great composer, suffered from hearing loss while he was writing some of his best works? When he died he was almost completely deaf. Today, scientists believe that Beethoven could have been helped by modern day hearing aids or by surgery.[1]

10-4 A HEALTHY SMILE

> ### "If I knew then what I know now, I would have listened..."
> #### A personal testimony
> #### by Susan Boe
>
> "Brush and floss your teeth," my mother would say to us as we began our bedtime routine. My two sisters and I shared a bathroom with one sink. It became a rush to the bathroom to get myself ready at night or in the morning before school. Brushing my teeth became a duty and I learned to save time by doing a "rush" job. Flossing? Well, that was only done the day I had to go to the dentist so when he asked me "are you flossing?" I could honestly say, "yes, sometimes."
>
> I didn't seem to have any problems with my teeth as I grew older. Each time I went in for my regular check-up my dentist would say, "no cavities, you have great looking teeth." What I did not realize was that I was developing some "sleeping giants."
>
> At a recent dental appointment my dentist found that I needed two crowns and one root canal. I just returned from a root canal specialist (endodontic specialist). After spending an hour and fifteen minutes in the dental chair I wish I would have taken better care of my teeth. Sometimes we have to learn our lessons the hard way. If I knew then what I know now, I would have listened to my mother.

Clean teeth, healthy gums and fresh breath communicate to others that you have good health habits.

You can say a lot about yourself without saying a word. Your smile not only shows off your face but it tells people how well you care for your teeth and gums. Clean teeth, healthy gums and fresh breath communicate to others that you have good health habits. Just like the personal testimony you have just read, you may not think about the future condition of your teeth, but in a few years you may begin to experience problems with your teeth. Just spending a few extra minutes a day can give you a healthy smile.

YOUR TEETH

The teeth you have now as a teenager must last you the rest of your life. When all your permanent teeth and molars have come in, you will have 32 teeth as an adult. The four kinds of teeth in your mouth each have a different function. The **incisors** are the front and center teeth. They are responsible for cutting and tearing food. The four pointed teeth next to the incisors are your **canine** teeth (or cuspids). They are responsible for tearing food to prepare it for chewing. Your **premolars** (or bicuspids) and your **molars** are located in the sides and the back of your mouth. Their job is to grind and chew your food.

Your teeth are supported by the periodontium. Your **periodontium** consists of your jawbone, gums and ligaments. There are three parts of a tooth: the crown, the root and the pulp. The **crown** is the part of the tooth that you can see. It is made up of enamel, which is the hardest substance in the human body. The **root** is the part of the tooth that is below the gums. It is basically made up of **dentin**, which is a layer of hard tissue (about the hardness of bone). The **pulp** is inside the tooth and is composed of blood vessels, nerves and connective tissue.

Careers
- **Dentist:** *a doctor who treats teeth.*
- **Orthodontist:** *a dentist who specializes in treating irregularities in the teeth.*
- **Dental hygienist:** *specializes in cleaning the teeth.*

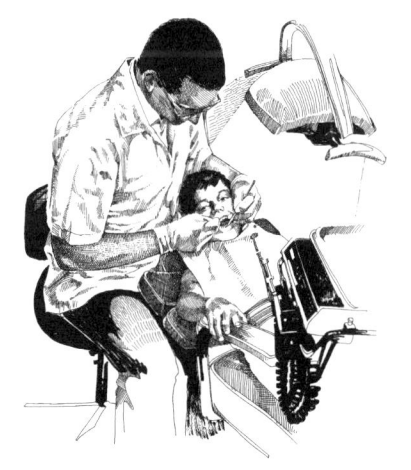

The Do's And Don'ts Of Tooth Care

Do

1. Do brush and floss regularly, after each meal if possible, at least twice a day.
2. Do avoid sugary foods, especially candies or cookies that stick to your teeth.
3. Do replace your toothbrush after you have had a cold or flu.
4. Do replace your toothbrush every few months or if the bristles become worn.
5. Do floss your teeth after you brush rather than before.
6. Do have regular dental check-ups, every six months or once a year.
7. Do eat a healthy, balanced diet.
8. Do use a toothpaste that has fluoride.

Don't

1. Don't overbrush your teeth. Overzealous scrubbing with a toothbrush can cause damage to the gums.
2. Don't use toothpastes that claim to whiten your teeth. The harsh abrasives may damage your teeth.
3. Don't smoke or use chewing tobacco; these can irritate gums and can lead to cancers of the mouth.

Problems With The Mouth And Teeth

Over 300 different bacteria live in a human mouth. This bacteria is the cause of bad breath and gum disease. When bacteria begins to attack your gums, gingivitis results. **Gingivitis** is a gum disease caused by a build up of plaque and tarter on the teeth. Food caught between the teeth, if not removed, may cause infection. If you experience swelling, bleeding gums it may be a sign of gingivitis. Seeing your dentist regularly will help to spot gingivitis before it turns into **periodontal disease** (more advanced gum disease).

Plaque is a grainy, sticky coating that is constantly forming on your teeth. It consists of saliva, bacteria and food particles.

Plaque should be removed with daily brushing and flossing. The hard substance that is formed on your teeth is called calculus or **tartar**. You often feel this with your tongue behind your lower teeth. Once tartar forms, brushing will not remove it. Tartar should be removed at your regular dental appointments.

You hear a lot about plaque and tartar from commercials for toothpastes that claim to fight them. These toothpastes are effective but should not keep you from a regular routine of flossing and brushing. Toothpastes only clean on the exposed surface of the teeth, but flossing will get between teeth where the bacteria can build-up. The bacteria that live in your mouth and add to the build-up of plaque can form an acid that destroys tooth enamel and irritates your gums. Tooth decay occurs when this acid eats a hole through the enamel on your teeth. This hole is called a **cavity**.

If the decay spreads deeper into the tooth and affects the nerve, you can suffer from a painful toothache. Generally a root canal is needed. During a *root canal* your dentist or specialist will drill a hole in the tooth and remove the exposed root. Then an artificial *crown* is made to fill the tooth.

Malocclusion is a condition where the upper and lower teeth do not properly line up. Slight malocclusion is common but severe irregularities can be treated by orthodontic treatment (wearing braces). When overcrowding is the cause, some teeth may need to be extracted (pulled). Malocclusion usually develops in childhood, when the teeth and jaws are growing. Heredity, thumb-sucking and overcrowding of the teeth are causes of malocclusion. By seeing your dentist regularly, you can avoid many problems with your teeth.

A dentist once said to one of his patients, "If you choose to eat candy, I would rather have you eat a candy bar and get it over with than munch on M & M's or suck on a constant source of sugar throughout the day."

SOMETHING TO THINK ABOUT

Did you know that stress can affect your teeth? Do you find yourself clenching your jaws or grinding your teeth at night? This habit can cause cracks in your teeth and a sore jaw. Your dentist can fit you with a night guard that will protect your teeth.

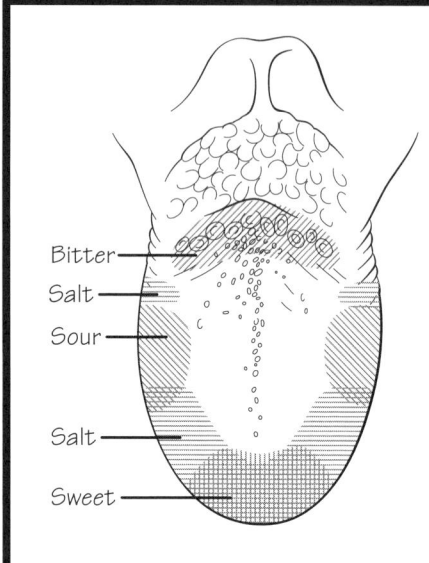

SOMETHING TO THINK ABOUT

The four primary tastes: salty, sweet, sour, and bitter are easy to recognize when the source of the taste is strong. For example: take something sweet and place it on the tip of your tongue. The taste buds that are sensitive to sweetness are located here. Near the tip of the tongue just behind your sweet sensation, are the taste buds sensitive to salt. Next, take a piece of lemon and place it on the sides of your tongue. This is where sour taste buds are located. The bitter taste is probably easiest to detect, its strong sensation is detected by the taste buds in the back of the tongue.

Bitter
Salt
Sour
Salt
Sweet

10-5 STANDING TALL

Just as your smile can say a lot about you, so can your posture. Your **posture** is the way you carry yourself. There are many reasons for poor posture. If you are depressed, sad or lacking confidence, you are more likely to slouch. Why is your posture a reflection of your mood or self-image? Often times, a person does not even know what it feels like to have good posture. If this is your problem try this easy exercise to remind you:

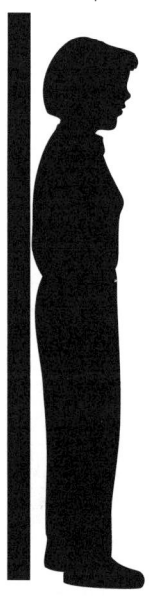

- Stand with your heels a few inches from a wall and about six inches from each other. Make sure your weight is evenly distributed.
- Keep your lower back near the wall as you straighten your upper back. Lift your hands up over your head keeping them in contact with the wall.
- Keep your head resting against the wall with the chin tucked in slightly.
- Concentrate on flattening your lower abdomen by pulling the muscles up and in. Breathe normally as you keep the muscles tight for about 10 seconds. Release and repeat several times.
- Lift your heels off the floor so you are balancing on your toes.

262

Why Should You Have Good Posture?

Being conscious of how you carry yourself is not only good for your physical health but it is good for your mental and social health as well. How you hold yourself influences how others see you and how you feel about yourself. Having bad posture takes away from your appearance and at the same time weakens important muscles and ligaments.

Good posture improves your breathing efficiency by strengthening the muscles and ligaments used in inhalation and exhalation. When you practice good posture you are also helping your circulatory system and internal organs function properly. Although it may be a strain for you to make yourself stand tall or sit up straight, your bones and muscles will adjust and you will find it a very comfortable and natural position.

Do You Have Good Posture?

Stand in front of a mirror, turn sideways and examine the way you are standing. Is your head and neck falling forward? Is your stomach pushed out? Do you generally look like you have a slumping posture? Now imagine a line extending through your body from your head, shoulder, hip, knee and ankle. The line is pulling you up straight like a plumb line (a vertical line that has a weight at one end). How does this change your profile?

Your posture is also important when viewing yourself from the front. Turn and face the mirror. Are your shoulders level with each other? How about your hips? If they are not even with each other you may need to consult a physician.

You should be able to maintain good posture throughout the day whether you are standing, sitting or walking. Answer the following questions:

_____

Why is your posture a reflection of your mood or self-image?

_____

☑ Do you lean on an elbow on your desk while in class?

☑ Do you find yourself tipping your chair either forward or backward to change positions?

☑ Do you find yourself tired and falling asleep in class?

☑ Do you carry your books in a bookbag on one shoulder on the same side of your body?

☑ Do you lean over without bending your knees and keeping your back straight when you pick up something?

If you answered yes to the questions, you need to make changes to improve your posture. Having good posture can help you stay alert in class and improve your energy.

A Word About Your Feet

Think about it. Over a lifetime, your feet carry several million tons and cover enough distance to circle the earth more than two and a half times. When standing on both feet, each bears half the body weight. When walking or running the amount of pounds exerted on each foot dramatically increases. These two feet that held you up when you took your first steps must serve you the rest of your life. Most people are born with healthy feet but after much "abuse" and without proper care, foot problems can develop.

Your feet play an important role in your posture. Have you ever worn shoes that were so uncomfortable that standing or walking was unbearable? Although style has much to do with your choice of shoes, comfort should have a high priority.

- Choose shoes that are flexible and supple but firm in the arch. Pick up a shoe and bend it. Does it feel flexible?
- Choose shoes that have laces or adjustable straps because they can keep the foot from sliding.
- Choose shoes that are at least half an inch longer than the feet and wide enough to allow the toes to move comfortably.
- Choose shoes only after you walk around in them. Remember to put on *both* shoes at the same time. One foot may fit differently in the shoes.

Taking proper care of your feet does not have to take a lot of time or money. Wear comfortable socks with your shoes to help absorb the moisture and protect your feet from blisters. Wash your feet thoroughly during your daily bath or shower. A simple foot bath in the sink or bathtub will make you feel refreshed even if you do not have time for a full shower or bath. Use a foot powder to help control perspiration and foot odor. Because high heel shoes put an added strain on your feet, change your shoes once throughout the day to a lower heel to give your feet a break and always wear the correct shoes for sports.

Common Foot Problems

- **Blister:** caused by shoes rubbing against the foot, usually from poorly-fitted shoes. A water-filled pouch forms at the sight of the irritation. Blisters can lead to corns.
- **Corn:** an overgrowth of the skin on the toe. Corns are usually caused by poorly-fitted shoes. If corns get too thick they must be cut away by a foot specialist.
- **Callus:** a hard, thick part of the skin on the foot. A callus is caused by the foot rubbing against the shoe.
- **Bunion:** a bunion is a bump on the inside of the foot near the big toe. They are caused by shoes that are too tight.

- **Athlete's foot:** a problem caused by a fungus growing in the warm, moist places of the foot. Itching and irritation along with redness occurs. Athlete's foot is very contagious and can be treated with over-the-counter medications.
- **In-grown toe nails:** when the nail cuts into the skin. Caused by improperly cutting the toe nails and shoes that are too tight.

CHAPTER REVIEW

DEFINE

Sebum

Acne

Whitehead

Blackhead

Pimple

Warts

Dandruff

Head lice

Keratin

Cuticle

Hangnails

Balance

Incisors

Canine

Premolars

Molars

Periodontium

Crown

Root

Dentin

Pulp

Gingivitis

Periodontal disease

Plaque

Tartar

Cavity

Malocclusion

Posture

EXPLAIN

1. Explain how your appearance affects your self-esteem.
2. Explain why acne occurs and what you can do to help your skin.
3. Explain why it is important to keep your hair clean and nicely groomed.
4. Explain why not everyone can wear the same hair style and look good.
5. Explain the meaning of Matthew 10:29–31.
6. Explain why the Lord wants you to be careful what your eyes see.
7. Explain the symptoms that may mean you have a problem with your eyes.
8. Explain the structure of the ear and the responsibilities of each.
9. Explain how your ear is responsible for your balance.
10. Explain what can happen if you do not take good care of your teeth now.

11. Explain why good posture can help keep you alert and improve your breathing efficiency.
12. Explain why wearing poorly-fitted shoes can affect your posture and the condition of your feet.
13. Explain why people experience motion sickness.

DISCUSS

1. Discuss the meaning of Matthew 5:14–16.
2. Discuss how acne can affect a person's social life and self-esteem. What would you tell someone who was depressed over his/her acne?
3. Discuss the do's and don'ts of dealing with acne.
4. Discuss how a good hairstyle can improve your overall appearance.
5. Discuss how you can help a friend who wants to stop biting his/her nails.
6. Discuss the analogy of spiritual ears and natural ears.
7. Discuss the negative aspects of using headphones.
8. Discuss how important first impressions are and what you notice first in a person.
9. Discuss why students often have bad posture while sitting in class. What can you do to improve your posture while in class?
10. Discuss how a person should pick out a good pair of shoes.

SUGGESTED ACTIVITIES

1. **Key Concepts:** Outline the chapter and make a study guide for yourself. You can work in groups and each student can be responsible for one section.

2. **Looking Good, Feeling Good:** Write a report on how your appearance affects your self-esteem.

3. **First Impressions:** Make up ten questions concerning what people notice when they meet someone for the first time. Hand the questionnaire out to other students and then collect them. Organize your findings and present them to the class. What do your findings say about personal hygiene?

4. **Wanted: A career in the health field:** There are certain careers in the fields dealing with this chapter. Pick one or two careers and do a report on each one. Present this to the class as an oral report. Include what the qualifications are and the preparation needed to enter this career.

5. **Interview:** Prepare some common questions teenagers may have about their skin and acne. Interview a dermatologist (skin specialist) and present the findings to your class.

6. **Spiritual eyes and ears:** Write a report on the analogy of spiritual eyes and ears. How does the Bible discuss the importance of seeing and hearing?

7. **Communicate with me!** Learn a portion of sign language and teach it to the class. Include a report on sign language.

8. **Dental Hygiene:** Research the proper way to brush and floss your teeth and present your findings to the class.

Risky Business

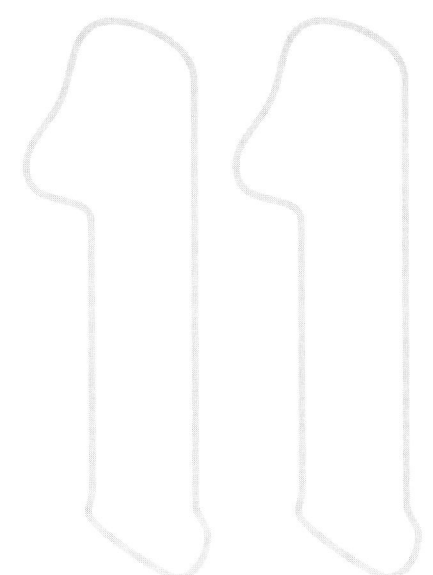

11-1   TAKING A RISK
11-2   SAFETY FIRST
11-3   BASIC FIRST AID
11-4   EMERGENCY!

11-1   TAKING A RISK

"I dare you!" Have you ever been the victim of this one-liner? Many young people view risky activities as fun and adventurous. Consequently, accidents have become one of the leading causes of death among people from one year to 38 years old. Look at the definition of the words *risk* and *accident* according to Webster's Dictionary:

Risk: to expose to hazard or danger
Accident: unexpected, harmful events that occur by chance

No one wants an accident to occur, but the chances greatly increase when you participate in risky activities. The fact that teenagers are notorious for taking unnecessary risk adds to the grim likelihood that a fatal accident may happen.

Teenagers and Risk

More young people die of accidents because they take more risks. Taking risks gives some people a feeling of excitement. Your adrenaline increases as the challenge gets greater, and when you "beat" the odds, an unrealistic sense of confidence clouds your decision making. The attitude that many teenagers share about taking chances is a main factor in their risk taking. As a general rule, the following statements are true concerning why teenagers

When you "beat" the odds, an unrealistic sense of confidence clouds your decision making.

take unnecessary risks:

- Teenagers believe that they are in the peak of health; they are indestructible.
- Teenagers do not think about the possible consequences; as a result they do not make careful decisions.
- Teenagers are "thrill-seekers."
- Teenagers do not want to appear cowardly to their friends.
- Teenagers are unwilling to face the fact that there is a possibility of danger.

What is your attitude about taking risks? Do you tend to fall into the "thrill-seeker" category, or are you more cautious? Whatever your attitude, it is important to know that your life is not the only life affected by your choice. The people you take chances with, as well as your family and friends, will all be involved in the result of your actions. The potential danger often outweighs the potential excitement.

Preventing Unnecessary Accidents

You can still participate in fun and challenging activities, but avoid the unnecessary risks involved. Before you decide to participate in something "questionable," ask yourself the following questions:

- How much is known about the activity? (what *exactly* are you going to do?)
- What risks are involved?
- What can I do to reduce those risks or substitute a less risky activity?
- If I cannot reduce the risks or substitute a less risky activity, is the activity still worth doing?

If, after honestly answering those questions, you decide to participate in the activity, you should make sure an adult knows what you are choosing to do. If you feel you cannot tell an adult what you are planning...then you probably shouldn't do it!

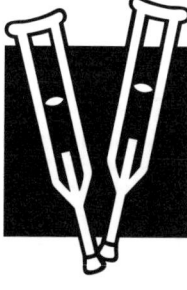

The condition of all aspects of your health affects your risk taking. You need to know your physical limitations. How is your skill, your efficiency, and your ability to make quick responses? If you are taking any medication or failing to eat right, you lose the ability to respond. Furthermore, when you are physically fit, you are better able to handle physical challenges.

You also need to know your emotional state of mind. When you are emotionally upset you are less likely to make wise choices (for example, worrying about a test and not paying attention to traffic). It is difficult to fully concentrate on what you are doing or what is going on around you. Your social health also affects your ability to make wise choices. Are you trying to impress your friends? Peer pressure is a dangerous, but common, reason why many teenagers take unnecessary risks. Can you think of examples where this is true?

What does God think about your taking risks? Do you think He is going to protect you in every activity in which you are involved? The Lord's protection is not absolute. You must take responsibility for your actions. The state of your spiritual health affects the way you handle risky activities. When you lack wisdom you are more likely to participate in questionable activities.

> The Lord's protection is not absolute.

SOMETHING TO THINK ABOUT

Are you safe from crime?

Sometimes people take risks and do not realize that it can put them in a dangerous situation involving crime. Taking part in a crime is going not only against the law but against your obligation to respect the rights and property of others.

Sometimes your own personal safety is threatened by crime. You can take precautions to help you avoid being a victim of criminal action.

- Travel in groups.
- Keep your doors and windows locked (car included).
- Avoid dark streets and unpopulated areas.
- Always look and ask who is at your door before opening it.
- Avoid interactions with strangers.
- Avoid giving any information over the phone to a stranger.
- If something "feels" wrong, find an adult or police officer.

THE UNEXPECTED

It is important to discuss the issue of rape because it is a crime that can unexpectantly affect you. The crime of rape may happen to you or to someone you know. It is very traumatic for the victim. Although the crime generally happens against girls, boys can also be victims. **Rape** is forcing another person to have

©DG 1990

sexual intercourse without consent. **Attempted rape** is an assault in which sexual intercourse is attempted but does not occur. **Statutory rape** is when an adult has sexual intercourse with a minor (under the age of consent) *with* the minor's permission.

Rape is the most unreported crime in America. It is the fastest growing violent crime in the United States and a rape occurs every 6 minutes; that's 80,000 per year! Anyone can be raped, male or female, overweight or underweight, young or old. The rapist does not discriminate; he does not care if you are married or single. Even with these grim statistics, it is good to remember:

Although anyone can be raped, most women will never be raped. [1]

The key for you is to act wisely and take "lifestyle" precautions. This means to practice these precautions for the rest of your life.

- Avoid situations where you are open to attack.
- Avoid being alone; go places in groups. Rape is a crime of privacy.
- Do not let anyone touch you inappropriately.
- Walk with confidence. Have a purpose to your stride. Do not act like a victim.

If a rape does occur, the victim should get help immediately — call the police. A rape victim advocate will come and be with the victim throughout the legal process. Rape is not something that just "goes away" or something that a person can easily forget. What has happened is not "fair," "good," or "right," but the Lord is a person's hope and strength (II Corinthians 5:7, II Timothy 1:7, Psalm 20:7 and Hebrews 13:5).

Rape is not the victim's fault. Rape counselors know the trauma that the individual experiences and respects their privacy.

SOMETHING TO THINK ABOUT

"It won't happen to me"
Although you can be raped by a stranger, you can also be violated by someone you know. When **date rape** occurs the victim is forced to have sexual intercourse by someone on a date. You must take special precautions when you begin dating. Your date may seem like a gentleman and do all the "right" things, but when it comes to sexual involvement, he may demand something from you that you do not want to give. The best advice is to never get into the situation where you find yourself alone, in a private area where your date

could take advantage of you. Never feel you must give in to this person because you are "friends." Whatever the situation, rape is a crime and a violation against you.

Accidents will, but do not have to, happen!

11-2 SAFETY FIRST

Accidents happen unexpectedly. You may be walking down the stairs in your home like you have done a million times, and just this once, you miss a stair and fall. You may think nothing of taking a bath, until one day you step out of the bath and slip on some water on the floor. If you do not take precautions in your everyday living, you or someone you love, may be the victim of an accident. *Accidents will, but do not have to, happen!*

SAFETY AT HOME

About one-fourth of all accidental deaths occur in the home. Knowing how to prevent home accidents is important — not only for you, but to all the members of your family.

Fire Safety

The best fire safety in the home is "prevention." The best place to start is to install and maintain smoke detectors. Smoke detectors can warn you of a fire in time for you to escape. They should be installed on every level of the home and checked every month to make sure they are functioning properly. Change the battery once a year.

If a fire occurs in your home, you must act quickly! You and your family should have two escape routes out of every room planned and practiced. Choose a meeting place outside and once you are out of your home, do not go back in!

Everyone should know this rule if your clothes catch on fire: *stop, drop, and roll.* Do not run! Cover your face with your hands and stop where you are, drop to the ground, and roll over and over to smother the flames. When traveling in a smoke-filled home, the safest way to move is to crawl low to the ground under the smoke.

- Be careful while cooking. Never leave the area while you are cooking. Make sure pot handles are turned inward to avoid being knocked over. Keep the cooking area clear of any combustibles (flammable objects) and wear tight fitting sleeves. If a grease fire occurs, carefully cover the pan with the lid to smother the flames, then turn off the burner. Oil and water do not mix. Do not use water on a fire caused by grease!

276

- Keep electrical wiring in good working order. Don't over-load extension cords and never run extension cords under carpets, through doors or over nails.
- Keep matches and lighters out of the hands of children.
- If there are smokers in the house, be extra cautious concerning fire hazard. Always use ashtrays for cigarettes and never smoke in bed or when you are resting.
- Throw out old newspapers and other combustibles. Keep oily household rags in tightly-covered metal containers, including kerosene, gasoline, and paint thinners.
- Space heaters need space. Keep space heaters at least three feet from anything that can burn. Always turn them off when you leave your home or when you go to bed.

SOMETHING TO THINK ABOUT

Do you have a first-aid kit?

A first-aid kit will prepare you to treat minor injuries and to deal with more serious injuries until the person can get medical help. Do you have a first-aid kit in your home?

- First-aid manual
- Rolls of sterile gauze bandages in various sizes
- Adhesive bandages, various sizes
- Roll of adhesive tape
- Scissors
- Elastic bandage
- Cotton swabs
- Cotton
- Syrup of ipecac (to induce vomiting)
- Tweezers
- Hydrogen Peroxide
- Bar of plain soap
- Antibiotic ointment
- Antiseptic wipes
- Dosage spoon or eye-dropper

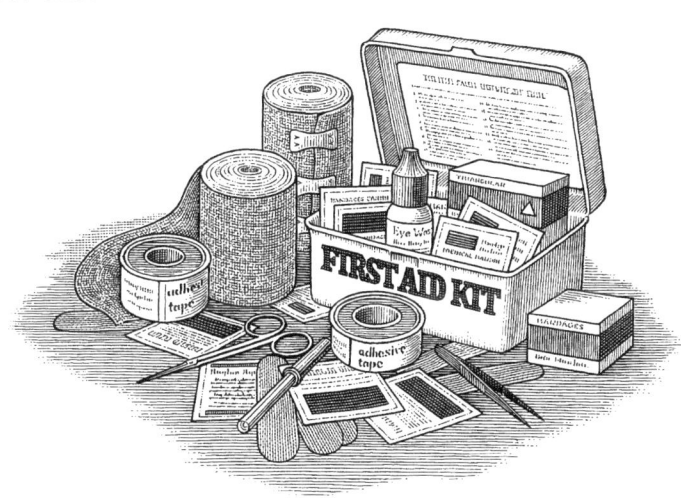

Poisoning

Poisons in the home are a real threat, especially for young children. Many common household items are poisonous. Cleaning supplies, insect sprays, gardening and household chemicals and medicines are all potentially hazardous. Poisoning involves not only ingesting products, but smelling the gases and vapors as well.

Keeping these items in their original containers and out of the reach of children (preferably in a locked container) is the best precaution. Make sure you keep all the labels on medicines so the dosage and precautions can be read. Throw out drugs and prescriptions that have passed their expiration date.

First aid for a person you suspect has swallowed a poison is:

- Call the Poison Control Center: the number to your local poison control center should be on the inside cover of your phone book. If you can, take the bottle of substance and the victim to the phone with you so you have all the information for the emergency operator. Do what you are told by the center.
- Call the 911 emergency operator and explain the situation and all that the poison control center told you to do. An ambulance may come and take the victim to the emergency room.
- Save the container of substance and give it to the medical team when they arrive.
- Wipe the mouth clean: take a clean, moist cloth and wipe the mouth of the victim clean of any excess substance around or inside the mouth.

Falls

You have heard the warnings, "don't run in the house" or "someone is going to get hurt." These verbal warnings are usually correct; within minutes someone is hurt and crying. Falls are a common accident. These accidents can usually be prevented by following a few safety rules:

- Keep toys and other objects out of the traffic areas of your home.
- Clean up spills on the floor thoroughly.
- Use a non-skid mat in your bathtub and shower.
- Avoid running and "rough-housing" indoors.

Gun Safety

People have guns in their homes for various reasons. A gun is not a toy. No matter how curious you might be about a gun, do not handle a gun unless an adult has taught you how to handle one safely and gives you permission. An adult should also be there to supervise the situation. Guns should always be locked securely and should only be loaded when it is to be used. Above all else — never point a gun at anyone!

Making the Call

Your local emergency number can be located at the front of your telephone book. Keep this number near all phones. Better yet, have it memorized. When the assistants on the other end of the phone answers, give them the following information. Speak clearly and do not rush.

- The site of the emergency (give street names and cross streets).
- The number of the telephone you are using to make the call.
- Your name.
- What happened to the victim(s) (fire, accident etc.).
- The number of people injured.
- The victim's condition and any obvious injury (bleeding, head wounds, etc.).
- Any first aid currently being given.
- DO NOT HANG UP THE PHONE.

SAFETY AT SCHOOL

Traveling to and from school may seem like a daily routine to you, but it can be dangerous if you do not take precautions. If you walk or ride your bike any of the distance you should take special care as to where you travel. Always use main roads. If you  must travel at dusk or dark always use well-lit streets. There is safety in numbers, so as much as possible, travel with a group of other people.

If you find yourself in a hurry in getting to and from school, remember, it is better to get there a little late than to not get there at all. During school hours you may find yourself hurrying from class to class. Try not to rush. The risk of any accident happening is great where there are a number of people. Always follow the rules and play within your ability when you are involved in a sports activity or during Physical Education class.

SAFETY OUTDOORS

Safety rules are made to help protect you from accidents. Most of them are a matter of common sense, but if you do not take them seriously or you do not respect the principles they stand for, you could be a victim of an unnecessary accident.

Safety on the Road

Whether you walk, jog, ride your bike or drive a car, the road is a very dangerous place. When accidents happen to **pedestrians** (people who travel on foot), it is not always the driver's fault. As a pedestrian there are certain precautions you need to take to act responsibly.

- Always be aware of what is going on around you (avoid wearing headphones or playing loud music).

Safety rules are made to help protect you from accidents.

- Always use the designated crosswalk, do not jaywalk (cross the street in the middle of the block).
- Always stop, look and listen before you cross the street.
- Always wear reflective gear when traveling at dusk or at night.
- Always assume that the driver will not see you.
- Always use a sidewalk, but if there is not one, walk facing the traffic.

Bicycle riding has become a very popular mode of transportation. It is low-cost as well as being beneficial to your health. The possibility of an accident can be reduced if the biker obeys the rules of the road.

- Always ride on the right side of the street (with the flow of traffic) in single file.
- Always obey the traffic signals.
- Always look back over your shoulder frequently and pay extra attention when passing driveways, parking lots, and schools.
- Always use proper hand signals for turning. Yield to cars and to pedestrians.
- Always keep your bike in good working condition.
- Always wear a helmet.
- Always use reflectors and reflective clothes when riding.

Motor vehicle accidents are the leading cause of accidental deaths among teenagers. Precaution needs to be taken by the passengers as well as by the driver. Driving defensively is an important principle to learn. To drive defensively also means to obey all the traffic laws and to be aware of the other drivers, bikers, and pedestrians that share the road. Watch for the unexpected. Be aware, another driver may not be obeying the law and may be putting you at risk of an accident.

Wearing your safety belt is an important rule of the road. Make the passengers in your car wear their safety belts. If you are the driver, do not daydream or window shop as you are driving. Avoid unnecessary distractions in your car by keeping the radio low and the passengers from being too loud. If you are taking a long trip, take frequent rest stops and switch drivers when you need a break. Remember, do not drink alcohol or take drugs that can cause drowsiness.

Safety in the Water

The second leading cause of accidental deaths among teenagers is drowning. Some of these accidents could have been prevented if people followed some basic rules.

The number one rule for water safety is, do not enter or play around the water unless you know how to swim. It is never too late to learn how to swim. You do not need to be an expert swimmer to enjoy the water. The second most important rule for water safety is, do not swim or boat alone. You may be an excellent swimmer but when the unexpected happens you need someone there to look out for you and to get help. Whenever participating in recreational activities on the water, be sure to wear a life jacket.

Tips for swimming safety:
- Learn to swim.
- Do not swim alone.
- Check the depth of the water before diving.
- Swim where there is a lifeguard.
- Avoid swimming when you are tired, sick or overheated. When you get a cramp, change your stroke, float, or apply firm pressure to the cramped muscle.
- Avoid swimming after eating a heavy meal.
- Never swim during a storm.

Tips for Boating safety:

- Take a boat out only if you can handle it safely.
- Make sure you have all the legal equipment on board and working properly.
- Do not place more weight in the boat than is recommended for that size.
- Never drink alcohol or take drugs that can cause drowsiness when around water.
- Always scan the water ahead of your boat for objects or people in the water.
- Check the weather and water conditions.

11-3 BASIC FIRST AID

THE VALUE OF HAVING FIRST AID TRAINING

Natural disasters can occur without any time to prepare, accidents can happen without any warning, and illness can strike without any indication. If you are trained in the basic principles of first aid then you are equipped to give help to yourself, give help to others, prepare for a disaster, and have reliable safety awareness. You may never encounter a time when your knowledge is called upon, but giving proper first aid, just one time, can mean the difference between life and death.

First aid is the immediate care given to a person who has been injured or has been suddenly taken ill until qualified medical care can be supplied. If you are not the victim, you could be the first-aider. The person giving first aid is called the **first-aider.**

First aid begins with *action.* When you show confidence to a victim that you know what to do and what not to do, it gives the person a sense of well-being. Proper action has a calming effect for both you and the victim and if you remain calm, the victim is more likely to remain calm.

When you realize that someone needs first aid, you must take action and check out the situation. Every second you save by acting quickly could save a person's life. Read the following situation. With the first aid knowledge you have now, would you stop to help, and if you did, would you know what to do?

You and a friend are driving home one night and you come upon an automobile accident. You stop to help and survey the situation and this is what you find:

_____

First aid

begins with

action.

_____

A two-car accident. One car has victim #1 who was thrown from the car and is severely bleeding. Victim #1 is conscious but very weak. From the other car, you find victim #2 who is unconscious and you cannot find a pulse. He has no obvious external wounds but he is still in the car. Victim #3, the driver of the car, has an obvious broken leg and a serious head wound. He is in and out of consciousness. You and your friend are the first to arrive on the scene of the accident. You are at a normally busy road, but it is late and you have not seen a car come by since you arrived — you must act now! Who would you treat first? Second? Third? How would you administer first aid?

Don't worry if you do not know how to respond to the situation described. After reading this chapter, you will have the knowledge to act quickly and administer basic first aid until help arrives.

First, Check it Out!

When you find yourself in a crisis situation, take a deep breath, clear your head, and try to relax. You will be surprised at how much first-aid knowledge that you have stored in your memory will come back to you when you need it. The first action you need to take when you arrive at a scene is to check it out or survey the situation. To survey the situation means to quickly view all of the victims and their condition as you see it. Then do the following as they are listed in order of importance:

#1. Rescue the victim.
#2. Check the victim's breathing.
#3. Control severe bleeding.
#4. Get help!

#1. Rescue the Victim

Move a victim only if his life is in danger if he remains where he is. If you see any sign of head, neck or spine injury do not move him. If the victim needs to be rescued from water because of drowning or from a fire because of the risk of burns and smoke inhalation, or if a person in a car is endangered from oncoming traffic, then remove the person.

#2. Check the Victim's Breathing

Look, Listen And Feel: If the victim is unconscious, check to make sure he/she is breathing. Place the victim on his or her back and place your ear over the mouth and *look* at the chest to rise as he/she is breathing. *Listen* and *feel* for air from the mouth or nose. If he or she does not seem to be breathing, make sure nothing is obstructing the airway. Remove anything that may be blocking the victim's breathing. If he or she is still not breathing, administer mouth-to-mouth or mouth-to-nose **artificial respiration** (sometimes called rescue breathing). This is a substitute

When you find yourself in a crisis situation, take a deep breath, clear your head, and try to relax.

for normal breathing in which someone forces air into the victim's lungs. A victim without oxygen to the brain has approximately 4–6 minutes until permanent damage occurs.

Artificial respiration does not help if the heart of the victim has stopped completely. When this occurs, the combination of artificial respiration and cardiopulmonary resuscitation is necessary.

The **ABC's** of artificial respiration for adults and older children are:

Airway
Breathing
Circulation

Airway

a. Open the airway by tilting the head backward. Place one hand on the forehead and one hand under the chin. While gently pressing down on the forehead lift up the chin. Clear out the mouth if any foreign object is blocking the airway.
b. Look, listen and feel for breathing.
Look for chest to rise.
Listen for exhalation.
Feel for breath against your cheek.

Breathing

a. Pinch nostrils with hand resting on forehead.
b. Take a deep breath and with your mouth open widely, seal your mouth tightly over the victim's mouth. Give four quick breaths.
c. Look, listen and feel for breathing to start.
d. Repeat if not breathing, giving about 12 breaths per minute.
e. Repeat steps if breathing does not start.

Circulation

a. Check for pulse: on side of neck feel for pulse at carotid artery.
b. If no pulse is felt administer cardiopulmonary resuscitation.
c. Re-check pulse and breathing every minute.

For small children and infants the procedure is slightly different. For an infant or child between the ages of 1 and 8, do not tilt the head back as far as an adult. Support the infant's head in your hand and cover the child's nose and mouth with your mouth. For children 1 to 8 years give one breath every 4 seconds and for infants, one breath every 3 seconds. Do not breathe as hard as you would for an adult because the lungs could be damaged.

#3. Control Severe Bleeding

If a person is breathing and there is a pulse then the next step is to control any severe bleeding. The sight of blood may be traumatic for you but don't let it distract you from what you need to do. Severe bleeding may lead to shock or, in a short amount of time, death. Control bleeding by doing the following:

- **Apply direct pressure:** Press down hard on the wound with an absorbent material. If no material is available, use your hand. Do not remove the dressing if it becomes soaked, just add more material to the top of the dressing. If the bleeding stops, do not lift the dressing off the wound.
- **Elevate the wound:** If possible raise the wounded area above the level of the victim's heart. If the victim has a broken bone, do not elevate the area.
- **Use a pressure point:** If the bleeding does not stop, combine direct pressure with pressure on a main artery leading to the wound.

If the victim shows the following signs he or she may be in shock. Victim's breathing is shallow and uneven, the skin is pale and clammy, the pulse is weak or cannot be felt, and the eyes may be dull and pupils dilated (wide open).

Shock is a dangerous condition in which the body functions slow down dramatically. Any traumatic experience can cause a person to go into any degree of shock. It is important that you treat the victim for shock by laying him or her on the back with their feet elevated 8 to 12 inches off the ground. Do not raise the feet if there is a head injury. Cover the person with a blanket or other wrap to keep the body temperature from dropping.

Pressure Points

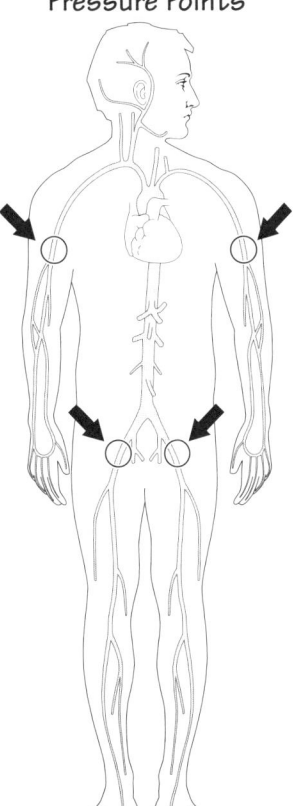

The sight of blood may be traumatic for you but don't let it distract you from what you need to do.

#4. Get Help!

When you arrive at the sight of an emergency and you are not alone, send someone to get help. Tell them by name, "Sue, go call 911." Be expected to give the following information over the phone:

Your name, the location of the accident, the number of persons involved, the telephone number where you can be reached (at that moment and later at your residence for further information). Do not hang up the phone until after the other party hangs up!

Test your knowledge: Go back to the car accident described in the beginning of this section. Read through it. Test your first aid knowledge. Can you answer the questions?

11-4 EMERGENCY!

Common emergencies happen everyday. While you are at school students get nose bleeds, sprained ankles and may even faint. The school nurse can help in these emergencies, but there may be times when you will need to administer first aid to a person or to yourself.

"I Feel Faint"

Have you ever felt faint? It is a feeling you don't easily forget. At first you may feel light headed, then a bit dizzy. When you see those black spots you know you're heading to the floor!

Fainting (a temporary loss of consciousness) occurs for many reasons (illness, stuffy room, over-exhaustion, not eating). When the blood supply to the brain suddenly decreases, a person feels faint. If a person says he feels faint, do not try to hold him up. Have the person sit down and place his head between his knees. If this does not help, gently ease the person to the ground on his back. Make sure the person is breathing and has a pulse (look, listen and feel). Elevate the feet 8 to 12 inches above the ground and loosen the clothing. Use a cool, moist cloth on the person's forehead and face. If the victim does not regain consciousness, get medical help.

Burns

There are three categories of burns. They are: first-degree, second-degree and third-degree. Burns are classified by their severity. No matter what the degree of burn a victim has, never place butter, oil or ice on the burn.

First-degree burns affect only the outer layer of skin. A person can suffer a first-degree burn by briefly touching a hot object or having a minor sunburn. The symptoms of a first-degree burn include: red skin and pain and/or swelling in the area of the burn. To treat this type of burn, hold the burn area under cold running water or immerse the burn in cold (but not iced) water for 15 to 30 minutes. Keep the burn area above the heart if possible and apply a clean dressing to the burn.

Second-degree burns damage not only the outer layer of skin but also the layer beneath it. A person can suffer a second-degree burn from severe sunburn and contact with hot liquids. The symptoms of a second-degree burn include: red skin, pain, swelling, and blisters, which may appear along with peeling of the skin. To treat this type of burn do all that you do for a first-degree burn but also remember not to pop the blisters. See a doctor if the burn covers more than two inches or if it becomes infected.

Third-degree burns are very serious burns in which all the layers of skin are damaged. In severe cases even the fat cells, muscles, and bones are damaged. Causes of third-degree burns include: electric shock, burns from fire, and contact with hot liquid. The skin looks white and charred and it is likely that the person will suffer from shock. The best first aid for a person who has a third-degree burn is immediate medical care. Do not put water or ointments on the burn area. Also do not remove any burned clothing. You may cover the burned area with a sterile dressing. If the person is conscious, you may give him/her small sips of water. If the person is not breathing, give artificial respiration.

Nosebleeds

Nosebleeds are common because the capillaries inside the nose are close to the surface. A bump to the nose, a cold, or exposure to high altitude can all cause the capillaries to break. Most nosebleeds are more of an inconvenience than an emergency, but action should be taken to stop the bleeding. If you have a nosebleed sit down and lean slightly forward. Breathe through your mouth and pinch the nostrils firmly. Hold the nostrils shut for about 5 to 10 minutes without stopping. You can hold a cold cloth to your nose while you pinch it. Although these steps should stop a nosebleed, there are exceptions. If the bleeding does not stop, get medical attention. If the nosebleed was caused by a head injury or a hard blow to the face, get medical attention.

Heat Exhaustion and Heatstroke

Exercising in hot weather or being exposed to high temperatures can cause heat exhaustion or life-threatening, heatstroke. Symptoms of heat exhaustion include: abundant sweating, pale and clammy skin, dilated pupils, weakness, nausea, muscle cramps, headache and a rise in body temperature. When a person suffers from heat exhaustion, the profuse sweating actually helps keep the body temperature down. It is when the sweating stops that heatstroke can occur.

The actions to take for a person suffering from heat exhaustion would be to cool the person off by moving him or her out of the sun, lay the victim down, loosen the clothing and elevate the feet. Give the victim sips of cool water.

Heatstroke is life-threatening because the body's cool-

> Exercising in hot weather or being exposed to high temperatures can cause heat exhaustion or life-threatening, heatstroke.

ing system shuts down and the body temperature gets dangerously high. In heatstroke any or all of the following may occur: the person may be flushed with hot, dry skin, and may have rapid pulse, dizziness, confusion, hallucinating, loss of consciousness and sudden rise in body temperature.

The first action to take for a person suffering from heatstroke is get medical help immediately. While waiting for help to arrive, remove the victim's clothing and place him or her in a cold bath. If this is not possible, spray the person with cool water, wrap him or her in cool sheets or towels, fan the victim or use an electric fan. It is important not to get the person shivering cold. Keep a close watch on the victim's body temperature.

Hypothermia

Hypothermia is a dangerous condition caused by prolonged exposure to the cold. Besides having a low body temperature, he or she might also suffer from the following symptoms: drowsiness, irritability, slurred speech, stiff muscles, red skin and loss of consciousness. To treat a hypothermia victim, get medical help immediately. Make sure the person is breathing and has a pulse, take the person to a warm location and remove any wet clothing. Wrap the person in blankets (do not use electric blankets), have the victim lie down and do not massage the person. Massaging the person and having them move around will cause the blood to draw away from the vital organs. If the person needs more warmth, lie down next to him or her. If the person is conscious, give sips of warm liquid.

Choking

Each year about 3,000 deaths occur in the United States as a result of choking. Choking occurs when the airway becomes obstructed. Unless a person who is choking gets immediate first aid, he or she can die within minutes. You could be the one to save a person from choking to death. The warning signs of choking include, gasping for breath, inability to speak, waving the hands, change of skin tone to blue, and clutching the throat. Everyone should know the universal sign for choking: grab your throat between the thumb and forefinger.

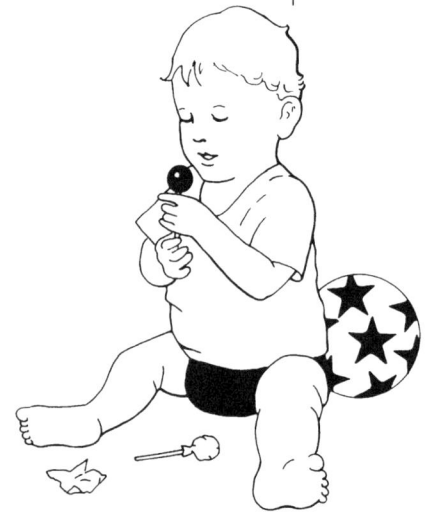

The **Heimlich Maneuver** is used to dislodge an object from an adult's or child's throat. First aid for infants and small children who are choking involves a different procedure. With your forearm under the infant, place the baby on your knee and give four firm blows between the shoulder blades. If this does not work, turn the baby over on his or her back. Press two fingers into the middle of the child's chest, just below the nipples. Repeat this procedure if the object is not released. For children under eight years old, do the four blows on the back but when you turn the child, press two fingers into the middle of the child's abdomen just above the navel and below the ribs.

If you think someone may be choking ask them "are you choking?" If you get no answer or a "yes," then move behind the person and do the Heimlich Maneuver. This method is also called *abdominal thrusts*.

1. Stand behind the victim. Put your arms around his or her waist. Place your fist with the thumb side against the abdomen, just above the navel but below the ribs.
2. Holding your fist with your other hand, give up to five quick, forceful thrusts. Use only your fists and do not squeeze the ribs. Once the object is dislodged, give rescue breathing if necessary.

If you are choking and you are alone, you can administer abdominal thrusts to yourself. Make a fist and thrust it quickly into your upper abdomen. If this does not work, press your stomach forcefully over the back of a chair. Repeat until the object is removed.

CPR (Cardiopulmonary Resuscitation)

CPR is a technique that combines artificial respiration and chest compressions to revive victims who have no pulse. Artificial respiration puts oxygen in the blood while the chest compressions force the blood throughout the body. Make sure that you learn this technique well. Only someone professionally trained in the correct procedure should administer this technique because the chest compressions, if done incorrectly, can damage a person's ribs and internal organs.

If you see someone who you has collapsed, you should do the following:

- Check for responsiveness: "Are you O.K.?"
- Tell someone to get help.
- Follow the ABC's of artificial respiration.
  Airway: look, listen and feel for breathing.
  Breathing: if there is a pulse, but not breathing, give artificial respiration.
  Circulation: if there is no pulse, only someone trained in CPR should carry out this procedure.

Tips for Babysitters

- Ask the parents where the first-aid kit is in the home.
- Make sure all important phone numbers are posted near the phone, including the poison control center.
- Have a brief medical history of each child available to you.
- Take a first-aid course.
- Have available the phone numbers of a trusted neighbor or family member.
- In case of an electrical outage or some other disaster, know where the fuse box and flashlight are located.
- Make sure you are aware of any allergies or health problems the child may have.
- Do not spend lots of time on the telephone or watching T.V. when you can be distracted from watching the child or children.
- Do not take any medications in front of the children, and never call medicine "candy."

CHAPTER REVIEW

DEFINE

Risk

Accident

Rape

Attempted rape

Statutory rape

Date rape

Pedestrians

First aid

First-aider

Artificial respiration

Shock

Fainting

First-degree burn

Second-degree burn

Third-degree burn

Hypothermia

Heimlich maneuver

Cardiopulmonary resuscitation

EXPLAIN

1. Explain why more young people are more likely to take unnecessary risks.
2. Explain how a teenager can still have fun but avoid the unnecessary risks involved in an activity.
3. Explain the meaning of the phrase, "The Lord's protection is not absolute."
4. Explain what is meant by taking "lifestyle" precautions concerning rape prevention.
5. Explain how you can help prevent accidents at home.
6. Explain the proper procedure when you think someone may have swallowed a poisonous substance.
7. Explain how you can prevent accidents while riding your bike.
8. Explain what is the value of having first-aid training.
9. Explain exactly what you would do when you came upon the car accident described in this chapter. What would you do first? Who would you treat first, second and third? What first aid would you administer to each victim?
10. Explain the correct first-aid procedure for artificial respiration or rescue breathing.
11. Explain the correct first aid for controlling severe bleeding.
12. Explain the correct first aid for treating each degree of burn.
13. Explain what the universal sign for choking is, and what

you would do to administer the Heimlich Maneuver to an adult.

14. Explain what you would do if your infant brother was choking.

15. Explain why it is important that only persons trained in CPR should administer this technique.

DISCUSS

1. Discuss some of the specific ways that teenagers take risks. If you were encouraged to do an activity that was "questionable," how would you handle the situation?

2. Discuss why it is important for everyone to take precaution against rape and other attacks. Why do you think rape is the most unreported crime in the United States? How can a woman protect herself from date rape?

3. Discuss how you can take precautions to protect yourself from crime.

4. Discuss why gun safety is so important. Why do you think that the issue of guns has become a major issue in society today? Years ago young people played with play guns and it was not such a "big deal." Why do you think this is different today?

5. Discuss why being in a hurry can be a major factor in an accident. How can a person change this "in-a-hurry" lifestyle?

6. Discuss why it is important for you, the first-aider, to remain calm at the sight of an accident. What about explaining the person's injury in detail to him or her? For example, "this is so bad, you are really bleeding!" How does this make the victim feel? How can you reassure the victim instead of frightening him or her?

7. Discuss why it is important to survey an accident. How do you do this?

8. Discuss how you, as an older brother or sister, or as a baby-sitter, can better prepare yourself for an emergency.

9. Discuss the verse James 1:5 and how it applies to acting in an emergency situation.

10. Discuss the meaning of the phrase, "accidents will, but do not have, to happen."

SUGGESTED ACTIVITIES

1. **Key Concepts:** Outline the chapter and make a study guide for yourself. You may work alone or in groups.

2. **Take Precaution:** Call your local Rape Prevention Hotline through your local police. Interview them concerning the issue of rape prevention. What can you do to protect yourself against rape and other attacks? What should you do if you think someone is following you? What should you do if you are attacked? Add to this list of questions and share your findings with the class.

3. **Act it Out!:** Get in groups of 2–3 and put together a skit concerning an issue from this chapter. For example, deciding not to take risks, what to do to protect yourself against crime, rape, accidents, or what to do when you come upon a car accident. Plan the skit out carefully so you can accurately teach the class what to do.

4. **Do it Now!** Get a good-sized box (slightly bigger than a shoe box). Prepare it as a first-aid kit for your home. Make sure you have all the items listed (and even more!) in this chapter. Place the box in a safe, dry place in your home, out of the reach of small children. Present your first-aid box to the class to show them how it is done and what each item is used for.

5. **Fire Prevention:** Interview a local firefighter and ask him or her about the necessary precautions you can take to help prevent fires in your home or school. Share you findings with your class and make a poster listing all the things that you learned.

6. **A Picture Talks:** Make a collage on the topic "safe living." Add pictures and words that will teach others how to live safely. Place your collage in your classroom and notice how, even though each is unique, they all share similar principles of safety.

7. **Fire!** Map out two fire exits from each room in your home. Make a map on paper of the floor plan of your house. By using arrows, show your fire escape routes on the paper. Do this activity with your family so everyone knows the routes. Then practice the fire escapes.

8. **"Don't Shoot!"** Write a report on gun safety. Include in your report what the government is recently doing to enforce gun safety. Include any rules your school has about guns and weapons. Find some statistics on gun accidents involving children. Your local police department would help you with this information. Include in your report how people who hunt can take precautions with guns. Also include what your opinion is on children playing with toy guns (there is no right or wrong answer here, just support your opinion).

9. **Meet Mr. Yuk:** Ask your poison control center to send you several Mr. Yuk stickers. Place them on all the poisonous products in your home. "Introduce" your younger brothers or sisters to Mr. Yuk and explain to them the dangers of poisons.

What's Your Responsibility?

12-1 IT'S IN THE ATTITUDE
12-2 RESPONSIBILITY AS A CHRISTIAN
12-3 RESPONSIBILITY AS A PERSON
12-4 RESPONSIBILITY AS A CITIZEN

12-1 IT'S IN THE ATTITUDE

Do you want freedom without responsibility? That combination will not work. If a person is not yet ready to accept all the responsibilities of living, then he is not ready to handle unrestricted freedom either.[1]
Dr. James Dobson

Throughout this text you have read that your attitude determines your actions and your actions reflect your values. It is often difficult to put into words an attitude. An **attitude** is a feeling or emotion toward something. What is your feeling about taking responsibility for your behavior?

Teenagers have strong feelings about freedom, how much unrestricted "space" they are allowed by adults. One 13 year old puts it this way: "It all comes down to independence, and this lack of independence probably causes most of the problems between teens and their parents. Independence to me, is being able to do what I want to do, when and how I want to do it. One thing I know is when I do get it, my world will expand."

Yes, your world will expand when you are given more independence. With this "enlargement," however, will come success or defeat. Do an "attitude check." Are you ready to develop the attitude that is the basis for success? Do not fight against the limitations but submit to them and know that God is preparing you for action — action that will result in victory. Your lifestyle may seem directly opposite to what society portrays as "success-ful." Pride, position, and power is the message that society wants you to hear. These words speak selfish ambition and defeat. God has a different message — love, submission and obedience. These words speak Godly ambition and victory.

Dr. Dobson says that the combination of freedom without responsibility will not work. It is like oil and water — they do not mix. Soon, you will experience the type of freedom you are desiring. You will be "on your own." No one will tell you what time to go to bed, when to get up for school, or what you should eat. Your attitude however, about that "freedom" will determine whether your life will result in chaos or order.

A parent of a young teen says: *"freedom is not really valued for its true worth unless it is earned."*

So, what's your attitude? Is your faith going to make a difference in your lifestyle? It will all stem from your attitude; the way you think and feel about God and life.

God has a special plan…no one can stop it, but many can miss it! [2]
Pastor Wendell Smith

12-2 RESPONSIBILITY AS A CHRISTIAN

Steward: a manager, supervisor, superintendent; to hold the office of oversight of another's property or affairs.

As each one has received a gift, minister it to one another, as good stewards of the manifold grace of God.
I Peter 4:10

God wants you to be a good steward of the life you have received from God. He has bestowed on you unique gifts that are a part of fulfilling your destiny. Carrying out your spiritual responsibilities as a Christian is part of good stewardship.

When you choose to follow Christ, you also choose to take on responsibility — the kind of responsibility that comes with being a solider of Jesus Christ. A soldier's primary responsibility is to follow the orders of the commander. Your commander is Christ and His orders are the Word of God. What are some of the responsibilities of the Christian life? Being a Christian means following the Word of God.

- Love God (Deuteronomy 6:5; 2 Corinthians 5:14).
- Love One Another (I Peter 1:22).
- Extend the Kingdom: Share the Gospel (Matthew 28:19; Mark 16:15).
- Obey His Commandments (Deuteronomy 10:12,13; 13:4; 30:8,16).
- Be An Example in Word and Deed (1 Timothy 4:12).

Just as there are many soldiers in a natural army, there are many soldiers in God's army. You do not have to bear the burden of the responsibilities alone. There is strength in numbers. Archibald Naismith describes the Christian attitude toward responsibility best:

Responsibility *for the Christian has been defined as "your response to God's ability."*

There are five possible attitudes:
#1. You may shirk your responsibilities.
#2. You may shelve your responsibilities.
#3. You may shoulder your responsibilities.
#4. You may shed your responsibilities.
#5. You may share your responsibilities. [3]

#1. You may shirk your responsibilities

 To *shirk* means to avoid the performance of an obligation or duty. When you shirk you do anything in your power to avoid fulfilling your duty. To avoid the responsibilities of a Christian life, a person avoids fulfilling the commands of the captain of the army. You are still a part of the army but you are not in "active" duty. What does this attitude do to a Christian soldier? As a result of this attitude, you never grow and mature from being involved in the action and you do not experience the full joy of participating in God's army.

#2. You may shelve your responsibilities

 To *shelve* means to put them off the "to do" list and place them on the "waiting" list. When you put off your Christian responsibilities for another time you are missing out on the action. You are wasting valuable time hoping that in the future you may be able to fulfill them. What does this attitude do to a Christian soldier? As a result of this attitude, you miss out on all that God has for you right now. Others will experience growth in God, but you will remain "in the back" of the ranks.

#3. You may shoulder your responsibilities

 To *shoulder* means to assume the burden or responsibility alone. When you take on the duties by yourself you are placing too much pressure on yourself. You go to the front lines without any protection! This is not the way God's army is designed. What does this attitude do to a Christian soldier? As a result of this attitude you are welcoming attack from all sides. And if you do have moments of triumph, you will take the credit yourself. At some point you will, most likely, get wounded and burn out from spiritual exhaustion.

#4. You may shed your responsibilities

To *shed* means to rid oneself of temporarily or permanently as unwanted. This could happen after you have attempted to fulfill your responsibilities but failed. Discouragement, lack of faith or disinterest can cause a Christian to give the responsibilities back to God with an "I don't want it" attitude. What does this do to a Christian soldier? As a result of this attitude you don't respond to the commander. You give *back* to Him the call He has placed on you. You never reach your destiny. Others march ahead and you are not in the ranks.

#5. You may share your responsibilities

To *share* means to partake of, use, experience, or enjoy with others. When you share the responsibilities of the Christian life with others, you receive strength. The army is strengthened by your position and when you are weak, others can take up the slack. With this attitude you are better able to reach your destiny in God because you have the guidance and protection of other soldiers in the army. It is following this principle that you will best be able to live a successful Christian life and bring Glory to God.

Bear one another's burdens, and so fulfill the law of Christ. For if anyone thinks himself to be something, when he is nothing, he deceives himself. But let each one examine his own work, and then he will have rejoicing in himself alone, and not in another. For each one shall bear his own load.
Galatians 6:2–5

SOMETHING TO THINK ABOUT

I often have a dream about a friend of mine. We have known each other much of our lives and I would consider us good friends. The pictures in the dream are foggy, the images are a little dim, but the words that I hear my friend say to me are very clear. "Why didn't you tell me about Jesus" she yells to me as I am entering the light of heaven and she is fading into the darkness of eternity.

You see, I am scared to tell my friend about Jesus. When I look at her life — the money, reputation, career and possessions — I have a hard time sharing with her the simple love of God. I remember I tried one time. She laughed and said "that's all right for you but I am happy with my life." When I see my friend, I am reminded of my reoccurring dream. In reality, my friend is poor and I am rich. I need to share the wealth.

12-3 RESPONSIBILITY AS A PERSON

PHYSICALLY: WHAT YOU CAN DO

The first and most important key to a healthy life is to accept responsibility for your physical health. One aspect of your lifestyle is how you care for your body. Certain factors such as the environment, heredity, and the actions of others are out of your control. However, the foods you eat, the exercise you get

and the way you respond to stress are areas affecting your physical health that are in your control.

The better physical health that you experience the more energy you will have to give to God and to others. What motivates you personally to make the lifestyle choices that would improve your physical health? Imagine you can see into the future. At the age of 75 you see that you are going to have a heart attack and die. If you knew that a change in diet and an increase in exercise now would lessen your chances of having that heart attack, would you begin to do it? Your physical body is important to God. The Bible sheds some light on the spiritual and physical condition of the human body.

The habits that you are forming right now positively or negatively affect the future health of your physical body. Research shows that your diet can play a major role in the effective function of each system of your body. Remember how closely linked each system is to one another? Having a balanced, nutritious diet is taking responsibility for your physical body.

The benefits of exercise are almost too numerous to list. Even a short walk each day can add years to your life. Not only is a longer life one of the many benefits of exercise, but feeling good while you are living is a strong motivating factor.

You have heard the phrase, "count your blessings," but did you know that counting your blessings can affect your physical health? Having a grateful heart can turn your worst circumstances into positive experiences. God says to give thanks in everything (2 Thessalonians 5:18).

The next time you find yourself in a fit of anger, reacting to everything and everybody, remember that you can change. People who typically are uptight can teach themselves to relax, deal positively with confrontations and learn to see the positive instead of the negative. Learn to have a thankful heart and daily count your blessings. This is not just a spiritual principle, but a prescription for good health.

If you insist upon being mistrustful and angry and showing your anger, remember; the scientific data suggests that as a result, you are running risks with your life.[4]
Earl Ubell

MENTALLY: WHAT YOU CAN KNOW

You live in a world that highly respects power, riches and knowledge. But after seeking all these, nothing is of eternal value. Paul warns people of gaining the *wrong* kind of knowledge:

…Beware lest anyone cheat you through philosophy and empty deceit, according to the tradition of men, according to the basic principles of the world, and not according to Christ. For in Him dwells all the fullness of the Godhead bodily…
Colossians 2:8,9

To **cheat** means to rob or to spoil, to lead away from the truth. In the introductory chapters of I Corinthians, Paul discusses the contrast between the wisdom of God and the wisdom of man. The Tyndale New Testament Commentary on the book of Colossians describes the philosophy of man as being deceitful because of its attractive presentation. As a result, it carries people *away* from the truth of God. Gaining knowledge is not wrong. However, being drawn into a way of thinking that is not in line with God's wisdom is dangerous.

Wendell Smith says, "being able to intelligently approach life situations with wisdom and knowledge enables you to be a better representation for the Kingdom of God. You need to cultivate your abilities to read, write, reason, and articulate." So, although your degree(s) in school will not be among your "heavenly treasures," it is a means to fulfilling your destiny in God and influencing society for Christ.

You have a responsibility to be the best you can be, not only physically and spiritually, but also mentally. Develop the gifts that God has given to you. As God directs you, pursue the "natural training" that is necessary to have a Godly influence. Men may applaud a learned and gifted presentation, but only those who love and know God will turn men's hearts toward Him.

> Although your degree(s) in school will not be among your "heavenly treasures," it is a means to fulfilling your destiny in God and influencing society for Christ.

Some years ago a great actor was asked at a drawing-room function to recite for the pleasure of his fellow-guests. He consented and asked if there was anything they specially wanted to hear. After a minute's pause an old minister of the Gospel asked for Psalm 23. A strange look came over the actor's face; he paused for a moment, then said, "I will, on one condition — that after I have recited it, you, my friend, will do the same."

"I!" said the preacher, in surprise, "I am not eloquent, but, if you wish it, I shall do so."

Impressively the actor began the Psalm. His voice and intonation were perfect. He held his audience spellbound, and, as he finished, a great burst of applause broke from his guests. As it died away, the old man rose and began to declaim the same Psalm. His voice was not remarkable; his tone was not faultless; but, when he finished, there was not a dry eye in the room.

The actor rose and his voice quivered as he said, "ladies and gentlemen, I reached your eyes and ears; he has reached your hearts. The difference is just this; I know the Psalm but he knows the Shepherd" (Psalm 23:1, 2 Timothy 1:12).[5]

SOCIALLY, WHAT YOU CAN BE

The view and location sold the house. The home is elegant in its decor and the yard is spotless. A nice family has moved in and the first thing they do is — put up a fence. People place both natural and emotional barriers up for "protection." People desire "privacy."

John Donne illustrates how contrary this feeling of privacy is from fact. "No man is an Island, entire of it self; every man is a piece of the Continent, a part of the main...." No person can live without touching the lives of others. No matter how hard you try, you cannot live a solitary life.

What is your social responsibility? God has called every believer to show the love of God. It is the kind of love that causes you to care deeply for others. It can be a "feeling," but, more importantly, it is also a sacrificial love. This is the same love that Jesus shows toward you. The best gift you could give others is the knowledge of the love that Jesus has for them. Having the love of God become a reality for you will motivate you to pursue your destiny in God. Ask God to help you know His love and to give that love away to others.

> No man is an Island.
>
> John Donne

Beloved, let us love one another, for love is of God; and everyone who loves is born of God and knows God. He who does not love does not know God, for God is love.
I John 4:7,8

This is My commandment, that you love one another as I have loved you. Greater love has no one than this, than to lay down one's life for his friends.
John 15:12,13

How well you get along with others will affect how much you enjoy life. Friendships and close relationships will bring you both joy and heartache. It is hard to comprehend that God wants you to love others the way He does — with heartfelt emotion. This includes your family, friends, adults, teachers, and strangers! No life is unimportant to God. His love does not

discriminate against race, sex, appearance, wealth or social status. Can you love people the way God does? It seems an impossible task. If you ask Him, God will place in you a new love and you will have greater influence in the lives of others. Since God is in the people business, so are you!

> Society is destroying the very "paradise" that God gave to mankind to enjoy.

12-4 RESPONSIBILITY AS A CITIZEN

> There was a certain rich man who had a steward, and this steward was reported to him as squandering his possessions. And he called him and said to him. "What is this I hear about you? Give an account of your stewardship, for you can no longer be steward."
> Luke 16:1–2 (NAS)

"ME, AN ENVIRONMENTALIST?"

God has given the responsibility of the environment to mankind. God created it, and God gave it away. What an awesome possession; what an awesome responsibility. An **environmentalist** is someone who is concerned about the quality of the human environment. Everyone lives within the **environment**, that is, within all the living and non-living things, conditions or influences. God was the first environmentalist. When He created the earth, all living and non-living things, He considered it "very good." He placed one restriction on mankind and that was not to eat from the tree of life. Man disobeyed and sin entered the human race. With sin came the pollution in man's heart and pollution in man's environment. The Garden of Eden was never the same when man polluted it through disobedience.

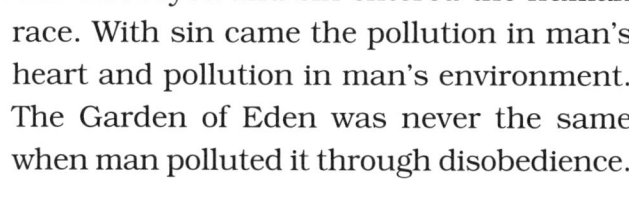

Pollution is contamination. The majority of the pollution on the earth is made up of man-made waste. Society is destroying the very "paradise" that God gave to mankind to enjoy. Today, the increase of population and the technical and industrial progress has caused pollution to become a significant health hazard. The world will never be like the Garden of Eden again, but things can be done to slow down the negative effects of pollution on the earth. Taking good care of the earth is part of the responsibility you have as a citizen.

The Air

You see it move the trees, you feel it in the wind and you need it to live; air is a mixture of invisible, odorless, tasteless gases. Unfortunately, the air you need to live, can also make you sick. It is not the air itself that is harmful, it is what is *in* the air that can be hazardous to your health. Many people who suffer from allergies or other lung ailments can tell right away when pollutants are in the air.

The main causes of air pollution are smoke and exhaust. These fumes come from the burning of coal, oil and natural gas that are used in car engines and factories. Chemicals used on farmland to kill insects and the smoke from burning trash and debris also pollute the air.

Not only is dirty air bad to breathe, it can also damage the earth itself. The **greenhouse effect** is a warming of the earth's temperature. When the carbon dioxide goes into the air it acts like a blanket that smothers the earth. The warm air is trapped inside the atmosphere and the temperature rises. This rise in temperature may cause melting of the ice in the northern and southern parts of the earth. This water will travel to rivers and oceans and may make them dangerously high.

The **ozone layer** is a form of oxygen that is formed naturally in the upper atmosphere. This layer protects the earth from the harmful effects of the sun. Many years ago, being exposed to the suns rays was not considered so dangerous. Today, however, with the decrease in the protection of the ozone layer due to the air pollution, the rays from the sun are more intense and as a result, more dangerous.

After a rainfall the air seems fresher. When it rains, the water washes the pollutants to the ground. This may be good for the air, but bad for the trees, plants, soil and water life. The rain that contains these pollutants is called **acid rain.**

What is your responsibility? The best thing you can do is to be responsible for how you add to the air pollution. Use public transportation, ride your bike or walk when it is possible. People often form car pools to help with school, sports and other activities. You can also use less energy, and as a result, cut down on the amount of fuel that needs to be burned for energy. Be responsible in your home and school by following basic, environmentally-safe guidelines.

The Water

Why are people worried about water shortages when almost 70% of the earth's surface is water? The answer is, only three percent of that water is able to be used as drinking water. Much of the water that covers the earth is salt water and almost all of the fresh water is frozen in polar ice. This is one reason why it is so important to keep the water supply free from pollutants.

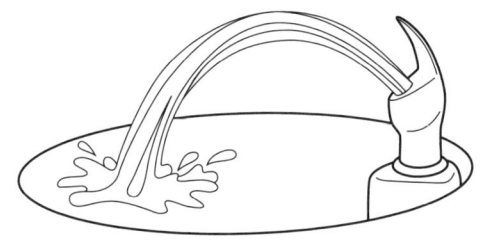

Every living thing needs water to survive. You probably think you couldn't live without your summertime water activities. If the water was not clean, recreational activities that you may take for granted would not be possible.

Water pollution is caused by many things. Chemicals used on the soil and in factories seep into the ground and eventually end up in the water supply. Rivers can be polluted by accidental spills such as oil and gasoline from traveling supply tankers. Think of your own home. Sewage, household cleaners, detergents and all that you place down the drains or toilets, must go somewhere. Now imagine all the office buildings, factories, malls, and recreational areas that use water and discard waste. Where does it all go? Extensive pipe systems carry the waste to specified locations where it can channel into the water.

What is your responsibility? You can be responsible for how you keep your water clean. Avoid putting strong detergents and cleaners down the drain. Read the labels on the containers and purchase environmentally friendly products. Some products are said to be **biodegradable**, that is, they can be broken down in the water without causing a problem. Saving water will also help the environment. Take shorter showers, turn off the water when you are not using it, repair leaky faucets and use less water when watering your yard.

Reduce, Reuse, Recycle

Becoming wise with your waste is popular today. This is not a temporary trend that will go "out" in a few years. Researchers are finding new ways to reduce, reuse, and recycle much of the solid waste that is in your garbage. The landfills that are used to contain the garbage that society "trashes" are full, full, full. Out of necessity, recycling is a must. It is estimated that over 80% of the solid waste that is thrown out could be recycled. Many communities have recycling programs that make it easier for families and businesses to be responsible. Is there a recycling program in your community?

Reduce: To **reduce** means to decrease in size, amount, extent or number. One way you can reduce your solid waste is by changing your purchasing habits. Purchase products that are packaged in recyclable packaging. Many household products come with a refill system that reduces the amount of garbage. You can reduce the amount of wasted paper by using both sides of a sheet. Use recycled paper products and always keep your scraps of paper that you can use for another purpose. You can use less shampoo and less soap and you will still be as clean as a whistle!

Reuse: When you **reuse** something you are decreasing the amount of solid waste that will add to your garbage. For example, many grocery stores give you a 5-cent credit if you reuse their brown grocery bags. Once you reuse it, you can then recycle it. You can reuse many plastic containers for school projects or use them around the house for other purposes. When you reuse you save yourself money while you are helping the environment.

Recycle: **Recycling** is a process that takes material that would otherwise be garbage and regains it for human use. It is hard to keep up with all the products that can be recycled today. Many communities provide curbside pick-up for recyclable materials. Once you get into the habit of recycling, it becomes a natural part of living. Recycling also decreases your household garbage and this saves you money too! You can recycle: certain plastics, aluminum, empty aerosol cans, paper, newspaper, corrugated cardboard and brown paper bags, oil, glass, magazines and steel (tin) cans. If the law provides you an opportunity to take your pop cans to the grocery store, you will receive your deposit and they will take the responsibility to recycle the cans.

Adopt a Highway Program
Have you seen the signs on the road in your community? A business or group adopts sections of the highways and provides litter pickup at least twice a year. If this were not done, the roads would be lined with the garbage of those who carelessly litter.

SOMETHING TO THINK ABOUT

Trash talk

- Oregonians throw away enough garbage each day to cover one acre of land with garbage eight feet deep. How about your state?
- Nearly 400 glass bottles and jars are used each year by every person in America. Using 50% recycled glass in the manufacture of new glass saves 370,000 barrels of oil that can heat 15,000 homes for one year.
- Did you know that there is no supply of tin in the United States? It must be imported or recycled from old cans and other items.
- If the newspapers thrown out in a medium-sized city in a month were recycled, 34,000 pine trees would be saved.

"ME, A CONSUMER?"

Do you consider yourself a consumer? A **consumer** is anyone who purchases goods or services. When you pay to see to a movie or pay to see a sporting event, you are purchasing a service. When you buy items such as food, clothing and school supplies you are purchasing goods.

Many of the goods and services that you purchase are directly related to your health. If you see a doctor, you are buying his medical care for you; if you buy cough drops you are purchasing a health product. What are other examples of health care goods and services that you purchase? Because total health includes more than your physical health, products that affect your mental, social and spiritual wellness, can also be considered "health" products.

Consider the following list of goods and services that teenagers typically purchase. What area of your total health does each item influence,

physical, mental, social or spiritual? Does any one category affect more than one area of your health?

- Music tapes, CD's
- Rental or bought movies
- Clothes
- Sunglasses
- Other fashion accessories
- A hair cut
- Workout at a club
- Swim at an easement or swim park
- Snacks, food, lunch at school
- School supplies
- Books
- Cosmetics and grooming products

What's Your Responsibility?

God has entrusted to you the power to make money. He has also given your parents or guardians the ability to care for you. When you get the "independence" that you desire, being a consumer will become more of a reality for you. You will learn that the money you earn must first be used for basic needs (shelter, food, clothing) and your wants (entertainment, fashionable clothing, etc.) will be "extra." Becoming a wise consumer does not happen overnight. It is a learned skill. You may learn by observing the positive and/or negative consequences of how others use their money, or you may learn by making your own mistakes. You can, however, learn the skills necessary to become a wise consumer.

What does God think about how you use your money? Being a good steward or manager of what He gives you is very important to Him. If you show responsibility with your, or your parents' money now you are more likely to handle your finances better when you are on your own.

> **Building your consumer skills makes you a better steward of what God gives you**
> 1. Use your money wisely, getting the most out of your dollar.
> 2. Buy goods and services that help you have good health.
> 3. Do your homework! When shopping for an expensive item, comparison shop.
> 4. If you have a problem with goods or services that you purchased, don't ignore it, get help.
> 5. Take good care of the items that you have already purchased.
> 6. Be a good influence on your family and peers by helping them make wise choices.
> 7. Avoid peer pressure or the pressure to conform when spending your money.
> 8. Avoid buying when you are in a hurry; don't make rash decisions.
> 9. Avoid grocery shopping without a list or when you are hungry.
> 10. Pray for wisdom when spending your money.

He who is faithful in a very little thing is faithful also in much; and he who is unrighteous in a very little thing is unrighteous also in much. If therefore you have not been faithful in the use of unrighteous mammon, who will entrust the true riches to you? And if you have not been faithful in the use of that which is another's, who will give you that which is your own?
Luke 16:10–12 (NAS)

Making Choices

Tom is shopping for some ski equipment for a trip his class is taking. There are many brands displayed in the store. He sees new as well as used equipment with the prices ranging from inexpensive to very expensive. Tom is confused because he does not know what will best suit his needs. Most of his friends who are going on the trip already own expensive equipment that cost much more than he wanted to spend. Because the trip is tomorrow he must make a decision today. It is up to Tom. What is he going to do?

Tom, like many consumers, finds that too many choices make decision-making more difficult. What are some of the influences that may affect Tom's choice in ski equipment?

- *The cost:* is the price in his budget?
- *The advertising:* what gimmicks in advertising will sway Tom to a specific brand?

- *The knowledge and skill of the salesperson:* does the store want to sell a specific brand over other brands?
- *The features of the product:* what special features meet Tom's specific needs?
- *The quality:* does Tom want to spend the money on equipment that is made well and will last?
- *The convenience:* does Tom have the time to shop for a better buy or wait for a sale?
- *The warranty or guarantee:* what if the equipment is faulty after Tom buys it? Is there a written warranty to handle repairs or a guarantee of his satisfaction?
- *The peer pressure:* will Tom give in to buying the most expensive equipment because his friends have it?

Tom is in a difficult situation because he did not give himself the time to **comparison shop** (to compare the price and quality of similar goods and services). What can Tom do to make the best decision under the circumstances? When you shop for health products or services, the same factors can influence your decisions. The difference is that with the purchase of a health product or service, your money and your health are at risk.

The Power Of Advertising

Sometimes more money is put into a product's advertising than into the product itself. It is the strongest influence on your purchasing choices. **Advertising** is sending messages to the public about a certain product or service. If the advertising is done well, the product will sell. Consider the following techniques used in advertising:

- Bandwagon: "Everybody is doing it." For example: Join the Pepsi Generation.
- Snob Appeal: "Eat Imperial margarine and feel like a King."
- Glittering Generality Appeal: "End all headaches" or "the safest way to…"
- Testimonial Appeal: Michael Jordan and basketball shoes.
- Brand Loyalty: "They tried to make me switch from Tide, but I wouldn't."
- False Image Appeal: "If you use this shampoo, your hair will look like…"
- Humor: "I can't believe I ate the whole thing." or "Where's the beef?"
- Scientific Evidence Appeal: "In a recent hospital survey, it was found that…"
- Sex Appeal: smoking commercials, cosmetic commercials, ads for Coca Cola® and exercise videos.
- Lifestyle Appeal: the commercial shows people having a good time and then shows the product. Nothing is said about the quality of the product. They just want you to think you will have fun if you use it.

Can you think of other techniques advertisers use to get you to "buy" their product? The important thing for you to know is to be aware of their gimmicks and make sure you read labels and do some comparison of your products or services. Watch out for products or services that claim "always" or "never" or "the best." If they say it, make them prove it!

Exploitation of Consumers

Exploitation means to make unethical use for one's own advantage or profit. You see it in commercials directed toward certain age groups (Saturday morning cartoons and the commercials directed toward children). You see it in radio stations and the disc jockeys vying for your listening ear. You see it in stores that draw you in on "sales" and then raise the cost of the other items in the store. "Let the buyer beware." This old saying is right. You must watch-out for goods and services that claim something that they cannot fulfill.

Modern day "quacks" exist, trying to deceive people out of money. A **quack** is an individual who boasts that he or she has medical skills or a scientific remedy, but in fact has none. A quack is a fake — an impostor. The dishonest actions of a quack are called quackery. Although it is against the law to make false claims about a product such as drugs or cosmetics, quacks still make money off people every day.

Some examples of modern-day quacks include, unsubstantiated diet aids, beauty products that claim to "take years off" your appearance, or miracle cures such as those that claim to cure baldness.

Quackery can be spotted several ways, often through the mail, door to door, or on the television. There is pressure, hype and the need to mail it right away before a specified date or call in before the "special offer" is over. In order to survive, quackery needs ignorant, fearful people. If you are careful, alert and informed, you won't become a victim of a quack.

The phrase "buyer beware" is especially important when shopping for health care. At this time in your life, your health care is probably the least of your worries. Your parents or guardians think about it and are concerned about the qualifications of the care you receive. When your life "expands" as a result of more independence and freedom from home, you will have to understand the health care system. Here are a few pointers to get you thinking. You may not care about it now, but when the time comes for you to choose your own medical care, you will want to be knowledgeable and prepared. You want to be a wise health-care consumer by getting the best care you can find, for a reasonable price and at a location that is convenient for you.

Choosing a Health-Care Provider

- Read thoroughly and understand your health insurance information.
- Ask a friend or family member to recommend a doctor or facility to you.
- Check the name of several doctors with your insurance plan to make sure you will be covered.
- Call the service facility and ask questions over the phone: price, how they bill patients, hours they are open, what doctors cover if yours is unavailable, how long they have been practicing, and do they give a free consultation.
- Call for a consultation.
- Prepare a list of questions for the doctor concerning his practice.

When it comes time to make a choice, be sure you feel comfortable not only with the doctor, but with the nurses and the way the office makes you "feel." You might be familiar with the term family doctor. Most people get their main health care from a **family doctor** who provides basic health care to people of all ages.

When you have a special medical need, you should see a trained specialist in that area. **Specialists** are doctors trained to treat particular kinds of patients or health needs. Your family doctor will usually recommend a specialist for you to see.

Your parents or guardians know that financing health care is a big concern. **Health insurance** is a program in which a person or group of persons pays a fee on a regular basis to a company that agrees to pay for some or all of their health care needs. When you look for a job, make sure you know the health care coverage. This information may be an important part of your job benefits. Some people are covered by HMO insurance. **HMO** or **health maintenance organization** is a program where many different types of doctors give health care to their members. The members pay a yearly fee to participate in an HMO plan.

"ME, A CITIZEN?"

A **citizen** is a person living in a town or country, who owes allegiance to a government and is entitled to the rights, privileges and protection of it. You are a citizen of the Kingdom of God, giving devotion to and entitled to the rights and privileges of being a part of it. Moreover, you are a citizen of the earthly government that rules your country. You are not of the world, but you must live in the world (John 15:19). Your responsibility as a natural citizen includes obeying the governing laws to the best of your ability and exercising the freedoms you receive as being a part of the country. Taking responsibility as a citizen includes: becoming a knowledgeable voter, writing letters to the appropriate governing officials of issues you are concerned about, and praying for your country.

In all areas of your life — as a Christian, as a person and as a citizen — you can experience the love of God and be a good steward of what He has given you.

Chapter 12 What's Your Responsibility?

CHAPTER REVIEW

DEFINE

Attitude

Steward

Responsibility

Cheat

Environmentalist

Environment

Pollution

Greenhouse effect

Ozone layer

Acid rain

Biodegradable

Reduce

Reuse

Recycle

Consumer

Comparison shop

Advertising

Exploitation

Quack

Family doctor

Specialists

Health insurance

HMO

Citizen

EXPLAIN

1. Explain why freedom is not really valued for its true worth unless it is earned.
2. Explain why freedom without responsibility does not work.
3. Explain what it means to *shirk*, *shelve*, *shoulder* and *shed* your responsibilities.
4. Explain why it is best to *share* your responsibilities.
5. Explain what it means to be a good steward of your physical body.
6. Explain what it means to be a good steward of your environment.
7. Explain why it is important for a Christian to be a good citizen.
8. Explain how a teenager can show the love of Jesus to others.
9. Explain how teenagers can be good stewards of the money they earn or of their parents' money.
10. Explain the meaning of the verse in Luke 16:10–12, and how does it relate to a teenager.

DISCUSS

1. Discuss ways that teenagers can earn more "freedom" and what kind of attitude is necessary to accept the responsibilities of living.

2. Discuss how your faith can make a difference in your lifestyle. Include how the way you think and feel about God affects the life of a teenager.

3. Discuss why people are to love God with all their heart and soul and might. How does this love affect the way teenagers can live (Deuteronomy 6:5)?

4. Discuss the definition of responsibility: "your response to God's ability." How can this definition affect how you face life?

5. Discuss how teenagers shed their Christian responsibilities. How does this affect the way they live their lives?

6. Discuss how a teenager can share his/her Christian responsibilities (Galatians 6:2–5). What are some of these responsibilities?

7. Discuss why being able to intelligently approach life situations with wisdom and knowledge enables teens to be a better representation of the Kingdom of God.

8. Discuss the role that school and training has in the life of a teenager.

9. Discuss how teenagers can learn how to be wise consumers. Why is this important to learn now at your age?

10. Discuss the specific ways that advertising targets teenagers. How can "buyer beware" help in your choice of purchases?

SUGGESTED ACTIVITIES

1. **Key Concepts:** Outline the chapter and make a study guide for yourself. You can work in groups and each student be responsible for one section or do the study guide on your own.

2. **Know His Love and Give it Away:** Do a study on the love of God. Find several scriptures where the Bible discusses this love. How can you know His love for you? Why is this so important for living a successful Christian life? Why does the Bible say to love your neighbor? Who is your neighbor?

3. **Give Me Freedom:** Write a paper on what you would do with more "unrestricted" space if it were given to you. What could this "freedom" do for you positively? negatively? Include in your answer why freedom without responsibility does not mix.

4. **Attitude Check?:** Sit down with your youth pastor or parents or guardians and ask them what kind of attitude they think you have about responsibility. Be ready to hear and listen without getting defensive. It takes maturity to do this project and learn from it. Share your findings with the class if you feel comfortable with it.

5. **Picture This!** Make a collage of pictures and words that show teens taking responsibility for different areas of their lives. You may use a camera and take specific pictures and then mount them in a creative poster. Hang it up in the class for others to see.

6. **Put it to Memory:** Choose 3–5 Scriptures dealing with the love of God toward you and/or how you are to love God. Write them down on 3x5 cards and place them in your locker or at home where you can see them often. Try to memorize these verses. Share with the class how this has affected the way you feel about God's love.

7. **Extending the Kingdom:** Choose a few close friends and form a prayer team. Pray together once a week or once or twice a month. Spend time praying for each other, your school and friends. Include people you know who do not know the love of Jesus. Keep a journal of your time together so you can be reminded of the faithfulness of God.

8. **Taking Responsibility:** Do a self-inventory. Consider the areas where you have not taken proper responsibility. Make a list of these areas and how you will choose to make positive changes.

Maturity: What's it All About?

13-1 "VOLUMES" OF CHOICES
13-2 MORE THAN JUST SAYING "NO"

13-1 "VOLUMES" OF CHOICES

The human brain is a complex organ and is the highest part of your human design. Its functions are endless and its importance is immeasurable. Among its countless functions, your brain has the capacity to store information, to draw conclusions from that information, to send messages of feeling and sensation to the body, to cause body movements, to make difficult decisions and to discern between right and wrong.

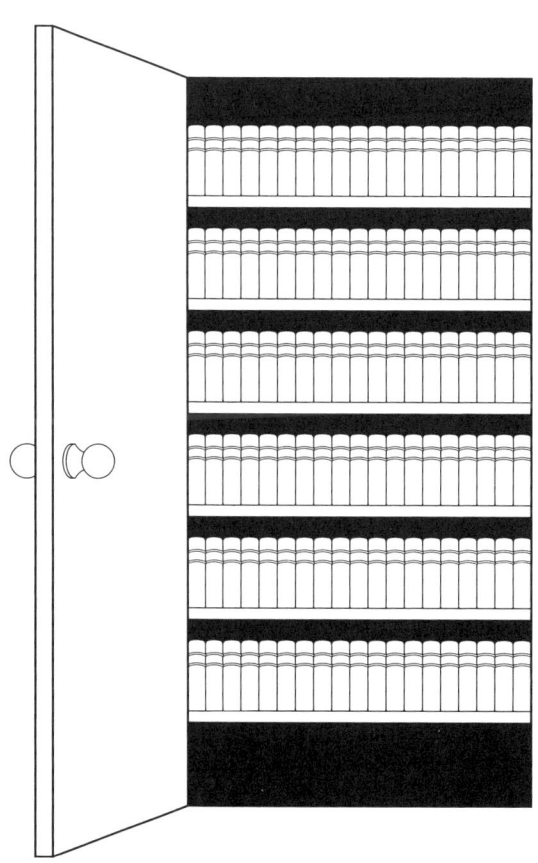

Imagine for a moment if your brain were like a library with endless shelves of books. Volumes of information are stored on the "shelves" of your brain. What you receive in your mind, you categorize and store in these volumes. When you need the information, you can draw from the stored knowledge and make decisions. Not everyone's library looks the same or holds the same number of volumes containing the same information. However, mixed in with these rows and rows of knowledge and stored information are volumes of wisdom and common sense that the Creator has given to the human race.

The human race is unlike any other living being…You are capable of reflecting on all that makes your life different, for example: how you came to be, where you want to go, how you want to live and what you want to do. I could talk all day to a giraffe but it wouldn't be any wiser in the end![1]
Dr. Paul Brand

So, what does this mean to you? God created *you* with the ability and free will to make your own decisions and choices. How are you going to make positive choices? The information you gather into the "library" of your brain will influence these decisions.

Imagine taking a walk in your "library." Volumes and volumes of stored information lay before you, you don't even know what all the books contain. Somewhere amongst your "volumes" you have stored information concerning social and personal issues. As you read this chapter, you may want to "store" much of this information for another time when you will need to draw from it. You may also want to replace some of your already existing "volumes" of information with the information you "take in" from this chapter. Whatever your situation, have an open mind as you read and try to understand the principles behind the words.

VOLUME I: MAKING TOUGH DECISIONS

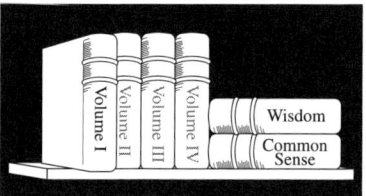

Read *Making Tough Decisions* on the facing page. Think about the situation with Susan and Bill. Susan was parked in a car with a guy she thought she really liked. She did not take time to write down the positive and negative consequences of her decision. Something inside her told her that what she was doing, or going to do, was wrong. In many instances you don't have the time to weigh the consequences; you must go by your "gut" feeling.

Making Tough Decisions
A personal testimony
By Susan Boe

When I entered High School I thought I should feel and act differently, more mature and sophisticated. I was prepared for the academic and athletic challenges, but I was not prepared for the social pressure. I was surprised at myself. I found myself attracted to a guy in the senior class. I knew he could never like me, a freshman, but I still found myself watching him from a distance. By the middle of the year, Bill (name changed), had begun to "hang around" me. It made me feel special and important, but I still knew that he would never really like me. This "crush" dominated my thoughts my whole freshman year. Then it happened. He asked me out on a date! I thought this was the greatest thing that could ever happen. My parents gave me permission to go out with Bill. They knew how I had liked him and they reassured me that they trusted my judgment.

It was a Friday night; Bill and I were going to go to dinner and a movie. I carefully picked out my clothes and I took an extra long time getting ready. When Bill arrived, he came in for a brief moment to meet my parents. When we walked out to the car I didn't even notice that he did not open the car door for me, but at that point I don't think I would have cared. The dinner and movie went fine, although there was not a lot of conversation. I was too nervous to initiate any talk and he didn't seem too interested in conversation.

On our way home Bill suggested we take a different route, "a place were we could see the city lights," he said. I was still so nervous that I went along with it. We arrived at a place called The Heights, a common place for couples to "park." We shared some small talk and then Bill made "the move." I felt uncomfortable with what was happening but I was so torn by my feelings for him that I didn't know what to do. This whole school year I had waited for this date and now I had found myself in a compromising situation. The thought raced through my head, "if I don't go along with this, Bill won't like me anymore." My "gut" feeling told me what was happening was not right. In an instant decision, I pushed Bill away, and said, "I think you better take me home"....

As a result of Susan's decision, Bill never asked her out again. You may experience similar rejection as you make tough decisions in your life.

We live in an "instant" society....But this "right now" mentality can be dangerous....Right choices, on the other hand, often require waiting for better long-term results.[2]
Josh McDowell

Fortunately, Susan made a positive choice. However, the benefits of making right choices are not always instantaneous. It is often difficult to think seriously about how your choices will affect your future. Consequently, when you feel the pain of a wrong decision, it helps you make a better choice next time. Experience is a good teacher. Unfortunately, some experiences produce much pain and heartache, and what people often overlook is the fact that many of the decisions you make affect others. Hopefully as an individual matures — physically, mentally, socially and spiritually — his decisions have more positive consequences.

When you reach into your "library" ask God to give you volumes and volumes of wisdom to help you in the decisions in your life. The Bible says that wisdom is better than gold (Proverbs 3:13–15), if you lack wisdom, ask God and He will give you wisdom (James 1:5).

VOLUME II: WHAT DOES IT MEAN TO BE MATURE?

One aspect of maturity is the ability to make wise decisions. Consider Susan and Bill. It took a lot of maturity for Susan to stop what was happening and tell Bill, who was older than she, to take her home. Measuring an individual's maturity level is very difficult. Just as your total health includes your physical, mental, social and spiritual health, so it is with your total maturity.

Physical Maturity

When you mature physically, you enter the time of life called puberty. **Puberty** is the stage of growth and development at which males and females become physically able to reproduce. Unlike physical maturity, mental (emotional), social and spiritual maturity are hard to recognize right away. For example, have you ever met someone who *looked* mature physically and after you got to know them you realized they were not *really mature* at all?

Physical maturity is marked by *secondary sex characteristics.* Each sex produces both male and female hormones. Men produce a greater amount of the male hormone than the female hormones; women produce a greater amount of female hormones. These hormones cause the more obvious physical changes that occur. The physical changes are called secondary sex characteristics.

Male: Testes produce hormone testosterone which results in muscle development, voice change, facial, pubic and body hair.

Female: Ovaries produce hormones estrogen and progesterone which result in growth of breasts, widening of pelvic bones, pubic and body hair, added weight and menstruation cycle.

Along with the obvious physical changes, come the emotional, social and spiritual changes. Your hormones affect not only the way you feel about yourself but also the way you feel about the opposite sex.

Emotional Maturity

During puberty the hormonal highs and lows make it difficult to control your feelings and moods. It also causes you to become more concerned about your appearance and about what others think of you. Sometimes your mind may be consumed with thoughts of a person of the opposite sex. These changes that you experience are all normal, but learning to control these feelings is part of the process of maturity. Nobody, not even an adult, always succeeds at controlling his emotions. Remember, maturity is not something you "arrive at" during your lifetime, *maturity is a process.*

In some cultures young men and women must perform a task to prove their maturity. Other cultures believe that turning a certain age determines the level of maturity. Maturity itself is a difficult concept to define. It is often easier to notice signs of emotional immaturity in a person than signs of maturity.

Social Maturity

Social maturity is the ability a person has to relate to others in a proper way. You can learn to have manners and learn to treat others with respect but social maturity, just as other areas of maturity, is a process. It is true, however, that as you develop a closer relationship with God, you are better able to deal with relationships at every level with more maturity. As you become more concerned about your "social life," it is important to remember that you can trust God to do the very best for you. He can bring to you good wholesome friendships with the same, as well as the opposite, sex. Keep reminding yourself that God can join you with the person who is best for you — if you allow Him to!

Spiritual Maturity

Your life here on earth is only the beginning of an eternally developing relationship with God. Your spiritual maturity is the area of maturity that will take you into eternity. Therefore, it should concern you the most. What are signs that a person is growing in spiritual maturity? It is often difficult to know for sure the level of spiritual maturity of a person but a good measuring rod is the fruit of the Spirit — love, joy, peace, patience, kindness, goodness, faithfulness, gentleness, and self-control (Galatians 5:22–23).

Signs of Maturity

- Has self-control: thinks through things before acting, controls words, anger, love, and other emotions.
- Recognizes godly values: makes good judgments concerning money, time, friends.
- Recognizes the importance of setting goals: realizes that there is value in preparing for the future. For example, studies not only for grades but for learning.
- Stands up for what is right even when persecuted: does not go along with the crowd.
- Assumes responsibility for actions: does not place blame on others.
- Avoids compromising situations.
- Avoids being judgmental or critical of others: does not gossip about others .
- Is able to be trusted: able to keep confidential information private.
- Respects others: forms mature relationships with others.
- Has more concern for others: not so self-centered and selfish.

Think for a moment and evaluate your own level of maturity, keeping in mind that you cannot "become mature" in your own strength. *Maturing* is what it means to move forward in the process, and growth in every area shows that Christ is working in you. When you think of someone who seems mature, what characteristics do you notice? These are not signs that everyone consistently shows on their own. Ask the Lord to help you in the ongoing maturing process.

Forming Boundaries

A boundary is something that indicates a limit, something that is not to be crossed or passed through. A fence is a form of boundary for defining a particular area. Parents place limits on children to keep them from an accident. Some 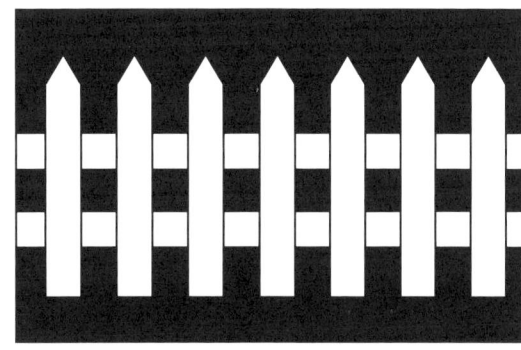 boundaries are very clear and accepted, while others are more difficult to accept. Adults try to help you shape your own convictions about certain issues by placing boundaries in your life. As you grow older and show more responsibility, those boundaries are often lifted or extended. How much you allow God and others to influence your life will help fine tune your "gut" feeling or conscience.

God does not place boundaries in your life so He can watch you fail. He gives boundaries to protect you. More importantly, God's laws *are realistic* for your life. Others may not always understand how hard it is to stay on the straight and narrow path, but you can be assured that God knows. Don't try to handle things on your own. A sign of spiritual maturity is acknowledging that you cannot overcome on your own strength. God and others are there to help.

> God does not place boundaries in your life so He can watch you fail. He gives boundaries to protect you.

WARNING: Danger Ahead

A father and a mother watch as their four year old rides his bike down the road. The father anxiously calls, "look how fast you are going, you are doing great." The mother, on the other hand, nervously calls, "watch out for the cars — you don't want to crash." There are two different perspectives, the father who loves to see his son have fun on the bike and the mother who sees the potential danger ahead. Both perspectives are needed. Often young people only see the fun and don't look ahead to see the risks of their behavior (see Proverbs 7:6–12).

Dealing With Curiosity

As youngsters grow up they have a natural curiosity that causes them to investigate things. An infant explores toys by placing them in his mouth, a toddler uses his imagination and creates a world of make-believe. As teenagers, your curiosity in the areas of sex is normal. It is what you allow yourself to think about and investigate that can cause you problems.

When God made Adam and Eve, He knew He made something good. His desire was that they would be fruitful and multiply. Does the Bible describe how Adam and Eve were to multiply? Genesis 4:1 in the New King James Translation states: "Now Adam knew Eve his wife, and she conceived and bore Cain...." The New American Standard Bible translation puts it this way: "Now the man had relations with his wife Eve, and she conceived and gave birth to Cain...." Do you think that God had to explain to Adam and Eve what to do to conceive a child?

The closest thing in the Bible to an explanation of the act of sex is in the Book of The Song of Solomon. Solomon describes a beautiful display of love and passion toward a man and a woman. The key to this book is that it speaks about love between a bride and groom. This physical expression of love is natural between a husband and wife.

> As teenagers, your curiosity in the areas of sex is normal.

332

Don't believe it if someone tells you that you need to know everything about sex before you are married. God made man and woman with natural passion and desires. There will be a strong physical desire for intimacy with the one you marry. You won't need a how-to manual for sex. As for curiosity, it's natural.

13-2 MORE THAN JUST SAYING "NO"

VOLUME III: WHAT ABOUT SEX?

Throughout your life your parents or guardians have tried to protect you from things that could harm you. From the time you heard "don't run in the street" to "don't stay out too late," you have been bombarded with commands. You now understand that the choices that you make will come from the convictions you have of what is right and wrong. Do not be deceived by society in believing that there is no absolute truth. There are definite right and wrongs in life. Not only are there biblical reasons to abstain from sexual activity before marriage, but there are physical, emotional, mental and social reasons as well. You do have the freedom to make the choices you want, but if you make negative choices negative consequences will follow you. Those consequences follow you right into adulthood.

At this point it is important to make something very clear. Sex does not only mean intercourse. Sex is the activity that arouses the desire for *more* sexual activity with the completion or end being intercourse. It is important to understand that God made the human body, both male and female to find pleasure in the *total* sexual involvement, not only intercourse.

Abstinence Is Not the Only Goal

A health teacher began the lesson dealing with sex education when a student raised her hand and said, "all I want to know is

> Not only are there biblical reasons to abstain from sexual activity before marriage, but there are physical, emotional, mental and social reasons as well.

how far is too far"? In response the teacher stated, "You will find different opinions to this question. Unfortunately, people usually ask until they find someone who gives them the opinion they *want* to hear."

You may not understand the intensity of sexual pressure now, but it will increase as you get older. When you graduate from high school, leave home or begin a steady relationship, the advice that people have been giving you will become more practical. Any physical contact can begin the arousal of sexual feelings. This is the way your body is supposed to work. Holding hands might be all you do now. But physical sexual activity is progressive. If you start the motor running, it is not meant to shut off! You may be saying, "I understand that sex is to culminate with intercourse, but I can stop anytime." That may be true, but abstinence from intercourse is not the only goal!

Unfortunately, many young people go "too far" without "going all the way." That is, they engage in sexual physical activity but do not have intercourse. You may say this type of activity is all right as long as you don't "go all the way." Scott Talley, the author of *Talking With Your Kids About The Birds And The Bees* puts it this way:

Abstinence from intercourse is not the only goal!

…they (teenagers) pride themselves on having refrained from intercourse. Sexual experience is gained, but virginity is preserved. This kind of activity is so widespread that a new term has been coined by psychologists and counselors to describe the teens in this category as "technical virgins"…Biblically speaking, they are observing the letter of the law but not its spirit. Since the Bible forbids only sexual intercourse anything but intercourse is considered fair game (in the teens' minds).[3]

Being a Christian means more than observing only the letter of the law. The Bible teaches us to live by spirit and principle. Consider the following scriptures in relation to the principle of purity.

For this is the will of God, your sanctification: that you should abstain from sexual immorality; that each of you should know how to possess his own vessel in sanctification and honor, not in passion of lust, like the Gentiles who do not know God…For God did not call us to uncleanness, but in holiness.
I Thessalonians 4:3–7

But I say, walk by the Spirit, and you will not carry out the desire of the flesh. For the flesh sets its desire against the Spirit, and the Spirit against the flesh; for these are in opposition to one another, so that you may not do the things that you please. But if you are led by the Spirit, you are not under the Law. Now the deeds of the flesh are evident, which are: immorality, impurity, sensuality…
Galatians 5:16–19

Moral purity means more than just abstaining from intercourse. Furthermore, if you allow yourself to violate your conscience, even a little, you will be more likely to violate it again, a little more. It becomes easier to allow yourself to "go a little further" each time you give in to sexual pressure. Remember also that if your body is feeling the sexual arousal that can lead to further activity, you know that the person you are with is experiencing similar if not stronger feelings. To **defraud** someone means to arouse sexual desires in another which cannot be righteously satisfied.

Sex is not like tennis. Practice does not make perfect; it only leads to more practice.

Paul Pearsall,
Super Marital Sex:
Loving for Life

...no one should take advantage of and defraud his brother in this matter, because the Lord is the avenger of all such, as we also forewarned you and testified.
I Thessalonians 4:6

If you truly care about the person you are with, you will value and respect him/her. When you are in a relationship and desire sexual activity to fulfill your own desires, you are acting out of selfishness. Scott Talley puts it this way, "selfish use of others for personal gratification violates the basic message of Christianity."[4]

SOMETHING TO THINK ABOUT

What a great question!

During a high school health class a student asked the question: "why did God give us such a strong sex drive when we are not able to fulfill it and if sex is so great and our bodies are ready, why do so many people say it's wrong to do it"?

In response, the teacher replied, "the temptations you face today will still be with you as an adult. Learning self-control during this difficult time will help you face the same temptations as an adult. Furthermore, a relationship with another person is built on more than just sex. Relationships are built mainly on love, commitment and respect for the other person. It is normal to have sexual feelings at your age, but there are physical and emotional consequences to sexual behavior."

Although some temptations seem more difficult during puberty, adults also deal with similar temptations but are often better able to handle the feelings. Why ?

What temptations are typical during adolescence? Does the fact that these are normal temptations justify yielding to them?

Why Wait?

Quoting scriptures to help motivate you to moral purity may not be enough for you. There are many reasons, other than the commandment for purity, that make a good case for abstinence. God did not give us restrictions and boundaries to keep us from having fun in life. On the contrary. Obeying God and His commandments while having a personal relationship with Him is fulfilling. Many things you would like to experience often bring pleasure only for a moment, with the consequences lasting a lifetime (Hebrews 11:25).

You are aware of the *physical* consequences to having sex, the risk of getting Sexually Transmitted Diseases, AIDS, or an unplanned pregnancy. However, the *emotional* consequences of becoming sexually active are often overlooked.

As boys and girls, your physical and emotional natures are different. Boys tend to respond in a much more physically demanding way than do girls. Girls tend to respond more to the emotional needs of security and closeness. Boys face a more physical want for sex, whereas girls face a more emotional desire for closeness and intimacy.[5]
James Dobson

With this difference in mind, imagine what can take place between two young people who have such strong feelings for each other. Sexual intimacy during the teen years ultimately results in broken hearts and strong feelings of depression and loss. James Dobson describes the "connection" between two people sexually active as being traumatic.

You see, the sexual relationship bonds two people physically and emotionally. Breaking up when you've shared your body and soul with someone is profound and traumatic….Sex connects our minds and bodies in a way that, once connected, they can never be separated again.[6]

When you cross the boundaries that the Lord has set for you in the area of physical intimacy, it affects your personal relationship with Him. Remember, God understands the strong feelings that you experience — He is waiting to help you and give you the grace you need to wait.

Why Wait [7]
by Josh McDowell

- Purity protects from unplanned pregnancy and provides a healthy atmosphere for child-rearing.
- Purity protects from sexually transmitted diseases and provides for peace of mind.
- Purity protects from sexual insecurity and provides for truth.
- Purity protects from emotional distress and provides for true intimacy.

How To Wait

You may find yourself confident right now saying, "I have already decided abstinence is my choice." I want to reassure you  that just because you know the right thing to do, does not mean you always have the strength to do it. Overcoming sexual temptation is very difficult if you set yourself up for testing. Paul says that even he did things he knew he should not (Romans 7:15).

Going on group dates is a good alternative to dating. Being in a group gives you the opportunity to get to know the person you like and protects you from any feelings of social pressure.

Your hormonal codes are wonderful but your creative mind (which is the highest part of the human design) with its wisdom and knowledge can override these hormones. You can say to yourself, "I have a higher quality in me that can think about who I am and can think about what I want to do and I can make good decisions based on what I know and understand. Other people may be helped by what I decided or may be harmed by my choices — and I am ultimately responsible."…You can develop the moral sense, which is the basis for all civilization.[8]
Dr. Paul Brand

How To Wait [9]
by Josh McDowell

- Set standards beforehand and share these standards with your dates.
- Be accountable to your parents or to another person regarding your dating behavior.
- Let your lifestyle show through conversation, body language and clothes.
- Know yourself and be your own person.
- Choose companions carefully; hang around people with the same values.
- Seek others' wisdom; get counsel or advice when you are involved in a friendship.

Finding Help In Time Of Crisis

An unplanned pregnancy raises a lot of emotional feelings not only for the girl who is carrying the child but for the families involved. Someone close to you, a family member or friend, may have found herself in this situation. This is not a time for passing judgment, but a time for love, acceptance and support.

The choice has already been made not to wait until marriage to have sex. Now the choice is what to do about the pregnancy. There are four choices available to a pregnant teenage girl: give the baby up for adoption, have an abortion, raise the child alone or get married. Unfortunately she must face this alone because studies show that more than 85% of the boys who father a child abandon them.

Abortion

Abortion is one of the most divisive subjects discussed. If you have never had to take a personal stand on the issue, you probably do not realize the emotional, as well as political, issue it has become. What would you tell a pregnant teenager who was considering an abortion? When pregnancy becomes a reality for a teenager and her family, the thought of an abortion may become an option. For some, an abortion seems to be a quick and easy solution.

Teenagers need to be told that abortion is not as simple or as easily and quickly forgotten as they might think. Guilt can be a devastating emotion, especially when spread over an entire lifetime.[10]
Scott Talley

Do you know exactly what it means to have an abortion? In medical terminology, the word **abortion** means either spontaneous abortion (or miscarriage) or medically induced termination of a pregnancy. Somehow the unborn child must be killed within the mother's womb. Up to the twelfth week of pregnancy, an elective abortion can be done in many states. After the twelfth week, many states regulate abortions. After the 24th week of pregnancy, some state laws regulate and may even prohibit abortion except where the mother's life may be in danger. Consider the stages of development of an unborn child keeping in mind that God knows this little life from the moment of conception.

Stages of Development

6 weeks
Facial features (eyes, ears, nose, and mouth) are forming. Internal organs have begun to form and the heart is beating. Arms and legs are growing rapidly. The embryo is approximately 1/2 inch long.

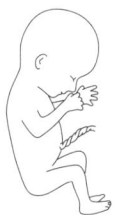

3 months
The fetus is kicking and moving its arms, but the mother probably doesn't feel this yet. Eyelids now cover the eyes and the fetus can frown or smile. The fetus is approximately 2 1/2 inches long.

9 months
The head is positioned down for birth. Organs have matured to prepare the baby to survive on its own. Fat is added. The average baby weighs about 7 pounds and is about twenty inches long at birth.

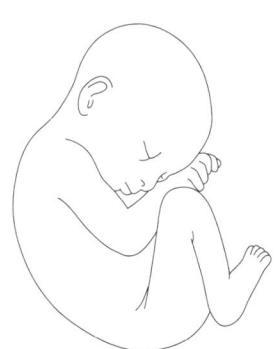

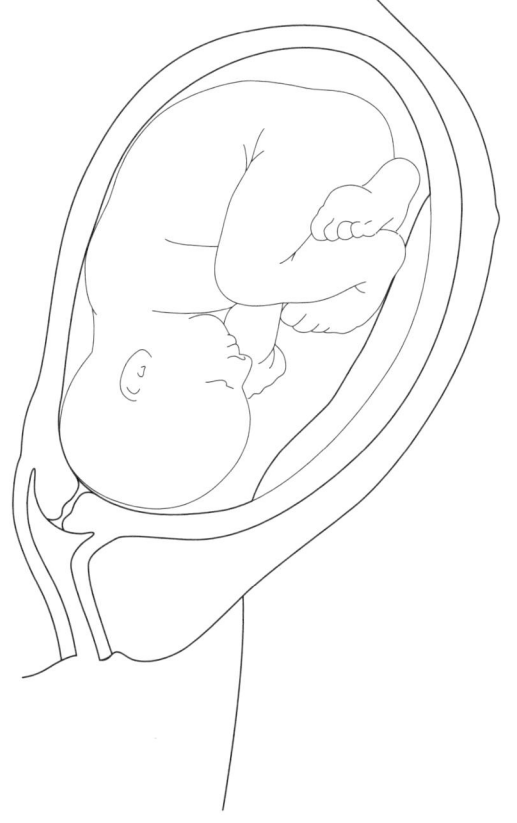

6 months
Hair, eyelashes and eyebrows begin to grow. Fingernails and toenails begin to appear and the fetus can suck its thumb. The ear has developed and can hear sounds from outside the uterus. The fetus is approximately 12 inches long.

Before I formed you in the womb I knew you;
Before you were born I sanctified you…
Jeremiah 1:5

Hopefully you will not experience an unplanned pregnancy. But if you do, or you know someone who does, you need to be fully convinced of your stand on abortion. Do you view abortion as an alternative? You may believe that you are totally opposed to abortion but sometimes convictions change when the crisis becomes personal.

The reaction of your parents or friends to the news of the pregnancy can be more frightening than the pregnancy itself. It is important to understand that many families and friends would be supportive and forgiving. God is a God of love and forgiveness. A child is a blessing, not an inconvenience and would bring great joy to a childless couple. There are positive options for a pregnant teenager. Take the time to seek help. Remember, all life is precious, born or unborn. Space does not allow a lengthy discussion of abortion, but if you find yourself or a friend considering this as a solution to your problem, think again, and get help. In your local area there are

A Tribute To My Niece
For Shaina

Your mother and I used to sit on her bed and talk about "girl" things. She would help me through the trials of high school and always give me the encouragement I needed.

Now it was my turn to be by her side. When you were born I was there. Friends and family were waiting outside the door to hear when you arrived. When your little head began to appear we could see your beautiful black hair and within a few minutes you were here. After the nurses took care of you, I got to hold you and carry you to your mother.

Shaina, from the beginning of time the Lord knew you would be born into our family. Every child is a miracle, but you, Shaina, are a true miracle. You see, your mother was not married when she gave birth to you. But she chose to bring you into this world — into our family. I cannot imagine our family without you!

P.S. Your four year old cousin Steven thinks you're AWESOME!

Crisis Pregnancy Centers that will help you explore all the other options available.

The Gift

Imagine finding just the right person and being totally and completely in love with that person. After a time of engagement the two of you decide to get married. It will be a marriage between two wonderful people who are very much in love. What would be the most precious gift you could give that special person? A gift more precious than anything money could buy — a unique gift that is valuable because it is a part of yourself? The most precious and valuable gift you could give your future loved one is your virginity. It is precious because it is a part of you and can only be given once. When it has been given, it can never be given again (Scott Talley).[11]

> The most precious and valuable gift you could give your future loved one is your virginity.
>
> Scott Talley

Imagine a present beautifully wrapped. You don't know what is inside but it looks so beautiful and those who have seen it tell you it is wonderful. Your curiosity is so great, all you want is just a "peek" inside. The card has your name on it but you are not to open it until the right time. If you were to take only a little peek inside the package, you would spoil the surprise — not to mention the wonderful anticipation that comes with waiting to open the gift.

Sex is like that package. Even the anticipation of enjoying it on your honeymoon is exciting. Don't spoil the surprise given by God by peeking inside before its time. Experiencing that special intimacy with the one you marry is worth waiting for!

VOLUME IV: WHAT ABOUT TOBACCO, DRUGS AND ALCOHOL?

Learning From Experiences

Twenty years ago teenagers worried about having the right clothes, having a date for a dance, being on time to class, being respectful to the teachers, and at worst, sneaking a beer or a cigarette. Today, teenagers are at risk from drugs, alcohol, crime, gangs, suicide and sexually transmitted diseases.

It has been said that experience is often the best teacher. That is, after you experience the consequences yourself, you learn from your mistakes and are less likely to make the same mistake. Generally, people do learn from their mistakes; however, it would be great if people learned first from the mistakes of others. Pastor Ron Mehl from Beaverton Foursquare Church in Beaverton, Oregon, calls learning from others experiences "guided experiences." If a person tells you what will happen if you make a certain choice, you could listen and take his advice — or you could try it anyway and see for yourself. Unfortunately, the latter is usually the choice.

If your curiosity is too great to ignore, and you believe that "trying" something can't hurt, just remember that it only takes one time to start a deadly habit. The best teacher for you could be "guided experience" rather than "personal experience." You may be the "borderline" type. That is, you have not made a decision about the use of tobacco, drugs or alcohol. No matter what people tell you, it is your choice. If you were confronted with the decision today — what would you say?

Tobacco

It used to be "cool" to smoke, but today people are catching on to the health risks related to smoking. Unfortunately, most of the studies of tobacco deal with cigarette use and not pipe, cigar, or chewing tobacco, all of which are unhealthy. More research shows that smoke also harms the nonsmoker when subjected to second-hand smoke. It is now a common sight to see nonsmoking signs in restaurants, airplanes and

other public places. A habit like smoking is not "cool" anymore.

What is in Tobacco?

Did you know that one puff on a cigarette exposes you to over 3,000 chemicals? Tobacco is more addictive than either heroin or cocaine — that is why it is so difficult to quit. Some of these chemicals are more harmful than others; however, three of them are particularly harmful.

Nicotine: The substance that causes addiction to tobacco. **Nicotine** is a drug that acts like a tranquilizer and stimulates the release of epinephrine into the smoker's body. This increases the heartbeat and raises the blood pressure. It can also cause dizziness and upset stomach.

Tar: The substance that is produced when tobacco burns. **Tar** is a thick, dark liquid that produces chronic irritation of the respiratory system of a smoker. It is the main cause of lung cancer.

Carbon monoxide: The gas that is produced when tobacco burns. **Carbon monoxide** gas passes from the lungs into the bloodstream where it interferes with the oxygen in the bloodstream. It attaches to the red blood cell and then it is not released by that cell until the cell dies. Pregnant women who smoke deprive the fetus of oxygen, therefore the baby is often born underweight. Carbon monoxide is what makes the exhaust fumes of cars poisonous.

The Harmful Effects of Tobacco

Whether tobacco is smoked or chewed, the drugs in tobacco are all harmful. Lung cancer is probably the best known harmful effect of smoking. The tar and carbon monoxide damage the bronchi, the passageways to the lung tissue. Lung cancer results when the cells become damaged. The cancerous cells then grow out of control.

Cancer is not the only disease caused by smoking. Emphysema is a disease that occurs when the small air sacs called alveoli are damaged or destroyed. A person with emphysema experiences breathlessness and coughs up sputum. Although breathing is a

Did you know that one puff on a cigarette exposes you to over 3,000 chemicals?

natural and easy function of the body, to a person with emphysema it is a difficult task.

The Harmful Effects of Tobacco

Brain: smoking affects the arteries of the brain which may lead to a stroke.

Mouth: smoking dulls the tastebuds, causes bad breath and can lead to cancer of the mouth, lips and throat.

Teeth: smoking stains the teeth.

Larynx: smoking can cause cancer of the larynx.

Skin: smoking ages the skin, causes wrinkles by depleting the body of moisture.

Lungs: smoking causes the lungs to have to work harder. It can cause diseases such as cancer and emphysema as well as chronic bronchitis.

Heart: smoking damages the arteries, causes high blood pressure and increases the risk of coronary artery disease.

Digestive system: smoking and chewing tobacco can cause ulcers and damge to the small intestines.

Bladder: smoking increases the chance of cancer of the bladder.

Legs: smoking seriously affects the arteries of the legs. Peripheral vascular disease is when the blood vessels are constricted. Amputation is sometimes necessary.

SOMETHING TO THINK ABOUT

Smoking affects your lifestyle

Take a deep breath. Do you feel your lungs expand and fill up with air? This easy task that you often take for granted is not so easy to a smoker. Because a smoker's lungs become damaged from the effects of carbon monoxide and tar, taking a deep breath is often difficult. How do you think smoking would affect your active lifestyle? For example, a person who smokes may find it difficult to walk up a long flight of stairs.

Do you think that smoking affects your social life? Is the effect positive or negative? Are you attracted to people who smoke or is it an instant "turn off"?

A person who smokes may also experience frequent bouts with bronchitis. Furthermore, a virus or flu can settle in the lungs because of their weakened condition.

Have you ever noticed that the smell of tobacco smoke seems to cling to your clothes? You don't have to be a smoker to experience the smell of tobacco on your clothes. Smoking also affects your appearance. It not only looks "uncool" to smoke, but it also damages your skin. The chemicals in tobacco rob your body of nutrients and needed moisture. People who smoke are more likely to have wrinkled and dry skin.

Smoking is also unhealthy for unborn babies. A pregnant woman who smokes is putting her baby at risk. Babies born to mothers who smoke are more likely to be smaller and less likely to survive. Even after birth, the children who live with smokers are more likely to suffer from asthma or other respiratory disease and are more likely to become smokers themselves.

Why stay away from Tobacco

- Tobacco stains your teeth and makes your clothes smell bad.
- Tobacco can cause many serious diseases.
- Tobacco use is expensive.
- Tobacco use is often banned in public places and in schools.
- Tobacco use dulls your sense of smell and taste.
- Tobacco use can become addictive.
- Tobacco use is not so "cool" anymore.

SOMETHING TO THINK ABOUT

If you smoke one pack of cigarettes each day, you could be spending over $500 in a year. Can you think of better ways to spend your money?

What about Chewing Tobacco?

You may think that you are safe from the harmful effects of smoking by using smokeless tobacco. Snuff is a packet of finely ground tobacco that is placed between the teeth and gum or a wad of tobacco is chewed. In either case, smokeless tobacco can cause serious diseases.

Cancer of the mouth is the most common problem with the use of smokeless tobacco. When the tobacco or saliva carrying the tobacco juice is swallowed, the poisons are carried to the stomach, intestines and bladder. Smokeless tobacco also causes bad breath and stains the teeth. Because chewing tobacco also contains nicotine, the habit of smokeless tobacco can be addictive.

Drugs

Drugs have changed the health of the American people. Their influence has been both positive and negative. Consider where people would be without the use of drugs such as antibiotics (for

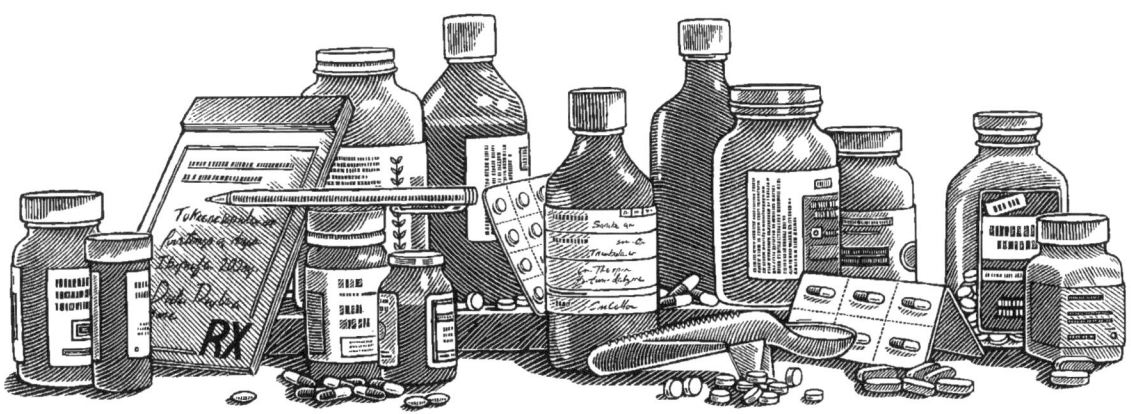

example, penicillin) and immunizations. Not all drugs are bad. **Drugs** can be defined as: any chemical substance that alters the function of one or more body organs or changes the process of a disease. Many foods and drinks contain small quantities of substances classified as drugs. For instance, coffee and cola drinks contain caffeine which is both a stimulant and a diuretic drug. A drug can also be considered a medicine. **Medicines** are drugs that are meant to cure or prevent diseases and other conditions.

Misuse and Abuse of Drugs

Medicines are positive advances in the medical field. However, certain drugs are manufactured that can produce dangerous results. *Drug abuse* occurs when a person uses an illegal substance or misuses a legal substance.

The most common drugs that are abused and misused are stimulants and depressants. These two categories of drugs affect the nervous system. **Stimulants** are drugs that speed up the body's functions. Stimulants cause the blood pressure to rise, increase the rate of breathing and the rate of heart beat. The use of stimulants can cause dangerous side effects and may also become addictive. An **addiction** is a physical or mental need for a substance.

Certain stimulants such as caffeine seem harmless. However, research shows that too much caffeine can produce negative side effects. More dangerous stimulants that are abused are amphetamines and cocaine. These drugs are often used to get "high." Amphetamines and cocaine are killers. They are highly addictive and even one use can kill a person.

Depressants are drugs that slow down the body's functions and reactions. Many depressants are prescribed by doctors to help a person cope with difficult situations. However, depressants can be addictive and have many negative consequences. The main groups of depressants are tranquilizers, barbiturates, and hypnotics. Alcohol is often thought of as a stimulant, but it is actually a depressant.

Choosing to be Drug Free

Many drugs have no beneficial use. These drugs are often called "street drugs" because they are manufactured to buy and sell on "the streets." These drugs are not only illegal but highly dangerous.

As a teenager you face many choices. One choice you may have had to make is whether to try drugs. It is a choice you must make before you are faced with the temptation. If you say "it won't hurt me" or "I can stop anytime I want to," you are mistaken. You cannot control drugs — drugs control you. The damage that many drugs do to your body, mind and spirit are permanent.

Positive peer pressure can help when you or a friend are confronted with the decision to try drugs. If you choose your friends wisely, and stay clear from situations where you think there might be drug use, you are making positive choices for a healthy lifestyle.

Alcohol

"Before I'll ride with a drunk, I'll drive myself"
Stevie Wonder, Famous Blind Musician

Alcohol is a depressant. It is a drug that is produced from the fermentation of carbohydrates by yeast. Alcohol is the main ingredient in beverages such as beer, wine and hard liquor.

Once the alcohol enters the bloodstream it begins to affect the brain and the nervous system. A person becomes less able to control his/her body. A person who drinks alcohol usually does things he would not normally do. Although the effects of alcohol are obvious when a person becomes intoxicated, the health problems that occur as a result of alcohol are not visible.

SOMETHING TO THINK ABOUT

What can I say?
- "No thanks, there's more to life than drugs."
- "I don't do drugs."
- "If you were really my friend, you would stop asking."
- "I don't want to hang around you if you are going to do drugs."
- "Call me when you decide you want help."
- "Doing drugs is your choice, but I've decided not to."

Alcohol-Related Health Problems

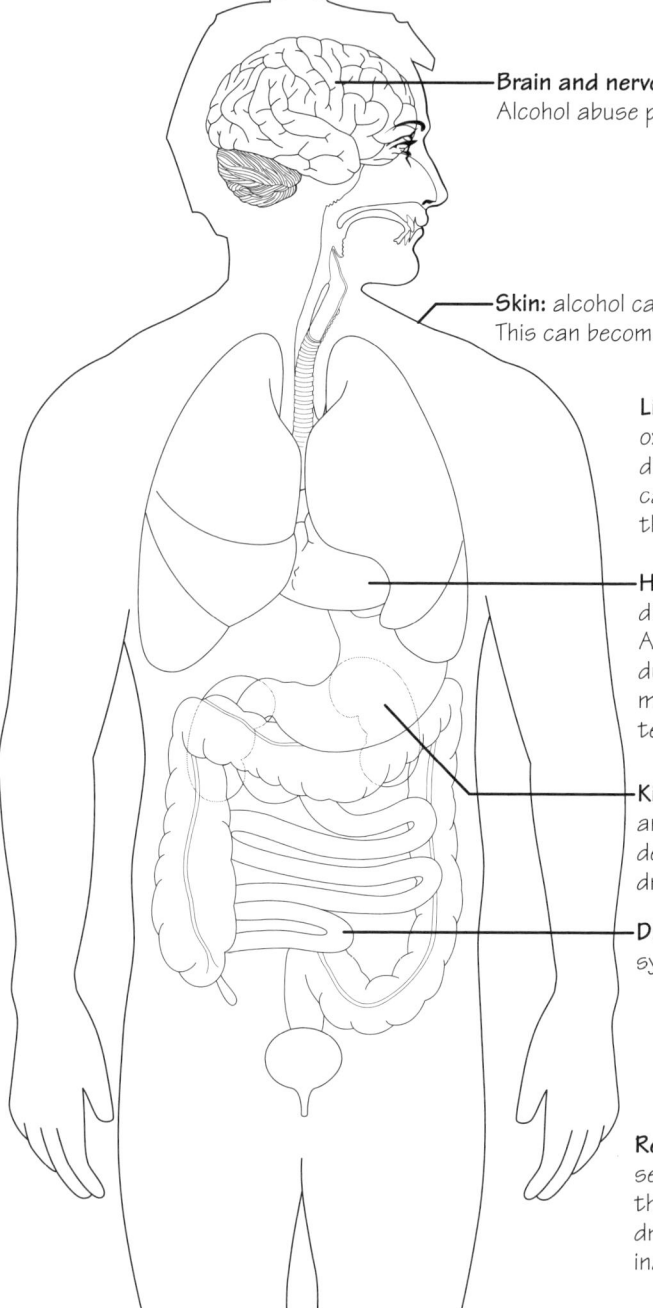

Brain and nervous system: alcohol depresses the nervous system. Alcohol abuse permanently impairs brain and nerve function.

Skin: alcohol causes flushing in the face (a pink to red skin tone). This can become constant in heavy drinkers.

Liver: alcohol must pass through the liver. The liver oxidizes the alcohol (changes it into water and carbon dioxide). If too much alcohol is consumed, the liver cannot function properly and cirrhosis (scarring) of the liver occurs. This condition is deadly.

Heart and bloodstream: alcohol can cause heart disease, hypertension, heart failure, and stroke. Alcohol also gives a person the sense of being warm due to the enlarged blood vessels from alcohol. This is misleading and may actually cause the body temperature to drop.

Kidneys: alcohol acts like a diuretic and increases the amount of urine that is produced. Drinking can cause dehydration of important body fluids and prolonged drinking can cause kidney failure.

Digestive system: alcohol irritates the digestive system and can cause gastritis and ulcers.

Reproductive system: alcohol increases a person's sexual confidence which can cause a person to do things he/she normally would not do. Heavy, prolonged drinking can also cause impotence for males (physical inability to engage in sexual intercouse).

SOMETHING TO **THINK** ABOUT

Use your brain and don't drink

Did you know that drinking alcohol over an extended period of time destroys millions of brain cells? Other body cells can be replaced but brain cells cannot be repaired or replaced. So, use your brain and don't drink…before it's too late.

Alcohol and Teenagers

For many teenagers, drinking is a social activity. Most don't enjoy the taste of hard liquor but drink only because they feel the pressure from their peers. The "cool" image you may think comes with drinking is not so "cool." For someone who is trying to live a life pleasing to God by abstaining from alcohol and obeying the law, it is "cool" to say "no."

As a teenager your body is experiencing many physical changes. These important changes are hindered by the use of alcohol. The law prohibits the use of alcohol for teenagers, not to punish you, but to protect you from something that can do you great harm. You may feel that taking a drink once or twice won't hurt you. However, drinking alcohol can be habit-forming. Teenagers who drink alcohol tend to need more and more to feel the desired effect. This habit of drinking can turn into an addiction, where you experience a physical and mental need for alcohol. Studies show that people who begin drinking at an early age are more likely to become addicted to alcohol later in life.

Why do teenagers choose to drink? Pressure from peers to drink can start at a young age. Teenagers who give in to peer pressure are allowing their "friends" to make their choices for them. Do you think that drinking makes you look more mature? Think about this, is it "cool" to have your head hung over a toilet vomiting your guts out because you thought it was mature to drink? NO THANKS!

Drinking does not take away your problems, it only creates more for you.

Many teenagers drink to avoid their problems. It is an escape from the "real" world. However, drinking does not take away your problems, it only creates more for you. What would you tell a friend who wanted to try drinking? What would you tell someone if he/she wanted you to have a drink?

If you struggle with drinking or drugs, there is help and accountability is the key. Open up a conversation with your parents or a significant adult whom you trust. Drinking alcohol or trying drugs only magnifies your desire for isolation. Do not allow the fear of disappointing those you love to keep you from reaching out for help. You might be surprised at the love and understanding you get from your family.

How are you different?

You know the truth — let your life show it!

Live life, then, with a due sense of responsibility, not as men who do not know the meaning of life but as those who do....Don't get your stimulus from wine (for there is always the danger of excessive drinking), but let the Spirit stimulate your souls.
Ephesians 5:15–18 (Phillips Translation)

Protect Yourself And Others

- Never drive with someone who has been drinking.
- Do not get into an argument with someone who has been drinking.
- Never say "I promise not to tell" when trying to help someone who has a drinking problem.
- Do not protect the drinker by lying for him/her or by making excuses for his/her behavior.
- Do not feel responsible for the drinker's behavior.
- Avoid situations where you feel drinking may take place.
- Be the strong one by saying "no" when pressured to take a drink.
- Pray to God for strength to overcome the temptation to drink. If you fail, pick yourself up and try again.

Alcoholism

Alcoholism or alcohol dependence, is an illness characterized by habitual, compulsive, long-term, heavy drinking of alcohol. Withdrawal symptoms occur when the drinking stops. Researchers cannot find one specific reason why a person becomes an alcoholic. Many believe that a person has a tendency to become alcohol dependent if he/she comes from a family with a history of alcoholism. Nevertheless, drinking alcohol is a choice. If you feel you could be a candidate for having a drinking problem, then don't take that first drink. Make the choice that will benefit you the rest of your life — avoid drinking alcohol.

Families of those who are alcoholics must deal with unique circumstances. Alcohol abuse as well as drug abuse affects those who know the alcoholic. If you find yourself in a difficult situation with someone you care about, family member or friend, get help. There are support groups specifically designed for alcoholics and their families. *Alcoholics Anonymous (AA)* has had success in helping alcoholics beat their addiction. *Alateen* is a group designed to help the children of alcoholic parents. *Al-Anon* is another group that helps the husbands, wives and friends of alcoholics.

SOMETHING TO THINK ABOUT

Fetal Alcohol Syndrome

A pregnant woman not only hurts herself by drinking alcohol but also harms her unborn child. When a pregnant woman drinks, the alcohol is passed through her bloodstream to the fetus. As a result of this, a condition known as **Fetal Alcohol Syndrome (FAS)** can result. This disorder consists of physical and mental problems such as cleft palate, heart defects, abnormal limb development, and lower-than-normal intelligence.

The sad thing about Fetal Alcohol Syndrome is that the unborn child had no choice in what entered its body. The mother made the choice for the child.

A Tribute To A Brother
by a loving sister
Names have been left anonymous to protect the family involved

My brother used to always tease me. I guess that is normal for a big brother to always pick on his little sister. As I grew up I noticed things were not always "right" in our home. My mom and dad used to make excuses for my brother's behavior. When he came in late or did not come in at all, there was always a "good" reason. It was not uncommon for my brother to sleep half the day and then stay up late at night. He also did not communicate much with the family. When I tried to strike up a conversation he would either ignore me or snap at me and tell me to leave him alone. My brother isolated himself in his room or downstairs in front of the television set. And when he was sick to his stomach, he always had the flu.

By the time I finished high school I knew my brother had a drinking problem but it was never mentioned in our house. It was like if it was ignored it would go away... but it only got worse. I remember one night when my brother called home. He was calling from a pay phone across town. I could tell from the sound of his voice he had been drinking and he wanted help. After we got off the phone with him my sister and I took off in the car to look for him. We never found him but found his car in a bar parking lot. The next day he came home.

It all came to a head when a close friend of my brother's asked him "do you want to kill yourself, because that is what you are going to do"? A few days after that my brother admitted himself into an alcohol treatment center and began to faithfully attend Alcoholics Anonymous. I suppose some people have to reach rock bottom before they look up.

I am very proud of my brother. He has been sober for ten years and is still attending his AA meetings. I am glad his friend had the guts to confront my brother, because I never did...

354

CHAPTER REVIEW

DEFINE

Puberty
Defraud
Abortion
Nicotine
Tar
Carbon Monoxide
Drugs

Medicines
Stimulants
Addiction
Depressants
Alcohol
Alcoholism
Fetal Alcohol Syndrome

EXPLAIN

1. Explain why you don't always see the consequences of your decisions until later in life.
2. Explain how the "right now" mentality can be dangerous. How does this affect the choices you make?
3. Explain why the time of puberty for teenagers can be a difficult time physically, emotionally and socially. Do you think this is a difficult time spiritually as well? Explain your answer.
4. Explain how a teenager should handle his/her curiosity about sex?
5. Explain why abstinence from sexual intercourse should not be the only goal.
6. Explain how a teenager can show respect for one another in the area of sexual desires.
7. Explain why God allows teens such a strong sex drive and then commands them to abstain from sex.
8. Explain the meaning of the term "technical virgins."
9. Explain some of the alternatives to an abortion.
10. Explain how a teenager can learn from other people's experiences and avoid making poor decisions.
11. Explain the harmful effects of using tobacco.
12. Explain the difference between drug abuse and drug misuse.
13. Explain the harmful effects of using alcohol.
14. Explain why some teens may choose to drink alcohol.
15. Explain the effects of cigarette smoke on nonsmokers.

DISCUSS

1. Discuss the situation with Susan and Bill. What were the negative and positive choices she made that night. How could she have avoided the heartache altogether? What might have happened if Bill refused to take Susan home? Could date rape have occurred and how could it have been avoided?

2. Discuss the reasons why you think God has placed boundaries in your life. Why is it a sign of maturity to have limits for yourself? Is it a sign of being a "wimp" when you pray and ask God for strength to overcome temptations? Explain.

3. Read 1 Thessalonians 5:12. Discuss why it is important to avoid the appearance of evil.

4. Discuss the meaning of maturity. What are signs of maturity?

5. Discuss why you think there is no "guide to sex" in the Bible.

6. Discuss why being a Christian means more than only observing the letter of the law concerning sex. Why does the Bible discuss purity, and what does it mean to be morally pure?

7. Discuss why it is a wise choice to wait for sex until marriage.

8. Discuss how a teenager can wait for sex until marriage. Do you believe that it is realistic to practice abstinence until marriage?

9. Imagine you have a friend who just found out she was pregnant. How would you comfort her? Discuss the alternatives she has to an abortion.

10. Discuss the pressures teens face concerning drugs and alcohol. How might you handle those pressures?

11. Discuss how smoking cigarettes can negatively affect your lifestyle? Do you think that smoking positively or negatively affects your social life?

12. Discuss ways you can say "no" to drugs and alcohol when faced with the pressure.

SUGGESTED ACTIVITIES

1. **Key Concepts:** Outline the chapter and make a study guide for yourself. You may work alone or in groups.

2. **Time to Talk:** Make a list of questions you have concerning sexuality. Make a date with one or both of your parents to discuss the questions you have. Be open to their answers and if they need time to answer the questions, give them the list and then take a "rain check" and meet with them again.

3. **Standing Out:** Do a skit on Christian teenagers who stand out of the crowd by saying no to the pressures of sex, smoking, drugs and alcohol. Use real-life teenage situations to make the skits realistic.

4. **It's in the Book:** Get together with a group of other students and select two or three scriptures concerning purity. Keep each other accountable to memorize the Scriptures. Try to recite the Scriptures by memory one each week. When you have reached your memory goal share with the class how it has helped you in your walk with Christ. Challenge each other to make Scripture memory a regular part of your life.

5. **Hidden Messages:** Write a report on the influence of advertising on sexual promiscuity, tobacco and alcohol use. Look for the hidden messages in the pictures and in the words that are used. You may make a collage if the pictures are appropriate to show to class. For example: The Marlboro Man is healthy and strong and smokes cigarettes. Is this a realistic image?

6. **Write a Letter:** Imagine yourself as a parent. Write a letter to your teenagers, one to your daughter and one to your son. Include in your letter your views on sexuality and abstinence. Share with your teenager why you believe the way you do and what you hope they will choose for themselves.

7. **Get M.A.D.D.:** Do a report on the Mothers Against Drunk Driving organization; who founded it and why, and how have they influenced the laws concerning drunk drivers.

   What are the goals of M.A.D.D. You can contact the organization by writing directly to their headquarters: M.A.D.D., 669 Airport Freeway, Suite 310, Hurst, TX. 76053.

8. **Be an Example:** Imagine you were asked to speak to the 7th grade class on the dangers of alcohol. Write your speech as if you were speaking directly to them. Hand it in to your teacher.

9. **Please Forgive Me:** Do a study on the mercy of God. Find at least five Scriptures dealing with God's mercy and forgiveness. For each verse write what it means to you personally. How might this apply to someone who has fallen into immorality? How might we learn from the way God forgives?

Changing Relationships

14-1 WHEN FRIENDSHIPS BECOME RELATIONSHIPS
14-2 WHEN TWO BECOME ONE
14-3 WHEN TWO BECOME A FAMILY
14-4 WHEN DEATH MEANS LIFE

14-1 WHEN FRIENDSHIPS BECOME RELATIONSHIPS

The basis for a successful relationship with others is a successful relationship with Him.[1]
Glenda Malmin

THE DATING GAME

You have heard throughout this text that your relationship with God affects all areas of your life. Your relationship with others is no exception. God is involved in your personal relationships. From your choice of casual friends to your choice for a marriage partner, God cares about each level of friendship in your life. Bill Gothard in his *Institute in Basic Youth Conflicts* seminar identifies each level of friendship. The pyramid illustrates that the number of friends naturally decreases as you go up the pyramid levels.

Four: Intimate Level
Based on commitment to the development of each other's character

Three: Close
Based on mutual life goals

Two: Casual
Based on common interests and activities

One: Acquaintance
Based on casual contacts

Evaluate your present friendships. Mentally place them in the level at which you think they belong. As you evaluate your friendships with the opposite sex, it is important to recognize that the close and intimate levels of friendship are reserved. That is, they are to be "saved" for a person with whom you are considering marriage.

Let's Go Out!

The time of dating for you can be an exciting and fun time or it can be a time of heartache and depression. Because of the potential problems associated with dating, you and your parents must decide together your personal dating standards and guidelines. Try not to compare your dating agreement with that of other teens and their parents. Each family is different and has its own convictions about certain issues. Your parents may feel it is not time for you to date. Trust them, *dating does not always equal fun.* You can have fun without the social pressures that come with dating. When you choose not to single-date, you also can be more focused on academics, school activities, family, friends and your relationship with the Lord.

Dating does not always equal fun.

SOMETHING TO THINK ABOUT

Excuses that compromise your dating standards

- "He's not a Christian, but he is nicer than some Christians I know."
- "I'm sure she will become a Christian; she has even started going to church."
- "We have so much fun together."
- "She is not the type I would want to marry; we are just having a good time."
- "My parents don't really care for him, but they don't really know him like I do."
- "Our relationship is different; we really love each other."
- "I know I should break up with him, but I don't want to hurt his feelings."

You may have already set guidelines for yourself concerning dating, or your parents may have already set them for you. Stick to your convictions, knowing that the way you handle friendships now will influence the way you deal with relationships later. Consider the following suggestions when making your decision about the "dating game."

- *Group dating* is going out with a group of friends. Many youth pastors encourage group dating instead of single dating. There may be couples in the group, but not necessarily. It can even be an uneven number of friends. There are many reasons why this is a positive choice. Group dating allows you to get to know people of the opposite sex without the social pressures that come with being alone on a date. When you are with a group of people, you can get to know people on a casual basis. You don't have that awkward feeling of being alone, not knowing what to say or do. Group dating also gives you the opportunity to get to know many friends of the opposite sex at the same time. Being able to watch your friends in different situations will help you determine if you may or may not be interested in them.

- *Make specific plans* for your date. Whether you are going on a single-date or a group-date, it is important to plan your time. *If you fail to plan, you plan to fail.* You will not impress your date if you just "see what happens." Plan dates in advance and be creative with what you choose to do. Always make a set time that you should return so you do not get into trouble just "passing the time."

- *Be creative* in what you and the others plan to do. If you try hard enough you will come up with some great activities in your own town. Others will be impressed because you did not do the same thing every time. The book *Dynamic Dating* by Barry St. Clair and William H. Jones gives many suggestions for fun activities.[2]

> Group dating allows you to get to know people of the opposite sex without the social pressures that come with being alone on a date.

Let's Go Out!
Helpful hints for having "good, clean fun"

Sporting ideas:
miniature golf
golf
pool
ice/roller skating
basketball game
horseshoes
walking
tennis
racquetball
bowling
jogging
frisbee

Outdoor ideas:
boating
rafting
fishing
horseback riding
canoeing
sightseeing
mountain climbing
sailing
hiking
biking
visiting the zoo
visiting an amusement park
flying kites
going to a rodeo

Crazy ideas:
going on a hayride
going to a fair
going on a double date with parents
having a water pistol fight
planting a garden
doing something special for an elderly person
having a water balloon fight
making a video
going to the airport
learning to drive a stick shift

362

Why Date?

Ask yourself these questions: "Why do I want to date?" "What do I hope to get out of dating"? "What do I want to have happen on a date"? "How can I get to know the other person"? These questions should be addressed *before* you begin to get involved in dating. Discuss them with your parents, counselor, or youth pastor. What is the purpose of dating? Do teenagers date to have fun, get to know someone better, or to learn how to have positive male/female relationships? All of those reasons are in some way correct but there is one reason for dating that is often overlooked. *The real purpose of formal single dating is to pursue a marriage partner.* Friendships at each level are important. When friendships progress up the chart, two people can *gradually* reach a marital commitment. As a result, two friends enter the marriage with a foundation built on a strong friendship.

Kingdom Relationships

When discussing relationships with the opposite sex, there is a tendency to jump right into discussing the physical relationship. God's order for a successful relationship is given as a guide to protect you and lead you into a godly relationship.

When you begin dating, the temptation exists to reverse the order and begin with physical involvement. The result is an unhealthy emotional bond and guilt. Taking the time and energy to know someone spiritually and emotionally seems difficult, but the rewards are lifelong. Even if the relationship ends, the spiritual foundation leaves a basis of respect and continued friendship.

Undoubtedly, you have entered your teen years anticipating dating. The friendships you have with the opposite sex will begin to change as you find yourself attracted to someone special. If you have not yet experienced the countless feelings that come with changing

Taking the time and energy to know someone spiritually and emotionally seems difficult, but the rewards are lifelong.

Divine order for relationships

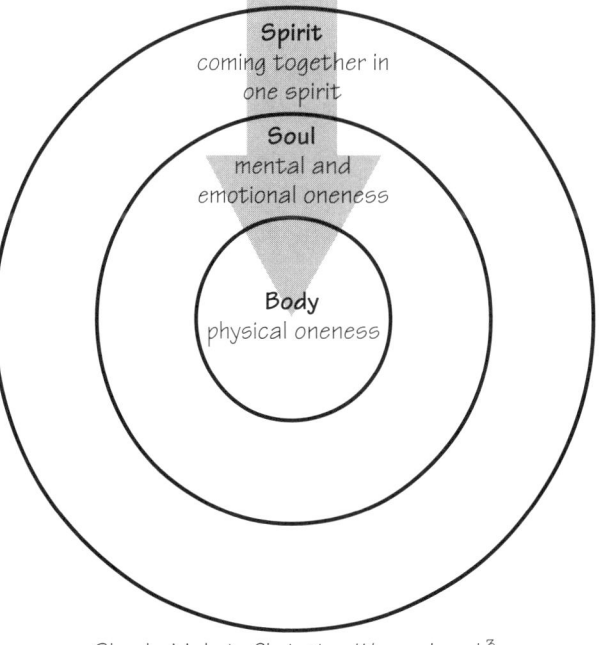

Glenda Malmin Christian Womanhood [3]

friendships, you will soon. You may feel confused, excited, anxious, and afraid all at the same time, and in there somewhere, you will wonder if these feelings mean you have fallen in love. Do not be persuaded to follow after society's methods for dating and relationships. The culture you live in today, embraces a "self-centered view" of everything. The seeds of this mentality trickle down into the most important relationship between two people — marriage. "Do not use the world's way to relate...or you will have the world's result" (Wendell Smith).

The following chart is taken from *Confronting Our Culture*.[4]

God's Ways of "Kingdom Relationships" *God-centered relationships*		Culture's Way of "Dating": *Self-centered relationships*	
Basis:	Wholesome attraction Commitment to God Friendship	**Basis:**	Natural attraction Feelings, desires
Goal:	Mutual edification and fulfillment of God's will	**Goal:**	Mutual gratification and fulfillment of self-will
Qualities:	Giving attitude Absolute moral standards Focus on Spirit and Soul Taking time to get to know each other Relationship inclusive of the Body of Christ	**Qualities:**	Receiving attitude No absolutes, no standards Focus on Body and Soul Moving quickly to take advantage of each other Relationship exclusive and possessive
Results:	Stronger relationship to the Lord and others Healthy self-image Character development for better Greater motivation Increased fulfillment Good example to others Peace, joy and abundant life	**Results:**	Weakened relationships with God and others Unhealthy self-image Character change for worse Draining of motivation Decreased fulfillment Influence others to sin Confusion, strife and heartache Emptiness and sorrow

"I Think I'm in Love"

No matter what your age, the desire for closeness, affection, and acceptance are real and natural desires. Everyone feels the need to be loved. As a teenager, you may find yourself having such strong feelings for a person of the opposite sex that you think you are in love. People often overuse this word, not knowing what genuine love really is. A deeper study of the word love in the Bible reveals that there are different types of love.

- **Agape**: the most common word of all forms of love in the New Testament. Expresses love from God the Father to Jesus, God to man, man to God, and man to his neighbor. Jesus' whole life, from birth to death, was divine love (agape) in action.
- **Eros**: more naturally used as intimate affection and liking to do things which are pleasant.

The difference between the phrases "I love God" and "I love ice cream" are obvious. However, when love and infatuation (having a "crush" or strong admiration for someone) get confused, there can be disastrous results.

The search for intimacy, coupled with an inability to differentiate between infatuation and real love, can lead to sexual involvement by teens. In many instances, sexual activity was not originally planned or desired. A relationship began, based on romantic feelings and infatuation, and continued because of a desire for intimacy.[5]
Scott Talley

"How will I know when I'm in love"? This is a common question that deserves an answer. You have probably heard the response, "Oh, you will *just know* when you are in love." This is not very comforting when trying to sort out all the feelings you may have. The first thing to recognize is that love and sex are not the same.

Sex and love are not synonymous. They are two separate concepts. Sex is an act performed by two people committed to loving each other for life, while love, in varying degrees, can be felt by anyone. Love is not an act; love is a commitment.[6]

Josh McDowell

Sex and love

are not

synonymous.

Josh McDowell

"Don't Fall For The Line..."

Line 1: Everybody's doing it.
        Reply: That's great. Then I guess you won't have any problem finding someone else.

Line 2: If you love me, you'll have sex with me.
        Reply: If you love me, you'll respect my feelings and not push me into doing something I'm not ready for.
        Reply: If you love me, you'll wait.

Line 3: If you won't have sex with me, then I don't want to see you anymore.
        Reply: Well, if that's the way you feel, I'm going to miss seeing you, but that's the way it's going to be.

Line 4: It's just part of growing up.
        Reply: Having sex doesn't mean you are grown up. Being grown up to me means deciding what I believe and then sticking to those beliefs.

Line 5: Don't you want to try it to see what it's like?
        Reply: What is this? Some kind of commercial ad? Try it; you'll like it! I do plan to try it with my husband (wife).

Line 6: But I have to do it.
        Reply: No you don't. If I can wait, you can wait.

Line 7: We had sex once before, so what's the problem now?
        Reply: I have a right to change my mind. I've decided to wait.

Line 8: If you care about me, you'll have sex with me.
        Reply: Because I care about you, I want to wait.
        Reply: There are many ways to show someone you care.

Line 9: You just don't know what you're missing.
        Reply: That will make two of us. You won't know what you're missing either.

Line 10: Want to go to bed?
        Reply: No thanks, I just got up.

Excerpts taken from *How To Help Your Child Say "NO" To Sexual Pressure.* By Josh McDowell [7]

When casual friendships change into romantic relationships, a whole new world opens up to you. It is often very difficult to understand the many emotions you are feeling. Parents and adults will try to help give you the proper perspective, but it may be difficult for you to accept. If you don't sort through your emotions and test the relationship, you may make a terrible mistake. Dr. Dobson sums it up this way:

To my knowledge, there is only one way to distinguish puppy love from the real thing: give yourself time to test your emotions. You will gradually come to understand your own mind and know what is best for the other person. How long will this process take? It differs from person to person, but in general, the younger you are, the longer you should wait.[8]

14-2 WHEN TWO BECOME ONE

Getting married is easy.
Staying married is more difficult.
Staying happily married for a lifetime
would be considered among the fine arts.[9]

THE MYTHS OF MARRIAGE

"Marriage Is Just Not Worth it"

A teenager is talking to her friend about boys. "I never want to get married," she says to her friend. "Men are all alike and marriage is not worth the effort, and besides, it will probably end in divorce." "Why do you feel that way"? her friend asks. "Marriage is not all it's cracked up to be," she responds. My mom has been married two times and she is still not happy...."

Unfortunately, this is what some teenagers believe about love and marriage. It doesn't help that six hours of the daytime television shows are soap operas dealing with "love," divorce, abortion, homosexuality, abuse,

367

lying and cheating. Even the prime-time "family" programs portray unstable family life and unresolved marriage conflicts. As a result, a young person grows up with the assumption that all marriages end in divorce and that avoiding the marriage commitment altogether is the answer.

"But, I Thought It Would Be Different"

Another myth about marriage is that marriage is the answer to all of life's problems, the key to success and happiness. Marriage is a wonderful gift from God, but if you are looking to marriage to get you out of your troubles or to be the answer to loneliness — you are mistaken.

Many people enter marriage with expectations that cannot be fulfilled. Engaged couples are so in love that they often do not see the "real person" they are marrying. They walk around with a permanent grin and have "stars in their eyes." Dennis Rainey, author of *Staying Close* puts it this way:

> Many couples think marriage promises fun that will never end. Nothing in the world arouses more false hope than the first four hours of a diet or the first day of the honeymoon.[10]

"If It Doesn't Work Out, I Will Just Get A Divorce"

The myth that divorce is the answer to a troubled marriage is also a mistake. To think that if you have problems you will just divorce is like punching holes in your boat and saying, "If the boat sinks, I will just swim to shore." When you enter the marriage agreement with this in mind, you better start swimming because the boat has already begun to sink!

"I Have it all Planned Out"

Do you and your friends ever talk about how your life is going to be? Do you find yourself saying, "I will get married when I'm 22 years old. After two years we will start a family and have four children, two boys and two girls. I will have a great job and life will be wonderful." Do you ever consider that you may not meet

Many people enter marriage with expectations that cannot be fulfilled.

the right person until later in life or that you may have difficulty conceiving children right away? God doesn't frown on making plans and having goals and dreams. But planning things that you have no control over can leave you open for great disappointments.

> …you do not know what will happen tomorrow. For what is your life? It is even a vapor that appears for a little time and then vanishes away. Instead you ought to say, "If the Lord wills, we shall live and do this or that."
> James 4:14–15

Seek God and develop a strong personal relationship with Him. It's not important to know *what* the future holds, but to know *who* holds the future.[11]

BECOMING ONE

You are probably tempted to skim over this chapter on marriage. The decision to get married may seem far off to you now, but I assure you the desire to get married will someday occupy your thoughts.

The decision to marry is so important that you need to be prepared *before* it becomes reality to you. When you plan a trip, you prepare far in advance. You purchase your airline tickets early to get the best price. You shop for special clothes and items that you will need for the trip. You even plan what you will do when you get to your destination — you get prepared. When you shop for a car, you search for the best price, check out the best models and do your homework so you won't make a mistake — you get prepared. A trip and a car are temporary purchases, but when you decide to get married, you are making a decision to last a lifetime. You want to be prepared.

It's not important to know what the future holds, but to know who holds the future.

What is marriage? To some, it is a convenient way to save money or a means of getting a tax write off. The *Zondervan Pictorial Bible Dictionary* gives the following definition for marriage.

Marriage is an intimate personal union to which man and woman consent, consummated and continuously nourished by sexual intercourse and perfected in a lifelong partnership of mutual love and commitment.

Wow! Even the definition reveals the intensity of the marriage agreement. Why get married? For sex? For romance? For money? For security? To have children? All of these answers may be right, but God has designed marriage for a bigger purpose. Dennis Rainey in his book *Staying Close*, gives five reasons for marriage.[12]

- To mirror God's image.
- To multiply a godly heritage.
- To manage God's realm.
- To mutually complete one another.
- To model Christ's relationship to the church.

God sees marriage as a covenant agreement, a solemn pledge between two people agreeing to fulfill certain conditions. When covenants between men were made in the Bible, God was asked

to be present as a witness. In the covenant of marriage, God is the witness. A covenant agreement is not made to be broken.

All the dynamics involved in marriage are a mystery. When you commit yourself to another person in marriage, you become one in body, mind and spirit. This is the mystery of 1 + 1 = 1.[13] When you *leave* your home you become independent of your parents. When you *cleave* to your spouse, you form a permanent bond together (Genesis 2:24).

The physical oneness in sexual intercourse is the easiest way to become one. Sex is intended to be a beautiful union between a husband and wife. It is an expression of love, commitment, trust and loyalty. The interesting part about marriage is that if you are not becoming one in mind and spirit, your sexual relationship can suffer. God creatively designed each form of oneness to affect the others.

All areas of oneness are important to a marriage. However, spirit oneness is the one area that will hold a marriage together. Dennis Rainey says this about being one in spirit, "As two people grow upward in their relationship with God by walking in the Spirit, they grow together as one."[14] The spiritual area in a marriage is, unfortunately, the one area that is often overlooked.

How can you prepare yourself for the commitment of marriage? Grow in your relationship to the Lord, developing the character qualities that will make you the best marriage partner you can be. Ask the Lord to prepare you for marriage, and if remaining single is His will for you, pray that He will prepare you for that lifestyle as well. Remember, the key to life is not marriage but your relationship to God. Never quit in your desire to become more like Christ. God's plan for you may not happen in the timing that you have "set" for your life, but His timing is right.

> The key to life is not marriage but your relationship to God.

14-3 WHEN TWO BECOME A FAMILY

PARENTING

The need for love, support and companionship begins at the moment of birth. God desires the family to be the place to meet those needs. When a husband and wife fulfill the commandment to "be fruitful and multiply" either by having their own children or through adoption, the dynamics of a family begin.

Most young people assume that they will be parents someday. When a couple gets married their life changes, but when a couple has a child, their life *really* changes. Parenthood involves constant care and attention to a child who is totally dependent. Parenthood offers many rewards while at the same time, requiring responsibility, time and love. Teenagers are not ready to be parents for many reasons. Most teens don't have the money and resources to provide what a child needs. Shelter, food, and clothing are only part of the responsibility that comes with having a child. During your teen years you are still learning who you are and what you want to do in life. Having a child when you are not emotionally ready is both damaging to you as well as to the child.

Having a healthy lifestyle before a baby is conceived and maintaining it during pregnancy and immediately after birth, will help the newborn and the parents have the best possible start. Children are a blessing from God. In any circumstance, a baby is a precious life waiting for someone to love and care for it. Good parents recognize their enormous responsibility and seek to do the best job they can. Raising a child to love God and respect others is a huge undertaking. Don't worry now about being ready to parent, when you get married and the time comes to have children, others will stand by you and God will give you the wisdom you need.

SOMETHING TO THINK ABOUT

Try this job!

Being a parent is a full time job. To see what kind of demands are on you as a parent, try this for one day. Have someone in your family set an alarm in your house to go off at various times, without telling you what time it is set.

When you hear the alarm, stop what you are doing, whether it is talking on the phone, eating or sleeping. Then do house work or some other job for about 10–15 minutes. Then return to whatever you were doing. Repeat this throughout a day. This is what it is like to be "on call" when you have a baby!

CONFLICTS, CONFLICTS, CONFLICTS

What do you argue about in your home? Does it seem that "just about everything" causes a major conflict? Think about this: if you have at least one brother or sister, that means that you have a potential of at least six interpersonal relationships exploding. Everyone experiences conflict of some kind. What makes it a bearable learning experience is handling each situation properly.

The teenage years can be filled with conflict. The changes that you are experiencing and the intense emotions are almost too much for you and your family to handle. The most important thing to do when dealing with conflict in the family is to keep communication open. This does not just mean talking, although friendly conversation does help keep families kind to one another. Dennis Rainey says this about communication: "Nothing is as easy as talking, nothing is as difficult as communicating."[15]

Communication skills are important in any relationship. How you deal with conflict in your home will be the basis for how you deal with it in the workplace, your marriage and any other situation involving people.

A Personal Testimony
By Susan Boe

I have two older brothers and two older sisters. Do we all love each other? Of course we do! Have we always showed that we love each other? No.

I shared a room with my older sister Ann until she entered high school. During the day we could avoid each other. The only conflicts seemed to be sharing clothes and keeping the room clean.

The problems occurred at night. Ann wanted to go to bed after I did so no matter what, I would end up in bed first. The light would be off and of course, she would have to turn it on to come in. Then it was time to exercise. Sit ups on the floor and various exercises awakened me (that is, if I was asleep). I thought I would nearly burst with anger. Once Ann got into bed, she had to listen to her radio. After I complained about the noise, Ann used an ear phone. This didn't help because I would be mad at her anyway!

Nothing is as easy as talking, nothing is as difficult as communicating.

Dennis Rainey

The key to the story of Ann and Susan is the last line: "I would be mad at her anyway." This is usually the case with family members. It doesn't have to be a big thing to get you angry, any little thing would do. Do you ever find yourself mad at someone in your family and you don't even know why? Most of the time the conflicts are due to the roller coaster ride of emotions you are feeling. Do you want to deal with the conflicts positively in your home? Check out the helpful hints to getting along.

Helpful hints to getting along...and loving it!

1. Avoid serious conversations when you know you are already upset.
2. *Communicate* clearly what you feel *before* you lose your temper.
3. *Really listen* when the other person is sharing.
4. Avoid using phrases like "you never..." or "you always..."
5. Use other opportunities to *build up* your family members by complimenting them, building their self-esteem.
6. Use phrases like: "this makes me feel," or "I am feeling" or "are you saying that...?"
7. *Be honest;* that means, share how you really are feeling. Avoid holding feelings in until you explode.
8. *Try praying* for the person with whom you are angry. Pray for them a little each day during your devotions or on your way to school, whenever you can.
9. If there is something specific to discuss, pick a time to sit down and talk about it apart from the moment of the argument.
10. Remember to say often: "I am sorry," "I was wrong," "please forgive me" and "I love you."
11. Avoid the temptation to "get back" at the person or "punish" them for something they have done.
12. Make time to communicate with your parents...alone. Share with them what you are feeling and make an effort to listen to them.

You may be thinking that "this would never work in my family." If you are experiencing difficulty with your parents, guardian or brother or sister, talk it over with an adult you can trust. A pastor, parent of a friends, teacher or counselor at school will listen.

It is a fact that the American family is changing all the time. Whatever family situation you face, whether it involves relatives, step-relatives, an adopted family, or a foster care family, these people care about you. Even in difficult times they are the most important people in your life. Make the most of your situation and don't forget to tell them you care.

Dear Lord,
Help me to love myself — but not too much;
Help me to love others — but not too little;
And help me to love You more and more.
Amen.

14-4 WHEN DEATH MEANS LIFE

Most assuredly, I say to you, he who hears My word and believes in Him who sent Me has everlasting life, and shall not come into judgment, but has passed from death into life.
John 5:24

THE GOLDEN YEARS

A daughter, while glancing through her mother's wedding pictures, comments, "mom, you look so young!" The mother responds, "well, I was young once too."

Young people often forget that senior citizens were young once just like them. They have gone through adolescence (and survived!), made difficult decisions, learned from their mistakes, experienced hardships and had a first love. Older adults have feelings just like you; they feel joy, sadness, depression, and heartache. *They have been where you are and you will be where they are.*

How Do You Treat the Elderly?

Do you have grandparents or older relatives? Much of how you feel toward the elderly is formed by how you view your own adult family. Do you respect adults? Do you respect senior citizens?

If your answers to the questions below reveal a negative attitude, consider whether these actions are true to the way you treat older people that you know or are related to. When you treat people as stereotypes, you lose opportunities for close relationships. Young and old share the basic human needs for warmth, understanding, support, dignity, and companionship.[16]

Do You:
- Avoid elderly people?
- Believe they can't make reasonable decisions?
- Show impatience toward them?
- Overprotect them by withholding information about health or other matters?
- Show disrespect by ignoring them or laughing at their physical problems?
- Do you talk down to them or talk over their heads?

Or Do You:
- Make allowances for their age and mobility?
- Seek their advice?
- React enthusiastically to their plans or thoughts?
- Involve them in your activities?
- Tell them they are important?

Older adults have much to share about life. Encourage your parents or grandparents to share their stories of childhood. Their advice may increase your faith and help you lead a victorious life.

SOMETHING TO
THINK
ABOUT

Making a Difference...

- *Noah Webster, published his famous dictionary in 1828, at the age of 68.*
- *Mother Teresa of Calcutta, won the first Pope John XXIII Peace Prize in 1971 at the age of 61 and the Nobel Peace Prize eight years later.*
- *Eleanor Roosevelt became Chairman of the United Nations Commission for Human Rights in 1946 at the age of 61.*
- *Winston Churchill began his second term as British Prime Minister in 1951 at the age of 77.*
- *Benjamin Franklin helped frame the Constitution of the United States in 1787 at the age of 81.*

When you think of aging, you probably imagine yourself wrinkled and gray. Actually, the physical changes that come with aging begin in your mid-twenties. Your body processes begin to slow down. People experience both physical and mental aging, but the rate and degree follow no set timetable and vary with each individual. Some physical signs of aging include:

- **Skin and hair:** a gradual loss of elastic tissue in the skin causes the skin to sag. Hair loses its color, and the skin may develop "aging" spots.
- **Skeleton and muscles:** height decreases with age, the joints become stiffer, the bones lose calcium which causes them to become more brittle, and the muscles become weaker.
- **Heart and circulation:** the heart has to work harder to pump the blood through the body, the arteries harden and thicken inside. Blood pressure may rise, and the circulation of blood through the body gets worse.
- **Lungs:** breathing ease is reduced because the tissues in the lungs become less elastic.
- **Abdominal organs:** the organs lose their efficiency and the kidneys are slower to filter the impurities from the body.
- **Senses:** a slow weakening of the senses. Especially the ability to focus on nearby objects. Hearing loss is also common. The ability to sense temperature changes may also occur resulting in a person dressing improperly for the weather conditions.

There are mental changes as well as physical changes that occur as you grow older. Just like the physical problems, the mental effects of aging are different from person to person. Many older adults have very active and alert minds. Some mental signs of aging include:

- **Memory:** short-term memory begins to fail.
- **Alzheimer's disease:** Alzheimer's disease is a form of mental slow-down. People who suffer from Alzheimer's lose their memory over a period of time. They may also lose their physical ability to move and to control their speech. Alzheimer's can also attack people in their forties and fifties although it is more common to affect those over 65.
- **Dementia:** **Dementia** is a disease that interferes with the normal working of the mind. It is often caused by small strokes that have occurred in the brain. Most people who suffer from this disease are in their sixties and seventies.

A Positive Attitude

Adopting healthy lifestyle choices as a young person can help to alleviate some of the physical results of the aging process. Staying active and physically fit, as well as eating a healthy diet, is also important. Of equal importance however, is having a positive attitude about growing older. People have called these years the "golden years" because they finally have the time to pursue things they have wanted to do all their lives.

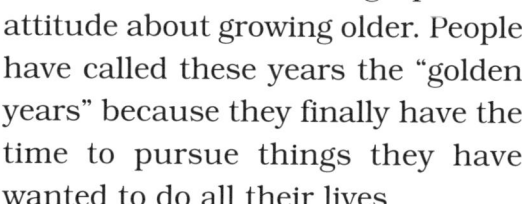

You will not be able to avoid many of the physical changes that come with aging, but your state of mind and heart will keep you motivated to pursue challenges. The challenges of adolescence prepare you for young adulthood. Being a young adult prepares you for middle adulthood which prepares you for late adulthood. Each stage in life is a journey to prepare you for the next stage. If you look forward to the future with enthusiasm and anticipation, you will enjoy the journey and keep the "spark" for living within you.

WHEN DEATH MEANS LIFE

Handling Death and Grief

Of all the living animals on earth, humans alone know that they will someday face death. Not everyone spends his days thinking about death and dying, but it is a fact that you cannot escape. If you have experienced the pain of having someone close to you die, then you have been touched by one of the strongest feelings humans can experience — grief.

Grief can be defined as: all the feelings of sorrow and deep distress over a death of a loved one. There are no words to describe

A Personal Testimony
By Susan Boe

After being married for two years my husband and I wanted to start having a family. I never thought I would have any problems getting pregnant or having a successful pregnancy. My mother had five children in ten years with no physical problems so I thought pregnancy would be uncomplicated for me.

I had two miscarriages before I got pregnant with our first son, Steven. I never realized what it was like to experience a loss such as a miscarriage. It is something that words cannot accurately describe. When Steven was two years old we wanted to try to have another baby. When I got pregnant I was excited, yet apprehensive, about the pregnancy.

When signs of complications began in the pregnancy, I counseled myself that everything would be all right. At 25 weeks I went into the emergency room due to strong contractions. When the doctor examined me he found that the baby had died. Later that morning I delivered a perfectly-formed baby weighing 14 ounces and measuring 12 inches in length. We held our little boy, took baby pictures and named him Samuel.

The purpose of this testimony is to share what it was like to have a miscarriage at such a late stage of pregnancy. Any miscarriage is difficult because you lose someone you love, someone who is a part of you. Each time November 10 comes, I think about Samuel and what he would have been like. But I know that he is in a greater place; he is with the Lord and his two brothers or sisters in heaven.

the feelings that come with grief. They are deep and personal. The way people respond to grief varies from person to person, but there are five common reactions to experiencing a loss.

- **Shock:** After the loss of a loved one, many people do not express their emotions. It is not that they do not want to, but they feel a sense of separation from their feelings, a feeling of numbness.
- **Anger:** It is common for a person who has lost a loved one to experience feelings of anger at the circumstances surrounding the death (for example, anger toward the disease, the person responsible for an accident, etc.) People also may feel anger toward God for allowing the person to die.
- **Longing:** The deep feeling of a loss brings a strong desire or yearning for the loved one to come back. Saying that you miss the person isn't even strong enough words to describe this intense feeling.
- **Depression:** The reality of the death brings a feeling of depression. The person knows her loved one is not coming back.
- *Going On:* After a period of time after the loss, the person can go on with his/her life. He still misses the person, but the strong grief he felt is lessening.

Grieving takes many forms. If someone you know experiences a death of a loved one but does not cry or seem "hurt" by the loss, do not judge them and think "they don't care." People express their grief in different ways and at different times. Some people get over losses quickly while others take more time. Do all you can to be a friend. Don't worry about giving them counsel or trying to answer the question of "why." Just being with someone when she feels alone is being a strength to her.

Afraid of What?

Do you have feelings of fear when you think of dying? Maybe you fear *how* you will die or what will happen to you *after* you die. No matter what you fear, there is reassurance that in physical death there is spiritual life.

SOMETHING TO THINK ABOUT

How to help someone cope with a loss

Read the following situation. Is Tom's response a helpful one? What would you say to Lisa?

Tom: "I just heard that Lisa's dog got run over by a car yesterday. She is really depressed and didn't come to school today. That's too bad, but at least it wasn't a person in her family. She will just have to snap out of it. She can always get a new dog."

- *Encourage them to express their feelings.*
- *Respect your friend's right to feeling sad or depressed.*
- *Give them the time they need to "move on."*
- *Help the person to remember the good things about his loved one.*

A Chinese girl who saw a man before he was shot, heard someone ask him the question, "Aren't you afraid?" "No!" he replied, "I am not afraid. If you shoot me, I shall go straight to heaven."[17]

Afraid? Of What?
To feel the spirit's glad release,
To pass from pain to perfect peace,
The strife and strain of life to cease —
Afraid — of that?

Afraid to see the Saviour's face,
To hear His welcome and to trace
The glory gleam from wounds of grace?
Afraid — of that?
Afraid — of what?

A flash, a crash, a pierced heart;
Darkness, light — O Heaven's art
A wound, of His the counterpart.
Afraid — of that?

To enter into Heaven's rest,
And still to serve the Master blest,
From service good to service best —
Afraid — of that?

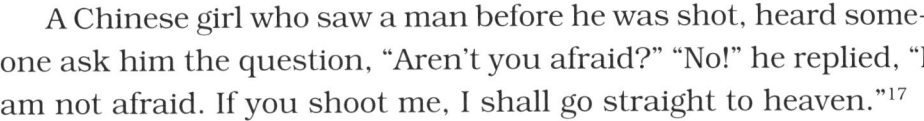

CHAPTER REVIEW

DEFINE

Agape
Eros
Marriage
Dementia
Grief

EXPLAIN

1. Explain the four levels of friendships and what type of friendship is at each level.
2. Explain why dating may not always equal "fun."
3. Explain why it is important to set dating standards. Include in your answer why it is important to set them *before* you begin dating.
4. Explain what group dating is, and why it is a good alternative to single-dating.
5. Explain the meaning of the phrase, "if you fail to plan, you plan to fail."
6. Explain the real purpose of single-dating and relate it to the levels of friendships chart.
7. Explain why it is important not to have physical involvement in a relationship.
8. Explain the difference between Agape love and Eros or Phileo love.
9. Explain why it is important to give a relationship time before making the marriage decision.
10. Explain the five reasons for marriage as given by Dennis Rainey.
11. Explain how to overcome a conflict between you and a family member.
12. Explain how younger people can treat older adults with respect.

DISCUSS

1. Discuss your feelings concerning dating. Do you have any fears? What do you expect from dating?

2. Discuss the possible consequences for making excuses that compromise your dating standards. For example, what might happen if you date someone who does not have the same Christian values as you do?

3. Discuss the meaning of the chart, "God's Ways of Kingdom Relationships." How can this chart help you in your dating standards?

4. Discuss how you can know when you are in "genuine love."

5. Discuss why sex and love are not synonymous (mean the same thing).

6. Discuss the four myths concerning marriage. Which myth do you find yourself believing?

7. Discuss practical ways you can prepare yourself for marriage now.

8. Discuss how each area of oneness (body, mind and spirit) can affect each other in a marriage relationship.

9. Discuss why teenagers are not ready to become parents.

10. Discuss what a "family" means to you. Why is your family the most important people in your life?

11. Discuss what a teenager can do if he/she has a difficult family life.

12. Discuss your feelings concerning growing older and dying. What fears do you have, if any? How do you want to be treated as an older adult? How would you like to be remembered after you die?

SUGGESTED ACTIVITIES

1. **Key Concepts:** Outline the chapter and make a study guide for yourself. You can work in groups or by yourself.

2. **"My Dating Standard":** Talk with your parents or a significant adult. Make a list of your dating standards. Keep these standards in your room or other place where you can see them often.

3. **Qualities I admire:** Make a list of qualities you would like in the person you would like to marry. Make another list of qualities you think someone of the opposite sex would like to see in you. How many of these qualities do you have already? How can you begin to develop those qualities?

4. **Interview:** Prepare some questions about dating and qualities teens like to see in teens of the opposite sex. Combine this and share it with the class or make it available for the rest of the high school to read. It may be done in a survey form.

5. **Help me understand!:** Find two older adults from each age category (50–60, 61–70, 71 and older). Prepare 10 questions about their view of growing older. For example, how do they feel others treat them. You may put the questions together as a class and then compare answers.

6. **"What about your generation?":** Interview a grandparent or another person of that generation. Ask the person what family life was like when he/she was your age. Include questions about what he did for entertainment, what she did if she went on a date, how he met his spouse, how she resolved conflicts.

7. **Act it out!:** Get in groups of two or four. Put together a skit concerning an issue from this chapter. For example, negative peer pressure on a date, positive peer pressure, resolving family conflicts, treating senior citizens positively

or negatively, or helping a friend with a loss of a loved one.

8. **Let's Go Out!:** Put together a list of fun things to do in your community. These should be appropriate for teens. The list can be placed in the classroom to give others ideas for group or single dates.

SPIRITUAL HEALTH

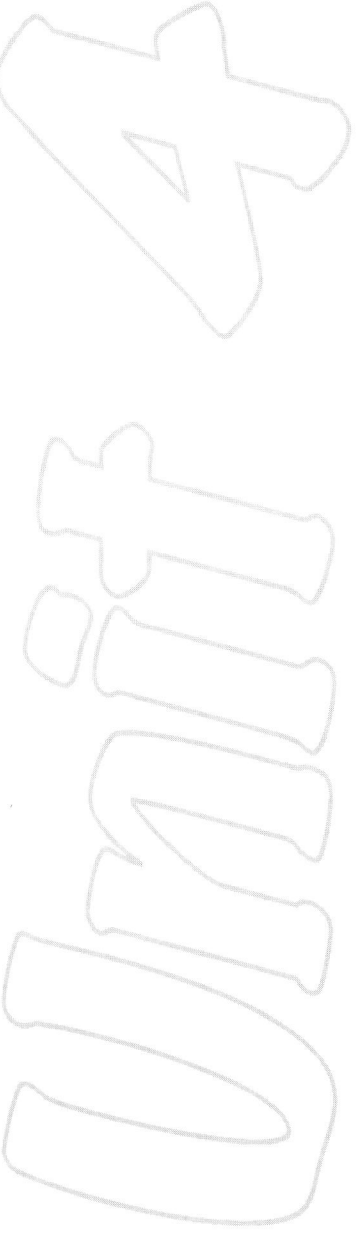

All Scripture is inspired by God and profitable for teaching, for reproof, for correction, for training in righteousness; that the man (or woman) of God may be adequate, equipped for every good work.
II Timothy 3:16,17
(parenthesis added) (NAS)

CHAPTER 15   BUILDING YOUR SPIRITUAL MUSCLES

CHAPTER 16   REACHING YOUR POTENTIAL

15 Building Your Spiritual Muscles **389**
  15-1 Keys to Spiritual Fitness 389
  15-2 Keys to Consistency 402

16 Reaching Your Potential **411**
  16-1 In Hot Pursuit 411
  16-2 Seeing Through the Darkness 415
  16-3 In My Father's House 421

Building Your Spiritual Muscles

15-1 KEYS TO SPIRITUAL FITNESS
15-2 KEYS TO CONSISTENCY

15-1 KEYS TO SPIRITUAL FITNESS

MAKE A CHOICE

Get Off the Fence!

A fence is a barrier used to mark a boundary. Imagine two property lines. On one side of the fence you have those who want to serve God and on the other are those who want to serve themselves. The fence is the position of neutrality or indecision. Are you riding the fence? Are you trying to decide whether you want to live life to please God or live life to please yourself? It is time to get off the fence of indecision and make a choice. Take a moment right now while you are reading this and evaluate where you stand with God.

Is every thing all right between you and God? If the answer is "no," ask God right now to help you have an open mind and heart to Him. Then, take a moment alone — just you and God — and tell Him you want to get off the fence because you have decided to walk with Him. If you are struggling with a lack of desire to know God, then your prayer might be, "Lord, give me the *desire* to desire more of You." If you pray for more hunger for the things of God, watch out! He will be faithful to give it to you!

Are you riding
the fence?

SPIRITUAL FITNESS

The meaning of the word exercise in the New Testament is: to exercise or to train the body or mind with a view to godliness.

...and exercise yourself rather toward godliness. For bodily exercise profits a little, but godliness is profitable for all things, having promise of the life that now is and of that which is to come.
I Timothy 4:7–8

Does the Scripture in I Timothy 4:7–8 mean that all things related to the health of the physical body are useless? No. However, the most important area of life is the condition of your spiritual health. If your physical body is strong and healthy, then you can give God more years of your life on this earth to serve Him.

An athlete exercises his/her muscles to keep them toned and strong. If an injury occurs or the athlete stops training, muscles that were once strong can become weak. Over a period of time with no exercise to a muscle, atrophy can occur. *Atrophy* is a wasting away or progressive degeneration of a muscle.

Think of yourself as a spiritual athlete. You have spiritual muscles that must be exercised in order to keep them fit. If you do not pay attention to your spiritual muscles, you will experience **spiritual atrophy** and you will find yourself weak and unprepared for spiritual activity.

Signs of Spiritual Atrophy:
- Have you been feeling like God is far away?
- Have you been struggling with temptation and sin lately?
- Have you had difficulty getting along with someone? Maybe a family member?
- Have you had little desire to read the Bible?
- Have you had little desire to pray?
- Have you had little desire to attend church or church activities?

If you can answer yes to any of these questions, then you have joined many other Christians suffering from spiritual atrophy. You have neglected the spiritual exercises necessary to live a victorious Christian life. Fortunately, getting back on a workout schedule will solve the problem and those weak muscles will soon be strong again.

Training in Righteousness

...But you, O man (and woman) of God, flee these things and pursue (seek) righteousness (virtue, uprightness), godliness, faith, love, patience, gentleness.
I Timothy 6:11 (parenthesis added)

It is common practice for a coach to post a training schedule for each group of athletes on the team. For a track team, the sprinters' training schedule may look like this:

Sprinters' Training Schedule

- warm up
- 440 pyramid 3 x
- practice starts with blocks
- practice technique
- 4 x 100 sprints
- warm down

Each day the workout is posted and the athletes are expected to complete the training. The coach knows what it takes to make an athlete ready for competition, but it is up to the athlete to follow the coach's plan.

It is a daily struggle to keep spiritually fit just as it is a daily struggle to keep physically fit. When you watch a skilled athlete

perform you see the result of hours of physical training. Similarly, spiritual fitness demands hours of training. The disciplines of a devotional life are small steps toward becoming the spiritual athlete God wants you to become. According to the New Bible Dictionary, **righteousness** is conformity to the law, mind, and will of God. Training in righteousness is a lifestyle, not a temporary achievement. God knows what it takes to be a strong athlete and the Bible is the training manual for spiritual fitness.

Read Isaiah 40:28–31; Philippians 4:6–9; Matthew 6:6–13; Psalm 1. It requires discipline to follow all that the Bible says about knowing God. You can listen to sermon after sermon and read book after book about how to have a strong devotional life, but unless you discipline yourself to *be a doer of the Word and not only a hearer,* you will not grow in your relationship with Him. It has been said:

It is more important to know Him than to know how to know Him.

If you draw near to Him in a personal relationship, He will draw near to you and cause you to desire more and more of Him. The following are the basic keys to spiritual training.

God knows what it takes to be a strong athlete and the Bible is the training manual for spiritual fitness.

Training in Righteousness

○ Bible reading and meditation on the Word
○ private prayer times and being quiet in His presence
○ fellowshipping with other believers; church and other activities
○ GIGO: God in — God out; serving and telling others about God
○ praise and worship

BIBLE READING AND MEDITATION ON THE WORD OF GOD

…But his delight is in the law of the Lord, And in His law he meditates day and night. He shall be like a tree Planted by the rivers of water, that brings forth its fruit in its season, Whose leaf also shall not wither; and whatever he does shall prosper.
Psalm 1:2–3

If you are not familiar with the Bible, do not be overwhelmed. It is the "book of books" and in its pages are the inspired words of God. The Bible is a book from God and about God. It was written by men of various background who were moved on by the Holy Spirit and wrote what they were inspired to write. The true purposes of meditating (reflecting on or thinking about) on the Word of God is to know God, to know Jesus Christ whom the Father God sent to die for mankind, and to know the will of God for your life.

Biblical meditation will transform your life by transforming your thoughts and your heart. The problems of the world will seem less troublesome as you place God's Word on the throne of your heart.

> Biblical meditation will transform your life by transforming your thoughts and your heart.

Practical Steps To Bible Reading

Step One: Have your own Bible. You should choose a translation (paraphrase or interpretation of Scripture) that you feel  comfortable reading. The following are suggested translations: New American Standard, New International Version or New King James. Go to your local Christian Book store and look over several Bible translations before you purchase your own.

Step Two: "Where do I begin reading?" Here are a few suggestions:

It is important to make a definite reading program for yourself. If you have a "system" you are following, you are more likely to stick to it. For example, you may want to read for a certain amount of time; if you plan to spend 15 minutes reading you may want to read five minutes in the Old Testament and five minutes in the New Testament and then five minutes during that time for prayerful thought on the scriptures. You may want to read by chapter: five chapters in the Old Testament and five Chapters in the New Testament. It is a good idea to read some from both the Old and New Testaments each day. Some people read Proverbs. Since there are 31 Proverbs, you can read one each day, then read a few chapters beginning in Genesis and a few chapters beginning in Matthew. You can also choose to study by topic. Pick a word, "faith" for example. Find the passages that deal with faith, meditate on them and put a few to memory. Whatever way you decide to read the Word, make it a regular part of your day.

Step Three: Choose a specific time of day (preferably in the morning or the beginning of the day so His word can help you through your day).

Step Four: Pray, ask God to help you as you read. He may inspire you to go away from your daily schedule and lead you to other verses that may minister to you personally.

Step Five: Mark your Bible or take notes in a notebook when a Scripture speaks to you about something specific.

Step Six: Put the Bible to memory. Choose Scriptures that encourage you and begin to memorize them. You not only need to know Scripture in times of hardship but also when sharing with others and for your own personal edification.

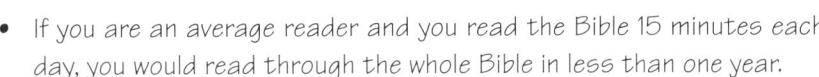

Interesting facts from Campbell McAlpine's book, Alone with God:[1]

- If you are an average reader and you read the Bible 15 minutes each day, you would read through the whole Bible in less than one year.
- If you read for 71 hours you could read the whole Bible through. The Old Testament would take 52 1/2 hours, the New Testament 18 1/2 hours.
- If you read by chapters, you could read the whole Bible in 18 weeks by reading 10 chapters a day.

…If you abide in My word, you are My disciples indeed. And you shall know the truth, and the truth shall make you free.
John 8:31–32

PERSONAL PRAYER AND QUIET TIME

Be anxious for nothing, but in everything by prayer and supplication, with thanksgiving, let your requests be made known to God; and the peace of God which surpasses all understanding, will guard your hearts and minds through Christ Jesus.
Phillippians 4:6–7

Although the Word of God is revealed within the pages of the Bible, the heartbeat of God is found in His presence. Spending time with God can bring you into an intimate and personal relationship with Him.

The desire to pray is not something that you can make yourself feel. Just as the desire to read the Bible must come from God to your heart, so it is with the desire to pray. Take a moment right now and ask the Lord to plant the desire in your heart to spend time in prayer.

Only the heart that is melted in devotion
is pliable in My hand.[2]
Frances J. Roberts

Answers to Common Questions

Why pray?

There are many good reasons why you should spend time in prayer. Prayer gives you strength to face the challenges of life. Prayer causes you to see yourself as you truly are; in deep need for God. Prayer helps you to be more kind and loving to others. And prayer can bring health and healing to bodies and minds. Most importantly, prayer causes you to become more like Him. Prayer is one of the hardest disciplines of the Christian walk. It receives little recognition and the results are not always evident right away.

> *I do not ask you to take time for Me with the intention of placing a burden upon you in requiring you to do so. Rather than adding a requirement, I seek to lift your load. Rather than burdening you with a devotional obligation, I desire to take from you the tensions of life.*[3]
> *Frances J. Roberts*

> *Prayer is one of the hardest disciplines of the Christian walk.*

What if I don't have time?

You have heard that every one has the same number of hours in a day and if you really want to do something, you can fit it in. It just depends upon your priorities. Think about this: take five minutes to pray in the morning before you get ready for school or before you start the day. It might seem like an effort to give Him the time. Stick with it and those five minutes will increase because you enjoy spending time with God.

> *Wait not for an opportunity to have more time to be alone with Me. Take it, though you leave the tasks at hand. Nothing will suffer. Things are of less importance than you think. Our time together is like a garden full of flowers, whereas the time you give to things is as a field full of stubble....*
> *Seek Me above all else.*[4]
> *Frances J. Roberts*

What if I have sinned?

Bill Bright says that whenever you stumble and sin you face a choice. You can let it go, in which case you will continue to be troubled by spiritual unrest and ineffectiveness; or you can make things right with God and others and clean the slate.[5]

God is faithful to forgive you of your mistakes if you confess them to Him. Saying "I'm sorry," and "please forgive me," are some of the hardest words to say. But when you release that burden, God forgives you and never brings it up again.

If we confess our sins, He is faithful and just to forgive us our sins and to cleanse us from all unrighteousness.
I John 1:9

In order to stay physically healthy, we must exhale to cleanse the waste air from our systems (carbon dioxide) and then inhale to replenish the good air (oxygen). In a similar fashion, Christians need to "breathe spiritually" to stay spiritually healthy. The moment the Holy Spirit convicts us of sin, we should "exhale" by confessing that sin to God….After exhaling the impure, we can "inhale" the pure…
and receive God's forgiveness.[6]
Bill Bright

What if I don't feel like praying?

Feelings and emotions are hard to control. Feeling tired, depressed, anxious, in a hurry, and angry are real feelings that can keep you away from prayer. If you come to your prayer time each day and ignore your feelings, you will reap the benefits of spending time with God. Remember, prayer is work; it takes commitment and discipline. Your feelings change with each day but your commitment to prayer should not.

What if I am distracted during prayer?

Having mental distractions during prayer is common. Confess to God that you have a lot on your mind, then give your concerns to Him.

What if I don't think God will answer me?

Faith or lack of faith for answered prayers is a battle that every Christian faces. Faith comes from hearing the Word of God, so read what He says about His faithfulness to answer prayer. Remember, God will answer your prayers, but it may not be the answer you might have wanted or expected.

Now this is the confidence that we have in Him, that if we ask anything according to His will, He hears us. And if we know that He hears us, whatever we ask, we know that we have the petitions that we have asked of Him.
I John 5:14–15

What if I don't think God cares about me and my problems?

Your problems, no matter how small, are a concern to God.

...casting all your care upon Him, for He cares for you.
I Peter 5:7

For I know the thoughts that I think toward you, says the Lord, thoughts of peace and not of evil, to give you a future and a hope. Then you will call upon Me and go and pray to Me, and I will listen to you. And you will seek Me and find Me, when you search for Me with all your heart.
Jeremiah 29:11–13

Practical Steps to Prayer

Step One: Tell God how great you think He is! If you do not know what to say, read Psalm 47 and 48 out loud to God. This is praise and worship!

David, in the book of Psalms, is a good example for you when learning how to pray. He cried out to God, confessing his sins, telling Him his fears, and speaking faith in God through worship and praise. David sang songs, prayed out loud and through everything he remained honest and humble before Him in prayer. That is why David is called, "A Man after God's Heart." If you want to get to know David, read II Samuel and the book of Psalms.

Step Two: Pray for forgiveness. Think of the areas in your life that God might not be pleased with. Confess them honestly believing that God forgives your sins. Then ask Him to give you strength to overcome temptation.

Step Three: Pray for others. Pray for your family and those who are close to you and pray for people who don't know God. Pray for problems in your country as well as those in places around the world.

Step Four: Pray for the areas that affect your life. Tell God about the things that concern you. Do you have any needs? What problems do you face today, tomorrow, in the future?

Step Five: Pray the Word of God — the Bible. When you speak the Word of God out loud in prayer, you know God hears you because it is God's will written for you. Speaking the Word of God out loud in your prayer time will increase your faith in all that God can do!

When you meet with the Lord, will He know you as an intimate friend or a casual acquaintance?

Step Six: Be quiet before God. The Bible says to "be still and know that I am God" (Psalm 46:10). Being still in God's presence allows Him to speak to you. You can focus on the goodness of God and ask Him to speak to your heart. You will learn to hear His voice as you practice being still before Him.

SOMETHING TO THINK ABOUT

Do you have a hard time knowing how to pray? Follow this easy-to-remember format and you will be on your way.

A   **Adoration:** *to worship and honor God for who He is.*
C   **Confession:** *to ask God for forgiveness for thoughts, actions, behaviors that have not pleased Him.*
T   **Thanksgiving:** *to give thanks to God for all He has done for you.*
S   **Supplication:** *to bring concerns, worries and petitions before Him. To ask for guidance and provision for yourself and others.*

RELATIONSHIPS WITH OTHERS

With whom you choose to "hang around" affects your spiritual fitness. When you spend time with people who do not hold the same values as you, it is like slowly changing the wind direction on a sail. You won't see the effects right away, but pretty soon you will find yourself off course! Get involved with a good youth group so you can be encouraged and strengthened to follow after God's heart.

The Bible tells us to "not forsake the assembly of believers" (Hebrews 10:25). Attending a church is part of being spiritually fit. In church you experience corporate prayer, worship and you hear the Word of God (I John 4:20,21; I Peter 1:22; I Peter 4:7–10 and I Corinthians 7:32–35).

G.I.G.O — GOD IN, GOD OUT

The acronym **G.I.G.O.** can be used to show that your relationship with God is not only meant to bless you but to bless others.[7] God wants you to get "filled up" with Him and His goodness and then give it out to others. The following are some ideas for practicing G.I.G.O.:

- volunteer when there is a need
- send notes or make phone calls to encourage people
- visit the elderly in nursing homes
- visit people who might be in the hospital
- lead a Bible study at your school or through your youth group
- tell people what the Lord is doing in your life
- share an encouraging scripture with a friend
- write a teacher a thank you note for all he/she does for you
- buy a small gift for someone special
- can you think of any other ideas? _____

PRAISE AND WORSHIP

People praise and worship the Lord in different ways. Get into the habit of expressing your love to God. Thank Him for all He has done for you and all He is doing for you now. Read the book of Psalms to understand how David gave praise and worship to God. Even if you do not think you can carry a tune, sing songs to God songs because all singing is beautiful to Him!

You can also praise God with your time and money. When you give of your time in a sacrificial way, He knows that you are doing it for Him. When you give your money to the needs of the church and to others in need, He knows that you are sacrificing for Him. Praise Him with joy in your heart and a giving attitude.

15-2 KEYS TO CONSISTENCY

The only consistency in human nature is inconsistency.

THE BATTLE WITHIN

Have you ever felt as if you were being pulled in two different directions? The apostle Paul knew what it felt like to be struggling with choices of right and wrong. Paul speaks to the church of Rome about the struggle:

For that which I am doing, I do not understand; for I am not practicing what I would like to do, but I am doing the very thing I hate....So, now, no longer am I the one that is doing it, but sin which indwells me. For I know that nothing good dwells in me, that is, in my flesh; for the wishing is present in me, but the doing of the good is not.
Romans 7:15–18 (NAS)

Paul realized that there was a war going on in him. One part wanted to do right, his spirit; and another part wanted to do what was wrong, his flesh. When you become a Christian and believe in the Lord, you have been set free from sin; that is, you now have the power to do what is right, you are not a slave to do what is wrong (Romans 6:11).

Christianity is not a do-it-yourself project!

You may be asking yourself, "what good is it then, if you say I am free from sin, but then I am still harassed and often defeated by sin in my heart?" The key here is that you are not left to fight this battle alone. If you have God on the throne of your heart, then you also have the enabling power of His Holy Spirit. Christianity is not a do-it-yourself project! You have the power of Christ in you to help you live a life that is pleasing to Him.

God gives you a free will to make your own choices. Imagine you have a control tower inside of you. From this control tower come the instructions you are to follow for daily living. Your control tower is the Word of God. For you to know your instructions for living, you must read and meditate on the Word of God. When you yield to temptations and sin you are not allowing the Word of God to be in your control tower and help guide you out of the situation.

KEYS TO CONSISTENT CHRISTIAN LIVING

The Bible gives some divine principles for living the Christian life *consistently.* Consistent can be defined as: possessing firmness; free from irregularity, variation, or contradiction. So, living a Christian life *consistently* would mean *having a solid and stable lifestyle pleasing to God.* Although the Bible contains many principles for living, the following are five keys to help you live a consistent Christian life.

 **Renewing the Mind**

And do not be conformed to this world, but be transformed by the renewing of your mind, that you may prove what is that good and acceptable and perfect will of God.
Romans 12:2

Part of any training is practice, practice, and more practice. You have heard that practice makes perfect? However, if you practice the skill improperly you will never perfect your skill. *Remember, perfect practice makes perfect!* In the same way, if you allow your mind to think on things that are not pleasing to God, you will be deceived (to lead away, to trick or to mislead) and after deception comes the act or behavior — sin (James 1:14,15). But if you fill your mind with godly thoughts, your lifestyle will reflect the peace of God.

Finally, brethren, whatever things are true, whatever things are noble, whatever things are just, whatever things are pure, whatever things are lovely, whatever things are of good report, if there is any virtue and if there is anything praiseworthy — meditate on these things. The things which you learned and received and heard and saw in me, these do, and the God of peace will be with you.
Philippians 4:8–9

When you yield to temptations and sin you are not allowing the Word of God to be in your control tower.

God does not expect perfection when it comes to your thought life or your behavior. He has, however, called you to godliness. Godliness springs forth from the heart of man (all your soul: mind, will and emotions). The mind feeds the soul (Proverbs 4:23). If you fill the mind with thoughts that are pleasing to God, your heart will not deceive you and you will be better able to live a victorious Christian life (2 Corinthians 10:5).

Many times the temptation to do something you know is wrong begins in your thoughts. If you fill your thoughts with the Word of God you have more strength and power to overcome the temptations that you will face.

Practical Steps To Renewing Your Mind

Step One: Study, meditate and memorize the Word of God

Step Two: Spend time in prayer

Step Three: Listen to edifying (uplifting) music

Step Four: Read edifying material

Step Five: Discipline your tongue to only speak what is edifying

 **2 Growing in Christian Virtues**

But also for this very reason, giving all diligence, add to your faith virtue, to virtue knowledge, to knowledge self-control, to self-control perseverance, to perseverance godliness, to godliness brotherly kindness, and to brotherly kindness love. For if these things are yours and abound, you will be neither barren nor unfruitful in the knowledge of our Lord Jesus Christ....for if you do these things you will never stumble; for so an entrance will be supplied to you abundantly into the everlasting kingdom of our Lord and Savior Jesus Christ.
II Peter 1:5–11

Wow! Does God expect you to develop all of these qualities? If you thought that your life with God was a list of only "do's and don'ts" then you would be discouraged from the very start. God wants each one of His children to pursue (seek after) these good virtues. Growth in all areas of the Christian life is progressive, that is it is worked out over a period of time and the growth is never finished.

The great thing about seeking godly virtues is that Jesus is your source of power. He enables you to "put on" godly character. Your responsibility is to make a commitment to seek Him. Do not focus only on developing those traits through your own strength but focus on your relationship with God and you will develop the character of Christ.

Practical Steps to Developing Godly Virtues

Step One: Recognize the source of your strength is in Jesus.

Step Two: Ask God to keep your motives pure (not for selfish gain)

Step Three: Keep your expectations of yourself reasonable. When you make a mistake (which you will!) pick yourself up and try, try again!

Step Four: Study Proverbs 2 and ask God to give you His divine wisdom in your life.

 Discipline

Webster's Dictionary defines discipline as: "training that corrects, molds, or perfects the mental faculties of moral character."

Training in a sport or specific skill is hard work. You must apply yourself to certain skills and discipline yourself to practice these skills. You learn as you go along. In the same way, spiritual fitness requires that discipline to develop godly skills. You will learn how to pray, how to develop godly character, how to praise Him and how to read the Bible. It is not easy, but the rewards are great.

The great thing about seeking godly virtues is that Jesus is your source of power.

 **Perseverance (Patience)**

By perseverance the snail reached the ark.
Charles Spurgeon

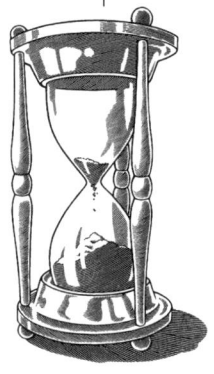

The snail, although slow in his pace, persevered to reach his destiny — the ark. The way to spiritual fitness and godliness may seem a hard and tedious journey for you. However, just as with the snail, you are not alone, God is with you. He is helping you along the way. Be patient with your progress. There may be times you slip back and lose ground or you fall and stumble. Others may pass you. If you hold steady and endure the hardships you will reach the destination God has planned for you.

 **Have a Vision (a Motivating Cause) for Your Life**

If the snail that traveled so slowly to the ark did not have a drive or motivating cause for his journey, don't you think he would have quit? The Bible says in Proverbs 29:18 that without a vision, the people perish. Think about your own personal life. In practical ways you try to keep a vision ahead of you to help keep you motivated. For example, does the thought of a vacation or holiday help keep you motivated in school? How about with a job? If you can see that there is an end to a project or a responsibility then you have more motivation to finish.

Wendell Smith says that when there is no vision, or motivating cause, people grow careless and apathetic. Do you have a sense of destiny for your life? Do you know that you have a specific purpose on this earth? Read on to learn why having a vision for your life will help keep you motivated to pursue the things of God.

CHAPTER REVIEW

DEFINE

Spiritual atrophy
Righteousness
G.I.G.O.

EXPLAIN

1. Explain why it is important to get off the "fence" of indecision. How can staying on the fence negatively affect your life?
2. Explain the meaning of I Timothy 4:7–8. How can your spiritual and physical health be a positive part of God's plan for your life?
3. Explain what is meant by atrophy and how does this relate to your spiritual condition.
4. Explain the meaning of the phrase "it is more important to know Him than to know how to know Him." How can this phrase help you in getting to know God?
5. Explain how meditating on the Word of God can transform your life.
6. Explain the true purposes of meditating on the Word of God.
7. Explain each of the six steps to Bible reading.
8. Explain what is meant by the phrase, "God may answer your prayers but not the way you expected or wanted." How does this affect the way you pray?
9. Explain why attending church and a youth group is good for your spiritual health.
10. Explain why G.I.G.O. is important for spiritual fitness.
11. Explain the importance of renewing your mind when it comes to spiritual fitness. How can a teenager renew his/her mind?

DISCUSS

1. Discuss some of the signs that a teenager is "riding the fence" of Christianity.

2. Discuss ways that teenagers can "pursue righteousness." How can this be practical in your everyday life?

3. Discuss some of the struggles teenagers might have with keeping a devotional life. How can you overcome these struggles?

4. Discuss the meaning of "spiritual breathing" and how it can help keep you spiritually fit.

5. Discuss why David was called "a man after God's heart." What can you learn from David's life?

6. Discuss how certain "friends" can get you off course if you are not careful.

7. Discuss Romans 7:15–18 and tell how you can overcome this battle. How did Paul deal with his struggles and temptations. How can Romans 6:11 help you?

8. Discuss why it seems so hard to walk a consistent Christian life.

9. Discuss what is meant when a person says he/she is deceived. How can deception creep into a teenager's life and what are some of the signs?

10. Discuss why having a vision for your life might help you stay motivated about the things of God.

SUGGESTED ACTIVITIES

1. **Key Concepts:** Outline the chapter and make a study guide for yourself. You may work alone or in a group.

2. **Your Spiritual Workout:** Pray that God would help you develop a plan for daily devotions: reading the Word and prayer. Then write down a spiritual "workout" schedule and ask God to help you stick to it.

3. **Keep a Journal:** Buy a notebook and begin keeping your prayers to God in that notebook. Write down how your prayers were answered. Looking over your notebook will help you remember God's faithfulness to you.

4. **"Where Two or More Are Gathered":** Ask a few of your closest friends to form a prayer group. You don't have to pray together every day, just give each other a list of things you would like them to pray for. When you can, pray together. There is power in numbers!

5. **Consistently Inconsistent:** Do a written report on the word consistency. What does it mean to be consistent and how does inconsistency affect your life and the life of others?

6. **It's In the Book:** Choose 2–3 scriptures to memorize. Ask someone to hold you accountable so you stick with it. You may recite them to the class for credit or keep them in a prayer journal.

7. **Praise and Worship? What's That?:** Define the meaning of the terms praise and worship. Use more than one dictionary. Try to use a Bible Dictionary also. Then write a paper on how teenagers can praise and worship God, and why it is important.

8. **Study the Word:** If you don't already have your own Bible, go out and buy one. You can also get a Bible dictionary or handbook, a concordance and a notebook to write down

what you learn as you study the Word of God. Ask some-one for help (teacher, parent or youth pastor) if you want to learn how to study the Bible using these tools.

9. **After God's Heart:** Study David from the Bible. Find out about his life and write a report. After you give your report to the class, pick four Psalms that he wrote and read them aloud to the class. Choose Psalms that represent different emotions he experienced.

10. **Learning From the Word:** Choose a chapter in your Bible to read. Before you start, pray to God that He would speak to you from His Word (maybe start with the book of Matthew). After you finish reading the chapter, sit quietly and think about the verses. Then ask yourself these questions:
   • What did I learn from God today?
   • What did God speak to me about through this chapter?
   • What did I learn about myself?

11. **Learning How to Pray:** This is the day you can start to have devotions and put into practice what you have learned. Follow the steps here and make them personal for your life:
   • Be still in His presence (find a quiet place). Kneel, sit or stand.
   • Begin to thank Him for all He has done for you.
   • Think of the things that you have done that may not be pleasing to Him and ask for forgiveness.
   • Praise Him for who He is (read Psalm 104 or 113 or another Psalm that praises God).
   • Ask God to help you today. Ask Him to help others. Be specific, use names.
   • Ask God to guide you tomorrow and in the future.
   • Ask God to speak to you from His Word. Then read a chapter in the Bible.
   • Thank God for answering your prayers according to His will.

Reaching Your Potential

16

16-1 IN HOT PURSUIT
16-2 SEEING THROUGH THE DARKNESS
16-3 IN MY FATHER'S HOUSE

16-1 IN HOT PURSUIT

What keeps athletes motivated to endure hours of strenuous workouts? What keeps athletes motivated to sacrifice time, money, and fun to compete in an event? The answer is *vision*. Athletes have a vision of reaching certain goals. They know that hard work and sacrifice will pay off when it is time to compete. With their eyes on the vision, the distractions that can hinder concentration and negatively affect performance are reduced to a minimum.

Do you have a vision for your life?

IN PURSUIT OF A VISION

Vision: unusual foresight: an image or idea of spiritual nature seen or obtained under the influence of a divine…agency.
Random House Dictionary

Do you have a **vision** for your life, that is, a motivating cause given to you by God that gives you a purpose for living? The Bible says that "Without a vision the people perish" (Proverbs 29:18). Wendell Smith, founder of Generation Ministries says this about vision:[1]

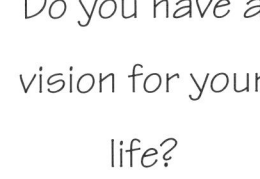

Our generation needs a fresh understanding of purpose — where they came from — where they're going and why in the world they're here!

There is a deep sense in a Christian that each believer has a purpose for living, a purpose beyond existing for selfish gain. God created all things for a purpose. In Revelation 4:11 John writes:

Thou art worthy, O Lord, to receive glory and honor and power: for thou hast created all things, and for thy **pleasure** they are and were created. (KJV)

You are worthy, O Lord, To receive glory and honor and power; For You created all things, And by Your **will** they exist and were created. (NKJV)

To get a grasp of the power of this verse, compare the two words *will* and *pleasure.* All the verses in the New Testament translation come from the original Greek language. If you compare the Greek meaning of these two words you see a powerful connection.

Pleasure: a determination, a choice, specifically a purpose or a decree, a volition, inclination, desire, or will.

Will: To determine, a choice, to prefer, to wish, to be inclined to, to delight in, to love.

Just by reading these two Greek definitions you can see that God chose to create you for a specific purpose. His will (desire) for you is that you find *His* purpose, walk it out in your lifetime, and ultimately reach the potential God has planned for you. This gives Him great pleasure!!

Just Love the Lamb

As the definition of the word vision states, vision is obtained from a divine source. Jesus Christ is the Lamb sacrificed on the cross for your life. If you were the only person on the earth He would have suffered for you alone. What you make of your life is of great interest to Him! He wants to reveal His purpose to you. He does not want you to be "in confusion" concerning your life, but rather for you to pursue Him, and in doing so, receive a clear vision.

Many people get "hung-up" on issues that take away from the purposes of God. Philip Yancey tells about an experience he had when searching for answers about the way God cared for His people:

I began my search for answers during a solitary two-week retreat at a mountain cabin in Colorado. Slowly, carefully, I reread the Bible from beginning to end. Again and again, I discovered evidence for God's caring for his people. But still the answers eluded me. How could a loving God allow such terrible things to happen? Then in one of those rare bursts of insight, I began to understand what God wants from human beings.

God doesn't want to be analyzed. He wants to be loved.[2]

Seeking a purpose for living means seeking the creator of that purpose, the Lord Himself. When you learn to love God and draw close to Him, He reveals things to your heart. You may not receive an illustrated picture of all the things you are to do for God's Kingdom, but you will get a divine sense of purpose that will motivate you to be in "hot pursuit" of the things of God.

> Seeking a purpose for living means seeking the creator of that purpose.

Stone by Stone

When a brick layer builds a wall he cannot put it up all at once, he must build it one stone at a time. Each brick, when placed in just the right place at the right time, provides extra strength to the structure. As you work to build your life by placing the right principles and commandments together, you will fashion a strong fortress that can withstand the elements.

In the same way that a wall is built, stone by stone, you find and walk out your destiny in God a little at a time. "He who is faithful in a very little thing is faithful also in much" Luke 16:10 (NAS). So, as you walk out the basic principles for living the Christian life, you will find yourself walking in the very purpose God has planned for you.

The commandments of God are the life-giving procedures that lead us to the fulfillment of His Vision…So, when we are seeking to discover our calling and destiny in God, we must go to the Bible, which is the revealed Will of God, and ask the Holy Spirit to guide us in that personal discovery.[3]
Wendell Smith

> The great thing about having a destiny in God is that your future is in the best hands!

IN PURSUIT OF YOUR DESTINY

Destiny: something that is to happen to a particular person or thing. The predetermined course of events.

…being predestined according to the purpose of Him who works all things according to the counsel of His will.
Ephesians 1:11

And we know that all things work together for good to those who love God, to those who are the called according to His purpose. For whom He foreknew, He also predestined to be conformed to the image of His Son…
Romans 8:28,29

As you pursue God and "catch-His-vision" for your life, you will find yourself fulfilling the destiny that God has planned for you. Do not get lost along the way by various detours and miss out on *all* that God has for you. The key here is realizing that it is *His* plan for your life, not *your* own plan that is your destiny in God.

You may want God to show you the "whole" picture all at once, but He often gives you a glimpse. The small visions that God gives you motivates you to fulfill your destiny in God. The great thing about having a destiny in God is that your future is in the best hands! Wendell Smith says the following about trusting God with your future:

We may struggle at times in deciding to do the will of God, but we must come to the place where we trust Him with our lives. If He made us, then He knows what is best for us — and what will bring us the greatest fulfillment.[4]

You don't have to wait until you are "older" to begin to walk out the vision God has given to you. Practice what you know now. Begin to set your heart and mind to move out and do great things for God. God's hand is on you now, right where you sit. Do you feel a sense of destiny? Decide to pursue God's vision for your life. Change your focus concerning your future. "Your goal in life is not to decide what you want to do, but to discover what He destined you to do!"[5]

Let no one despise your youth, but be an example to the believers in word, in conduct, in love, in spirit, in faith, in purity.
I Timothy 4:12

SOMETHING TO **THINK** ABOUT

The destiny of a shepherd boy [6]
In calling David, God — sought a man (1 Samuel 13:14), chose a shepherd (Psalm 78:70), found a servant (Psalm 89:20), commanded a captain (1 Samuel 13:14), and provided a king (1 Samuel 16:1–13).

16-2 SEEING THROUGH THE DARKNESS

But when I looked for good, evil came to me; And when I waited for light, then came darkness. My heart is in turmoil and cannot rest...
Job 30:26,27

THE IMPORTANCE OF "GOD-FOCUS"

Joe just finished a great "pep" talk in the locker room with his teammates before the competition was to begin. He is feeling confident that all his training will pay off today. Joe makes his way to the gymnasium and his intensity and enthusiasm is felt by the other team members. As he enters the gymnasium he glances over and sees the immense physical stature of his opponent. Joe immediately hangs his head in discouragement. The competition is lost before it even began.

This scene is very common among individual competitors as well as athletic teams. At one moment Joe was feeling so confident and sure of himself, and the next moment, he felt defeated. Joe let the outward circumstances affect his inward motivation to pursue his goal. Many Christians are just like Joe. They let the circumstances of life dictate how they feel and ultimately how they live.

When you begin to set your mind to seek your destiny in God, difficulties will come that will discourage you. One day the vision may be completely clear. The following day your vision may seem cloudy and the next thing you know all you can see is darkness. You cannot avoid times like these; however, having the right perspective will allow you to see through the darkness.

In your daily walk with the Lord, it is important not to "borrow trouble." This means that you must not worry about things that you don't even know will come to pass! In an article from the *Mental Edge*, Bill Meyer and Dan Zadra speak about the jitters that come with athletics: "Sometimes we spend so much time thinking about how we might lose, that we forget to think about how we might win. Instead of thinking about how well we're going to do, we spend all our practice time thinking up imaginary disasters for ourselves."

Do you find yourself "borrowing trouble"? Do you often think of what bad thing might happen to you rather than concentrating on the promises of God? The important thing to remember is that you are on a winning team. There is no way you can lose — that is — if you stay on God's team. During even the most difficult times in your life, keep God at the center of your mind and heart. Train yourself to speak encouragement to yourself, speaking out the promises of God. This mental discipline is being "God-Focused."

John Wesley was one day walking along the road with a friend who, sore vexed and troubled, expressed his doubts of God's goodness. "I don't know what I shall do with all my worries and troubles," said he. Wesley noticed a cow looking over a stone wall,

> Do you find
> yourself
> "borrowing
> trouble"?

and put the question, "Why does a cow look over the wall?"

"Because he can't see through it, I suppose," replied his friend.

"Precisely!" said Wesley. "So, if you can't see through your troubles, try looking over them: and look up to God."[7]

DISAPPOINTED WITH GOD

Everyone experiences it, even adults feel it at times. It is the feeling of being disappointed with God. Think about it; do you ever feel like God is unfair? Do you feel He ignores you sometimes? Or maybe you have the nagging question: "If God cares, why doesn't He do more for people?" It is normal to feel disappointed with circumstances in life — you don't understand the problems and you don't understand God.

Questions and doubts like these steal from you the vision that God wants to place in your heart. Yes, these questions are normal, but it is what you do with these questions that can make the difference. This is where faith comes in. Faith is firm belief in something for which there is no proof. Faith is the substance of things hoped for, the evidence of things not seen (Hebrews 11:1). It is the distinctive mark of the saints of the Bible. According to Philip Yancey, a kind of faith that goes hand-in-hand with trust is fidelity. This is a deep loyalty to God. Fidelity is that "hang-on-at-any-cost" faith.[8]

We may experience times of unusual closeness, when every prayer is answered in an obvious way and God seems intimate and caring. And we may also experience "fog times," when God stays silent, when nothing works according to formula and all the Bible's promises seem glaringly false. Fidelity involves learning to trust that, out beyond the perimeter of fog, God still reigns and has not abandoned us, no matter how it may appear.[9]
Philip Yancey

Hindrances to the Pursuit

Do you want this "hang-on-at-any-cost" faith? Begin to draw close to God and you will sense this loyalty grow in you. When things don't seem to go right, remember that life is full of trials. Be alert! Many of the challenges that you face may become hindrances to reaching your destiny. Can you think of some challenges that might keep you from your full potential in God?

The Bible says that part of being a Christian is taking up your cross.

...If anyone desires to come after Me, let him deny himself, and take up his cross daily, and follow Me. For whoever desires to save his life will lose it, but whoever loses his life for My sake will save it.
Luke 9:23

Wendell Smith explains the meaning of the cross in the life of a Christian as the crossing of two wills, yours and God's: *The "suffering" that often occurs in our life is the inward struggle between our will and God's will. Suffering is saying "no" to self and "yes" to God. This crossing of wills is a critical part of discovering your destiny.* [10]

This "crossing of the wills" can be a major hindrance for you. You may be asking yourself "Why does it have to be so hard?" As you try to follow God's way, He is right along with you, giving you the power to "take up your cross" and pursue His destiny for you. The trials that you go through and the disciplines of the Christian life make you stronger. God allows them for your sake, not His (James 1:2,3). Consider the story of Job. Through all that he suffered, he endured. He had the kind of loyalty that gave him the power to triumph in the end. Though the darkness shown all around him, and the feeling of hopelessness overwhelmed him — he was "God-focused" and deeply devoted.

More specific hindrances to reaching your destiny are things such as lack of motivation, laziness, rebellious attitudes and lack of discipline. The lack of discipline is the strongest hindrance that will keep you from your destiny. James Dobson says that if he could only tell families and young people one thing it would

---

Suffering is saying "no" to self and "yes" to God.

---

be, "learn to discipline the flesh." God can help you overcome these difficulties but you must choose to do your part.

Ron Mehl, Pastor of Beaverton Foursquare church in Beaverton Oregon, says, "sin and temptation will always affect your vision." Look at the story of Samson in the Bible. He had the spirit of God on him and that great power was evident in his physical strength. He, however, allowed a lack of discipline of the flesh to be his downfall at the end of his days. He had the Holy Spirit on him and was touched by God but still gave into his desires. He made his choice, but you can learn from his life (Judges 16).

Only you and God know the personal weaknesses that can keep you from your destiny in God. If your life is weakened by music, then alter what you hear. Be careful what you expose yourself to. If movies affect you negatively, then alter what you see. Don't tolerate temptation — resist it (Judges 16). Samson tolerated Delilah and ultimately gave in to her continual temptation. Read the story of Samson in the Bible. Do you think he reached his full potential in God?

The greatest deterrent to sin is not religious rules, but vision.[11]
Wendell Smith

> *Shortcuts usually lead away from growth, not toward it.*
>
> *Philip Yancey*

There Are No Shortcuts

The American way is "the faster and easier the better!" However, this is not always how God works. Things that take hard work, discipline and time often produce the best results. Do you find yourself in school wanting as many shortcuts to learning as possible? Do you look in the back of your book for definitions of words instead of reading the material? How about in math class. Are you tempted to look in the back of the book for answers to the homework problems? There is something in everyone that wants instant results, ultimately avoiding the process of learning. Philip Yancey says, "shortcuts usually lead away from growth, not toward it."[12]

God does not promise that you can avoid or *skip over* the trials. He does, however, promise to be with you as you walk *through* them. Keeping the promises of God in your heart as you go through disappointments will help you reach your God-given potential.

Just Wait

Are you weary? Not necessarily physical weariness but spiritual weariness? Being tired in your spirit is more dangerous than being tired in your body. Many times Christians can feel "worn-out" and exhausted from trying to do all the "right" things. You get harassed from all sides. Pressure from friends, family and society are hard to withstand. Even more difficult is the pressure you can put on yourself. Can you relate? Paul understands and because he knows what it is like to grow weary, he gives his advice:

And let us not grow weary while doing good, for in due season we shall reap if we do not lose heart.
Galatians 6:9

But as for you, brethren, do not grow weary of doing good.
II Thessalonians 3:13

God knows that the struggles are hard and that you will become spiritually exhausted! He also gives you the source to renew your strength. Just wait on the Lord. Wait with patience, anticipation and with humility in His presence. In all your waiting the important thing is to wait expectantly. God never sleeps, He never gets tired, and He never stops walking by your side.

...The everlasting God, the Lord, The Creator of the ends of the earth, neither faints nor is weary. His understanding is unsearchable. He gives power to the weak, and to those who have no might He increases strength. Even the youths shall faint and be weary, and the young men shall utterly fall, But those who wait on the Lord Shall renew their strength; they shall mount up with wings like eagles, They shall run and not be weary, they shall walk and not faint.
Isaiah 40:28–31

Even more difficult is the pressure you can put on yourself.

420

16-3 IN MY FATHER'S HOUSE

Some time ago Charles E. Fuller announced that he would be speaking the following Sunday on "Heaven." During that week a beautiful letter was received from an old man who was very ill, and the following is part of his letter:[13]

Dear Pastor,

Next Sunday you are to talk about Heaven. I am interested in that land, because I have held a clear title to a bit of property there for over fifty-five years. I did not buy it. It was given to me without money and without price. But the Donor purchased it for me at tremendous sacrifice. It is not a vacant lot. For more than half a century I have been sending materials out of which the greatest Architect and Builder of the Universe has been building a home for me which will never need to be remodeled nor repaired because it will suit me perfectly, individually, and will never grow old. Termites can never undermine its foundations for they rest on the Rock of Ages. Fire cannot destroy it. Floods cannot wash it away. No locks nor bolts will ever be placed upon its doors, for no vicious person can ever enter that land where my dwelling stands, now almost completed and almost ready for me to enter in and abide in peace eternally, without fear of being ejected.

I hope to hear your sermon on Heaven next Sunday from my home in Los Angeles, California, but I have no assurance that I shall be able to do so. My ticket to Heaven has no date marked for the journey — no return coupon — and no permit for baggage. Yes, I am all ready to go and I may not be here while you are talking next Sunday evening, but I shall meet you there some day.

YOUR INHERITANCE

In My Father's house are many mansions; if it were not so, I would have told you. I go to prepare a place for you.
John 14:2

By adoption you are entitled to an inheritance from God your Father. You cannot earn this inheritance; it is given to you by God's grace because of your status in His family. His home in your heart is the only prerequisite for securing your place in His eternal house. The culmination of the fullness of your inheritance waits for you in heaven, but that does not mean that you cannot enjoy the blessings that come with being a child of God while you live on earth.

It is easy to lose sight of your "heavenly mansion" while you experience the trials of earthly life. Jesus wants to reassure you there is a glorious place waiting for you. You can experience great anticipation when you think about your eternal home with the Father. Because of the knowledge of your "eternal home" you can feel unceasing joy in the midst of your present struggles. Paul writes in Colossians 3:2 to set your mind on the things above. What awaits you in heaven is far better than what you have right here.

For to me, to live is Christ, and to die is gain....For I am hard-pressed between the two, having a desire to depart and be with Christ, which is far better.
Philippians 1:21,23

What Is Your Inheritance?

Your room in the Father's house is perfectly suited to you. He is having His carpenters make a sign for the door with your name on it! More importantly, it is a place of permanence. You don't have to move — you won't want to move! It cannot be invaded from the outside and it cannot be destroyed from the inside. He is preparing it right now, and it is intended for your enjoyment. In your new home there is no more pain, no more hunger, no more sorrow — just complete joy. How does that sound? This "place" for you is filled with blessings. The ultimate inheritance, however, is to enjoy Jesus Christ forever — He is the true treasure.

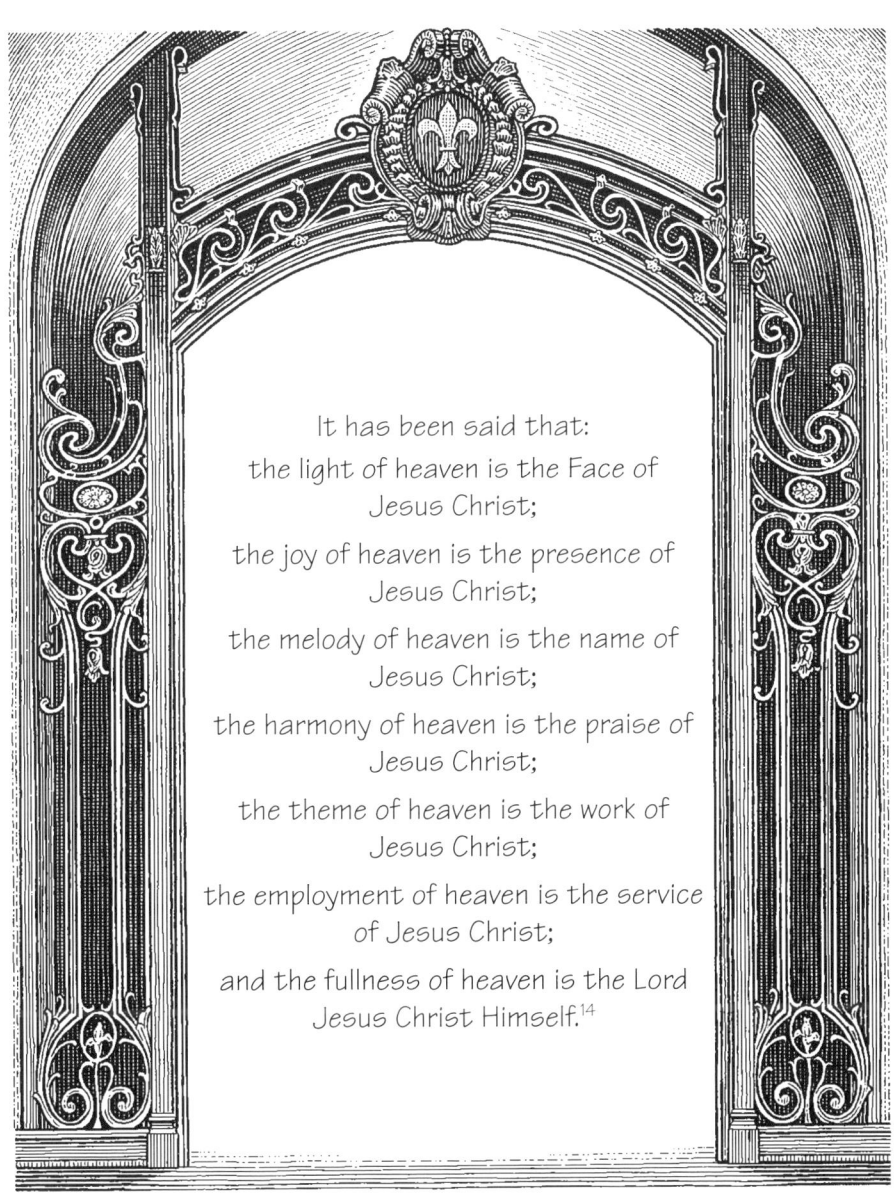

It has been said that:

the light of heaven is the Face of Jesus Christ;

the joy of heaven is the presence of Jesus Christ;

the melody of heaven is the name of Jesus Christ;

the harmony of heaven is the praise of Jesus Christ;

the theme of heaven is the work of Jesus Christ;

the employment of heaven is the service of Jesus Christ;

and the fullness of heaven is the Lord Jesus Christ Himself.[14]

CHAPTER REVIEW

DEFINE:

Vision

Destiny

EXPLAIN:

1. Explain the importance of having a vision for your life. Who is the source of your vision?
2. Explain the connection between the words pleasure and will as they are used in the two translations of Revelation 4:11. How does this relate to God's vision for your life?
3. Explain why it is important not to get "hung-up" on issues that can distract you from the purposes of God. What are some examples of these issues that might be unique to teenagers?
4. Explain why God may not give you the total vision for your life, but little pieces of the picture.
5. Explain what is meant by the phrase "take up your cross." What is the cross of your life?
6. Explain why it is so important to stay "God-focused" when you are going through times of despair and darkness.
7. Explain what is meant by the phrase don't "borrow trouble."
8. Explain how being disappointed with God can steal from you the destiny that God has for your life.
9. Explain the difference between faith and fidelity as Philip Yancey explains it.
10. Explain why there are no shortcuts in reaching your potential in God.

DISCUSS

1. Discuss practical ways that a teenager can be in "hot pursuit" of his/her destiny for God.
2. Discuss practical ways that a Christian teenager builds his/her life, stone by stone. Use Luke 16:11 as an illustration. What ways can a teenager show him/herself faithful in little areas?

3. Discuss Romans 8:28,29 and relate it to a teenager trying to live according to God's purposes.

4. Discuss why it is important to put all of your trust in God for your future. How can this help a teenager live a life of purpose?

5. Discuss how Christian teenagers may let the circumstances of life dictate how they feel and how they choose to live. Use practical examples.

6. Discuss how a teenager can experience "God-focus" even in the midst of difficulties. Why is this so important?

7. Discuss specific disappointments that teenagers might face and how these might hinder their walk with God.

8. Discuss some shortcuts in the Christian walk that many teenagers want to try. Why do Christians ultimately have to go through the "learning process"?

9. Discuss the meaning of the phrase "crossing of the wills." How does this relate to the lives of teens?

10. Discuss what you envision heaven to be like. Does the assurance of having a place in the Father's house make your life on earth easier? Why or why not?

11. Discuss how the ultimate inheritance of Jesus Christ Himself would affect a person's relationship with Him while living on earth. What would you tell non-Christians about heaven and the person of Jesus Christ?

SUGGESTED ACTIVITIES

1. **Key Concepts:** Outline the chapter and make a study guide for yourself. You may work alone or in a group.

2. **In the Driver's Seat:** Do a paper on the importance of disciplining the flesh. How can this discipline make all the difference in reaching your destiny in God? Include some examples that teenagers may face when disciplining the flesh.

3. **A Great Fall:** Do a study on Samson from the Bible (Judges chapters 13–16). Research his life and give a detailed report on how he allowed a lack of discipline to destroy the end of his life. How can you learn from his life?

4. **It's In The Book:** Get with a group of other students and pick two to five key Scriptures dealing with destiny, inheritance, or purpose for living. Keep each other accountable and try to recite them to each other once a week. Once you have all reached your memory goal, share with the class how it has helped you in your walk with Christ. Challenge each other to make scripture memory a regular part of your life.

5. **My Inheritance:** Make a collage representing the way you think heaven will be. You can use words, pictures and symbols. Put this up in your classroom with the title: "My Inheritance."

6. **Between Me and God:** Devote yourself to pursuing a vision for your life. It comes by spending quality time with Him and time meditating on the Word of God. Write down anything you feel comes from God. It could be only a slight inspiration to do something or it could be a "picture" of what you want to do in life. Whatever you sense, as long as you feel it comes from the right source — Jesus, then write it down. Don't share this with anyone unless you want to. It's just between you and God.

7. **In "Hot Pursuit":** Make a list of all the things that you can do in your life right now to cause His destiny for you to come to pass. How can you reach the potential God has for you? Make a plan of action and then make steps to pursue it. For example: if you felt that God wanted you to be a teacher, what could you do to bring that to pass? Or, if you felt that somehow you would work with teenagers when you get older, then think of things you can do right now to pursue that.

8. **Love the Lamb:** "God does not want to be analyzed, He wants to be loved." How can you love God more? Write a paper on what it means to love God. What are some practical ways teenagers can show their love for God.

9. **David the Shepherd Boy:** Do a report on David. Include each part of his life; as a man, as a shepherd, as a servant, as a captain, as a king. What can you learn from the life of David — failures and all? Did he struggle finding God's destiny for his life? What were some of his hindrances?

10. **When I Borrow Trouble:** Write a paper discussing the specific pressures you place on yourself as a Christian teenager. This can include academics, activities, as well as home life. Explain how the pressure you put on yourself can make you weary spiritually as well as physically. Include in your paper how you can overcome this pressure and how this will affect you spiritually and physically. Also include examples of how you "borrow trouble" and how these zap your strength.

Epilogue

...my movements seem mechanical as I start the race. I have practiced this race so often but at each hurdle I am afraid that I may stumble and fall. Then I feel that added strength. Something, no, Someone, is giving me the strength. I feel like I want to quit but I have made the choice to run in this race and I cannot quit. I am tired and my legs feel like dead weights, but I continue to run.

I glance upward. I can see the finish line in front of me. My coach and teammates cheer me on "you can do it!" With added strength I lunge forward ahead of my opponents....

Determine to run your race to win. Press on toward the goal for the prize of the upward call of God in Jesus Christ. He will give you strength when you feel you cannot make it. He will be there waiting for you at the finish line saying, "well done, thou good and faithful servant."

Notes

Introduction
   1 Jerry White, *Honesty, Morality and Conscience* (Navigators, 1979), 238.

Chapter 1
   1 John W. Hole Jr., *Human Anatomy and Physiology*, 2nd ed. (William C. Brown Co. Publishers, 1981), 11.
   2 Dr. Paul Brand and Philip Yancey, *Fearfully and Wonderfully Made*, (Zondervan, 1980), 26.

Chapter 2
   1 Dr. Paul Brand and Philip Yancey, *Fearfully and Wonderfully Made*, (Zondervan, 1980), 73.
   2 Ibid., 71.
   3 Ibid., 70.
   4 Ibid., 161.
   5 Ibid., 163.
   6 Norman W. Walker, *Colon Health: the KEY to a VIBRANT LIFE*, (Norwalk press, 1979), 1.
   7 Reader's Digest, *ABC's of the Human Body*, (Reader's Digest Association Inc., 1987), 234.
   8 Walker, *Colon Health*, 1.
   9 Ibid., 5.
  10 Richard Selzer, taken from, *Fearfully and Wonderfully Made* Dr. Paul Brand and Philip Yancey, 115.
  11 Dennis and Barbara Rainey, *Teaching Your Children About Sex*, FAMILY LIFE TODAY Audio Series.

Chapter 4
   1 Roger Rapoport, "Blasting Away at Body Fat," *Running* (March/April 1982): 20.
   2 Rob Sweetgall, "Walking for Long-Term Health," *Walking* (March/April 1993): 42.

Chapter 5
   1 *Surgeon General's Report to the American Public on HIV Infection and AIDS*, (Centers for Disease Control and Prevention, 1993): 1
   2 Ibid., 1.

Chapter 6
   1 Michael A. Wilson, MD, *Matters of the Heart* Newsletter, (The Heart Institute at St. Vincent's Hospital, Portland, Oregon).
   2 Ibid.,
   3 Brand and Yancey, *Fearfully and Wonderfully Made*, 59.
   4 Ibid., 20.

Chapter 7

1 S.I.McMillen, M.D. *None of These Diseases*, (Fleming H. Revell a division of Baker Book House Company, 1984), 98.
2 Ibid., 178.
3 Ibid., 178.
4 Wendell Smith, *Roots of Character*, (Bible Press, 1979), V.
5 McMillen, *None of These Diseases*, 123.
6 Leo Buscaglia, adapted from, *"LIFE There's Nothing Like It"* Pamphlet,(Christopher News Notes, New York, NY).
7 Dr. Mary Griffin, Carol Feisenthal, "A Cry for Help" taken from, "LIFE There's Nothing Like It," Pamphlet, (Christopher News Notes, New York, NY).

Chapter 8

1 Jerry White, *Honesty, Morality, and Conscience*, (The Navigators, 1979), 218.
2 McMillen, *None of These Diseases*, 125.
3 Smith, *Roots of Character*, 20.
4 Howard E. Ferguson, *The Edge*, a collection of quotes, poems, and selections, (Cleveland Ohio: Great Lakes Lithograph Company). 1-1.
5 White, *Honesty, Morality, and Conscience*, 230, 233.
6 Ibid., 62.
7 Dr. James Dobson, *Preparing for Adolescence*, (Regal Books, Ventura, CA 1989), 60.
8 Ibid., 123-124.
9 A. Naismith, *1200 Notes, Quotes and Anecdotes*, (Moody Press, with Pickering & Inglis Ltd. British publishers, 1962). 193.

Chapter 9

1 Mary Bronson Merki, *Teen Health, Decisions For Healthy Living*, (Glencoe, A division of Macmillan Publishing Company, 1990), 66.
2 Dobson, *Preparing for Adolescence*, 53.

Chapter 10

1 Reader's Digest, *ABC's Of The Human Body*, 212.

Chapter 11

1 Glenda Malmin, *Christian Womanhood*, (Bible Temple Publications, 1985), 211.

Chapter 12

1 Dobson, *Preparing for Adolescence*, 130.
2 Wendell Smith, *Dragon Slayer*, New Generation Seminar, (Generation Ministries of Bible Temple, 1987), 18.
3 A. Naismith, *1200 Notes, Quotes and Anecdotes*, 168.
4 Earl Ubell, "The Deadly Emotions," (*Parade*, February 11, 1990), 6.
5 A. Naismith, *1200 Notes, Quotes and Anecdotes*, 114.

Chapter 13

1 Dr. Paul Brand, *You Are Wonderful* Tape Series: Hormones. (Norlynn Audio Media Services, 1994).

2 Josh McDowell, "Help Your Teen Make the Right Choice." (*Focus on the Family Newsletter*, November 1994), 4.

3 Scott Talley, *Talking with Your Kids about the Birds and the Bees,* (Regal Books, A division of GL Publications, 1990), 166.

4 Ibid., 169.

5 Dobson, *Preparing for Adolescence,* 112.

6 Ibid., 113.

7 Josh McDowell & Bob Hostetler, *Right From Wrong; What You Need To Know To Help Youth Make Right Choices,* (Word Publishing, 1994), 157-161.

8 Dr. Paul Brand, "You Are Wonderful" Tape Series.

9 Josh McDowell and Dick Day, *"Why Wait?" What You Need to Know about the Teen Sexuality Crisis,* (Thomas Nelson Publishers)

10 Talley, *The Birds and the Bees,* 190.

11 Ibid., 168.

Chapter 14

1 Glenda Malmin, *Christian Womanhood,* 139.

2 Adapted from Josh McDowell *How To Help Your Child Say "NO" To Sexual Pressure,* 122. Barry St. Clair and William H. Jones, *Dynamic Dating,* (Here's Life Publishers, 1987).

3 Glenda Malmin, *Christian Womanhood,* 172.

4 Iverson, Smith, Scheidler, Malmin, *Confronting Our Culture,* (Bible Temple Publications), Lesson Five.

5 Talley, *Birds and the Bees,* 162.

6 McDowell, *Say "NO" to Sexual Pressure,* 37.

7 Adapted from McDowell, *Say "NO" to Sexual Pressure,* 137-139.

8 Dobson, *Preparing for Adolescence,* 98.

9 Taken from, Dennis Rainey, *Staying Close,* (Word Publishing, 1989), 3. Author Unknown.

10 Dennis Rainey, *Staying Close,* (Word Publishing, 1989), 61.

11 Adapted from McMillen, *None of these Diseases,* 70.

12 Rainey, *Staying Close,* 106.

13 Glenda Malmin, *Christian Womanhood,* 185.

14 Rainey, *Staying Close,* 126.

15 Ibid., 203.

16 Reader's Digest, *Complete Manual of Fitness and Well-Being,* (Reader's Digest Association, 1988), 239.

17 Naismith, *1200 Notes, Quotes and Anecdotes,* 53.

Chapter 15

1 Campbell McAlpine, *Alone With God,* (Bethany House Publishers, 1981), 58.

2 Frances J. Roberts, *Come Away My Beloved,* (King's Farspan, Inc., 1973), 149.

3 Ibid., 174.

4 Ibid., 13.

5 Bill Bright, *The Secret, How to Live With Purpose and Power,* (Thomas Nelson Publishers, 1989), 69.

6 Ibid., 70-71.

7 Frosty Westering, *Sports Motivation.* Class lecture notes.

Chapter 16

1   Smith, *Dragon Slayer*, 12.
2   Philip Yancey, *Disappointment With God*, (Zondervan Publishers, 1988).
3   Smith, *Dragon Slayer*, 14.
4   Ibid., 15.
5   Ibid., 15.
6   Naismith, *1200 Notes, Quotes and Anecdotes*, 50.
7   Ibid., 197.
8   Philip Yancey, *Disappointment with God*, 245
9   Ibid., 246.
10   Smith, *Dragon Slayer*, 15.
11   Ibid., 13.
12   Philip Yancey, *Disappointment with God*, 247.
13   Naismith, *1200 Notes, Quotes and Anecdotes*, 93-94.
14   Ibid., 94.

Bibliography

Devotional

Bridges, Jerry. *The Practice of Godliness.* Colorado Springs: Navpress, 1983.

Bridges, Jerry. *The Pursuit of Holiness.* Colorado Springs: Navpress, 1978.

Bright, Bill. *The Secret: How to Live With Purpose and Power.* Nashville: Thomas Nelson, 1989.

Iverson, Dick and Wendell Smith, Bill Scheidler, Ken Malmin. *Confronting Our Culture.* Portland, Oregon: Bible Temple Publishers.

Malmin, Glenda. *Christian Womanhood*: Course notebook from Portland Bible College, Portland, Oregon.

McAlpine, Campbell. *Alone with God: A Manual of Biblical Meditation.* Minneapolis: Bethany House Publishers, 1981.

Roberts, Frances J. *Come Away My Beloved.* Ojai, California: King's Farspan, Inc., 1973.

Smith, Wendell. *Dragon Slayer.* Portland, Oregon: Generation Ministries of Bible Temple, 1978.

Smith, Wendell. *Roots of Character.* Portland, Oregon: Bible Temple Publishing, 1979.

Westering, Frosty. *Make The Big Time Where You Are!* Big Five Productions. 1990.

Westering, Frosty. *Sports Motivation.* A collection of poems, quotes and personal notations.

Physical

Brand, Dr. Paul and Philip Yancey. *Fearfully and Wonderfully Made.* Grand Rapids: Zondervan Publishing House, 1980.

Center for Disease Control. Guidelines for Effective School Health Education To Prevent the Spread of AIDS. MMWR 1988;37 (suppl. no. S-2):[inclusive page numbers].

Center for Disease Control. "HIV/AIDS PREVENTION." (September 1992).

Hole, John W Jr. *Human Anatomy and Physiology*, Second Edition. Dubuque, Iowa: Wm. C. Brown Company Publishers, 1981.

McMillen, S.I. *None of These Diseases.* Grand Rapids: Fleming H. Revell, division of Baker Book House, 1984.

Merki, Mary Bronson. *Teen Health: Decisions For Healthy Living*. Mission Hills, California: Glencoe, a division of Macmillan Publishing Company, 1990.

Rapoport, Roger. "Blasting Away at Body Fat." *Running* (March/April, 1982), 18-24.

Reader's Digest Editors. *ABC's Of The Human Body: A Family Answer Book*. Pleasantville, NY: The Reader's Digest Association, 1987.

Reader's Digest Editors. *Great Health Hints and Handy Tips*. Pleasantville, NY: The Reader's Digest Association, 1994.

Reader's Digest Editors. *The Complete Manual Of Fitness And Well-Being*. Pleasantville, NY: The Reader's Digest Association, 1988.

Roy, Steven and Richard Irvin. *Sports Medicine: Prevention, Evaluation, Management, and Rehabilitation*. Englewook Cliffs, New Jersey: Prentice Hall, Inc., 1983.

Smith, Pamela, M. *Eat Well, Live Well*. Lake Mary, FL: Creation House, 1992.

Sweetgall, Rob. "Walking for Long-Term Health." *Walking* (March/April, 1993), 42-44.

Ubell, Earl. "The Deadly Emotions: They Can Shorten Your Life If You Let Them." *Parade* (February 11, 1990), 4-6.

U.S. Department Of Health And Human Services. "AIDS PREVENTION GUIDE: The Facts About HIV Infection And AIDS." (1992).

Walker, Norman, W. *Colon Health: the KEY to a VIBRANT LIFE*. Prescott: Norwalk Press, 1979.

Teen Issues

Dobson, Dr. James. *Preparing for Adolescence*. Ventura: Regal Books a Division of Gospel Light, 1989.

Gothard, Bill (instructor). *Institute in Basic Youth Conflicts*. Seminar.

Kidney, Debra. "Dare To Live." *This Week Magazine*.

"LIFE There's Nothing Like It." Christopher News Notes. No. 283.

McDowell, Josh. *How To Help Your Child Say "NO" To Sexual Pressure*. Dallas: Word Publishing, 1987.

McDowell, Josh and Bob Hostetler. "Help Your Teen Make the Right Choice." *Focus on the Family* (November, 1994), 3-4.

McDowell, Josh and Bob Hostetler. *RIGHT FROM WRONG: What You Need To Know To Help Youth Make Right Choices*. Dallas: Word Publishing, 1994.

McDowell, Josh and Dick Day. *Why Wait? What You Need To Know About the Teen Sexuality Crisis.* Nashville: Thomas Nelson Publishers.

Miller, Mike. "Dare To Live." *Newsletter.* Vancouver, Washington, 1989.

St. Clair, Barry and William H. Jones. *Dynamic Dating.* San Bernardino, California: Here's Life Publishers, 1987.

Talley, Scott. *Talking with Your Kids about the Birds and the Bees.* Ventura: Regal Books, a division of Gospel Light Publications, 1990.

Other

Brand, Paul. *You Are Wonderful.* Tape Series: Norlynn Audio Media Services, 1994.

Naismith, A. *1200 Notes, Quotes and Anecdotes.* Chicago: Moody Press, 1962.

Rainey, Dennis. *Staying Close, Stopping the Natural Drift Toward Isolation In Marriage.* Dallas: Word Publishing, 1989.

White, Jerry. *Honesty, Morality and Conscience.* Colorado Springs: Navpress, 1979.

Yancey, Philip. *Disappointment With God.* New York: HarperCollins Publishers, 1988.

Standard References

Advanced First Aid And Emergency Care, The American National Red Cross for the Instruction of Advanced First Aid Classes. First Edition. Garden City, New York: Doubleday and Company, Inc., 1973.

Clayman, Charles B. (Medical Editor). *Home Medical Encyclopedia, The American Medical Association,* Vol. One A-H. New York: Published by The Reader's Digest Association, Inc., with permission of Random House, Inc.

Clayman, Charles B. (Medical Editor). *Home Medical Encyclopedia, The American Medical Association,* Vol. Two, I-Z. New York: Published by The Reader's Digest Association, Inc., with permission of Random House, Inc.

Douglas, J.D, (Organizing Editor). *The New Bible Dictionary.* Grand Rapids: Eerdmans, 1962.

Nave, Orville, J. *Nave's Topical Bible:* Original Edition With Index. Grand Rapids: Baker Book House, 1981.

Random House Dictionary. New York: Ballantine Books, 1978.

Vincent, Marvin, R. *Word Studies In The New Testament.* Grand Rapids: Eerdmans, 1980.

Webster's New Collegiate Dictionary. Springfield, Mass., Merriam-Webster, 1977.

Glossary

Abortion. Spontaneous miscarriage or medically induced termination of a pregnancy. *339*.

Accident. Unexpected, harmful events that occur by chance. *271*.

Acid rain. The rain that contains pollutants. *310*.

Acne. A condition that occurs when the pores of the skin become clogged with oil. *244*.

Acquired immunity. The body's ability to adapt to certain invaders and then keep a memory of how to destroy them if they return. *49*.

Acute diseases. Those diseases that develop suddenly with symptoms that are often severe. *130*.

Addiction. A physical or mental need for a substance. *348*.

Advertising. Sending messages to the public about a certain product or service. *316*.

Aerobic activity. When the body demands more oxygen than normal. *103*.

Agape. The Greek word used in Scripture which expresses love from God the Father to Jesus, God to man, man to God, and man to his neighbor. *365*.

AIDS (acquired immunodeficiency syndrome). A result of HIV. *144*.

Alcohol. A depressant drug. *349*.

Alcoholism (alcohol dependence). An illness characterized by habitual, compulsive, long-term, heavy drinking of alcohol. *353*.

Allergen. A substance to which a person's body is particularly sensitive. *131*.

Alzheimer's disease. A progressive condition in which nerve cells in the brain degenerate and the brain loses its ability to function. *174, 378*.

Amino acids. The chief component of every protein. *62*.

Anaerobic activity. Short bursts of energy, without the use of oxygen. *104*.

Anatomy. The field of study dealing with the structure of body parts, their forms and arrangements. *15*.

Anemia. A condition characterized by a shortage of or an inadequate number of red blood cells. *29.*

Anorexia. A self-induced starvation resulting in extreme weight loss and characterized by an intense fear of gaining weight and becoming fat. *90.*

Antibodies. Special proteins produced by the lymphocytes in response to a foreign substance in the body. *132.*

Arteriosclerosis. A disease where certain arteries become hardened and obstructed, eventually limiting or stopping the flow of blood to certain organs of the body. Also known as hardening of the arteries. *29, 159.*

Arthritis. A condition characterized by pain, swelling, stiffness, and redness in the joints. Also known as inflammation of a joint or joints. *34, 171.*

Artificial respiration (rescue breathing). A substitute for normal breathing in which someone forces air into the victim's lungs. *285.*

Assume. To take on the particular character that others are saying whether it is true or not. *229.*

Asthma. A respiratory condition where the air passages in the bronchial tree swell and constrict. *31.*

Atherosclerosis. The most common type of hardening of the arteries in which there is a buildup of fat deposits on the artery wall. *159.*

Atrophy. A condition when a muscle is not used and it decreases in size and loses its strength. *111.*

Attempted rape. An assault in which sexual intercourse is attempted but does not occur. *274.*

Attitude. A feeling or emotion toward something. *299.*

Autoimmune disease. A condition that occurs when the body's immune system mistakes its own cells or tissues for possible intruders. *51.*

B-cells. Lymphocytes that make antibodies that attack germ cells. *133.*

Bacteria. One-celled tiny organisms that come in many shapes and grow everywhere. *126.*

Balance (equilibrium). The ability to remain steady and in control of one's body. *256.*

Basal metabolism. The ability of the body to use energy at a higher rate when the body is at rest. *72.*

Benign. The description of a non-cancerous tumor. *165.*

Biblical conviction. A strong belief based upon the Word of God. The framework that holds an individual's Christian walk together. *206.*

Biodegradable. Products that can be broken down in the water without causing a problem. *311.*

Biopsy. A test to diagnose cancer. A microscopic examination of tissues cells. *168.*

Birth defects. Abnormalities obvious at birth or detectable early in infancy. *156.*

Blackhead. A type of acne created when a pore is plugged with oil but is exposed to the air. *244.*

Blood pressure. The measure of the resistance to blood flow in the vessels and the efficiency of circulation. *98.*

Bronchitis. A swelling or inflammation of the bronchi. *31.*

Bulimia. A pattern of bingeing (eating large amounts of food) followed by self-induced vomiting or laxative abuse with or without weight loss. *90.*

Bursitis. The inflammation of the bursa and is usually due to excessive stress on the joint. *34.*

Calorie. A unit of heat the body uses for energy. *73.*

Cancer. A condition caused by abnormal cells growing without control. *164.*

Canine (cuspids). The four pointed teeth next to the incisors. *259.*

Capillaries. The smallest blood vessels that carry blood from the arteries to the body's cells and from those cells to the veins. *28.*

Carbohydrates. Energy producing foods such as starches and sugars. *63.*

Carbon monoxide. The gas that is produced when tobacco burns. It passes from the lungs into the bloodstream where it interferes with the oxygen in the bloodstream. *344.*

Carcinogens. The substances that cause cancer. *167.*

Cardiac output. The volume of blood pumped by the heart in one minute. *98.*

Cardiopulmonary resuscitation (CPR). A technique that combines artificial respiration and chest compressions to revive victims who have no pulse. *293.*

Cardiovascular fitness. The condition and health of the heart. *97.*

Carrier. A person who is carrying the germ but does not seem to be suffering from the illness. *130.*

Cavity. A hole in the tooth that is the result of tooth decay. *261.*

Cells. The basic building blocks from which all larger parts are formed. *18.*

Central nervous system. A complex system that controls and coordinates all the body parts so that they work as one flowing unit and responds to changes appropriately. *51.*

Cerebral palsy. A condition in which the cerebrum of the brain is damaged resulting in muscular spasms, poor balance or problems with vision, hearing and speaking. *52.*

Character. Moral excellence and firmness; the underlying qualities that are revealed in your actions and attitudes that set an individual apart. *204.*

Cheat. To rob or spoil, to lead away from the truth. *305.*

Chlamydia. The most common, yet the most difficult to discover, sexually transmitted disease in the United States. *140.*

Cholesterol. A waxy substance that is carried around the body in the bloodstream by lipoproteins. *65.*

Chronic diseases. Diseases that develop gradually and may persist for years. *130.*

Circulatory system. The group of body parts that transports the blood throughout the body to keep the body functioning properly. *27.*

Citizen. A person living in a town or country, who owes allegiance to a government and is entitled to the rights, privileges and protection of it. *320.*

Comfort zone. An area which a person will not go beyond; a place of security. *231.*

Comparison shop. To compare the price and quality of similar goods and services. *316.*

Complete protein. Protein that contains all the amino acids. *63.*

Complex carbohydrates. Starches made up of monosaccharide molecules and are broken down by the body into two or more sugars. *64.*

Conduct. A standard of personal behavior. *202.*

Conform. To adapt oneself to prevailing standards or customs: to be or become similar in form or character. *211.*

Congenital. Genetic disorders that are evident at birth. *155.*

Connective tissues. Groups of cells that are located in all parts of the body; they bind structures together, provide support and protection. *20.*

Consumer. Anyone who purchases goods or services. *313.*

Conviction. A personal belief upon which certain actions are based. *206.*

Countenance. The face as an indication of mood, emotion, or character. *233.*

Cross training. A principle of exercise that means to vary the exercise routine. *105.*

Crown. The part of the tooth that a person can see. *259.*

Cuticle. The portion of the fingernail which surrounds the nail and is made up of nonliving skin. *251*.

Dandruff. A condition that is characterized by a flaking of the outer layer of dead skin cells of the scalp. *249*.

Date rape. Occurs when the victim is forced to have sexual intercourse by someone with whom she is on a date. *275*.

Defraud. To arouse sexual desires in another which cannot be righteously satisfied. *335*.

Degeneration. A lowering of effective power, vitality, or essential quality to a worsened kind or state. *153*.

Degenerative diseases. The body's tissues break down and do not grow or function properly. Noninfectious diseases are said to be degenerative diseases. *154*.

Dementia. A disease that interferes with the normal working of the mind. *378*.

Depressants. Drugs that slow down the body's functions and reactions. *348*.

Depression. A condition characterized by a "sad and blue" feeling, overwhelming feeling of hopelessness and worthlessness, and disappointment leading to apathy and withdrawal. *193*.

Destiny. Something that is to happen to a particular person or thing. The predetermined course of events. *414*.

Diabetes (diabetes mellitus). A disease where the body cannot properly utilize the glucose (sugar) that it needs. *54, 169*.

Diabetes type I. A condition related to blood sugar in which those who suffer from it are dependent on insulin. *169*.

Diabetes type II. A condition related to blood sugar in which those who suffer from it are not dependent on insulin. *170*.

Digestion. The process by which food is broken down. *39*.

Digestive system. The organs that take in food and break it down into a chemical form that can be absorbed by the body. *39*.

Disease. Any condition that negatively affects the normal functioning of the mind or body. *125*.

Distress. Stress that reaches a point when feelings of depression, confusion and exhaustion replace the natural excitement and drive to meet a challenge. *186*.

Drugs. Any chemical substance that alters the function of one or more body organs or changes the process of a disease. *348*.

EKG (Electrocardiogram). Recording the electrical impulses set off by the heart. *102*.

Emotional fatigue. Feeling tired in the emotions as a result of tension, stress, frustration, fear or boredom. *117*.

Emphysema. A disease where the air sacs in the lungs become enlarged and lose their elasticity. *32, 344*.

Endocrine system. The group of body parts that uses chemicals (hormones) secreted by the glands to send messages to the cells in the body by way of the blood. *53*.

Enriched. A label given to foods that have added vitamins and minerals after some of the nutrients have been removed during processing. *83*.

Environment. The circumstances including all the living and non-living things, conditions or influences, by which one is surrounded. *308*.

Environmentalist. Someone who is concerned about the quality of the human environment. *308*.

Epilepsy. A brain disorder that results from a sudden burst of nerve action. *52*.

Epithelial tissues. Layers of cells that cover all body surfaces inside and out, forming the most obvious protective layer, the skin, as well as the inner lining of the body cavities such as the stomach and the intestines. *20*.

Ergogenic aid. Something that improves physical work performance. *106*.

Eros. The Greek word used in Scripture which expresses intimate affection, liking to do things that are pleasant, lust, selfish desire for physical pleasure. *365*.

Essential amino acids. The amino acids that must come from the foods people eat. *63*.

Excretory system. The group of body parts that provides ways for waste to be removed from the body. *43*.

Exploitation. To make unethical use for one's own advantage or profit. *317*.

Fainting. A temporary loss of consciousness. *288*.

Family doctor. A doctor who provides basic health care to people of all ages. *319*.

Fat. Chain of fatty acids that provide a concentrated source of energy. *64*.

Fat calories. The source of calories that come from fat in the diet. *86*.

Fatigue due to illness. Feeling tired when your body is fighting a sickness. *118*.

Fetal alcohol syndrome. A condition consisting of physical and mental problems in the fetus as a result of a pregnant woman's consumption of alcohol. *353.*

Fiber. The part of foods that is not a nutrient but passes through the body carrying with it unwanted waste. *73.*

First aid. The immediate care given to a person who has been injured or has been suddenly taken ill until qualified medical care can be supplied. *284.*

First-aider. The person giving first aid. *284.*

First-degree burn. A burn that affects only the outer layer of skin. *289.*

Fitness. The ability of the whole body to work together to the highest level possible. *97.*

Fortified. A label given to a product that has added vitamins above what it would have had naturally. *83.*

Fungi. An organism that usually causes diseases of the skin. *127.*

Gallstones. A condition which results when bile stored in the gallbladder hardens into small crystals. *42.*

Gamma globulin. A shot of protein that gives protection against the hepatitis disease. *139.*

Genetic disorder. A disease or condition caused primarily by a defect or defects in the inherited, genetic material within a person's genes. *155.*

G.I.G.O. (God In, God Out). An individual getting "filled-up" with God and then giving out to bless others. *401.*

Gingivitis. A gum disease caused by a build-up of plaque and tartar on the teeth. *260.*

Glucose. The result of the break down of carbohydrates into a type of sugar which provides fuel for the body. *63.*

Gonorrhea. The next common sexually transmitted disease after chlamydia. Sometimes called the "preventer of life" because it can cause sterility in both males and females. *141.*

Greenhouse effect. A warming of the earth's temperature. *309.*

Grief. All the feelings of sorrow and deep distress over death of a loved one or other significant loss. *379.*

Hangnails. Splits in the cuticle along the edge of the nail. *251.*

Head lice. Insects that can live in the hair and look much like dandruff. *249.*

Health insurance. A program in which a person or group of persons pays a fee on a regular basis to a company that agrees to pay for some or all of their health care needs. *319.*

Health maintenance organization (HMO). A program where many different types of doctors give health care to their members. *319.*

Heimlich maneuver (abdominal thrusts). A procedure used to dislodge an object from an adult's or child's throat. Quick, upward thrusts into the diaphragm. *292.*

Hemophilia. A disease in which the blood is lacking one or more of the elements (clotting factors) that cause the blood to clot. *29.*

Hepatitis A. Inflammation of the liver caused by a virus that is spread through fecally-contaminated food, water, or objects. *139.*

Hepatitis B. Inflammation of the liver that is caused by a virus that is spread through direct contact with the infected person or through infected needles. *139.*

Herpes simplex II. A sexually transmitted disease that causes a painful rash on the genitals (reproductive organs). *142.*

High blood pressure (hypertension). A common condition in Western societies that occurs when blood pressure is higher than normal for long periods of time. *30.*

High density lipoproteins (HDL). The good cholesterol because it is the cholesterol that is being removed from circulation and transported to the liver. *65.*

HIV (human immunodeficiency virus). The virus that causes AIDS (Acquired Immunodeficiency Syndrome). *144.*

Homeostasis. The process by which the body maintains a constant internal environment despite the external changes. *136.*

Hypoglycemia. A condition resulting in an abnormally low level of sugar in the blood. *169.*

Hypothermia. A dangerous condition caused by prolonged exposure to the cold. *291.*

Immune system. The group of organs and cells that works with the lymphatic system to fight germs. Also known as the body's natural resistance.*48, 132.*

Incisors. The front and center teeth. *259.*

Incubation period. The period of time from which a person becomes infected with a microorganism to the time when they actually have symptoms allowing them to recognize the disease. *129.*

Infectious disease (communicable diseases). All diseases that are caused by the spread of germs. *126.*

Insomnia. The inability to go to sleep. *120.*

Insulin. A hormone released from the pancreas to regulate the sugar in the body. *74.*

Integumentary system. Includes the skin, hair, nails, sweat glands and oil glands. *46.*

Isokinetic. A combination of isometric and isotonic. Muscle contraction with the resistance changing with the amount of force applied to it. *114.*

Isometric. Muscle contraction but no movement involved. *114.*

Isotonic. Muscle contraction against a fixed resistance. *114.*

Keratin. A tough, dead material of which fingernails are made. *251.*

Lean body weight. The weight of the muscles of the body. *99.*

Leukemia. A form of cancer characterized by an uncontrolled or abnormal production of white blood cells. *29.*

Lifestyle. An individual's whole way of living. *201.*

Lifestyle diseases. Those diseases caused by health habits. *157.*

Lifetime sports. Those activities that a person can participate in throughout life. *103.*

Low density lipoproteins (LDL). The bad cholesterol because it is the cholesterol that tends to be deposited in the arteries. *65.*

Lung cancer. Occurs when the cancer cells grow out of control and destroy the air sacs in the lungs. *32.*

Lymphatic network. Vessels that circulate a special body fluid called lymph. *133.*

Lymphocytes. White blood cells manufactured by the lymph nodes to travel through the lymphatic system to fight off germs. *133.*

Malignant. The description of a cancerous tumor. *165.*

Malocclusion. A condition where the upper and lower teeth do not properly line up. *261.*

Marriage. An intimate personal union to which man and woman consent, consummated and continuously nourished by sexual intercourse and perfected in a lifelong partnership of mutual love and commitment. *370.*

Medicines. Drugs that are meant to cure or prevent diseases and other conditions. *348.*

Metastasis. Tumors that spread to other parts of the body through the blood stream or lymphatic system. *165.*

Minerals. Inorganic substances essential for your body to help form bones, teeth and blood cells. *81.*

Molars. The teeth located in the sides and back of mouth. *259.*

Multiple sclerosis (MS). A disease in which the outer coating that protects some nerves is destroyed. *53.*

Muscle tissue. Groups of cells whose primary function is to contract, causing body parts to move. There are three types of muscle tissue: skeletal, smooth and cardiac. *21.*

Muscular system. The group of tissues that makes body parts move. *37.*

Natural immunity. An inborn resistance to certain diseases. *49.*

Nerve tissue. Highly complex structures that are located in the brain, spinal cord and nerves. They are very sensitive to changes, receive and transmit impulses to various parts of the body. *21.*

Nicotine. The substance that causes addiction to tobacco. A drug that acts like a tranquilizer and stimulates the release of epinephrine into the smoker's body. *344.*

Noninfectious diseases (noncommunicable). Diseases caused by heredity, the environment, and a person's lifestyle and are not passed on from one person to another. *154.*

Opportunistic infections. Those diseases that do not normally affect a person with a healthy immune system, but do take advantage of a person with AIDS. *146.*

Optimist. One who has the tendency to look on the more favorable side of happenings. *191.*

Organ. Two or more tissues grouped together and performing specialized functions. *22.*

Osteoporosis. A condition which results in a loss of bone tissue. *35.*

Overload. A principle of exercise that means to gradually do more than normal to improve performance. *104.*

Ozone layer. A form of oxygen that is formed naturally in the upper atmosphere. *309.*

Pathogens (germs). Microorganisms that cause disease. *126.*

Pedestrians. People who travel on foot. *280.*

Periodontal disease. More advanced gum disease. *260.*

Periodontium. A structure that supports the teeth, that consists of the jawbone, gums and ligaments. *259.*

Pessimist. One who has the tendency to see what is gloomy, or anticipate the worst possible outcome. *191.*

Physical fatigue. The muscles become exhausted from the work they have had to perform. *116.*

Physiology. The field of study dealing with the function of the body parts, what they do and how they do it. *15.*

Pimple. A clogged pore that has become infected and filled with pus. *244.*

Plaque. A grainy, sticky coating that is constantly forming on the teeth. *260.*

Pneumonia. A serious illness that occurs as a result of an infection of the lungs and causes difficulty breathing. *31.*

Pollution. Contamination. *308.*

Positive stress. Stress that challenges a person enough to face daily responsibilities and to pursue life goals. *186.*

Posture. The way an individual carries him or herself. *262.*

Premolars (bicuspids). The teeth located in the sides and back of mouth. *259.*

Progression. A principle of exercise that means to start with a little and add to it regularly as improvement is made. *104.*

Proteins. Nutrients needed by your body for building new tissue. *62.*

Puberty. The stage of growth and development at which males and females become physically able to reproduce. *328.*

Pulp. The portion inside the tooth that is composed of blood vessels, nerves and connective tissue. *259.*

Quack. An individual who boasts that he or she has medical skills or a scientific remedy, but in fact has none. *318.*

Rape. Forcing another person to have sexual intercourse without consent. *274.*

Recommended dietary allowance (RDA). An assumed percentage for the average non-pregnant adult. *79.*

Recycling. A process that takes material that would otherwise be garbage and regains it for human use. *312.*

Reduce. To decrease in size, amount, extent or number. *312.*

Regenerate. The ability of the body to be renewed or to be restored. *155.*

Reproductive system. The group of organs responsible for the continuation of the human race. *54.*

Resistance. The ability to fight the invading germ. *130.*

Respiratory system. The group of passages that exchanges gases in order for the body to function properly. *30.*

Responsibility. The quality of being reliable, trustworthy. A Christian's response to God's ability. *301.*

Resting pulse rate. The rate at which your heart beats, taken in the morning as you awaken. *98.*

Reuse. To decrease the amount of solid waste by making use of the product for a different or similar purpose. *312.*

Righteousness. Conformity to the law, mind and will of God. *392.*

Risk. To expose to hazard or danger. *271.*

Risk factors. Traits or habits that raise someone's chances of getting a disease. *157.*

Root. The part of the tooth that is below the gums. *259.*

Scoliosis. A condition that occurs when the vertebral column develops an abnormal curvature, so that one hip or shoulder is lower than the other. *34.*

Sebum. An oily substance produced that can clog the pores of the skin. *244.*

Second-degree burn. A burn that damages not only the outer layer of skin but also the layer beneath it. *289.*

Self-image. The view you have of yourself and the way you believe you are seen by others. *228.*

Self-talk. The mental "tape" running in one's mind, repeating all the positive or negative things one hears, sees, reads or imagines. *232.*

Set point theory. The theory that a body maintains a certain comfort zone, a weight that is difficult to break. *85.*

Sexually transmitted diseases (STDs) or venereal diseases (VDs). The diseases that pass from one person to another through sexual contact. *142.*

Shock. A dangerous condition in which the body functions slow down dramatically. *287.*

Skeletal system. The combination of joints and connecting tissues. *33.*

Sodium. An essential mineral found in salt that the body needs. *74.*

Specialist. Doctors trained to treat particular kinds of patients or health needs. *319.*

Specificity. A principle of exercise that means to do specific kinds of exercise to develop certain parts of the body. *105.*

Spiritual atrophy. A wasting away or progressive degeneration of one's spiritual fitness. *390.*

Statutory rape. When an adult has sexual intercourse with a minor (under the age of consent) with the minor's permission. *274.*

Sterility. Incapable of producing offspring. May occur in either male or female. *140.*

Steward. A manager, supervisor, superintendent; they hold the office of oversight of another's property or affairs. *300.*

Stimulants. Drugs that speed up the body's functions. *348.*

Stress. The body's response to external or internal changes. *183.*

Stressor. The stimulus that triggers the stress. *183.*

Stroke. The condition that occurs when the blood flow to one part of the brain is severely restricted or cut off. *29, 163.*

Stroke volume. The volume of blood the heart pumps at each stroke. *98.*

Symptoms. The changes in the body that signal that a particular disease is present. *137.*

Syphilis. The least common, yet one of the most dangerous, of the sexually transmitted diseases. Sometimes called "the great imitator" because it looks like so many other diseases. *141.*

Systems of the body. A group of related organs in the body. *22.*

T-cells. Lymphocytes that fight germs by several ways, that are different than the way the B-cells fight germs. *134.*

Tar. The substance that is produced when tobacco burns. A Thick, dark liquid that produces chronic irritation of the respiratory system of a smoker. *344.*

Target heart rate. A way to monitor the intensity of a workout, so the heart and lungs can benefit the most from a workout. *109.*

Tartar (calculus). The hard substance that is formed on the teeth. *261.*

Third-degree burn. A burn that damages all the layers of the skin. *289.*

Tissues. Groups or layers of similar cells that are specialized to carry on particular functions in the body. *19.*

Total health. Physical, mental, social and spiritual wellness. *3.*

Tumor. Groups of abnormal cells that may grow quickly and form masses of cells. *165.*

Type A personality (hurried sickness). A person who seems to exhibit intense drive, and extreme competitiveness. *185.*

Type B personality. A person who seems to exhibit patience, calmness and who is less hurried. *185.*

Ulcer. An open sore in the membrane lining the stomach and the small intestine. *42.*

Urinary tract. Expels waste in the form of urine. *43.*

Vaccine. A mixture of weakened or killed germ cells, given orally (by mouth) or through an injection. *134.*

Virus. Smaller in size than bacteria and responsible for more infections than any other pathogen. *127.*

Vision. A motivating cause given to an individual by God resulting in a purpose for living. *411.*

Vitamins. Organic substances the body needs to help regulate and coordinate functions of the body. *79.*

Wart. A growth on the skin caused by a virus. *245.*

Whitehead. A type of acne created when oil becomes trapped inside a pore. *244.*

Index

Page references in **bold** indicate charts or illustrations.

A

Abdominal thrusts 292
Abortion 339–342
Abstinence 333–336
Abundant life 2, 157
Accident 271
  preventing unnecessary 272–273
Acid rain 310
Acne 244
  caring for 245
Acquired immunity 49
Addiction 348
Additives 83
Advertising 316
Agape 365
Aging. *See* Elderly
AIDS 51, 144–147
  history of 145
  hotline number 141
  opportunistic infections 146
  prevention of 147
  transmission of 146
Alcohol 76, 349–353
  alcoholism 353
  fetal alcohol syndrome 353
  health problems 349–351
  peer pressure and 349
  teenagers and 351–352
Alcoholism 353
Alimentary canal 39
Allergen 131
Allergies 50
Alzheimer's disease 174, 378
Amblyopia 254
Amino acids 62
Anatomist 15
Anatomy 15
Anemia 29
Angina 160
Anorexia 90
Antibodies 132
Antioxidants 83, 167
Appearance 229

Appendix 43
Arteries 27
Arteriosclerosis 29, 159
Arthritis 34, 171–172
  osteoarthritis 171
  rheumatoid 172
Artificial respiration 285
  ABC's 286
Artificial sweeteners 74
Assume 229
Asthma 31
Astigmatism 253
Atherosclerosis 159
Athlete's foot 246, 266
Atrophy 111
  spiritual 390
Attempted rape 274
Attitude 299
  about responsibility 301–303
  freedom 299
  love 191
  of elderly 378–379
  society 300
  stress and 190–191
Autoimmune disease 51
Autonomic nervous system 52

B

B-cells 133
Baby
  stages of development **340**
Babysitting 293
Bacteria 126
Balance 5
  ears 256
Basal metabolism 72
Benign 165
Bible
  defense against disease 135
  reading 393–394
  stress and 188

Bicuspids 259
Bicycle safety 281
Bile 40
Biodegradable 311
Biopsy 168
Birth defects 156
Blackhead 244
Blister 265
Blood
  pressure 98, 160–161
  transfusion 29
Boating safety 283
Body
  needs of 16
  organization of 17
  systems of 22–23
Bone 33
Breast
  self-examination 165
Breath, bad 42
Bronchitis 31
Bruise 38
Bulimia 90
Bunion 265
Burns 289–290
Bursitis 34

C

Callus 47, 265
Calorie 73
Cancer 164–169
  antioxidants 167
  benign 165
  biopsy 168
  breast self-examination 165
  carcinogens 167
  cause of 165–167
  colon 45
  factors contributing to 166
  free radicals 167
  lung 32
  malignant 165
  metastasis 165
  of the female organs 56
  prevention of 167
  skin 48
  testicular 56
  testicular self-examination 167
  treatment of 168–169
  tumors 165
  warning signs of 168

Canine teeth 259
Capillaries 28
Carbohydrates 63–64
Carbon monoxide 344
Carcinogens 167
Cardiac muscle 21
Cardiac output 98
Cardiopulmonary resuscitation 293
Cardiovascular disease 79, 159–163
  arteriosclerosis 159
  atherosclerosis 159
  family history 161
  prevention 161–163
  treatment 161–163
Cardiovascular fitness 97–98
Carrier 130
Cataracts 254
Cavity 261
Cells 18
  characteristics of 18
Central nervous system 51
Cerebral palsy 52
Character 204–206
  chart **205**
  humility 205
  pride 205
Cheat 305
Chlamydia 140
Choices 192, 201
  consumer 315–316
  maturity 325–333
Choking 291–292
Cholesterol 65–66
Chronic overeating 90
Circulatory system 22, 27–30, **28**
  arteries 27
  capillaries 28
  heart **27**
  kidneys 28
  problems of 29–30
  veins 27
Cirrhosis 42
Citizen 320
Cold sores 47
Colon 43–44
Colon cancer 45
Color blindness 254
Comfort zone 231
Common cold 31, 136–138
  fighting 137
  preventing 138
  symptoms 137

treating 138
Communication skills 373
Compact bone 33
Comparison shop 316
Complete proteins 63
Complex carbohydrates 64
Conduct 201–204
Conflicts 372–375
   helpful hints to getting along 374
Conformity 211–212
Congenital 155
Conjunctivitis 253
Connective tissues 20
Consequences 6
Constipation 44
Consumer 313–319
   advertising 316
   choices 315–316
   comparison shop 316
   exploitation of 317–318
   health-care 319
   quack 318
Convictions 206–208
   how to develop 207–208
   temptation 207
Corns 47, 265
Countenance 233
CPR. *See* Cardiopulmonary resuscitation
Cramp 38
Creation 13
Cross training 105
Crown 259
Culture 7
Cuspids 259
Cuticle 251
Cystic fibrosis 172–173

D

Dandruff 249
Date rape 275
Dating 359–367
   activities 362
   group dating 361
   kingdom relationships 363–364
   sexual pressure 366
   standards 360
   why date 363
Deafness 257
Death 379–381
   fear of 380

Defenses
   physical 131–135
   spiritual 135, 154
Defraud 335
Degeneration 153–155
Degenerative disease 154
Dementia 378
Dental care. *See* Teeth
Dental hygienist 259
Dentin 259
Dentist 259
Depressants 348
Depression 193–194
   causes and signs of 194
Dermatitis 246
Dermis 46
Destiny 414–415
   hindrances 418–419
Diabetes mellitus 54, 169–171
   cause of 169–171
   diabetes type I 169
   diabetes type II 170
   treatment of 169–171
Diaphragm 31
Diarrhea 45
Diet 84–91
   anorexia 90
   bulimia 90
   chronic overeating 90
   eating disorders 90–91
   fat calories 86
   food journal 88–89
   reading labels 86–88
   Set Point Theory 85
Digestion 39
Digestive system 22, 39–42, **40**
   alimentary canal 39
   digestion 39
   esophagus 40
   gallbladder 40
   liver 40
   peristalsis 40
   problems of 41–42
   saliva 40
   small intestine 41
   stomach 41
Disappointment with God 417
Discipline 405
Disease 125
   acute 130
   antibodies 132
   bacteria 126

birth defects 156
cardiovascular 159–163
carrier 130
chronic 130
communicable 126
congenital 155
degenerative 154
environment and 156–157
fungi 127
genetic 155–156
germ theory 126
heredity 155–156
immune system 132–133
incubation period 129
infectious 126
infectious, fighting 136–140
infectious process 128–130
lifestyle 157
noninfectious causes 153–157
noninfectious, fighting 159–174
parasites 128
pathogen 126
physical defenses 131–135
regenerate 136, 155
resistance 130
risk factors 157
sexually transmitted 140–147
spiritual defenses 135, 154
vaccine 134–135
venereal 142
viruses 127
Dislocation 35
Distress 186
Divorce 368
Doctor, family 319
Drowning 282
Drugs 347–349
choosing to be free of 349
misuse and abuse of 348

E

Earaches 257
Ears 254–257
balance 256
caring for 255
infections 257
natural 254
problems with 257
spiritual 254
Eating disorders 90–91
Eczema 246

EKG 102
Elderly 375–379
Alzheimer's disease 378
attitude of 378–379
attitude towards 376–378
dementia 378
physical changes 377–378
Electrocardiogram 102
Emergencies 288–293
Emotions 215–217
family 216
friends 217
God 216
yourself 217
Emphysema 32, 344
Endocrine system 23, **53**, 53–54
problems of 54
Enriched 83
Environment 308
noninfectious disease and 156–157
Environmentalist 308
Epidermis 46
Epilepsy 52
Epithelial tissues 20
Ergogenic aid 106
Eros 365
Esophagus 40
Essential amino acids 63
Estrogen 329
Excretory system 22, 43–45
large intestine **43**, 43–44
problems of 44–45
urinary tract 43, **44**
Exercise
aerobic 103–104
anaerobic 103–104
atrophy 111
benefits of 113
cross training 105
goals 108
in heat or cold 115
misconceptions 106–108
motivation 112
overload 104
principles of 103–108
program 108–112
progression 104
specificity 105
stress and 190
target heart rate 109
warm-down 116
warm-up 115

weight control and 105–106
Expiration 30
Eyes 252–254
   careers 254
   caring for 252–253
   natural 252
   problems with 253–254
   spiritual 252

F

Fainting 288–289
Faith
   defense against disease 135
   suicide and 196
Falls 278–279
Family 8, 371–375
   communication skills 373
   conflicts 372–375
   feelings about 216
   health behavior of 8
   parenting 371–372
Farsightedness 253
Fatigue 116–118
   due to illness 118
   emotional 117
   physical 116
Fats 64–65, 75
   fat calories 86
Fears 222
Feet 264–266
   care of 265
   problems with 265–266
Fertilization 55
Fetal alcohol syndrome 353
Fever blisters 47
Fiber 73
Fingernails 250–251
Fire safety 276–277
First aid 283–288
   abdominal thrusts 292
   babysitter tips 293
   bleeding 287
   burns 289–290
   choking 291–292
   emergencies 288–293
   fainting 288–289
   first-aider 284
   heat exhaustion 290–291
   heatstroke 290–291
   Heimlich maneuver 292
   hypothermia 291

   kit 277
   nosebleeds 290
   poisoning 278
   pressure points **287**
   shock 287
   value of 283
First-degree burns 289
Fitness
   cardiovascular 97–98
   flexibility 99
   lean body weight 99
   lifetime sports 103
   muscular strength 98–99
   physical 97–99
   spiritual 389–401
   testing 100
Fixed commitments chart **220**
Flatulence 45
Flexibility 99
Follicles 247
Food 67–71
   anorexia 90
   bulimia 90
   chronic overeating 90
   diet 84–91
   eating disorders 90–91
   journal 88–89
   menu sample 71
   serving size 70
   snacks 78
Food Guide Pyramid 67, **68**
Fortified 83
Fractures 35
Free radicals 167
Friendships 212–215
   emotions and 217
   evaluating 214–215
   levels of 212, **359**
Fruit of the Spirit 330
Fungi 127

G

G.I.G.O.
   garbage 203
   God 401
   good 203
Gallbladder 40
Gallstones 42
Gamma globulin 139
Gas 45
Genetic disease 155–156

Gingivitis 260
Glaucoma 254
Glucose 63
Goal(s)
  exercise and 108
  higher 2–3, 222
  principles for setting 221
  time management 219
God-focus 415–417
Gonorrhea 141
Greenhouse effect 309
Grief 379–381
  coping with loss 381
Guided experiences 343
Gun safety 279

H

Habits 6
Hair 247–249
  care of 248
  follicles 247
  hairstyle 248
  problems with 249
  types of 247
Halitosis 42
Hands 250–251
Hangnails 251
Happiness 182
HDL 65
Head lice 249
Health
  Christian view 3
  insurance 319
  mental 181–182
  secular view 3
  total 3, 187
Health maintenance organization 319
Health-care provider 319
Heart 27
  cardiac output 98
  disease. See Cardiovascular disease
  stroke volume 98
  target heart rate 109
Heartburn 41
Heat exhaustion 290–291
Heatstroke 290
Heimlich maneuver 292
Hemophilia 29
Hepatitis 139–140
Hernia 56
Herpes simplex I 246

Herpes simplex II 142
High blood pressure. See Hypertension
High density lipoproteins 65
HIV. See AIDS
HMO. See Health maintenance organization
Homeostasis 15–16, 136
Hormones 53
Human body
  needs of 16
  organization of 17
  systems of 22–23
Humility 205
Hygiene 241–266
  ears 254–257
  eyes 252–254
  hair 247–249
  hands 250–251
  nails 250–251
  skin 242–247
  teeth 258–261
Hypermetropia 253
Hypertension 30, 160
Hypoglycemia 169
Hypothermia 291

I

Immune system 23, 48–51, 132–133
  acquired immunity 49
  autoimmune disease 51
  B-cells 133
  immunodeficiency disorders 50
  lymphatic system 48, **133**
  lymphocytes 133
  natural immunity 49
  opportunistic infections 50
  T-cells 134
Immunity 49
Immunodeficiency disorders 50
Impetigo 246
In-grown toe nails 266
Incisors 259
Incubation period 129
Indigestion 41
Infections 52
Influences 208–212
  conformity 211–212
  peers 209
  society 211
Inguinal hernia 56
Inheritance 422–423

Injuries
    prevention of 113–116
    RICE acronym 114
    skeletal system 35
Insomnia 120
Inspiration 30
Insulin 74
Insurance, health 319
Integumentary system 22, 46
    dermis 46
    epidermis 46
    functions of 46
    problems of 47–48
Intelligence 230
Intestine
    large **43**, 43–44
    small 41
Isokinetic 114
Isometric 114
Isotonic 114

J

Jock itch 246

K

Keratin 251
Kidney stones 45
Kidneys 28, 44

L

Labels, reading 86–88
Large intestine **43**, 43–44
Lazy eye 254
LDL 65
Leeuwenhoek, Anton van 14
Leukemia 29
Lifestyle
    character 204–206, **205**
    choices 201
    conduct 201–204
    convictions 206–208
    G.I.G.O. (garbage, good) 203
    G.I.G.O. (God) 401
    management of 201–208
    mind 203
    self-control 202
    self-discipline 202
    tobacco affects 346
    winning 2

Lifestyle disease 157
Lipoproteins 65
Liver 40
    cirrhosis 42
Love 191
    how will I know 365
    of Jesus 412–413
    types of 365
Low density lipoproteins 65
Lung cancer 32
Lungs 30
Lymphatic system 48, **133**
Lymphocytes 133

M

Malignant 165
Malocclusion 261
Marriage 367–371
    divorce 368
    God and 370
    myths of 367–369
    oneness 370
Maturity
    abortion 339–342
    alcohol 349–353
    boundaries 331
    choices 325–333
    curiosity 332–333
    defraud 335
    drugs 347–349
    emotional 329
    how to wait 338
    making decisions 326–328
    physical 328–329
    pregnancy 339–342
    puberty 328
    purity 335
    secondary sex characteristics 329
    sex 333–342
    sexual pressure 366
    signs of 330
    social 330
    spiritual 330–331
    tobacco 343–347
    what does it mean 328–333
    why wait 336–337
Media 8
Medical history 174
Medicines 348
Meditation 393–394
Menstruation 55–56

Mental health 181–182
  careers in 195
  depression 193–194
  happiness 182
  suicide 194–196
Menu sample 71
Metabolism 72–73
Metastasis 165
Microscope 14
Mind
  renewing 403–404
Minerals 81, **82**
Molars 259
Money 314
Mononucleosis 138–139
Motion sickness 257
Motor vehicle safety 281–282
Multiple sclerosis 53, 173–174
Muscle strength 98–99
Muscle tissue 21
Muscular dystrophy 173
Muscular fatigue 38
Muscular system 22, 36–38
  involuntary muscles 37
  problems of 38
  voluntary muscles 37
Myocardial infarction 160
Myopia 253

N

Nails 250–251
Natural immunity 49
Nausea 41
Nearsightedness 253
Nerve tissues 21
Nerves
  peripheral 51
  pinched 52
Nervous system 23, 51–53
  autonomic 52
  central 51
  peripheral 52
  peripheral nerves 51
  problems of 52–53
  somatic 52
Nicotine 344
Nosebleeds 290
Nutrients 61

O

Ophthalmologist 254
Opportunistic infections 50, 146
Optician 254
Optimist 191
Optometrist 254
Organ 22
Organizations 8
Orthodontist 259
Osteoarthritis 171
Osteoporosis 35
Ovaries 55, 329
Overload 104
Ovulation 55
Ozone layer 309

P

Parasites 128
Parenting 371–372
Pathogen 126, 129
Patience 406
Pedestrians 280
Penis 55
Periodontal disease 260
Periodontium 259
Periosteum 33
Peripheral nervous system 52
Peristalsis 40
Perseverance 406
Pessimist 191
Physiologist 15
Physiology 15
Pimple 244
Pinched nerve 52
Pinkeye 253
Pituitary gland 54
Plaque 66, 260
Pneumonia 31, 138
Poison Control Center 278
Poisoning 278
Pollution 308–312
  air 309–310
  reduce, reuse, recycle 311–312
  water 310–311
Positive stress 186
Posture 262–266
  feet 264–266
  importance of 263

Potential 411–423
    destiny 414–415
    God-focus 415–417
    hindrances to destiny 418–419
    inheritance 422–423
    vision 411–414
Praise 401
Prayer 395–400
    common questions 396–398
    defense against disease 135
    practical steps 399–400
Pregnancy
    fetal alcohol syndrome 353
    stages of development **340**
    tobacco and 346
    unplanned 339–342
Premenstrual syndrome 56
Premolars 259
Preservatives 83
Pressure
    negative 208
    peer 7, 209, 349
    positive 208
Pressure points **287**
Pride 205
Progesterone 329
Progression 104
Prostate gland 55
Protein 62–63
Psoriasis 246
Psychiatrist 195
Psychologist 195
Puberty 328
Pulled muscle 38
Pulp 259
Pulse 98
    target heart rate 109
Purity 335

Q

Quack 318

R

Rape 274–275
    help 275
    precautions against 274
Recommended Dietary Allowance (RDA) 79
Recycle 311–312
Reduce 311–312
Regenerate 136, 155

Relationships 400
Religion 7
Reproductive system 23, 54–56
    female 55
    male 55
    problems of 56
Resistance 130
Respiratory system 22, 30–32, **31**
    diaphragm 31
    expiration 30
    inspiration 30
    lungs 30
    problems of 31–32
Responsibility
    as a Christian 300–303
    as a citizen 308–320
    as a person 304–308
    consumer 313–319
    mentally 305–306
    physically 304–305
    possible attitudes 301–303
    socially 307–308
Resting pulse rate 98
Reuse 311–312
Rheumatoid arthritis 172
Righteousness
    training in 391–392
Risk 271–275
    accident 271
    God and 273
    teenagers and 271–272
Risk factors 157
Root 259

S

Safety 275–283
    bicycle 281
    boating 283
    falls 278–279
    fire 276–277
    gun 279
    home 276–279
    motor vehicle 281–282
    outdoors 280–283
    pedestrians 280
    poisoning 278
    road 280–282
    school 280
    water 282–283
Saliva 40
Saturated fat 65

Saturation 64
School 8
Scoliosis 34
Scrotum 55
Sebum 244
Second-degree burns 289
Secondary sex characteristics 329
Self-control 202
Self-discipline 202
Self-image 228–231
    appearance 229
    comfort zone 231
    countenance 233
    improving your 234
    in His image 234
    intelligence 230
    physical abilities 230
    self-talk 232–233
Semen 55
Seminal fluid 55
Senior citizens. *See* Elderly
Serving size 70
Set point theory 85
Sexually transmitted diseases 140–147
    AIDS 144–147
    consequences of 143–144
    fighting 142–144
    hotline number 141
    protection from 144
    sexual intimacy and 143
    sterility 140
    types of 140–142
Shock 287
Simple carbohydrates 64
Skeletal muscle 21
Skeletal system 22, 32–36
    compact bone 33
    injuries 35–36
    periosteum 33
    problems of 34–35
    spongy bone 33
Skin 242–247
    acne 244
    caring for 242
    nutrition and 244
    problems 245–247
    warts 245
Skin cancer 48
Sleep 118–120
    getting better night's 120
    insomnia 120
    stages of 119

Small intestine 41
Smoking 76. *See also* Tobacco
Smooth muscle 21
Snacks 78
Sodium 74–75
Somatic nervous system 52
Something to think about
    Abraham Lincoln 231
    AIDS and T-cells 134
    AIDS cases 144
    AIDS cure 146
    AIDS rate of infection 145
    alcohol and peer pressure 349
    alcohol and your brain 351
    appendix 43
    Beethoven 257
    Bible reading 395
    blood transfusion 29
    body temperature 16
    burning 300 calories 105
    change in history 85
    character 206
    compromising dating standards 360
    crime 273
    date rape 275
    David's destiny 415
    digestive system 41
    fertilization 55
    fetal alcohol syndrome 353
    fingerprints 47
    first-aid kit 277
    food poisoning 42
    give your heart a rest 99
    grief 381
    hairs are numbered 249
    horse vomit reflex 131
    lifetime distance walked 35
    lung air sacs 30
    medical history 174
    muscles 37
    nail biting 250
    pacemakers 163
    parenting 372
    prayer format 400
    Ring Around the Rosy 125
    senior citizen contributions 377
    sex drive question 336
    sharing your faith 303
    shoe shopping 265
    skin and nutrition 244
    smoking affects lifestyle 346
    smoking costs 347

sounds of the ocean 256
tastes 262
teeth and stress 261
tonsils 51
trash talk 313
Specialists 319
Specificity 105
Spiritual fitness, 389–401
Bible reading 393–394
discipline 405
growing in Christian virtues 404–405
keys to consistency 402–406
perseverance 406
praise 401
prayer 395–400
relationships 400
renewing the mind 403–404
spiritual atrophy 390
training in righteousness 391–392
vision 406
worship 401
Spleen 134
Spongy bone 33
Sprain 35
Statutory rape 274
Sterility 140
Steroids 106
Steward 300
Stimulants 348
Stomach 41
Strain 38
Stress 183–191
attitude and 190–191
Bible and 188
choice 192
coping with 188–192
definition of 183
distress 186
eating and 77
exercise and 190
factors that affect 184
fight or flight 185
negative 186
optimist 191
performance and **186**
pessimist 191
physical changes 185
positive 186
results of 186–187
stressor 183
teeth and 261
time management and 189–190

type A personality 185
type B personality 185
Stroke 29, 163–164
Stroke volume 98
Sugar 74
Suicide 194–196
faith and 196
help to prevent 195
warning signs of 196
Sweeteners 74
Symptoms 137
Syphilis 141–142

T

T-cells 134
Tar 344
Tartar 261
Taste buds 262
Teeth 258–261
careers 259
caring for 260
kinds of 259
parts of 259
problems with 260–261
stress and 261
Temptation 207
Testes 55, 329
self-examination 167
Testicular cancer 56
Testimony/Tribute
abortion 341
alcoholism 354
anorexia 91
dental care 258
family conflicts 373
grief 379
lifestyle diseases 158
making tough decisions 327
self-image 227
Testosterone 329
Third-degree burns 289
Thyroid gland 54
Time management 189–190, 218–221
fixed commitments chart **220**
goal setting 219
Tissues 19–21
connective tissues 20
epithelial tissues 20
muscle tissue 21
nerve tissues 21

Tobacco 343–347
    chewing 347
    harmful effects of 344–346
    lifestyle 346
    pregnancy and 346
Torn muscle 38
Total health 3, 187
Transfusion 29
Tributes. *See* Testimony
Tumors 52, 165
Type A personality 185
Type B personality 185

U

Ulcer 42
Unsaturated fats 65
Urinary tract 43, **44**
    infections 45
Uterus 55

V

Vaccine 134–135
Vagina 55
Vaginitis 56
Values 6, 9
    foundation for 9
Veins 27
Venereal diseases 142. *See also* Sexually
        transmitted diseases
Virtues
    growing in Christian 404–405
Viruses 127
Vision 406, 411–414
Vitamins 79–81, **80**
    antioxidants 83
Vomiting 41

W

Warm-down 116
Warm-up 115
Warts 47, 245
Water 76–77
Water safety 282–283
Weight control 72
    exercise and 105–106
Whitehead 244
Worship 401